BLACK RAGE IN NEW ORLEANS

BLACK RAGE
IN NEW ORLEANS

Police Brutality and African American Activism
from World War II to Hurricane Katrina

LEONARD N. MOORE

 LOUISIANA STATE UNIVERSITY PRESS   BATON ROUGE

Published by Louisiana State University Press
lsupress.org

Louisiana Paperback Edition, 2021

DESIGNER: Michelle A. Neustrom
TYPEFACES: Chaparral Pro, text; Vonnes, display

Cover photograph used with permission of *The Times-Picayune*.
Photo © 2009 The Times-Picayune Publishing Co., all rights reserved.

LIBRARY OF CONGRESS CATALOGING-IN-PUBLICATION DATA
Moore, Leonard N. (Leonard Nathaniel)
    Black rage in New Orleans : police brutality and African American activism from World War II
to Hurricane Katrina / Leonard N. Moore.
        p. cm.
    Includes bibliographical references and index.
    ISBN 978-0-8071-3590-7 (cloth : alk. paper) — ISBN 978-0-8071-3740-6 (pdf) — ISBN 978-0-
8071-4595-1 (epub) — ISBN 978-0-8071-7737-2 (paperback) 1. African Americans—Louisiana—
New Orleans—Social conditions—20th century. 2. Police-community relations—Louisiana—
New Orleans—History—20th century. 3. New Orleans (La.)—Race relations—History—20th
century. I. Title.
    F379.N557M66 2010
    363.2'32—dc22
                                                                                    2009030247

For Thaïs, Jaaucklyn, Lauryn, and Len

CONTENTS

TABLES

ACKNOWLEDGMENTS

It's hard to believe that this is my second book. But this book would not have been possible without a community of people.

I am particularly thankful to the history professors at Jackson State, Cleveland State, and the Ohio State University, for believing in me when few others did.

I am grateful for the support of outstanding librarians and archivists at the Louisiana Division of the New Orleans Public Library; the Department of Special Collections at the University of New Orleans's Earl K. Long Library; and the Amistad Research Center. And special thanks goes to Lynn Cunningham and Doug Parker at the *Times-Picayune* for assisting me with images.

At LSU Press, I want to thank Rand Dotson for his support of this project and believing in its importance.

This book could not have been written without the support of my students, who always keep me engaged. Seeing all of you on Tuesdays and Thursdays is one of the great privileges of my life.

My colleagues at the University of Texas at Austin have been truly supportive: Louis Harrison, Greg Vincent, Ted Gordon, Juliet Walker, Emilio Zamora, Toyin Falola, Alan Tully. To the entire Division of Diversity and Community Engagement (DDCE) family I cannot say thank you enough. In particular, Wanda Nelson, Ge Chen, Tiffany Tillis, Rian Carkhum, Francee Brown, David Ramirez, and Stella Escalante.

On a more personal level I want to thank the men that challenge me to be a better husband, father, and friend: Wayne Williams, Darren Kelly, Kevin D. Golden, Kevin N. Golden, Reggie Golden, and Geoffrey Golden,

Ron Sullivan, James Bright, Marcel Thompson, Garrett Scales, LaGarrett King, Samori Camara, Adam Williams, Spencer Platt, Jason Chambers, Sherwin Bryant, Sam Townsend, Christopher Sutton, Michael Dixon, Ronald Roberts, Kurtis Ellis, Keith Clark, Kevin Clark, Ralph L. Moore, Ralph D. Moore, Perry Robey, Carlos Thomas, Marcus Cox, Troy Allen, Lawrence Hart, Jr., and Adam Banks.

I am also indebted to the great community of people who make up the Soul Movement family. It is truly an honor for me to serve as your pastor.

Finally to the Moore and Bass family I say thanks. To Dad, we still miss you. Mom, Bev, and San, thank you for always being there for me. To my children, Jaaucklyn, Lauryn, and Lil' Len, who remind me on a daily basis what life is really about, I thank you for being wonderful children. To Bobbie and Papa, thank you for letting me marry your daughter. Thäis, you've followed me to Baton Rouge, now Austin, I think that Broadway is next! I appreciate you for being a wonderful wife, mother, writer, actress, and director. And of course I love you for marrying me.

ABBREVIATIONS

ACLU	American Civil Liberties Union
AHC	Ad Hoc Committee for Accountable Police
BOLD	Black Organization for Leadership Development
BOP	Black Organization of Police
BPD	Birmingham Police Department
BPP	Black Panther Party
BPPA	Black Police for Positive Action
CAC	Community Advancement Committee
CAN	Community Action Now
CAP	Committee for Accountable Police
CCNP	Citizens Committee on Negro Police
CCPM	Concerned Citizens on Police Matters of Police Brutality and Harassment
COC	Citizen's Observers Committee
COPS	community-oriented policing squad
CORE	Congress of Racial Equality
COUP	Community Organization for Urban Politics
CPPB	Committee to Prevent Police Brutality to Negro Citizens
CRC	community relations council
FAS	felony action squad
FEMA	Federal Emergency Management Agency
FOP	Fraternal Order of Police
HANO	Housing Authority of New Orleans
HRC	Human Relations Committee
HUD	U.S. Department of Housing and Urban Development
IAD	internal affairs department
LL	Liberation League

LVO   Louisiana Veterans Organization
MCC   Metropolitan Crime Commission
NAACP   National Association for the Advancement of Colored People
NCCF   National Committee to Combat Fascism
NIMA   Negro Interdenominational Ministerial Alliance
NOPD   New Orleans Police Department
NOUL   New Orleans Urban League
NUL   National Urban League
OBLC   Orleans Black Legislative Caucus
OMI   office of municipal investigation
OPPVL   Orleans Parish Progressive Voters' League
ORS   U.S. Office of Revenue Sharing
PANO   Patrolmen's Association of New Orleans
PBC   Police Brutality Committee
PBI   police bureau of investigation
PCPB   People's Conference on Police Brutality
PDC   People's Defense Council (Coalition)
PID   Public Integrity Division
RAM   Revolutionary Action Movement
SCIC   Special Citizens Investigating Committee
SCLC   Southern Christian Leadership Conference
SOUL   Southern Organization for United Leadership
SUNO   Southern University of New Orleans
TCA   Total Community Action
UFJ   United Front for Justice

BLACK RAGE IN NEW ORLEANS

INTRODUCTION
Police Violence, New Orleans, and the Postwar Urban Landscape

Police brutality has been a source of frustration, anger, and rage for African Americans throughout the postwar period. In the postwar migration of African Americans out of the rural South into the nation's urban areas in search of better social and economic opportunities, they came in contact with the most visible arm of the state: the police. African Americans throughout the country confronted repressive police departments that were threatened by black demands for equality after World War II and intimidated by an expanded black populace as whites fled to the suburbs. Law enforcement agencies across the country responded to the increased black presence with an iron fist. In many ways white police officers institutionalized an informal culture of police brutality toward African Americans and they emerged as the protectors of white privilege and the opponents of black progress. As Gail O'Brien notes in her study of police violence in Tennessee, "the police operated as the frontline guardians of an arbitrary criminal justice system and a social order that controlled black Americans in their relations with whites but that offered blacks little protection from whites or from one another." As the number of African Americans grew in the nation's cities, it did not take long for white officers to develop an "us versus them" mentality as they encountered African Americans on a daily basis. Consequently, they were often ready to let African Americans know who was in charge by utilizing any and all methods of police repression. Consequently, the term *police brutality* was all encompassing to African Americans during the postwar period. It included police homicides; unlawful arrests; assaults; threatening and abusive language; the use of racial slurs; sexual exploitation of black women; the beating of prisoners in police custody; racial profiling; police complicity in drug-dealing, prostitution, burglaries, protection schemes, and gun-smuggling; and the lack of justice available to black defendants in the courts. Although the New Orleans Police Department (NOPD) did not keep records of police brutality complaints and the mainstream media rarely covered incidents of police brutality against African Americans, the black press always highlighted cases of police mistreatment, and generally on the front page. Even a cursory examination of black newspapers in the postwar period reveals articles, at times on a weekly basis, detailing cases of police brutality. Likewise, the archives of local and national civil rights organizations are filled with thousands of affidavits and letters relaying first-person experiences of police brutality.[1]

In the urban South police departments adhered to a strict policy of segregation and its ideological pattern of white supremacy. The typical police officer in the urban South viewed African Americans as docile, fearful, cowardly, and deathly afraid of the police. But at the same time, they also viewed black men as criminals and black women as sexual aggressors. Consequently, while black men were often brutalized by the police, black women were often sexually violated by the police. While unfair encounters with law enforcement have been a fact of life for the African American community, these encounters become more intense in the postwar period for several reasons. First, as African Americans began to assert demands for freedom and democracy, white police officers viewed themselves as agents that existed for the protection of whites only. Although police departments were subsidized by all taxpayers, African Americans found themselves paying for fair and equitable police services that they seldom received. Thus, black residents needed the protection of the police while at the same time needing protection from the police. Second, as a consequence of white rural migration to nearby urban areas, white mob activity was replaced by police violence as a means of restricting black social mobility. While white supremacist organizations such as the Ku Klux Klan and White Citizens' Council were quite visible in the postwar South, they did not engage in lynchings and other forms of racial violence that were typical of the plantation South because of the urban setting. Instead, the local police department, with the support of politicians, segregationists, district attorneys, and judges, carried out extralegal violence against African Americans, realizing that black southerners had no visible means of redress. Third, as the black populace expanded and whites fled to the suburbs, local law enforcement agencies viewed black mobility as a threat. In some ways, the police department was expected to control black activity and limit their use of public space. Fourth, as African American police officers joined local law enforcement agencies en masse in the 1970s as a result of aggressive recruitment and affirmative action programs, they ushered in a new era of police violence toward fellow African Americans. Many black officers found it easy to brutalize other African Americans because they would be exempt from charges of police brutality, their white superiors would often reward them, and they would be seen as good cops in the eyes of their fellow officers. Finally, as urban violent crime rates continued to escalate in the postwar period, the black poor and working class became criminalized, making them easy targets for police violence.[2]

But African Americans did not quietly tolerate wanton police misconduct. Although they were poor, had no political voice, were often shunned by the black middle class, and had no visible means of redress against police violence, anti-brutality activists and their supporters sustained a level of protest throughout the postwar period. Shaped by the democratic ideas that enveloped the country during World War II, they challenged police brutality at every opportunity. Throughout the postwar period African Americans were determined to have fair and equitable treatment and they utilized a variety of tactics to protest police misconduct: sit-ins, boycotts, picketing, close supervision of police activity, armed confrontations, and, at times, killing and assaulting police officers. Further they demanded major police reforms, including more black officers, more African American police officers in supervisory positions, integrated patrols, a civilian review board, black police only in black neighborhoods, and federal intervention. Since police brutality was an issue that transcended class divisions, it served as a tool to unify the black community, and in particular the black poor and working class. Unlike education, employment, and housing discrimination, the black middle class was quite familiar with police brutality, although the black poor were the majority of its victims. Nonetheless, despite their familiarity with police violence and mistreatment, the black middle class was often reluctant to get involved in the anti-brutality struggle.[3]

Throughout the postwar period it was largely the black poor and working class who complained about harsh and brutal police behavior, largely because they were its primary victims. Black middle-class support for anti-brutality protest was determined by a number of factors, such as the nature of the protest, the background of the victim, and the political context. For instance, during the battle to integrate the NOPD, the black middle class led the fight, but they were largely silent on the issue of police violence when an African American occupied city hall. Consequently, the voice of the black middle class is not a consistent one in the postwar anti-brutality fight. One reason for their silence is that, like their white counterparts, middle-class blacks were often in favor of tough crime-fighting measures to protect themselves and their property from black criminals. Although this was rarely voiced for fear of "airing dirty laundry," their lack of leadership and visibility in these anti-brutality struggles is clearly evident. Another reason for their silence resulted from the close political ties between the mayor's office and certain black organizations. For instance, during the turbulent decades of the 1970s and 1980s, two of the city's most prominent black political organizations were largely silent concerning the issue of police brutality for fear of losing access to city hall patronage. However, their reluctance to get involved presented an opportunity for grassroots activists to assume leadership.[4]

Since members of the black poor and working class were the main victims of police brutality throughout much of the postwar period, it seems logical that the leaders of the anti-brutality protests would emerge from this group. Because they were not affiliated with the traditional civil rights organizations such as the National Association for the Advancement of Colored People (NAACP) and the National Urban League (NUL), they utilized protest techniques that were generally frowned upon by members of the more moderate wing of the African American community. Many of the anti-brutality activists lacked credibility, an institutional base, and a clear program. Hence, they were often reactionary, acted in an ad hoc fashion, and created organizations and developed constituencies as the need arose. This new generation of activists was suspicious of electoral politics, nationalistic in their outlook, and expressed doubt that black politicians would address the needs within the black community. Unlike their middle-class counterparts, this new strata of leadership preferred confrontational protest tactics over legal strategies. Anti-brutality activists were confronting an intergenerational problem and they found their base of support among the alienated, marginalized, dispossessed, unemployed, and angry underclass that had been ignored by the middle class as they sought political and economic empowerment. According to historian Charles Payne, this new type of leadership was not based upon class status, educational attainment, or connections to the white power structure. Rather, it was established on a commitment to helping others and the trust and respect of their constituency. However, in the eyes of the black middle class, they were simply rabble-rousers and "street niggas" looking for attention, particularly when they protested even in the case of unquestionably justifiable police homicides. Despite their motives and shortcomings, these activists kept the issue of police brutality at the forefront of the black freedom struggle in New Orleans for much of the postwar period.[5]

WHY NEW ORLEANS

This book explores how African Americans protested police brutality in the postwar period and it uses New Orleans as its vantage point for two reasons. First, the New Orleans Police Department has been arguably one of the most brutal, corrupt, and incompetent police units in the United States in the postwar period. In recent years the scandal-ridden department has been the subject of several national exposes, including a 60 *Minutes* segment and an *Investigative Reports* one-hour special feature. At the height of its corruption in the mid-1990s, the New Orleans department had the highest number of citizen complaints of police brutality in the country, and a 1992 Justice Department study reported that New Orleans citizens had lodged more complaints with federal officials about police abuse than residents in any other city between 1984 and 1990. The majority of these complaints came from the African American community. The second reason New Orleans is the focus of this book is because black New Orleanians have sustained a record of protest against police brutality since the 1940s. During the postwar period, working-class and lower-class African Americans in New Orleans established numerous organizations to protest police brutality since they were the main victims of police misconduct and since civil rights victories did nothing to alleviate these problems. The organizations they created to protest police brutality were the Citizens Committee on Negro Police (CCNP), the Committee to Prevent Police Brutality to Negro Citizens (CPPB), Concerned Citizens on Police Matters of Police Brutality and Harassment (CCPM), the Citizen's Observers Committee (COC), United Front for Justice (UFJ), the Ad Hoc Committee for Accountable Police (AHC), the Police Brutality Committee (PBC), the People's Conference on Police Brutality (PCPB), the Committee for Accountable Police (CAP), the Liberation League (LL), the People's Defense Council (PDC), the Black Panther Party (BPP), Soul Patrol, Community Action Now (CAN), the Community Advancement Committee (CAC), Black Police for Positive Action

(BPPA), and the Black Organization of Police (BOP). By keeping the issue of police brutality at the forefront of their agenda, working-class activists were able to force the middle class–based local NAACP and NUL chapters to get involved in the fight, albeit reluctantly. Consequently, residents in New Orleans were able to win some hard-fought reforms. Nonetheless, the struggle for equal police protection in New Orleans continues, particularly in the aftermath of the NOPD's failure during Hurricane Katrina. The NOPD made national and international headlines during the storm when 289 officers either failed to report, abandoned their duty, or defied orders during the storm and subsequent flooding of the city, while others continued the department's history of law-breaking and neglect by looting, stealing, and harassing evacuees.[6]

Although police brutality has been an integral part of the black urban experience, the issue has received very little attention from historians because national civil rights figures made integration and voting rights a higher priority. The only national civil rights organization to address police brutality was the Congress of Racial Equality (CORE). Throughout the 1960s, CORE chapters in St. Louis, Detroit, Brooklyn, Cleveland, Los Angeles, Seattle, and Kansas City, among others, launched vibrant protests against police brutality and mistreatment. Although these protests never became national in scope, CORE was instrumental in empowering local leaders to fight police misconduct. The other national civil rights organizations and their leaders ignored the fight against police brutality, believing that police reform would be an immediate result of black political power, while others felt that it was just an issue that confronted poor black folks. However, local activists throughout black urban America mounted a serious and sustained protest against their respective police departments in the postwar period. Many black community studies mention police brutality as it relates to the riots of the 1960s, but the lack of scholarship on police violence and community protest is surprising considering how police brutality was an unfortunate reality of twentieth-century black life. This work provides a much-needed historical context by focusing on the relationship between a police department and the black community in one particular city over an extended period of time. Local studies give us an opportunity to see "patterns of individual involvement, cycles of protest and politics," and the evolution of urban activism, social criticism, and political struggles in a particular place during a particular time period. To be clear, this is not a study of policing in New Orleans. Rather, my focus is on how ordinary African Americans protested police violence and sexual assault of black women by the New Orleans Police Department and in the process made the connection between fair police protection and democracy.[7]

One limitation of this study concerns the lack of reliable data on police brutality. In the case of New Orleans, the police department, the department's internal affairs division, the city's civilian review agency, and the city's legal department have resisted providing the public with pertinent data on police brutality, and have only released the statistics when threatened with legal action or when the data presents the department in a favorable light. For instance, during the mid-1990s, civil rights attorney and police abuse expert Mary Howell requested information about civil lawsuit settlements and civil jury awards paid by the city of New Orleans, but her requests were repeatedly denied. But this is not a problem endemic to New Orleans. Law enforcement agencies across the country have often denied the public access to police brutality data, although in most cases the law provides for it. In addition to denying public access, the separate city agencies in New Orleans often produced no annual reports and did not provide information relative to complaints, trends, sustained rates for each type of complaint, disciplinary actions stemming from these complaints, civil lawsuit payouts, and results of internal investigations. Consequently, I was forced to compile information from a variety of statistical sources to give a composite look at police brutality in New Orleans.[8]

THE COMPLEXITY OF POLICE VIOLENCE IN BLACK AMERICA

While the intersection of race and law enforcement occupies the focus of this study, the issue of police brutality is much broader and more complex than a simplistic black-and-white paradigm. The unique culture of police departments and a host of structural factors also explain why African Americans have been the primary targets of police brutality in New Orleans and across urban America. The problem of police brutality is rooted in the atmosphere, attitudes, policies, and practices of police departments. Like the majority of other urban police departments, the NOPD had a distinct institutional culture that emphasized an "us versus them" attitude toward the communities in which they served. In fact, police officers often thought of themselves as a minority group. This is a somewhat hidden culture among police officers that stresses group solidarity, a sense of loyalty, a sense of belonging, limited interaction with outsiders, and group segregation. Historically, this culture has been infused with obvious anti-black attitudes and feelings.[9]

The adoption of this culture represents an important component of the socialization process for new police recruits. Rookie officers soon realize that if they are going to have a future in the department, they must adopt the attitudes and actions of their less tolerant supervisors for fear of demotion, termination, or ostracism. For many members of the NOPD, a job on the police force was the only respectable one they could land, thus they were unwilling to jeopardize their employment by going against the prevailing attitudes of their supervisors. This culture sees African Americans as a potential source of crime, danger, and disorder. Since many white officers have had very limited contact with respectful, law-abiding, or college-educated African Americans, while having a great deal of interaction with black criminals, many officers feel that black people are inherent criminals. The criminalization of African Americans further encourages these attitudes and it forces officers to adopt an occupational attitude when they are policing black neighborhoods.[10]

Police attitudes often transcend race because although some African American officers joined the force to make a difference in their communities, they soon learned that being a good cop in the eyes of the rank-and-file meant being tough on their own people. Thus, a segment of the black police population embraced their identity as police officers who happened to be black, instead of being black police officers. Many black officers were quick to adopt this "white policing syndrome" that involved white perceptions of black communities. Throughout urban America and in particular in New Orleans, black police officers have committed some of the most egregious acts of brutality toward black civilians.[11]

A significant ideological component of police culture teaches recruits that any challenge to their authority from marginalized groups should be met with an iron fist. This helps explain why in New Orleans and in other cities the targets of police violence and brutality have changed over time. In the early decades of the twentieth century, white immigrants complained the loudest about police brutality, but as they assimilated, African American migrants became the target group. In the 1940s, returning black World War II veterans and other African Americans with heightened expectations in the immediate postwar period came under attack, while in the 1950s and 1960s traditional civil rights activists were often brutalized for demanding integration and voting rights. Toward the end of the 1960s, police officers became tolerant of integrationists with the emergence of the Black Panther

Party and other Black Nationalist organizations that challenged the authority of the local police department. During this period the daishiki, the black beret, the black leather jacket, along with the language of revolution led to a decade of confrontations between police and these self-styled revolutionaries. Purported gang members and residents of housing projects were the targets of police violence in the 1980s, and the war on drugs of the 1990s hastened police violence as police departments were served with community mandates to keep their cities safe from crime.[12]

A host of structural factors also helps explain the persistence of police brutality in New Orleans. Throughout the postwar period, New Orleans has been a relatively poor city. The city's white power structure has always favored limited local government, low taxes, and a laissez-faire attitude toward municipal services. As a result, the NOPD has historically been underfunded, understaffed, underpaid, and unprofessional. Low wages, outdated equipment, low hiring standards, nonexistent background checks, and a noticeable lack of professionalization have characterized the NOPD. Some of these factors have been the greatest obstacle to serious police reform. For instance, in 1990 the starting salary of a New Orleans police officer was a paltry $15,000 and veteran officers were barely making $25,000 to $30,000. By comparison, the starting salary for officers in Atlanta was roughly $30,000.

Because of low wages and poor working conditions, the NOPD was faced with two major issues. First was the inability to attract quality recruits to the department as the city's crime and murder rate skyrocketed in the 1980s. Instead, the ranks of the NOPD were filled by recruits with criminal records, DUIs, unfavorable employment records, and dishonorable discharges from the military. Their records were expunged and they were turned loose with guns, badges, and patrol cars. Second, to make more money, almost 80 percent of the force moonlighted at second jobs, which they referred to as "details." This generally involved providing security for bars, nightclubs, concerts, and other events. While details are not endemic to the NOPD, the situation in New Orleans was unique because there was no restriction or regulation toward off-duty work. Oftentimes, officers worked more hours at their details than they did for the NOPD. Further, many officers often came to work tired because they had worked a twelve-hour detail before their shift in the department. Details became such a part of the police culture that many officers pledged their allegiance to their details instead of the NOPD.

BLACK POLITICS

As the oldest African American urban community in the United States, New Orleans has been a focal point of migration and a hotbed of racial protest. During World War II, thousands of black rural migrants arrived in New Orleans looking for work in the shipyards. Although there was a severe labor shortage, local labor unions and company executives literally excluded blacks from lucrative industrial positions out of fear of a race war and also because they did not want to be accused of drawing black workers away from agricultural work. Consequently, the postwar labor shortage was an opportunity available only to white workers. The lack of employment available to black workers in the shipyards mirrored a larger issue: the inability of black workers to secure employment in the city's only industry, oil. Although during the two decades after World War I oil remained the preeminent industrial base of New Orleans, African Americans were still confined to the low-wage unskilled section of the labor force. Consequently, the majority of black men worked as stevedores, roustabouts, and manual laborers, while black women were only able to find work as domestics and maids.

Despite Jim Crow and large-scale employment discrimination, the city had a reputation for peaceful race relations. The Crescent City, so-called because it geographically resembles a crescent, is sandwiched between the Mississippi River and Lake Pontchartrain. It was by far the most unique city in the United States. The French, Spanish, African, and Caribbean influences throughout the city seemed to frown upon racial discrimination. Further, the city's strong ties to the Catholic Church also illustrate that although New Orleans was still in the South, it appeared to be a bit more progressive than other southern cities. Indeed, in New Orleans visitors would find a low level of residential segregation as blacks and whites lived in the same neighborhoods. Also, black domestics would lodge in adjacent shotguns just a stone's throw from some of the city's most prestigious addresses. Because of the city's reputation for being carefree, easygoing, and a place to have a good time, New Orleans was one of the few cities that did not have a major race riot in the twentieth century. The lack of visible racial problems made New Orleans seem akin to Atlanta, but beneath the surface the city's white power structure maintained a vice-grip-like hold on black folks. Since the bourbon period, New Orleans had been dominated politically and economically by a conservative elite, who were more preoccupied with social rituals, old money, and heritage than with economic growth for the city. They were fiscally conservative, very insular, and protective of power, so that whites with "new money" were excluded from these circles of influence.

The city's power structure maintained its control by limiting black access to the voting booth. The total 1940 population of New Orleans was approximately 495,000, of which roughly one-third was African American. However, only four hundred African Americans in the city were registered to vote. Thus, they had no say in city government. Consequently, they had no significant opportunity to protest discrimination, racism, and general mistreatment. However, black New Orleans did have a host of civil rights organizations that pressed for black demands. At the forefront of the protest effort was the New Orleans and Louisiana NAACP, the latter of which was under the direction of Alexander Pierre Tureaud, affectionately referred to as "A. P. Tureaud." As historian Adam Fairclough noted, "for most of the half-century Tureaud's name appeared on every school and university integration suit filed by the NAACP in Louisiana," as well as on court cases challenging virtually all other Jim Crow laws. Tureaud, who was the only black lawyer in the state until the 1950s, worked closely with Thurgood Marshall and the NAACP Legal Defense Fund. But while Tureaud was active across the state as the head of the Louisiana NAACP, he was also persistent in fighting police brutality at home. The files of the New Orleans and Louisiana branches of the NAACP are filled with hundreds, if not thousands, of police brutality complaints against the New Orleans Police Department.[13]

Despite persistent police brutality, employment discrimination, and Jim Crow, black migrants from the rural South looked at New Orleans as the promised land and in the two decades after World War II, the black population of New Orleans almost tripled. The large influx of black migrants during the second great migration altered the city's unique residential patterns in several ways. First, white flight took off as white residents headed to suburban cities such as Chalmette, Arabi, Mereaux, Metarie, and Kenner in the 1950s. During the next decade, another segment of the white population left the city and headed to Slidell, Mandeville, and Covington, after the Lake Pontchartrain Bridge was completed in 1956. During the mid-1960s, many of the remaining middle-class whites left the central city for New Orleans East. As whites escaped to the suburbs, black communities suffered as the black population came to represent a larger share of the overall population of the city. In 1940 New Orleans was roughly 33 percent black; 1960, 37 percent; 1970, 43 percent; 1980, 55 percent, 1990, 62 percent; and in 2000, 67 percent. With many black migrants piled up into the city's notorious housing projects, shanties, and shotgun houses, there was very little investment in the city in terms of economic development, jobs, housing, education, and law enforcement. Consequently, although New Orleans had experienced peaceful race relations throughout its history, it was becoming a city divided by race and class and African Americans looked at the New Orleans Police Department as a direct representative of the white power structure. Since white police officers were likely to be uneducated and unsophisticated, conflict was inevitable once African Americans began to fight and assert their rights in the postwar period. This book is about that fight.

Chapter 1, "Negro Police Will Aid in Law and Order," looks at how civil rights leaders in New Orleans waged a five-year battle to get blacks appointed to the police force at the close of World War II. After five years of steady resistance, city officials gave in to the demands and in 1950 two African American men were appointed to the NOPD. However, in reality they were only quasi-officers. They could not arrest whites, they could not wear uniforms, and they could only patrol black communities. Nonetheless, the first generation of black police officers served admirably and they opened the doors for other aspiring black police officers. Although the presence of black officers did decrease the high crime rate in the black community, they were unable to put an end to the wanton police brutality that confronted the city's African American community.

As the civil rights movement gained momentum in New Orleans, the NOPD intensified its brutality and lived up to its reputation as an oppressive force in the black community. As civil rights activists engaged in sit-ins, protests, boycotts, mass meetings, and other nonviolent protest, the NOPD did its best to discourage black protest through harassment, brutality, and unlawful arrest and detention. Conversely, when civil rights workers were harassed by whites, the NOPD offered little protection. In fact, on several occasions NOPD officers allowed black protestors to be brutalized by angry whites. The refusal of NOPD officers to protect black protestors during the civil rights movement encouraged black activists to demand more representation on the force. For instance, in 1965 black officers made up less than 3 percent of the officers within the ranks of the NOPD, and none were in supervisory positions. Because of persistent encounters between African Americans and the police there was a great deal of concern that New Orleans was sitting on a racial powder keg that could explode at any time. As other major cities, such as Watts, Newark, Detroit, and Cleveland, experienced race riots triggered by police violence, New Orleans had all of the necessary ingredients for a major civil disturbance. Chapter 2, "Or Does It Explode?" looks at the transition from civil rights to black power in New Orleans.

The arrival of the Black Panther Party in 1970 changed the nature of police-community relations in New Orleans. After setting up their head-quarters in the Desire Housing Projects and establishing a number of viable survival programs, the BPP quickly came to represent a threat to the NOPD. After several clashes between the BPP and the NOPD, the reputation of the BPP grew astronomically as black residents responded to point number seven of the Black Panther Party Platform "We Want an End to Police Bru-tality," the title of chapter 3. In one dramatic incident more than two thou-sand black New Orleanians confronted approximately three hundred police officers in front of Panther headquarters in the Desire Projects who had come to serve warrants against the leadership of the Panther chapter. Visi-bly outnumbered and humiliated, the police officers quickly retreated in the face of this unprecedented community support for the Panthers. Although the leadership of the Black Panther Party was arrested days after the stand-off and subsequently forced out of New Orleans, many of their sympathiz-ers and supporters remained.

Chapter 4, "The Politics of Self-defense," examines the sniper attacks that struck in 1973 when Mark Essex, a twenty-three-year-old African American male, laid siege to the city of New Orleans by killing nine, among them five police officers, including the second highest-ranking member of the New Orleans Police Department. While many observers labeled Essex crazy or insane, he had subscribed to an ideology that African Americans needed to take the law into their own hands to defend themselves and their communities from violent police officers. The Essex shootings enraged white America, who believed that the killings were part of a broader Black Nationalist conspiracy to kill white police officers. In fact, less than forty-eight hours after the shootings, Congress and the Louisiana state legisla-ture drafted measures to reinstate capital punishment for crimes that in-volved the killing of a police officer.

In the aftermath of the Essex shootings, the NOPD adopted aggressive police techniques that were part of a broader national movement to reduce crime, repress radicalism, and levy stiff sentences toward convicted crimi-nals. Chapter 5, "The Right to Organize," examines the post-Essex NOPD onslaught and discusses the ways in which the black community responded. One way they responded was by forming the BOP, which was established to address the specific needs of black officers as well as the public safety concerns of black residents. Shortly after its formation, the BOP filed suit in federal court charging the NOPD with racial discrimination in the hiring and promotion of African American police officers. While the suit was pending, the BOP held several highly publicized marches and protests in front of police headquarters. Simultaneously, anti-brutality activists took their concerns about police violence to the city council, which became the scene for some of the most volatile hearings in the city's history.

The election of Ernest "Dutch" Morial in 1977 as the city's first black mayor gave police reform activists and black officers much optimism. They were hopeful that Morial would bring the anti-black department under control and implement diversity programs to promote existing black officers and recruit more African Americans to the force. Chapter 6, "Black Power Politics," looks at the early years of the Morial administration and its attempts at reforming the NOPD. Although Morial took major strides to rein in the department, the low point of Morial's mayoral career came in 1980, when white police officers went on a rampage in the black community of Algiers, killing four, injuring as many as fifty, and brutally torturing several others in retaliation for the killing of a white policeman days earlier. In the aftermath of the Algiers killings activists repeatedly shouted, "We Are Living in a Police State," the title of chapter 7, and they demanded a civilian review board, a police brutality commission, and civilian control of the NOPD, which some were now referring to as the American Gestapo. As a compromise, Morial and the New Orleans city council created the office of municipal investigation, staffed by civilians, to handle police complaints. Prior to leaving office in 1985, Morial named African American Charles Woodfork head of the NOPD, making him the first black police chief in the city of New Orleans.

While black New Orleans was delighted about more African Americans joining the force, they grew pessimistic about the future of police-community relations since much of the burgeoning corruption and brutality came at the hands of black police officers. In many ways a segment of the black police population had no intention of providing the black community with fair law enforcement. In fact, some black officers soon realized that as long as they confined their illegal activity to black neighborhoods and black civilians, they would be protected from prosecution since they could not be accused of being racist. Thus by 1990, as the NOPD became almost 50 percent African American, police brutality complaints increased even though African Americans were now firmly in control of city hall. Chapter 8, "Black-on-black Crime," looks at the downward spiral of the NOPD under the mayoral administration of Sydney J. Barthelemy between the years 1985 and 1993, when New Orleans would gain notoriety as having perhaps the most corrupt police department in the nation. Barthelemy would confront a severe fiscal crisis, an economic recession, a racially divided police force, and a new generation of black police officers who were thugs in disguise.

The first half of the 1990s would perhaps represent the darkest days of the NOPD. In 1994, Officer Len Davis, an African American, ordered the execution-style killing of Kim Groves, an African American single parent who had filed a police brutality complaint against him. The Groves killing illustrated most clearly that black civilians were risking their lives in filing complaints against corrupt officers. Ironically, Davis's involvement was only discovered after federal officials tapped his phone in an already preexisting drug investigation. Months later, twenty-six-year-old policewoman Antoinette Frank robbed a Vietnamese restaurant and killed her off-duty partner, who was moonlighting as a security guard, and two employees. What made the Frank killings so sinister was that Frank moonlighted at the restaurant herself and that she responded to the 911 call as though she had no involvement in the crime. These were just two of the more horrific incidents involving black police officers. According to several reports, the corruption within the NOPD was systemic, pervasive, rampant, and institutional. Further, it was woven into the fabric of the NOPD from the leadership team to the newly appointed rookie. Low pay, ineffective training, outdated equipment, incompetent leadership, and poor benefits all contributed to the lure of corruption, which went unchecked throughout the first half of the 1990s. Consequently, officers on the NOPD soon acquired the nickname "Cop Killers."

When Mayor Marc Morial, Dutch's son, entered office in 1995, he made the reform of the NOPD a top priority. After his election, he hired Richard Pennington of Washington, D.C., to lead the scandal-ridden department. Upon assuming the position, Pennington took on the corrupt culture of the NOPD by firing a large number of officers, instituting background checks for new recruits, establishing a system to spot corrupt officers, and placing limits on off-duty employment. In the community Pennington instituted quality-of-life policing, which eventually shrank the overall homicide rate by more than 50 percent in just a four-year period. Pennington's success was hailed as "A New Day in Babylon," the title of chapter 9. However, after a failed attempt at becoming mayor of the city in 2002, Pennington became head of the Atlanta Police Department. Since his departure, the city's murder rate has escalated and it appears as if many of Pennington's reforms were short-lived.

Eddie Compass, an NOPD veteran and self-proclaimed street cop, took the helm as police chief in 2002. While Compass was a good street cop, he was not an administrator. Consequently, the NOPD once again fell into its old habits of harassment, brutality, corruption, and general lawlessness. The book's epilogue, "Policing Katrina," looks at how the historical ineffectiveness of the NOPD affected its ability to handle the greatest natural disaster in American history. During the storm, NOPD officers were caught looting, stealing, and vacating their posts. In fact, 289 officers either quit, failed to report for duty, or vacated their positions during the storm. However, those who stayed served heroically.

1 NEGRO POLICE WILL AID IN LAW AND ORDER
The Fight for Black Police in the Crescent City

In the immediate aftermath of World War II, African Americans across the urban South tested the region's commitment to democracy by demanding integration of local police departments. While black citizens had made similar requests during the interwar period, these requests became more serious and radical as black citizens looked at equal police protection as a critical component of democracy and as local police departments began to focus much of their attention on African American activity. Across the South, African Americans from various backgrounds argued with local white politicians that the hiring of black police would improve police-community relations, act as a form of protection against police brutality, reduce the high rate of crime in the black community, and create new economic opportunities. For instance, in Atlanta, the All Citizen's Registration Committee, which included Martin Luther King, Sr., held a protest march in 1946 with protestors holding signs reading, "Negro Police Will Aid in Law and Order," "For Negro Police," and "105,000 Negro Citizens Rate at Least 1 Negro Police." In Memphis, the rape and sexual assault of two African American women in 1945 galvanized the black community to vehemently protest police brutality and demand black officers as well. While these complaints had been echoed privately for decades, they were now voiced openly as black citizens made a connection between citizenship, democracy, and protection by the police as well as protection from the police. These protests were clear indications that all was not well between the city's black community and its law enforcement officers. As the postwar period got underway, black citizens would unify and rally around the issue of police violence and sexual assault. New Orleans fit this pattern.[1]

DEMANDING INTEGRATION

On Sunday, March 4, 1945, "thousands of civic-minded" black citizens gathered at Booker T. Washington High School in New Orleans and approximately three thousand of those in attendance signed a petition demanding that city officials appoint African Americans to the New Orleans Police Department (NOPD). The petition argued that since African Americans played an "important part" in the local war effort and were property owners, they were in need of proper police protection, which they argued, "must necessarily come from members of his own race." The petition also argued that in all-black neighborhoods, "orderly and well-meaning folks" would get better service from black officers. Further, black women and children who encountered the police would receive more sympathetic treatment, rather than neglect. The demand for black police that evening was even endorsed by the conservative New Orleans Ministerial Union, which gave its unwavering support to the petition to get African Americans on the force. That evening the letter was sent to Mayor Robert Maestri.[2]

The former Louisiana conservation commissioner and protégé of Huey P. Long entered city hall in 1936. Despite only finishing the third grade, Maestri was arguably the wealthiest person in New Orleans and its largest property holder. After taking over his father's furniture store and investing the profits in real estate, the young businessman turned to politics despite whispers throughout the city that most of his money came from prostitution and illegal gambling. He spent his first few years as mayor improving city services and listening and responding to citizen complaints. After a relatively easy reelection campaign in 1942, Maestri became bored with politics, and city services, including the NOPD, underwent a decline. During the war years, the NOPD was repeatedly criticized for not cracking down on prostitution, gambling, and other forms of vice, as crime rose throughout the city. Superintendent of Police George Reyer and Maestri repeatedly refused to address citizen complaints about the corruption within the NOPD. Into this context stepped the city's African American community, which wanted Maestri to integrate the New Orleans Police Department.[3]

The signed petition sent to Maestri was a clear indication that the city's black community was beginning to recognize its increased voting strength. Although throughout much of the early twentieth century, black activists pressed for black police officers, their lack of political power caused white politicians not to take their demands seriously. However, as black voting strength grew in the aftermath of *Hall v. Nagel* and *Smith v. Allright*, two court cases that outlawed the white primary and gave voting access to African Americans, white leaders could no longer ignore the call for black police officers. For instance, in 1940 there were only 400 African American voters in New Orleans, but by 1948 there would be more than 13,000 African Americans registered to vote. In making their request for an integrated NOPD, black leaders argued that the presence of African American police would not only act as a deterrent to police brutality, but it would also help reduce the high rate of crime in the black community and give blacks a say in how laws were enforced.[4]

Like many other police departments in the South, the NOPD was a haven for white working-class males. The typical officer was poorly educated, raised in a segregated world, was hostile to civil rights issues, hailed from a blue-collar background, had served some time in the military, and had joined the NOPD because it was the best job he could find. In segregated New Orleans the NOPD considered themselves to be the frontline defenders against integration and they were very protective of their status and identity as police officers. As the white middle class expanded after the war, white police officers came to represent the face of the white working class.

Upon receipt of the signed petition demanding the integration of the NOPD, Mayor Maestri agreed to consider the request. Black citizens were not that optimistic that Maestri would respond favorably since during his nine years as mayor he had paid very little attention to black concerns. As expected, no action was ever taken on the petition. When the mayor failed to respond to the demand for black police officers, the Negro Interdenominational Ministerial Alliance (NIMA), under the leadership of Reverend Abraham Lincoln Davis, decided to get involved. Davis was perhaps the best person to spearhead the drive to integrate the NOPD because as a well-respected minister and co-founder of the NIMA he was widely known across black New Orleans. The Bayou Goula native grew up as a pastor's kid and in 1941 the twenty-year-old Davis started pastoring in New Orleans with a practical theology that stressed black liberation. Unlike the majority of black pastors, educators, and professionals, Davis was outspoken and did not hesitate to voice the grievances of the community. So when Maestri denied the petition regarding black police officers, the young pastor made a thorough investigation of the civil service rules that governed the testing, selection, and appointment of new police officers. As Davis expected, local civil service rules said nothing about excluding African Americans—it was just custom that kept black folk off the NOPD. After presenting their findings to Maestri, Davis and the Alliance were assured by the mayor that if black candidates passed the requisite tests, they would be appointed to the force. Minimum qualifications for the NOPD dictated that the candidate be between the ages of 21 and 40, be at least 5'6" in height, weigh a minimum 150 pounds, have an 8th grade education, supply four "responsible references, and be a registered voter. The yearly salary was $1,600. In addition to the physical requirements, prospective patrolmen were also required to pass a battery of written tests on such subjects as moral character, health, education, and appearance.[5]

When Davis and the Alliance discovered that there were more than thirty vacancies on the force, they encouraged African Americans to take the police exam. They also passed out petitions under the headline, "Petition, Requesting the Appointment of Negro Police Officers." It read: "Because of the now and urgent NEED, as a Property Owner and Tax Payer, I favor and fully support the appointment of Negro Policemen as Law Enforcement Officers to help serve the 165,000 or more Negro Population of the City, and herewith registering my endorsement of the petition." The bottom of the petition gave clear instructions: "Please Sign—Get Others to Sign—Return Promptly." Despite their efforts few responded, and one year later they were still trying to persuade black citizens to take the exam. Under the headline, "Negro Policemen Are Possible," the *Louisiana Weekly,* the city's popular black newspaper, printed a statement by the Alliance outlining the procedure for gaining an appointment to the NOPD.[6]

When the Civil Service Commission announced that the next set of exams was going to be held on August 24, 1946, the Alliance recruited potential applicants. Members of the black community went on an aggressive recruitment drive for black officers because they felt that city officials were open to the idea of black police officers. Prospective applicants were told that since there were 125 vacancies on the NOPD, the mayor "might easily be influenced by the large number of Negroes who have registered in recent weeks."[7]

Of the approximately six hundred prospective applicants who took the test on August 24, 1946, twenty-five were African American. Otis Fisher was one of those who took the test. "I enjoyed taking the exam. We were all treated well." When asked by a reporter whether or not he and other black applicants finished their exam before or after their white counterparts, he stated that as a group black applicants finished ahead of the whites.[8]

The persistence of Davis and the efforts of the middle-class-oriented NIMA to desegregate the NOPD say a great deal about the politics of unfair police protection in New Orleans. First, it illustrates that police brutality cut across class lines and unified the community. In as much as the NIMA was filled with conservative black ministers who often preferred to work behind the scenes and broker deals with the city's business and economic elite, their willingness to spearhead the fight and their outspokenness about the necessity for black police officers show that many middle-class blacks held deep concerns about the city's police department. Second, it is an example of how World War II ushered in a new era of political activism for African Americans who had supported the war effort abroad, and who were now looking for victory at home. Despite being segregated in daily life and still being denied the right to vote, African Americans in New Orleans coalesced around the issue of police violence and in the process they were defining one aspect of freedom as the right to fair police protection.

As civil rights activists continued to observe the police testing process, they were closely watching the 1946 mayor's race that pitted a young reformer named Delesseps Story (Chep) Morrison against the incumbent Maestri. The LSU-trained attorney and state representative from New Roads, Louisiana, received the backing of prominent business leaders who were eager to see New Orleans develop commercially and industrially. They were also tired of Maestri and his connection to Longite politics. In a surprise election Morrison beat Maestri by 4,372 votes. This election signaled that the residents of New Orleans were ready for change, and black residents were eager to see if integrating and reforming the NOPD were on the young mayor's to-do list.[9]

Black activists were confident that Morrison was open to the idea of black police officers when he appointed a new police superintendent shortly after his election. Adair Watters, a former marine colonel and influential member of Morrison's campaign team, accepted Morrison's offer to lead the NOPD only after Morrison promised that he would not interfere or politicize law enforcement in New Orleans. Based upon a 1946 report by the local Bureau of Governmental Research, Watters would have his hands full because the NOPD was in shambles. The survey revealed a dysfunctional department characterized by uneven enforcement of the law, an institutional culture of corruption and graft, a weak administrative structure, and haphazard personnel procedures. Morrison biographer Edward Haas believes that the NOPD in 1946 "reflected decades of local indifference toward police administration and organization."[10]

Upon assuming his new position, Watters wasted little time in cleaning up the department. He raised salaries, recruited new officers, consolidated precincts, put more officers on the streets, transferred corrupt officers, cracked down on graft and corruption, and restructured the department to make it more effective. Watters was hopeful that an influx of young rookie recruits would ultimately change the culture of the department. But because protective civil service rules prevented Watters from firing police officers, new recruits quickly adopted the attitudes of their supervisors. In the midst of Watters's efforts to reshape the NOPD, black residents were hoping that the integration of the NOPD was a part of his program since it was learned that four black applicants had made the eligible list for appointment.[11]

As Morrison was settling into New Orleans city hall, it was revealed that four African American males had passed the police test: Otis Fisher, Ernest Raphael, James Russell, and Herwald M. Price. Although Price thought about staying in New York City after his discharge from the military and joining the integrated New York Police Department, he decided that it would be more constructive to come home "and fight it out here." These four were now eligible for appointment to the police force. New Orleans civil service procedure called for the highest-scoring applicants on the test to be ranked and then when police officials were ready to fill vacancies they would ask civil service officials to certify a certain number plus two extras. Their appointments were now in the hands of Superintendent Watters and Mayor Morrison. The *Louisiana Weekly* argued that it was now up to Watters and Morrison "whether or not New Orleans will follow the progressive example" of other southern cities such as Richmond, Charlotte, and Tampa, all of whom had black officers.[12]

When word reached the black community that four African Americans had passed the test, civil rights groups were eager to see them appointed. The Louisiana Veterans Organization (LVO), a black group, sent a strong letter to Mayor Morrison about the critical need for black police. "The current crime wave in New Orleans has grown so acute that citizens' lives are almost constantly in danger. We feel that the need for Negro policemen is badly felt at this time. Recently, a number of Negroes passed the city civil service examination and qualified for the police force. These men have met all requirements. We respectfully request that you disregard past precedents and recommend some of these men for appointment. We are certain that such action would be for the good of all."[13]

Although Morrison acknowledged receipt of the letter from the LVO, he made no mention of black police appointments. Instead, he denied the existence of a crime problem in the city and referred the issue of black police to Superintendent Watters. Black New Orleanians now felt as if they were caught in a classic case of catch-22. Undeterred, the LVO sent another letter to Watters two weeks later, but as Earl Mitchell, executive secretary of the LVO, remarked, "as before the letter has been ignored."[14]

Like the LVO, the *Louisiana Weekly* was eager to know the cause of the delay in their appointments because, according to the rules of the civil service commission, the eligible list for appointment was only good for twelve months. "Citizens Wonder What's Holding Up Appointment of Policemen Here," read the headline, which once again made a strong appeal for black officers. In mid-December the *Louisiana Weekly* sent a reporter to meet with Watters on the subject of black officers. When Watters was asked about the possibility of black officers, he gave a rather evasive response: "I am sorry I cannot answer that question. It will be up to my superior to answer whether there will be Negro Police or not."[15]

Despite their pleas, Morrison had no intention of appointing the candidates. Throughout the South the possibility of African American males serving as police officers sent shivers up and down the spines of white conservatives. The revolutionary consequences of seeing an African American on the city's police force, carrying a gun and with the power to *enforce* the law, was too much of a threat. One of the main concerns was the fear that African American police officers would harass and rape white women. The underlying argument against black cops was that since African Americans needed to be policed, and the police department functioned for the benefit of whites, then African Americans had no place on the police force.

Despite successfully passing the exam, the four black candidates never received an appointment to the NOPD. Nonetheless, black residents continued to apply pressure on Mayor Morrison. In the early months of 1947, Morrison gave black activists a glimmer of hope after Watters stated that he wanted to add more than six hundred new officers to the force. In his address, however, Watters made no mention of black police appointments. Increasing the black community's anger was that Watters repeatedly refused to meet with local civil rights organizations about the issue. Morrison's reluctance to appoint black officers was threefold. He did not want to seem soft on the integration issue; he knew that the rank-and-file of the NOPD would fight it; and he did not think that the white citizens of New Orleans were ready for it. Nonetheless, black activists continued to apply pressure on the mayor.[16]

Two incidents in January 1948 speak to the issue of the NOPD and its exclusion of African Americans. The first occurred when three black teachers at Booker T. Washington High School were arrested at the Freedom Train exhibit. The Freedom Train exhibit was a traveling exhibit for school-children designed to encourage patriotism and pride in America. Although the schools in New Orleans were still segregated, black students were in-vited to tour the train. The trouble began when a white woman, who re-sented having to wait in line behind black students, shouted at a white po-lice officer to put her in the front of the line. Embarrassed, the white officer instructed one of the teachers, Charles Speaker, to get out of line. Speaker refused to move and the police yelled "educated nigguhs" before arresting him for disobeying police. Maurice Provost and Bruce Neale, fellow teachers, were also arrested when they "attempted to learn the reasons for Speaker's arrest." One observer recalled that "officer 783 was very ungentlemanly in handling the whole affair and threatened to do bodily injury to each of us." After a brief trial, all three were found guilty and fined $5 or five days in jail. Despite the obvious reality that the teachers were directly responsible for the safety and well-being of their students, they were still arrested.[17] Later that week, a ninety-two-year-old African American woman was arrested for allegedly "cursing a policeman." The persistent cases of police brutality, misconduct, and unfair police protection caused C. C. Dejoie, Jr., publisher and editor of the black *Louisiana Weekly,* to write: "the present crop of po-lice officers are as sadistic, rude, brutal, down right thoughtless and lacking in the high and fundamental qualities of good law enforcement principles and techniques as any who ever received salaries from taxpayer's money."[18]

Dejoie's constant critique of the NOPD and his coverage of police vio-lence and sexual assault on the front pages of the *Louisiana Weekly* gener-ated a great deal of support for the integration of the NOPD. Well-respected by all segments of the community, Dejoie took his role as editor and pub-lisher seriously. His attention-grabbing headlines and weekly opinions helped shape black political thought in New Orleans. His willingness to ex-pose the brutality of the NOPD confirmed publicly what many residents had been complaining about privately for years. Since the city's main pa-per, the *Times-Picayune,* intentionally avoided coverage of black frustration, white residents were largely unaware of the tension between the black com-munity and the NOPD.

THE POLITICS OF POLICE APPOINTMENTS
The push for black officers in New Orleans gained momentum in April 1948, when Atlanta appointed eight African American males to its police force.

Atlanta was seen by many of its southern sisters as the jewel of the South. Black residents of New Orleans were hopeful that Morrison would copy the progressive action taken by the Atlanta city council. However, upon realizing the conditions that Atlanta's black police were subject to, black New Orleanians did not wish for Morrison to exactly duplicate those restrictions.

When Dejoie discovered that Atlanta's black officers were restricted to black neighborhoods and that they could only arrest African Americans, he was outraged. "This means that in Atlanta white persons may come into Negro neighborhoods which are under the protection of Negro policemen and perpetuate every manner of crime without fear of arrest. Furthermore, if two white thugs and a Negro accomplice are seen emerging from a business establishment after cracking and robbing a safe, the colored policemen could arrest the Negro accomplice, but the white thugs could go on their merry way. Some Policemen!"[19]

Months later Dejoie announced on the front page of his paper that six African Americans had successfully passed the civil service exam for appointment to the police force. Carlton Pecot, James Russell, Herwald Price, Joseph Beselin, II, John Raphael, and Earnest Raphael were the African Americans who had qualified for the eligible list for appointment. Despite their test results, many members of the black community were convinced that the NOPD would never appoint a black officer because it represented a threat to white supremacy since blacks were meant to be policed and not to be police officers. Others were optimistic even though they had witnessed previous black candidates get passed over on the list. In making the argument for black police, black city leaders passionately argued that black officers would reduce the city's black murder rate, relieve white police of the "burden" of policing black neighborhoods, keep order in the black community, improve the morale of the black community, and vigorously enforce the law. In making their demands for black police officers, civil rights leaders made it clear that they were not expecting black police officers to police whites. They were hopeful that by establishing limits on black police work their argument would be easier for hard-core segregationists to accept.[20]

In an effort to sway public support behind the effort the New Orleans Urban League (NOUL) conducted a survey of forty-three cities in the South that employed black police officers and found that in every city the question of employing black officers was initially met with strong opposition. "Yet in each of these cities, the actual appointment of Negro policemen has dispelled fears by reducing crime and bringing about better relations between the races."[21]

The survey was conducted in response to Watters's assertion that the employment of black officers by the NOPD would result in racial chaos. The NOUL found that same type of reasoning being used in other cities that refused to hire black police. Some of the typical comments were: "colored people won't have any respect for a Negro policemen . . . It takes a white policemen to have any authority in a colored section . . . It will lead to race trouble . . . What if a Negro policemen has to arrest a white person, white folks won't stand for that . . . White policemen won't work on the same force with Negroes . . . It's not in keeping with the southern tradition." Despite their concerns, a host of other cities had already integrated their police departments, but none in the Deep South.[22]

On September 10, 1948, police candidate Carlton Pecot, a twenty-two-year-old Dillard University student, received a call from Captain John Pinero inquiring as to whether or not he was still interested in joining the force. Pecot, one of the six black candidates on the eligible list of appointment, was told to report to the office of Superintendent Watters for an interview the following day. When Pecot arrived at the office, he encountered several white officers before asking if Pinero was present. Pinero, oblivious to the fact that Pecot was the person he had spoken to the previous evening, asked Pecot if he could help him. When Pecot responded that he was there for an interview, Pinero, bewildered at this point, told Pecot that they did not have any more openings. "We called your home Wednesday and left a message for you to report Wednesday. It's too late now. We've already appointed someone in your place. The forms just went out this morning." Pecot then reminded Pinero that he was called the night before and told to report. Pinero responded by telling Pecot that he was now at the top of the appointment list and that he would get a call for an appointment to the force sometime in the future. After realizing that he was getting the "double-talk brush off," Pecot headed for the door. Before exiting, Pinero asked Pecot to tell civil service that he had been "interviewed." Later, Pecot told Dejoie that he was going to utilize the court system to integrate the NOPD.[23]

The beating of Leroy Williams, Janette Dubose, Frank Charles, and Victor Henry in January 1949 gave black activists ammunition in the fight to integrate the NOPD. When Leroy Williams, a forty-four-year-old longshoreman, attempted to defend himself on a city bus after being confronted by two white passengers, he was taken to the Third Precinct police station, where he suffered "one of the worst beatings of his life" at the hands of white police officers. When the brutality was over, Williams had suffered three cracked ribs and had been charged with assault and disturbing the peace. Less than two weeks later, a twenty-nine-year-old expectant mother, Jeanette Dubose, was slapped, thrown to the ground, and threatened after an altercation with police over a parked truck. This particular act of brutality galvanized the local National Association for the Advancement of Colored People (NAACP) into action, which demanded that Watters take immediate steps to end the wanton police brutality in his department. "For the past two weeks, signed statements have been directed to you with a request that some definite steps be taken against parties guilty of practicing brutality in the various precincts of this city." As expected, Watters ignored the letter. Local residents were further outraged after learning that Frank Charles and Victor Henry, both African American, were taken to the First Precinct after being accused of stealing a piece of jewelry at their place of employment, the Jung Hotel. After Charles told detectives that he didn't know anything about the jewelry, the brutality began: "One policeman started beating me, hitting me in the stomach with his fist. Then about fifteen other policemen in the station began punching me in the stomach, back and side. One jabbed me in the ribs with a billy then hit me in the stomach back and side." Henry was next. He was hit in the face when he stated that he did not steal the jewelry. "He [the policeman] hit me again, behind the neck. About seven of them began beating me. They punched me in the stomach and the side." The next morning Henry was taken from the cell and punched until he was made to say that Charles had taken the jewelry.[24]

After this latest outbreak of police brutality, Watters finally responded to the NAACP letter by mentioning that all cases of police brutality would be fully investigated. In a written response he also stated that he issued a positive order to end police brutality. "If it continues against my orders I would appreciate your association insisting that complainants go to the District Attorney and file charges . . . this will bring the matter before the courts, who, I am sure, will give satisfaction." Two days later, Watters resigned. Morrison then appointed Chief of Detectives Joseph L. Scheuring as acting superintendent of police; he would immediately reverse many of Watters's reform efforts. Although black leaders could not confirm it, they believed that Watters was dismissed largely because of persistent complaints of police misconduct and brutality toward African Americans. However, it was later learned that his termination came because he enforced vice laws in the French Quarter and would not go along with systemic vice and corruption that was woven into the fabric of the NOPD.[25]

In response to the continued lack of concern toward black brutality complaints, the Second Ward Voters League, under the direction of Jackson V. Acox, convened a mass meeting to discuss the repeated brutality. Acox led off the meeting by arguing that when a law-abiding African American saw a police officer approaching "he [did] not know whether or not to take the attitude of security or if he should cross to the other side of the street for fear of the cop may molest him." Acox then reminded his audience that while he did not condone resisting arrest, he could understand it. "What man or woman, especially the one who has tried to stay within the law wants to be called a damn nigger, cursed and abused after having submitted to arrest? And if you happen to resent that type of treatment, you'll be punched, kicked and hit across the head by someone you are paying to protect you." In response to the constant police attitude that black suspects needed to be physically and brutally restrained upon arrest, Acox argued that white arrestees literally got away with murder. "I have read in the dailies time and again where white citizens have fought, bit, kicked, and destroyed a policemen's uniform . . . yet they were always dealt with respect."[26]

The dual system of law enforcement that Acox articulated had long been a grievance in black communities. Residents often complained that vice and crime were allowed to flourish in black neighborhoods, yet it was not tolerated in white spaces. Also, African Americans had often talked about witnessing whites resisting arrest and cursing police officers, yet they were still treated with respect. His critique summed up the feelings of many black residents who expressed fear, as opposed to safety, when a police officer approached.

In March 1949, Acting Chief of Police Scheuring surprised civil rights supporters when he stated that he would have no objections to hiring African American police officers. Scheuring's response was a far departure from the comments of his predecessor but he did not set a timeline. When a member of the black press asked Scheuring if the inherent racism within the NOPD acted as a deterrent to the appointment of black police, he quickly rejected that view. "If states such as Georgia, Tennessee, and others where racial prejudice is much stronger than in New Orleans can appoint Negroes to the police force we can do it here." Despite Scheuring's public statements, the appointment of black police was still not a priority.[27]

In an effort to pacify the black community, the NOPD established a Citizens Police Force of five hundred men and announced that Negroes would be selected. "The call is for a Citizens Police Force and it means just that.

There will be no attempt to discriminate. Negroes will be welcome as anyone else to serve this useful purpose." Not only would the Citizens Police
Force actively utilize blacks, but they would also be chosen in proportion
to their numbers in the respective wards and precincts in which they lived.
Although the members of the force would be given full police powers, the
mayor could only use them upon a special proclamation. Further, they
would be principally used to maintain public order. Black activists considered this proposal a gimmick and months later they took the issue to the
courts.[28]

The battle for African American police in New Orleans took a dramatic
turn on June 1, 1949, when Carlton Pecot filed suit in civil district court
asking the NOPD to show cause why he should not be employed on the
force. Filed by A. P. Tureaud, the noted civil rights attorney and NAACP official, Pecot had a strong case. He had scored a rating of 91.26 on the May
1948 exam, one of the highest marks in the history of the exam, yet he was
passed over repeatedly and other candidates with far lower test scores were
appointed. He filed his suit on the date his one-year eligibility for appointment expired. Black activists knew the broader ramifications of the lawsuit.
"If Pecot is successful in his suit, it is expected that he will have opened the
way for other Negroes to be employed by the NOPD," wrote Dejoie.[29]

While the suit was pending, Mayor Morrison was privately encouraged
to proceed with the appointment of black police officers. "An inevitable
necessity" is how public relations expert Scott Wilson labeled the employment of black police officers. On June 15, 1949, Mayor Morrison and the
Mayor's Advisory Committee called a special meeting to discuss the issue.
During the meeting the mayor agreed that black applicants were discrimi-
nated against, but that he favored the integration of the police force. After
much debate, it was agreed that the NOPD would hire black officers. Morrison's actions received the support of the district attorney and Scheuring.[30]

Morrison's decision to proceed with the integration of the police force
was a result of black demands, political pragmatism, and the threat of federal intervention. In 1948, the number of black registered voters stood at
13,000, and by 1950 that number would double, so Morrison clearly understood the value of the black vote considering that his election margin was
a slim 4,000 votes. By proceeding with the integration of the NOPD Morrison was certain that he could count on black support for years to come.
Further, Morrison did not want the courts to decide the issue. In the political aftermath of *Hall v. Nagel* and *Smith v. Allright,* city officials were confi-

dent that Pecot would win in court. Thus, they proceeded with the appointment to forestall intervention.[31]

Days after the Mayor's Advisory Committee supported Morrison's idea of integrating the police force, Herwald Price and James Russell, who had passed the May 1948 test, were called to NOPD headquarters for an "interview." Upon arriving at the office of personnel, they were given a form to fill out "on which they were to give preference for foot or precinct duty." They checked "either" so that there would be no misunderstanding. After the interviewer noticed their response, he then asked them if they could ride motorcycles. When they told him no, the official inferred that the only openings were for motorcycle patrolmen and that he would call them as soon as something became available.[32]

In an effort to expedite the appointment of black police, the African American community formed several citizens committees, such as the Committee on Race Relations and the Citizens Committee on Negro Police (CCNP). They were successful. In May, Mayor Morrison informed Tureaud that the appointments were imminent. Tureaud then told a group of journalists "off the record" that the city would be appointing at least two blacks to the NOPD in a matter of days. Although Tureaud's comments were supposedly off the record, the *Times-Picayune* reprinted the story, which ignited a firestorm of protest from white citizens.[33]

THE INTEGRATION OF THE NEW ORLEANS POLICE DEPARTMENT
Despite broad criticism from the white community, Morrison lived up to his earlier commitment when Carlton Pecot and John Raphael, ages twenty-three and twenty-eight, respectively, became the first black police officers in New Orleans since the turn of the century. But Morrison did "place the new black patrolmen carefully," according to one observer. The token integration of the police force was not without its problems. The officers were assigned to the juvenile division, where they were to "confine themselves primarily to the investigation of Negro youth"; they were not allowed to wear uniforms; and they were assigned to an all-black neighborhood, where they would have virtually no contact with white civilians. The separate and unequalness of the black appointments did not sit well with Pecot. After only seven months on the force, he quit. He was replaced by twenty-four-year-old George Williams. In 1952, two more African Americans, Herwald Price and George Dalmas, were appointed to the police force. However, like the first appointees, Price and Dalmas were not allowed to wear uniforms

and they were assigned to the juvenile division. Since police officers were historically seen as a sign of authority, Scheuring believed that white residents would get alarmed if they saw a black officer in uniform.[34]

Although black officers had to juggle the demands of Jim Crow police work, they quickly earned the respect of their superiors. The NOPD chief of detectives praised the work of black officers. "The effectiveness of the colored police officers walking in plainclothes have proven themselves in many instances. The Police Department is beginning to realize more and more that there is a definite place in the organization of the police department for plain clothes colored police officers." The detective chief was also hopeful that black officers would eventually become detectives.[35]

Just two years after they reappeared on the force, C. C. Dejoie began to publicly commend the officers for their work. Under the headline, "Officers winning Respect of Police Head, Citizens for Commendable Work," Dejoie described the performance of the black officers as "excellent and equal in every respect to that of anyone else charged with upholding the law." However, the editor then went on to defend the discriminatory actions of the NOPD, particularly the reality that they were assigned to all-black areas,

TABLE 1.

Year of First Post-Reconstruction African American
Police Appointment in Selected Southern Cities

CITY	YEAR
Charlotte	1941
Little Rock	1942
Miami	1944
Norfolk	1945
Richmond	1946
Dallas	1947
Atlanta	1948
Memphis	1948
Nashville	1948
New Orleans	**1950**
Montgomery	1954
Jackson, Mississippi	1963

Source: Dulaney, Black Police in America, p. 118.

could not wear uniforms, and were assigned to the juvenile division. Surely Dejoie did not agree with that treatment, but it appears that he could not expect too much too soon in the area of law enforcement. Dejoie closed out his lengthy editorial by making a direct appeal to the black community, asking that they begin to respect the black officers. "The attitudes and backwardness of their own people constitutes a problem," he wrote. "Try counting the number of times that Negro officers have been the vicious targets of abusive language and insults from 'bad Negroes' who have told them 'nigga take your hand off me' and meant it. What about the times when Negro officers have overheard street arguments to the effect that 'New Orleans has no real Negro Cops.'" Dejoie closed by stating simply "Negroes themselves must first learn to respect their officers and they in turn will be respected."[36]

Dejoie's editorial on the dilemma of black police officers was somewhat prophetic. Beginning with the first generation of black police officers in the twentieth century, black patrolmen were not readily accepted by their white counterparts, and they were seen by some in the black community as sellouts or, at best, junior police officers. Black citizens were quick to challenge or resist an arrest from a black officer, but they would show a great deal of deference toward white officers. This placed black officers in the proverbial catch-22. While they were proud to protect their community, they also felt disrespected by black residents who saw them simply as police officers and not as brethren who were there to protect them. After years of violent and inhumane treatment, black citizens developed an inherent distrust of the law, the police, and police authority. Black officers would have to earn the respect of their community.

By October 1952, the NOPD had ten African Americans in its ranks—but none were yet in uniform. However, on Sunday, November 16, 1952, "police history was made" when two black officers wore uniforms for their new assigned tour of duty in the Sixth District. Chief Scheuring selected black veterans George Dalmas and Ernest Raphael for the beat. In an interview Dalmas stated that he was up for the challenge: "I'm going to perform my duty to the best of my ability. We know that the Garden District is tough, but we're ready." Out of fear of alienating white citizens, Scheuring argued that a recent crime wave in the area necessitated the situation. It worked. When a white citizen was asked about the appointments, he responded, "We are not bothered about their race. What we want is good policing." In the following week's edition of the *Louisiana Weekly*, readers saw a front-page photograph of Dalmas and Raphael in their uniforms under the caption: "First in 50 years."[37]

But the celebration seemed a bit premature after a local journalist discovered the two officers were not walking a beat, as had been expected, but were merely "pulling guard duty" as watchmen in front of a construction site. Although they were initially supposed to patrol the Garden District, they were confined to the vicinity of the Calliope and Magnolia Housing Projects. Apparently they were not allowed to enforce the law outside of those boundaries. The journalist made a startling observation. "Hoodlums commit their crimes along LaSalle and Washington avenues and disappear quickly into areas where officers do not patrol. On one occasion I have noticed that thugs on Washington and LaSalle have looked at Negro officers and laughed because of geographical restrictions." The writer further discovered that the officers did not have the use of a patrol car nor a police radio. Thus, "if they jump a criminal and need the patrol wagon or help they have no telephone. They are forced to go into private homes or residents and use the phone at all times of the night." The criticism did not go unnoticed by the NOPD. In early March, the NOPD assigned two black officers to patrol the Claiborne area. "A check on Washington Avenue reveals that Aubrey and Dalmes are keeping a constant vigil over residences, Shakespeare Park, taverns and other establishments in the area." The writer failed to mention whether or not they were serving in uniform.[38]

By June 1953, there were twelve African Americans on the force but only six were in uniform. One year later, there were twenty-five African Americans on the force with many more serving in other capacities of the NOPD. But although African Americans were joining the ranks of the NOPD, they were forced to work under strict supervision and heavy scrutiny. Basically, they were closely monitored and any kind of misconduct on their part was considered a serious offense. In July 1953, Patrolman Warren Aubry and Herwald Price were suspended after their district commander found them sleeping in the hallway of Flint-Goodridge Hospital at 3:00 a.m. For Aubry, it was his second violation; he had been suspended for thirty days the previous May for conduct unbecoming an officer. Both Aubry and Price protested this latest suspension by arguing that "Aubry had complained of being ill and while he [Price] was on the phone making a sick report to district headquarters" the commander appeared. One year later, four African American officers were suspended and subsequently indicted by the district attorney's office on charges that they beat up a barber while investigating the mysterious drowning of a six-year-old girl. Although the officers were eventually acquitted, the black community was still upset because despite all of the charges of police brutality they had brought against white officers, the district attorney rarely indicted white offices. Now, however, the district attorney's office was quick to indict black officers on charges of police brutality and terminate them if necessary.[39]

Patrolman George Dalmas was fired from the NOPD in September 1954 after he kicked and cursed out a teenage boy who was resisting arrest. Even though he appealed his case to the New Orleans Civil Service Commission, his firing was upheld. The black community did not tolerate misconduct, but they wanted black officers to get equitable treatment. The heavy scrutiny of black officers continued when Officers Carlton Pecot and John Pitts were suspended for allegedly "mishandling" a murder investigation, just months after they were promoted from the juvenile division to homicide. After the eight-week investigation was complete, both Pecot and Pitts were fired, much to the anger of the black community. The infraction: they identified the wrong murder suspect. The firing of Pecot and Pitts caused some black residents to wonder whether the NOPD had been divided into two sections: "one section to investigate the criminal act and the other section to investigate the work of Negro police." The mistaken actions of Pecot and Pitts paled in comparison to the blunders of white officers.[40]

Some black officers appealed for their reinstatement when they felt unjustly dismissed. George Dalmas asked Morrison to reconsider his dismissal in light of the fact that his "time spent on the New Orleans Police Department was not all bad." After spending several paragraphs on his experiences as one of the first black officers in uniform, Dalmas told the mayor that some of his shortcomings as an officer came as a result of family problems and other issues. Although "he tried to get some time off to try and pull myself together," he was denied personal leave. He closed the letter by stating that he realized that there were many men on the NOPD who were better officers than "I will ever be. I don't ever think there was any prouder than I to wear the uniform of the New Orleans Police Department." Despite his appeal to the mayor, he was not reinstated.[41]

While black officers were forced to serve and protect under separate and unequal circumstances, they still faced the same day-to-day challenge as white officers, mainly the threat of being killed in the line of duty. Patrolman Percival Johnson, twenty-four years old and father of three, became the first African American police officer in New Orleans to lose his life in the line of duty. He was killed by a fellow African American male. After a disturbance at the intersection of S. Rampart and Girod, the assailant, who felt offended when Johnson told him to move on up the street, fired upon Johnson and his partner. "Hey you . . . you shouldn't have talked to me like that," said the assailant. The assailant then fired upon the officers before the officers returned fire while chasing their attacker into a doorway. When Johnson pushed the door to enter, he was shot in the groin and died minutes later. While in police custody, Johnson's attacker mentioned that he was unaware that Johnson was a police officer because he did not have on a uniform.[42]

At Johnson's funeral community leaders asked black residents to respect African American officers. One minister remarked that it was difficult getting black men to join the NOPD and that the disrespect they received from the black community needed to stop. During the ceremonies, many observers wondered why there was only one white officer at the service, why the NOPD did not give Johnson an official ceremony, and why the NOPD and the mayor had not sent his family an official letter of condolence. The NOPD's refusal to acknowledge Johnson at his funeral convinced many black officers that they were only quasi-members of the NOPD.[43]

In addition to the unfair treatment black officers received, they were also barred from joining the City Police Mutual Benevolent Association. Members of the whites-only association voted 529 to 42 against changing the group's bylaws and constitution to permit black members. The vote came after a request from black officers seeking admission. Captain Al Rankin of the NOPD commented on the situation, stating, "Despite the voting results, I feel that eventually Negroes will gain membership into the organization." He then argued that as more black officers joined the NOPD, the chances of them being allowed to join were higher. Like other similar benevolent organizations, the City Police Association was designed to help disabled and retired officers and the families of those killed in the line of duty. Since Percival Johnson had not been allowed to join the association, his wife did not receive the $3,000 death benefit the association had for its members.[44]

The exclusion of black officers from the benevolent association was a clear sign that although blacks were now on the force, they were still not accepted by the rank-and-file. For many white officers, the presence of black police officers was a threat to their occupational identity and they were willing to resort to any and all techniques to prevent their black brothers from thinking that they were really full-fledged members of the NOPD. By restricting their mobility, not allowing them to always serve in uniform, and disqualifying them from membership in the benevolent association, white officers were making it clear that black officers would be junior partners. Nonetheless, the first generation of black police officers in New Orleans served proudly.

Five years after African American men reappeared on the force, Beatrice Jones became the first African American woman to serve on the NOPD. After being sworn in on November 1, 1955, she immediately went on her beat with two African American male officers. One month later, Marguerite Bush and Rose Norfleet joined her. All three women wore uniforms. Black women were eager to join the NOPD because in many ways they would be able to safeguard black women from abuse, sexual exploitation, and rape from white officers, and they would be able to handle the cases of black women accused of sexual offenses.[45]

THE POLICE SCANDALS AND THE RESTRICTIONS ON PUBLIC SPACE

While African American police officers were joining the ranks, the NOPD was rocked by scandal in the early 1950s when the department's reputation for allowing gambling and prostitution reached new levels. Although the NOPD had the power to enforce local laws, it was common knowledge that many NOPD officers were on the take. Concerned citizens responded first by forming the Metropolitan Crime Commission (MCC) in February 1952 to monitor the NOPD and other public officials, and then by establishing the Special Citizens Investigating Committee (SCIC). Armed with subpoena powers, the SCIC conducted an in-depth administrative-criminal study into the NOPD. Chaired by Aaron M. Kohn, a lawyer and former FBI agent who had completed a similar study in Chicago, the committee interviewed hundreds of officers and politicians and held public hearings. Through his investigations Kohn discovered a "complex network of police graft and corruption that extended from the top to the bottom of the department as well as ample evidence of illegal liquor, gambling, and prostitution." While the report was more than 1,800 pages long, police brutality against African Americans did not occupy much space. In the aftermath of the hearings, the SCIC recommended that Chief Scheuring be fired. He was. On May 4, 1955, he was replaced by Assistant Superintendent of Police Provosty Dayries, a retired army officer who was described as "honest" but weak.[46]

In the aftermath of the *Brown* decision and the early years of the civil rights movement, the NOPD launched its own version of massive resistance, as African Americans and law enforcement clashed over what the NOPD considered to be white public space. As historian Kevin Kruse notes in his study on Atlanta, working-class whites were very protective of *their* playgrounds, libraries, parks, schools, swimming pools, and water fountains, and they expected the police department to protect that space. But motivated by the nascent civil rights movement, blacks in New Orleans often tested the limits of segregation. Consequently, conflict with the police was inevitable.[47]

A particularly outrageous case of police misconduct occurred over public space in March 1955, when the NOPD arrested fourteen children for using the whites-only McDonough playground in Algiers. The incident occurred after black students entered the spacious and unused playground. Police officers took them to jail, where they had to wait at least two hours before seeing their parents. Parents of the arrested children were then forced to sign statements charging their children with being delinquents. Witnesses to the arrests described the police tactics as "Gestapo-like," and "Nazism." As one small boy crawled under the fence to avoid arrest, "a policeman placed his foot on the child's head." All of the children had racist and profane obscenities shouted at them. Days later, it happened again when nine other children were arrested at the playground. What made the actions of the NOPD so questionable was that the whites-only playground had gone unused for years.[48]

Days after the incident, A. P. Tureaud fired off a letter of protest to Mayor Morrison. The letter read, in part, "It is the position of these parents that this playground should be available to them [African Americans] and therefore, there should be no police influence with the use of the playground." Tureaud then threatened legal action "because the police are putting forth every effort to carry out a policy of racial discrimination which is no longer valid." Tureaud closed the letter by asking Morrison to give the matter his immediate attention. Morrison ignored the petition.[49]

The actions at the playground caused an uproar by African Americans on the West Bank. On the Monday after the incidents, more than 450 "irate parents" jammed into the Masonic Temple and drafted a petition to city officials demanding that African Americans be given access to the playground. New Orleans NAACP President Arthur J. Chapital stated that if city officials failed to act on the petition, they would proceed with legal action. "We of the NAACP request that all recreational facilities be used on an integrated basis. As parents, Christians, Americans living in a democracy and as taxpayers, it becomes our moral and legal duty to have those things for our children without the fear of being arrested by police officers."[50]

As in many other southern locales, city buses were also a space for racial confrontation between African Americans and the police. In January 1956, the NOPD supervised the mass arrest of seventy-two African Americans on a city bus after a college student "floored a Jim-Crow sign" that divided the seating on the bus into black and white sections. The incident occurred in the aftermath of the Xavier and Dillard University annual basketball rivalry, when scores of college students boarded a city bus at South Carrollton and Washington avenues. As the students boarded the bus, words were exchanged between several students and the driver, thirty-six-year-old Francis Roux, over the racial division sign, although only one white passenger was on the bus at the time. Humiliated by the verbal exchange, the driver radioed a bus dispatcher, who then called police. Francis Carver, age seventeen, was singled out by the driver and when the other passengers heard the driver summon police to arrest her they shouted, "You'll have to take all of us." When the officers arrived, Carver laughed at them and so did the other passengers. The entire group was then taken to jail and while everyone was released within hours, Carver was booked with inciting a riot as well as disturbing the peace.[51]

In addition to their strict enforcement of Jim Crow laws, the NOPD also used black males, at times, as target practice. Sixteen-year-old John Sandville was fatally wounded by police after he refused to stop while being chased. The officer who fired the fatal shot argued that Sandville was holding a weapon in his hand at the time of the shooting. The alleged weapon was a pair of pliers. The only comment Sandville's mother offered was "they didn't have to kill my boy." In another unfortunate incident of police homicide, George Wright was killed "in cold blood," after being beaten with a blackjack and stomped in the stomach, all while being called a black nigger. However, before he was shot, witnesses testified that Patrolman Sanford Krasnoff ordered Wright to get up and run. As Wright ran away, Sanford took dead aim and shot him in the back, "as though he were an animal in a live hunt." As expected, the police version of events was somewhat different. The official version was that Wright pulled a knife and the officer fired in self-defense. The shots, which witnesses referred to as "the murder made by a young, trigger-happy cop, drunk with power," infuriated local residents, who told reporters that they would go to the FBI to secure justice. Days after the shooting, multiple witness went to NOPD headquarters to tell what they had seen and several reporters of the *Louisiana Weekly*, which broke the story, were called down to give testimony as well. The NOPD's efforts were strictly ceremonial. They had no desire to investigate the shooting.[52]

THE SEXUAL ASSAULT OF A BLACK WOMAN

The battle for equal protection was gaining momentum, but it still had not galvanized the entire community—even though literally every African American family had the potential to be affected by police brutality. However, the brutal rape of a twenty-three-year-old African American woman at the hands of three white officers in 1959 mobilized much of the community. In the early morning of Sunday, November 29, 1959, the unidentified woman was stopped by police shortly after 2:30 a.m. at the intersection of Treme and Lafitte. The woman was informed that she was being stopped for a minor traffic violation, but the officer allowed her to drive off without citing her. The officers followed her as she drove away, stopping her again several blocks away. Patrolman Anthony Saltalamacchia told her that she appeared to be too tired to drive and that she needed to let him drive. Once behind the wheel, Saltalamacchia instructed the other two officers to follow him to a "secluded spot." After driving to N. Dupre between Toulouse and Lafitte, the officer raped her while the other two officers remained parked. After the rape, officer Pete Callen was told by Saltalamacchia to go over to the woman's car and have sex with her. When Officer Callen approached the car, he found the woman crying. The police then drove off. However, in an act of carelessness, Saltalamacchia left his police hat on the front seat of the woman's car.[53]

The distraught victim drove to her uncle's house. He took her to the home of a prominent African American civic leader, who then called the police. In an act of swift justice, to the delight of the black community, the three officers, Saltalamacchia, Callen, and Ronald Raynes, were arrested, booked with aggravated rape, and dismissed from the force, after the victim identified her attackers.[54]

Richard Dowling, the Orleans Parish district attorney, upheld the case and filed aggravated rape charges against the three offices. After reading a statement from the victim and the three officers, including Saltalamacchia, who admitted having consensual sex with the victim, Dowling had little choice but to file formal charges. "From the information submitted to me, I could do nothing but accept charges of aggravated rape against all three men."[55]

In routine fashion the Orleans Parish grand jury indicted the officers in the rape and assigned the case to Judge J. Bernard Cocke of Criminal Court. District Attorney Dowling set a trial date for January, but he was still not committed on whether or not to seek the death penalty. Although grand jury indictments were somewhat of a formality, the presence of two African Americans on the grand jury helped. At their arraignment on January 6, 1960, all three former officers entered innocent pleas.[56]

As predicted, all African Americans who were interviewed as prospective jurors were challenged by the defense. Consequently, when the trial opened on March 21, 1960, the jury was all-white. When the victim took the stand, she identified her attacker and testified that he removed her pants and raped her and that she did not scream or yell because no one was around and because she had been afraid of the police since she was a child. The weeklong trial ended in a not guilty verdict for all three officers. Black spectators felt that the district attorney's office had not put forth a strong case. Regardless, only the most optimistic African American could have honestly believed that the all-white jury would convict three white police officers of raping a black woman. In the eyes of many, the acquittal upheld the traditional southern custom that the rape of a black woman did not constitute a crime. The acquittal of the three officers clearly demonstrated the institutionalization of police brutality against African Americans in New Orleans and it showed that blacks had very little recourse in their fight against police brutality.[57]

The killings of Sandville and Wright, and the rape and sexual assault of the unknown woman, illustrated the complicity of police officials, city politicians, the parish grand jury, the district attorney, and local judges in the institutionalization of police violence and sexual assault. While the rape case did go to trial, black observers were not confident that the officers would be found guilty. The African American community realized that the trial would be strictly ceremonial, considering that the victim was black, the police officers were white, and the jury was all-white.

With tensions still high after the acquittal, a disturbance at a local bar ended with a group of African Americans being arrested, brutalized, and charged with attempted murder of police officers. The scuffle began when two teenagers were searched by police who were looking for automobile thieves. When one of the boy's parents was notified by an onlooker that her son was being detained by the police, she arrived on the scene and was immediately brutalized. "They began beating me on the head," she recalled.

As onlookers poured out of bars and residences, about twelve additional squad cars arrived with officers brandishing sawed-off shotguns. The NOPD proceeded to conduct "a reign of terror" by arresting forty-nine African Americans on charges that they attacked police officers. In fact, the African Americans were the ones getting brutally beaten. Dorothy Melton, her son, and his friend were perhaps beaten the worst. All three suffered severe head injuries. Although the charges of attempted murder were eventually dropped, the incident provoked a great deal of community outrage.[58]

In the aftermath of the mass arrests, approximately fifty representatives of various civil rights groups formed the Committee to Prevent Police Brutality to Negro Citizens. Attorney Ernest N. Morial, the future mayor, was named chairman of the group. The involvement of Morial gave the committee instant credibility. The young creole attorney, armed with a law degree from Louisiana State University (LSU), was a political moderate and somewhat respected by whites. Since he was not seen as a civil rights agitator, it was politically safe for Morrison to meet with him. In a letter to Morrison, Morial explained that the community outrage served as the impetus for creating the committee. "Numerous persons have contacted various of our Negro leaders to do something about this dastardly thing. We found it necessary to call a 'Summit Conference of Negro Leaders' to discuss the grave issues involved and how to develop a program of action to prevent the recurrence of this violation of human rights." The mass arrests earlier that week, which they labeled "the worst case of police brutality and disregard of the rights of citizens in the last twenty-five years in this city," served as the specific catalyst for the creation of the committee. It was the committee's intent to call a meeting with Mayor Morrison; Dowling, the district attorney; and Councilman Fred Cassibry, who represented the district where the mass beatings and protests had occurred.[59]

At the committee's Monday meeting, Morrison, Dowling, and Cassibry denied that they had any knowledge of the Gestapo-like violence on the part of the police. At the meeting the committee asked the mayor to investigate police brutality charges and requested that the city council conduct open hearings on these charges. In defense, Morrison said his office was not aware of the brutality invoked in the local arrests. Morrison promised the committee that when the facts and evidence supporting charges of police brutality "are brought to my office, you can rest assured that definite action will be taken."

In spite of mass meetings in the black community on the subject of po-

lice brutality, black residents often expressed their displeasure to Mayor
Morrison over the department's long history of mistreatment of African
Americans in writing. In 1960, a man calling himself "Prophet A. M. Calhoun" sent the mayor a letter warning him of God's wrath on the NOPD
if they did not stop brutalizing black folk. Calhoun opened the letter by
stating, "This came from a Prophet of God. This message is on behalf of the
police force. It is God's request." The letter read: "God said you got a lot of
unconverted men on the police force. They are not qualified enough to even
be on police duty. They don't do anything but kick and stomp and beat up
and brutalize the colored people. You can pass by the precincts and hear the
licks and hear them pleading and asking them to please stop kicking them
in the stomach." Calhoun then specifically told the mayor that as soon as he
received this letter he had to act quickly. "As soon as you get this message
contact every police on the force and tell them that you received news from
heaven forbidding anymore beating or brutalizing 'my people' nor white nor
colored." If the mayor refused to stop it, he wrote, "God is going to stop it,"
because "the Lord thy God is angry with the police force. Never mind these
buildings, because when God moves upon this city there will not be one of
them left standing." Calhoun closed the letter by telling Morrison, "Don't be
a Jonah. Do as God commands you to do and have peace and be at ease."[60]

Part of the frustration expressed by Prophet Calhoun and others centered on the fact that black voters gave Morrison their unqualified support
during his fifteen years as mayor. With the help of Reverend A. L. Davis and
the Orleans Parish Progressive Voters League, Morrison was able to keep a
hold on the black vote by dispensing patronage benefits to Davis, Tureaud,
Avery Alexander's Consumers League, C. C Dejoie of the *Louisiana Weekly*,
and local labor organizer Dave Dennis, in exchange for black votes. While it
was widely known that Morrison wavered on the race issue, in a culture of
segregation he was a moderate politician. During his tenure, Morrison created a black advisory committee, integrated recreational facilities, removed
Jim Crow bathroom signs in city-owned buildings, integrated the city libraries, and gave Louis Armstrong a key to the city. Thus, despite the persistence of police brutality, African Americans in New Orleans believed they
had a friend in the mayor's office. The extent of that relationship would be
tested with the school desegregation crisis of 1960.[61]

2 OR DOES IT EXPLODE?
The Black Freedom Struggle Comes to New Orleans

While African Americans across the South were marching, sitting-in, and holding various forms of protest against segregation and disenfranchisement, television viewers outside the South saw the brutality of southern police departments that black southerners had complained about for decades. During the civil rights movement, many police officials understood that they had an obligation to keep black folks in their place since the urban setting did not allow for mob activity. Although massive resistance rhetoric may have been espoused by segregationist politicians and white community leaders, it was carried out by members of the local police department who were empowered by demagogues, segregationists, and the courts to use any means necessary to resist integration. In some cities police officials responded violently to black protest efforts, and in other locales white segregationists brutally attacked black activists as police officials stood by giving their consent.

The typical southern police department was filled with Klansmen and/or white supremacist sympathizers who cherished their working-class southern identity. Since the black drive for integration came, at times, at the expense of the white working class, they vigorously defended public space that they considered "theirs." The integration of restaurants, swimming pools, parks, libraries, and schools in working-class white areas led to a significant white backlash that was carried out in violent clashes between police officers and African Americans.

THE GENESIS OF THE CIVIL RIGHTS MOVEMENT IN NEW ORLEANS
On September 9, 1960, members of New Orleans Congress of Racial Equality (CORE) launched a sit-in at one of the Woolworth stores on Canal Street,

signaling the beginning of the direct-action civil rights movement in the Crescent City and a new era of black protest. After four hours, the New Orleans Police Department (NOPD) arrested the protestors and charged all seven with criminal activity. After the demonstrations, newly appointed police Chief Joseph I. Giarrusso, an NOPD veteran with a reputation for being a good administrator, issued a statement referring to the sit-in as "regrettable." He then mentioned how the NOPD would respond to direct-action: "As part of its regular operating program, the New Orleans Police Department is prepared to take prompt and effective action against any person or group who disturbs the peace or creates disorder on public or private property." The thirty-seven-year-old chief then made it clear that the NOPD and its personnel were "ready and able to enforce the laws of the City of New Orleans and the State of Louisiana."[1]

Throughout the next week protestors continued their sit-ins. However, Morrison instructed the NOPD to arrest them in violation of State Acts 70 and 80—two acts passed by the Louisiana legislature earlier that year to prevent demonstrations. The acts prohibited demonstrations that disturbed or alarmed the public, and Act 80 specifically prohibited the obstruction of public sidewalks. "It is my determination that the community interest, the public safety, and the economic welfare of this city require that such demonstrations cease and that henceforth they will be prohibited by the police department." According to Morrison, the sit-ins did not represent the feelings of most African Americans but rather "a small group of misguided white and Negro students." Police Superintendent Giarrusso added that he did not think that the demonstrators represented the more intelligent group of black folk. Morrison's directive to arrest the demonstrators came as a shock to black leaders, notably A. L. Davis; Clarence "Chink" Henry, president of the General Longshore Workers Local no. 19 and local political operative; and Reverend Avery Alexander, a pastor and head of the middle-class-oriented Consumers League. All three men were arguably the most powerful black leaders at the time and all three received patronage benefits through Morrison's Crescent City Democratic Association. However, in an effort to attract segregationist support for an upcoming gubernatorial bid, Morrison decided that the NOPD would hold the line of civil rights demonstrations to the disappointment of Davis, Henry, and Alexander.[2]

Giarrusso's public statements on the matter also came as a shock to black residents. Although they knew the chief had to obey Morrison, they were confident that he would express some sympathy for the demonstrations. After he was appointed in August 1960, he told the press that he would "dedicate all my efforts to giving you the type of police department which we can all be proud of." And during a speech at the police academy days later, he stressed to the recruits that "all of us must be kind and courteous to the public." Despite his pronouncements, Giarrusso would be unable to give black New Orleans the kind of law enforcement they needed.[3]

The formation of New Orleans CORE and the protest on Canal Street served as a signal of two things. First, relations between the races were not as harmonious or progressive as they assumed. Because of its international flavor, high degree of residential integration, and unique culture, many residents felt that New Orleans was exceptional—a place where blacks and whites peacefully coexisted with minimal racial tension. The *Times-Picayune* and its attitude of journalistic negligence contributed to this idea because by its refusal to cover black activism, protest, and frustration, it neglected to inform most whites about the frustration that ripped through black New Orleans. Second, the Canal Street protest also put the city power structure on notice that there was a different breed of leadership in the city who believed in direct-action and other forms of protest not usually seen in New Orleans. In a city that was now 40 percent African American, change was inevitable.

THE SCHOOL DESEGREGATION CRISIS

The first test of Joseph Giarrusso's tenure as police chief came in November 1960 as the Orleans Parish school board prepared to integrate its school system after an eight-year court battle that at times resembled a legal circus. In a May 1960 poll, 82 percent of white parents in the parish preferred closing the schools rather than accept integration. When U.S. District Court Judge Skelly Wright set the date for November 14, 1960, segregationist legislators, white citizens council leaders, and rank-and-file white parents set out to block integration by any means necessary. When the foes of integration failed to get a delay in the federal order, they accepted the inevitable. The schools marked for integration were William Frantz and John McDonough No. 19, both elementary schools that were all-white prior to the federal order. The choice of Frantz and McDonough No. 19 raised red flags since both of these schools were located in the Ninth Ward, arguably home to the city's poorest and least educated whites. However, when federal marshals ushered the three African American girls into McDonough No. 19 and the lone African American into Frantz, there was surprisingly no violence or disorder.[4]

The second day of integration would be a bit different as angry whites gathered at both schools in an effort to heckle and assault the black children. At McDonough No. 19 approximately 250 white youths surrounded the school until they were removed by the hundred police officers that were at the school. Another group gathered at Frantz and they, too, were removed by the police. Although the NOPD prevented the outbreak of violence, they did arrest twenty-one people for jeering and heckling. At times the NOPD was booed as well. After the second day of integration, black leaders were confident that the NOPD would protect black children and black parents in the integrated schools. In fact, the work of the NOPD in maintaining order and protecting innocent people did not go unnoticed. The editor of the *New Orleans States-Item* wrote, "In a potentially explosive school situation, New Orleans police have acquitted themselves admirably. With vivid memory of Little Rock, partly because of effective police work, police Supt. Joseph I. Giarrusso instructed his men well." The editor then mentioned that although Giarrusso was new in the "top police job, he has given an excellent demonstration of organization and leadership. Our praise to him and his men." Giarrusso's protection of the students illustrated to black leaders that the new chief would protect them from angry white segregationists. Giarrusso's apt leadership prevented an outbreak of racial violence. By protecting black children, having a significant police presence at the school, and arresting the hard-core segregationists, Giarrusso circumvented a duplication of the violence that had accompanied the integration of Little Rock's Central High School in 1957. While civil rights workers were delighted with Giarrusso's actions, hard-core segregationists were livid.[5]

That evening local residents were worked up into a racist frenzy at a citizens council rally that urged massive public resistance against the integration of local schools. Invited to get the crowd going was William Rainach, a state legislator, and Leander Perez, district attorney from nearby St. Bernard and Placquemines Parish. After verbally attacking Mayor Morrison, the National Association for the Advancement of Colored People (NAACP), and Federal Judge Skelly Wright, the speakers then attacked the NOPD for their role in making integration peaceful. Rainach stated that Morrison was a snake for making the NOPD guard the schools. "They would much rather have a mayor stand before you and pledge to support what you've been trying to do." The speakers made it clear what needed to be done. "Now you have to take the matter into your own hands," said Perez. John Wright, president of the citizens council of Jackson, Mississippi, told that audience that "checkerboard classrooms today mean blackboard jungles tomorrow. In the crisis you now face inaction is consent. Your battle for your sacred heritage depends on what you do in the next few hours."[6]

The next day hundreds of white teenagers mobbed the central business district, assaulting African Americans, verbally abusing police officers, and rampaging through city hall. Donald Campbell, nineteen, was returning to work when he was spotted by a mob yelling, "Get that nigger." He was beaten and stabbed by the mob as forty white youths fled the scene. Luckily, his wounds were not fatal. Twenty-six-year-old Theodore Lagarde was beaten as well while running an errand for his employer. He managed to break free and found refuge at the corner of Dryades and Lafatte, "where Negroes rushed from their homes with all types of weapons and stood the mob off." Eight of his ribs were fractured. One section of the mob then ran through city hall demanding to see Morrison, while another went into the state supreme court building looking for Judge Wright. The Confederate flag waving-mob was only subdued after the NOPD drove them back with water hoses, motorcycles, and horses, to the shock of protestors. "I hope all your children are black," a group of students shouted at Giarrusso.[7]

In the aftermath of the riots, Morrison, who had given the citizens council permission to use Municipal Auditorium for the rally, moved quickly to defend the actions of the NOPD from segregationists who suggested that Morrison was using the police department as a tool to crush segregation. "Student demonstrators were given every type of tolerance by the authorities. We continued our conduct of the ordinary business of the city and permitted these students to express their feelings." Ironically, Morrison admittedly let the white students protest, but when African Americans wanted to protest peacefully he was quick to issue an injunction. Further, it appears that Morrison wanted to allow some sort of protest but only stopped the madness when it reached riot proportions. Morrison was also angered by the verbal abuse heaped upon NOPD officers. "Officers of the department have been subject to continual abuse and name-calling for carrying out their duty of maintaining peace and order, which is so necessary to the future of our city."[8]

In conjunction with the riot, white parents at the two integrated schools launched a boycott and refused to send their children to school. Under pressure from segregationists who accused him and Morrison of being nigger lovers, Giarrusso allowed white protestors to harass white students and parents who chose to send their children to school. Giarrusso allowed the women, often referred to as "cheerleaders," to congregate every morning in front of the two schools so that they could abuse and harass the children and parents at the schools. NOPD officers often joked with the cheerleaders while forcing journalists to leave the area. Consequently, students and parents were forced to walk through a hate-filled gauntlet every morning and afternoon while entering and exiting the school. For example, Reverend Lloyd Foreman was pushed and shoved as he took his daughter into Frantz Elementary. Although the police cleared a path for him through the protestors, the NOPD did nothing when he was mildly attacked by the crowd. Minutes later, two women were assaulted in their car after dropping their children off at the school. The defiant cheerleaders were committed to a successful boycott. When asked how they intended to prevent anyone from reentering their children, one woman replied, "We'll get them. They just better not try." In both instances the NOPD did nothing to stop the heckling and the harassment. The following day the harassment continued as a Tulane University student was attacked, an American Civil Liberties (ACLU) director was mobbed, and a mother was pushed into a tree by the protestors. The NOPD took a tougher approach during the first week of December when it set up barricades three blocks from the school. It was now safe for children and parents to attend school. The boycott was weakened now that the NOPD had done its job. Black leaders could only conclude that if the NOPD had done its job throughout the integration crisis, the riots and demonstrations could have been avoided.[9]

The school desegregation riots and resulting violence during the fall of 1960 were avoidable. Some suggested that Morrison allowed the racial violence to take place so that he could gather segregationist support for his gubernatorial bid. During that campaign Morrison was accused by his opponent of being a proponent of integration because of his close ties to the black political establishment in New Orleans. Knowing that New Orleans was by far the most racially tolerant area in the state, Morrison attempted to ease the fears of segregationists across the state by playing the race card. The lack of police protection afforded to black students at the integrated schools was Morrison's way of sending a subtle message that he was not in favor of integration. By allowing the city to descend into racial chaos, Morrison was hopeful that he would be able to earn the votes of the state's most racially conservative voters in the 1960 gubernatorial race. His strategy failed. He lost the race.

AN INCREASED POLICE PRESENCE

Several police murders in 1961 ushered in a new era of police violence in the Crescent City. In January George Wilfred was shot twice in the chest by officers during a minor traffic stop. Wilfred and three passengers were pulled over by officers because his car did not have working headlights. When Wilfred opened the door and reached for identification, he was shot. Although Wilfred was an ex-convict, local citizens urged the NAACP to request a full investigation into the shooting. They did.[10]

The legal redress committee of the NAACP met with Giarrusso to talk about the Wilfred case and other cases concerning the mistreatment of African Americans. "We presented several documented cases, including one concerning six youths who were arrested apparently without cause, and one concerning the shooting of a motorist [Wilfred] who was apprehended on a minor traffic violation." Arthur Chapital, Jr., local NAACP president, made it clear that he wasn't against all police officers, just those who brutalized citizens. Shockingly, Chapital seemed convinced that the meeting was fruitful. "Giarrusso and Deputy Superintendent Joseph Guillot received us cordially, and promised to look into the matter immediately," he said.[11]

In May eleven-year-old Allen Bruce Foster was shot five times and killed by police as he fled the scene of a burglary at the Crescent Cigar and Tobacco Company on Lafayette Street. Patrolman Richard Martin said that he thought he saw a man atop a wire cage inside the store. He said he then saw something shining in the person's hand and ordered him to drop it. Martin then recalled seeing the boy jump fifteen feet to the floor and take off running. After Martin fired an errant shot, he then shouted to his partner, Robert Jackson, that the boy was armed and coming his way. As Foster ran into the street, he was gunned down and pronounced dead at the scene. This was the official police version.[12]

The community version of events was different. One witness was clear about what happened: "I heard one shot so I ran outside to see what was happening. I saw the child running toward a red automobile. Just as he reached it he was shaken violently as bullets tore into his body. The boy let out a piercing scream—one I shall never forget and fell to the ground. A policeman then stooped over the boy and said, 'Why didn't you stop when I told you to halt.' The boy never answered, never moved." The witness continued. "I never heard anyone tell the boy to halt. I saw everything that happened after hearing the first shot. I didn't see a pistol until photographers were taking pictures and that was after the boy had been taken to the hospital. And there is no way possible that I could have mistaken so small a boy for an adult. No one asked me for a statement."[13]

The black community was incensed when it learned that the victim was in the fifth grade. In response, a "protest funeral procession" was planned by the NAACP and the coordinating council of Greater New Orleans, and other local organizations requested an immediate investigation. To make matter worse, when Foster's mother ran to the scene after being told by neighbors that her son had been shot, she was told by an officer: "Now you want to know where he is; now you're looking for him; well, he's over at Charity (hospital), been there about 45 minutes."[14]

Hundreds attended Foster's funeral and approximately four hundred people voiced their protests at a mass meeting at St. Mark's Fourth Baptist Church the Sunday after the funeral. In the days after the shooting, Chapital requested that District Attorney Dowling present the matter to the grand jury to determine if there was any "improper police procedure" in the killing. When local residents discovered that Foster had been shot four times, with all of the bullets entering one side of the chest and emerging from the other side, they were convinced that Foster was shot in the back and not in the chest as had been previously reported. After a thorough grand jury investigation, police were cleared in the shooting, largely on the testimony of one of Foster's companions, who told investigators that Foster did have a toy pistol in his possession, which was almost an exact replica of a snub-nosed .38-caliber police special. As expected, relatives and concerned citizens were outraged at the grand jury's action and they were convinced that justice had "not been rendered" based upon the long history of tensions between the community and the NOPD.[15]

Two weeks later, twenty-one-year-old Ezell Ward was killed by police officers in his jail cell in an effort to subdue him. En route to the Sixth District police station on burglary charges, Ward attempted to escape and officers were obliged to use force to bring him under control. Three hours later, Ward was found dead in his cell. A citizens committee led by Chapital viewed Ward's body shortly after it was taken to Magee Funeral Home. Bruises were visible on both sides of the body. Dr. William Adams, a local physician, told reporters that "the bruises and contusions on the body are evidence of rough handling and could have been caused by a fight or beating of same quality by some person. The final cause of death, of course, depends upon the autopsy report. But a man apparently in good health would have had a more serious reason for dying than contusions and bruises."[16]

On the evening of Ward's wake, eight protestors staged a protest demonstration in front of the Sixth District police station as roughly two hundred spectators watched. The demonstrators carried signs that read "Are New Orleans Policemen Hired to Protect and Save Lives or Beat, Cuss and Kill My Community."[17]

The murders of George Wilfred, Alan Foster, and Ezell Ward followed a typical pattern that black New Orleans had unfortunately grown accustomed to. They were all unarmed, yet they were killed during encounters with police or in police custody; the police version of the incident was different from eyewitness accounts; there was no serious investigation into their deaths; there was no indictment by the district attorney, nor did the offending officers receive any form of punishment; and all of the officers involved were back patrolling the streets immediately after the killings. This pattern of violence and murder at the hands of the NOPD created distrust, hatred, rage, and anger. In the minds of many black residents, the police department had become the modern-day lynch mob.

As the direct-action phase of the civil rights movement erupted in New Orleans amid the latest outbreak of police violence, the NOPD on many occasions would arrest the demonstrators under orders from newly installed Mayor Victor Schiro, who was elected by the New Orleans city council to serve the unexpired term of Morrison, who had resigned as mayor to accept the appointment of ambassador to the Organization of American States. Schiro made it clear that he would not tolerate civil rights marches in his city. In December 1961, the NOPD "thwarted two protest marches" and arrested a total of 304 persons. On December 18, a group of Southern University–New Orleans and Dillard University students were arrested on Canal Street as they were walking to the state office building on Loyola Street from St. James African Methodist Episcopal Church. The group of 292 students was marching to protest the arrests of seventy-three students in Baton Rouge. Giarrusso said that he ordered the arrest because the marchers were violating a city policy by parading without a permit. The demonstrators were taken to the station in a paddy wagon; a total of fifty police officers and six wagons were needed.[18]

The students offered little resistance. However, one student was charged with carrying a concealed weapon after they discovered a long blade in his pocket. The students were bailed out by Clarence "Chink" Henry and the attorneys of ILA Local 1419. But the community was nonetheless outraged. Consumers League President Avery Alexander wired off an immediate protest to President John F. Kennedy, claiming that "nearly 300 students of Southern University and other colleges in this area were run down and hunted by dogs like animals, and were arrested while walking peacefully to a local state office building to protest the tear gassing and inhuman treatment of students at Southern University in Baton Rouge." Alexander also informed JFK that the Consumers League would soon be marching at the Orleans Parish voting registrar's office to protest against Schiro and the NOPD.[19]

Schiro was a former insurance executive who entered politics in 1950 as a Morrison protégé. In the 1954 and 1958 city council elections, he actively courted the black vote. With the threat of racial violence at integrated schools at the beginning of the 1961 school year, Schiro made it clear to segregationists that he would not have any racial violence in his city. He cordoned off integrated schools and placed sixty police officers at each school to protect black children. However, during the regular mayoral election of 1962, Schiro resorted to a race-baiting campaign strategy as he "outniggered" his opponents by attacking them as soft on integration, accepting the support of the local citizens council, reaffirming the city's racist tradition, ignoring the black vote, and not advertising in the *Louisiana Weekly*—and he was proud of it. "We did not, as our opponents, advertise in the Negro Press. I did not attend Negro meetings and I made little or no effort to attract Negro votes." That year black voters supported Adrian Duplantier, who met with members of CORE and members of the black professional class. According to historian Arnold Hirsch, Schiro's campaign was one of the most vicious race-baiting campaigns in Louisiana history, and it was successful, as he received 94,050 votes to Duplantier's 73,433 votes. After the election, Schiro told his inner circle that he would not tolerate any civil rights demonstrations in the city.[20]

From 1962 to 1963, black New Orleanians made steady progress toward integration. Because of Schiro's willingness to use the NOPD as a force in the massive resistance movement, activists instead worked through the court system. In July 1963, the New Orleans recreation department was forced to integrate the city's parks, playgrounds, swimming pools, and other facilities. Weeks later, Municipal Auditorium was desegregated as well. Historian Adam Fairclough suggests that "there was never much 'mass' in nonviolent direct-action in New Orleans." Instead, biracial groups such as the New Orleans Urban League, the Community Relations Council, and the Catholic Council on Human Relations, often worked behind the scenes, using the threat of mass demonstrations as a bargaining tool. In some instances it worked such as during Easter 1963, when Canal Street business owners agreed to hire seventy-five blacks as store clerks. Nonetheless, Schiro attempted to resist, even reneging in an August 1963 agreement to integrate city hall. His reluctance to follow through on the integration order, that he had signed, led to a highly publicized incident between the NOPD and civil rights activists during the spring of 1964 that galvanized black protest, generated considerable negative media attention on New Orleans, and caused the city's business leaders to intervene.[21]

That spring Reverend Avery Alexander was dragged by his ankles up two flights of stairs then out the door to a waiting police car while attempting to integrate the city hall cafeteria. According to U.S. District Court Judge Herbert Christenberry, it was a disgrace. "The man was dragged by his heels up two flights of stairs. I think the way this man was handled was a disgrace to the city, the police department, everyone concerned. If he was going to be arrested, he could have been picked up under the arms and carried out." Christenberry ordered the cafeteria immediately desegregated.[22]

The arrest and handling of Alexander created a great deal of anger toward the NOPD from the black middle class and from white business leaders. A polished, respectable gentleman, Alexander was in no way a troublemaker or a rabble-rouser. The photos of his handling and arrest in the *Louisiana Weekly* served as a catalyst to get other black moderates and the black middle class involved in the struggle for freedom, as they correctly assumed that their status as "respectable Negroes" meant nothing in the eyes of the NOPD. Further, as pictures of Alexander landed in papers and magazines across the country, it had begun to create a negative business climate in New Orleans, such that business leaders were concerned that New Orleans would gain a reputation akin to that of Birmingham. The city's business leaders told the mayor that he needed to take a milder approach to integration.

Despite the NOPD policy of breaking-up civil rights demonstrations, white officers in New Orleans were comparatively restrained in their handling of civil rights workers. In Birmingham, for example, the police department often attacked marchers with police dogs, high-pressure water hoses, and billy clubs. Further, throughout its history the Birmingham Police Department raped black women, castrated black men, and murdered black people. While the NOPD was certainly brutal throughout its history, Giarrusso at least showed some respect to African Americans. But he appeared incapable of providing the kind of police leadership the black community wanted and needed.[23]

The complexity of police brutality in New Orleans was woven into the fabric of city government. City hall, the NOPD's internal affairs division (IAD), and the Orleans Parish district attorney's office were all on one accord when it came to black complaints about police brutality and violence. The case of Morris Rowe provides a good example. After being fired from his job at Kirschman's Warehouse, Rowe was told to come back the following Monday for his final check. "While walking through the warehouse to the pay office, I saw Mr. Leblanc and he told me that he did not have time to fool around with me and he referred to me as a boy." While Rowe was waiting outside of the building for his check, two policemen pulled up and arrested him. "Where is the black nigger who is raising all of this trouble," they shouted. He soon received a ten-minute beating. "It seemed like the police beat me for ten minutes. I know they beat me until they got tired because the little short policeman was out of breath when he got back into the car. I was beaten with a pistol butt and billy." The brutality continued inside the Fifth District Station, when he was kicked in the genitals, stomach, head, nose, and mouth. During one of the episodes, one officer remarked, "I ought to kill you, Nigger."[24]

More than two hundred black citizens attended a protest meeting at Law Street Baptist Church to express outrage over the Rowe beating. At the CORE-sponsored rally, A. L. Davis told the crowd that Rowe's beating was "legalized battery" and that "Negroes are tired of being mistreated and of being denied their rights." New Orleans CORE Chapter President Oretha Castle read a letter CORE sent to Giarrusso and Mayor Schiro. Part of the letter read: "CORE vehemently protests the brutal treatment of Mr. Morris Rowe by Patrolman R. Calico and A. Dennis of the NOPD." Despite the request for an investigation, the district attorney saw no wrongdoing on the part of the officers.[25]

The inability of the NOPD and the district attorney to adequately and fairly investigate cases of police brutality was a clear indication that police brutality victims did not have any legitimate recourse or avenue to pursue their grievances. The IAD of the NOPD served as a whitewashing unit, as it rarely disciplined officers, and the district attorney's office rarely prosecuted officers because of their mutually dependent relationship. Created in 1953, the IAD was staffed by four police officers who served under the supervision of a director. The city charter called for investigations into police misconduct to be spearheaded by the officer's own unit. For instance, if a detective was accused of a violation, then the head of the detective bureau would conduct the investigation. Like many other units within the NOPD, the IAD was "loosely constructed, disgracefully underfunded, and unwisely administered," according to one local journalist. It produced no reports of its investigations and findings, operated with excessive secrecy, was virtually unaccountable to the public, and rarely prosecuted corrupt officers, if ever. Like many other similar units across the country the IAD appeared to exist for the purpose of protecting police officers rather than citizens. In addition to an ineffective IAD, NOPD officers learned quickly after joining the force that they could silence a future brutality complaint by charging victims with one of three charges: disorderly conduct, resisting arrest, or assault on a police officer. The charges allowed the officer to justify violence and, in some cases, the murder of innocent civilians.[26]

Police brutality victims also found the district attorney's office to be of little help in addressing complaints. Because of the mutually dependent relationship between the prosecutor's office and the police who worked together convicting criminals, the district attorney rarely indicted police officers. Further, the district attorney knew that it was hard to convince grand juries and trial juries that an officer had actually intended to commit a crime. Civil lawsuits were potentially a third avenue of redress and, although the NOPD paid out thousands each year in court cases, the officers were in most cases not even reprimanded or punished. So even if the victim got paid, the NOPD was still allowed to continue business as usual. Because of unfair internal investigations and the reluctance of the district attorney to indict police officers for misconduct, the local NAACP called for some sort of external check on the NOPD.

The increased incidents of police brutality in the 1960s were part of a white backlash to the civil rights movement. Just as their civilian counterparts expressed disgust and anger toward integration, white police officers felt even angrier. They perceived civil rights demonstrators as their enemy, a threat to their authority, and a menace to their hegemony over police jobs. Oftentimes, they took out their frustrations on the city's most defenseless residents.

CONCERNED CITIZENS ON POLICE MATTERS

With the passage of the 1965 Voting Rights Act, the nature of black protest against police violence changed. The local NAACP moved away from its traditional call for investigations. That month it called for a civilian review board. Although this had long been a demand from blacks in the North, it

was one of the first times that black southerners had suggested an external agency to review police conduct. The proposed review board would be
modeled on a similar board established years earlier in New York City and
it would hear charges brought against the NOPD. Horace C. Bynum, NAACP
president, stated, "There is an immediate need for a biracial independent
citizens' review board to investigate, conduct hearings, and report its findings and recommendations to proper authority . . . on charges brought by
citizens against law enforcement officers for police brutality, discourte-
ous treatment of citizens, and other misconduct which can be attributed
to race." He went on to state that "many a citizen and organizations have
made complaints to the police department of unwarranted action by police
officers only to be received courteously by the authorities who still took no
disciplinary action against the brutal officer." Bynum argued that the creation of a police review board would perhaps prevent a race riot or an all-
out attack on police.[27]

Bynum's rationale for the creation of a police review board was solid.
The previous summer persistent police brutality was the catalyst for the
Watts riots, the nation's worst urban disturbance in twenty years. During
the four-day riot in Los Angeles, there were thirty-four deaths, hundreds
injured, and more than $35 million in property damage. Although New Or-
leans had been able to dodge a major race riot up to this point, local leaders knew that as the relationship between the black community and the
NOPD continued to deteriorate, the scene in Watts could be duplicated in
New Orleans.[28]

In the aftermath of the NAACP's call for a civilian review board, community leaders formed the Concerned Citizens on Police Matters of Police Brutality and Harassment (CCPM). Their first plan of action involved a series
of public meetings to acquaint the people with recent acts of brutality. The
hearings would involve police brutality victims telling about their experiences at the hands of the NOPD. The CCPM understood that it was dealing
with a problem that dated back to the nineteenth century, but they were
convinced that something had to be done. By airing police brutality charges
publicly, they were hopeful that the media exposure could serve as a catalyst to some major police reforms.[29]

To spread the word about the new anti-brutality organization, members
of the CCPM passed out handbills at churches, community centers, parks
and recreational centers, and people's homes. The bills read: "As citizens,
members of the CCPM feel we must assume our civic responsibilities to de-

velop concrete steps to eliminate this problem. This can only be done by widespread involvement on the issue. If you have been a victim of such action by the police, or know of someone who has, or if you are willing to work on this issue please contact the Concerned Citizens on Police Matters."[30] The formation of the CCPM was important for several reasons. First, it represented the first time that the city had a local organization that would specifically fight police brutality. Second, it illustrated that the national civil rights organizations were not equipped or did not make police brutality a major civil rights issue. Third, it highlighted the growing importance of the black vote. No longer could political aspirants neglect black concerns. The CCPM made the issue of police violence and brutality a priority.

Police brutality victims soon took their complaints to the CCPM office on Dryades Street. Under the direction of Don Hubbard, a former CORE activist and businessman with a passion for big-city politics, the CCPM took affidavits from victims and then forwarded them to Chief Giarrusso. Attached to the affidavits was a standard letter from the CCPM requesting a "complete and impartial investigation. Upon completion of the investigation, we are requesting that the finding be made public." The CCPM's desire to function as an ad hoc police brutality investigation committee was greeted with great enthusiasm in the black community because the NOPD rarely failed to investigate complaints, nor did it have a safe mechanism by which blacks could lodge charges of brutality. Between 1964 and 1966, only thirty-four African Americans filed formal complaints with the NOPD. The total number of complaints filed across the city was seventy-two. Of those seventy-two complaints, only one case resulted in the firing of an officer. As the numbers illustrate, black residents were either intimidated by the process of going to the police station and filing a complaint, or they felt that it was simply a waste of time to report complaints since the NOPD clearly showed it had little desire to punish officers. The CCPM was certain that they could bring heat on the NOPD to investigate these complaints more thoroughly.[31]

"STOP AND FRISK"

In addition to airing charges of police brutality, the CCPM soon emerged as a viable force in the fight against police brutality when it came out against the proposed "stop and frisk" ordinance and "citizen inquiry card" that were pending in the New Orleans city council. In the aftermath of the long hot summers of 1965 and 1966, urban police departments across the county were successful in getting legislation passed that would allow them to effectively stop citizens without cause. The proposed ordinances were part of a broader crackdown on crime. The New Orleans ordinances would give police the right to stop persons and search for weapons without probable cause. Giarrusso supported it as an effective way to prevent crime. Don Hubbard and the CCPM came out angrily against the bill. Hubbard argued that the bill would create a police state by stopping any and all African Americans on sight that looked "suspicious," especially blacks that worked late and returned home at night. Hubbard also said: "Our committee is concerned about this situation because biased policemen still think all Negroes look alike." All African Americans would face the possibility of "being stopped and frisked on the street or in a public building at the discretion of a policeman." Hubbard then took aim at the newly proposed citizens' identification card. "Not only will people be stopped and frisked . . . but they will be given a card by the policeman stating that the person had been investigated on a certain day and has been 'helpful to the police' or words to that effect. CCPM says that people will become fearful of walking down the street without their 'card' which really only means they did nothing wrong at the time they were frisked."[32]

Hubbard and the CCPM were not the only civil rights groups to oppose the bill—CORE and the NAACP also expressed displeasure with the proposal. Isaac Reynolds, southern regional director of CORE, stated that the proposals were similar to the policies that had been used in South Africa. He further labeled the proposal "apartheid neo-nazi" like. "The stop-and-frisk ordinance along with the so-called citizen inquiry card can only serve as the seeds of discontent within our community. These are the tools of a tyrannical society against which we will use every lawful means to keep it out of the city of New Orleans." Likewise, Giarrusso's claims that the new ordinance would reduce crime was also questionable. According to Reynolds, the "stop and frisk "method would take another hundred years to reduce crime in New Orleans. Finally, Reynolds understood the grave consequences for African Americans if the bill passed. "Chief Giarrusso is wrong when he says that the stop-and-frisk ordinance will not affect any element in the community. History has shown us that there are policemen in the NOPD who have abused their authority in dealing with Negro citizens." CORE soon had petitions circulating throughout the black community and it also asked "everyone to be in the City Council chambers for the hearing Thursday morning at 9:30."[33]

The petitions by CCPM and CORE were aided by the possible unconstitutionality of the proposed ordinance. A similar law in New York was being challenged in the U.S. Supreme Court on two grounds: (1) whether a policeman could stop and search any person abroad in a public place on the basis of suspicion; and (2) whether the weapon could constitute a crime that could be used as evidence at trial.[34]

Despite black outrage and the alleged unconstitutionality of the legislation, the New Orleans city council passed the ordinance by a vote of 6–0. The bill gave officers the right to stop and frisk persons for weapons in public places who were believed to have committed, be committing, or about to commit a felony. Prior to the vote, Giarrusso reiterated that the new law was not against any segment of the community but against criminals. Although the law passed unanimously, several black organizations exercised their right in council chambers to voice objections. Representatives from the Algiers Teenage Youth Group, Algiers-Fischer Discussion Group, Youth For Progressive Action, Fischer Homes Tenant Council, Students for Human Advancement and Community, Desire Project Area, CCPM, and CORE all spoke out against the proposal but to no avail.[35]

Despite the controversial nature of the ordinance and the inquiry card, the enforcement of the laws did not appear to discriminate. Of the 15,767 persons stopped during the 2 months after the law went into effect, 9,702 were black and 6,065 were white. The NOPD arrested around 50 percent of all those stopped, both black and white. Further only 1,415 of the black detainees were arrested compared to 1,740 whites. So despite the concerns, the ordinance was not enforced in an overtly racist manner.[36]

While Giarrusso's support for the "stop and frisk" ordinance and the citizen inquiry card were met with hostility from black citizens, his creation of the community relations division of the NOPD was a way of improving the relationship between the NOPD and the African American community. While local civil rights groups such as the NAACP applauded the creation of the unit, they were concerned that it would be simply a window dressing unit. In a letter to Chief Giarrusso, Horace Bynum of the NAACP asked the chief to (1) beef up the personnel of the unit; (2) rotate the commanding officer periodically; and (3) have the unit report directly to the chief of police. In the summer of 1967, the community relations division launched an elaborate program in the black community and across the city all in the name of riot prevention. The summer program was based in the city's eleven housing projects. The curriculum had several components: athletic events, talent shows, tours, movies, and pistol training and self-defense for women. Black residents were hopeful that the creation of the community relations division would represent a new era in the relationship between the NOPD and African Americans, while city officials were hopeful that this would represent a good first step toward keeping New Orleans "cool" for the summer.[37]

From September 1966 to April 1967, the community relations division conducted a wide range of activities that included "assisting in the investigation of complaints of racial or alleged racial overtones," protecting Coretta Scott King during a visit to the city, and feeding needy families. While the community appreciated these efforts, the community relations division did not have any internal diversity training for the rank-and-file officer. Nonetheless, the creation of the community relations division was a progressive step toward improving the relationship between the NOPD and the black community.[38]

When Giarrusso suspended two white officers for their inactivity during a white attack on black swimmers, community activists were encouraged at the chief's efforts and felt that it was a direct result of the activities of the community relations division. At the June 1967 "going away" party for two Vietnam draftees, approximately sixteen African Americans were attacked by fifty white youths on Lake Pontchartrain. As the white youths approached the group, they yelled, "You black niggers, what are you doing here? This is for white people," while another yelled, "Get your black asses out of our section." In addition to being beaten with fists, sticks, and bottles, they were hit with rocks and threatened with knives. Although the police witnessed the altercation, they refused to break it up, arrest the attackers, and assist those who needed medical treatment. Marietta Camp, who witnessed the assault, recalled that the police did not assist in any way. She told NAACP officials that although the police were a few steps away from the fracas, "they took their time to stop the fight. They questioned me, but their main concern was if I was driving without a license." As expected, the NAACP requested an investigation. In a letter to Giarrusso the parents wrote: "We respectfully request your office to investigate this deplorable action by the white youths and the scandalous handling of this matter by the police on record." The protest and subsequent investigation was successful. Giarrusso suspended the two officers.[39]

THE ASSASSINATION OF MARTIN LUTHER KING, JR.

Police homicide reared its ugly head again just two days after the assassination of Martin Luther King, Jr., when white officers gunned down a

fifteen-year-old boy who was fleeing a burglary scene. The killing of Robert Lee Boyd alarmed residents and nearly triggered a riot in an already
racially tense city. The day Boyd was shot the NAACP was holding a leadership training conference in the city, and when word got to the delegates
that the fifteen-year-old boy had been killed by the police they immediately
scheduled a protest march for that Saturday. However, on that Friday evening Emmit Douglas, NAACP state president, cancelled the march when he
heard conflicting stories about the incident and after consulting with local
NAACP leaders. The decision to cancel the march was made also because
"we feel there might be elements that would infiltrate our ranks, elements
that we could not control. We want our marches to be peaceful." Douglas
was also encouraged by the sympathetic attitude taken by Assistant Superintendent of Police Treschair, who promised a thorough investigation. "We
are grateful for the attitude you have taken and we feel you won't give us
a whitewash job on the investigation. However, if we have indications of a
whitewash job we won't take the same stand." At the closing session of the
NAACP meeting, the body adopted a resolution condemning the homicide.
Immediately after the resolution was adopted, the delegates collected $112
to assist the youth's family with funeral expenses. The investigation was
apparently a whitewash because weeks later the Orleans Parish grand jury
exonerated the officer who did the shooting. The Boyd killing added fuel to
the racial fire that burned throughout the country in the aftermath of the
King assassination.[40]

Two days after the Boyd killing, approximately a hundred African
Americans surrounded two black police officers, yelling, "Nigger-uncle tom
cops." Across the street stood about twenty white officers with rifles, ready
to shoot. Things got tense when an unknown bystander started chanting,
"Burn, baby, burn." Miraculously, the crowd dispersed without any violence
and this was the closest New Orleans ever got to experience a 1960s-style race
riot. Several reasons explain why New Orleans averted racial trouble during
the long hot summers of the 1960s. First, 78 percent of the parish residents
were lifelong citizens of the city; thus they felt like a part of the city fabric. They were not as alienated like many southerners who had migrated up
North. Second, the NOPD's community outreach efforts helped ease racial
tensions. Because the NOPD reached out with a broad-based community
relations campaign, some black residents were able to have safe and peaceful interactions with members of the NOPD for the first time in their lives.
Finally, historian Kent Germany argues that the city's fledgling war on poverty programs brought community activists such as Don Hubbard of the

CCPM into city government, who used their strong ties to the black community to keep the peace.[41]

A DEMAND FOR CHANGE

In the midst of the nascent black power movement that gained momentum after King's death, activists began to call for more black officers and other reforms, while black patrolmen demanded an end to discriminatory assignments. The biracial community relations council (CRC) of New Orleans's ad hoc committee (AHC) on the NOPD argued that unless sweeping reforms were made, a civilian review board was the only way to stop the problem of police brutality. In a press release the CRC outlined a six-point program under the following categories: hiring practices, community relations, the NOPD academy, in-service training, budgeting and finance, and operational practices. However, much of their comments centered on the hiring and promotion of black officers, and they had good grounds. Although the city was roughly 40 percent African American, there were only 74 black officers out of a total force of 1,320. Further, there were no black supervisors, lieutenants, or captains, and only 10 sergeants out of 130. According to the CRC, part of the problem was related to testing. Only 18 out of every 300 applicants to the force were able to pass the written examination. The other problem was that the NOPD never actively recruited African Americans. The CRC requested that one out of every 3 appointed positions within the NOPD be reserved for African Americans. Finally, the committee recommended the creation of an advisory committee to the NOPD composed of civilians. Revius Ortique, CRC member and head of the New Orleans branch of the NAACP, explained that their suggestions did not mean they were anti-police. "In fact we all know we need a department we can respect. We are, in fact, seeking ways and means to aid the department."[42]

While the local NAACP was active in the anti-brutality movement at times, their actions reveal a reluctance to take on the police brutality issue. As one of the largest chapters in the country, their refusal to take more drastic action toward the NOPD meant that the black community did not present a unified front in the battle for police protection. Whenever complaints arose about an incident of police brutality, the NAACP generally sent a letter to city officials requesting an investigation, knowing that the investigation would rarely result in disciplinary action, an indictment, or a conviction. Anti-brutality activists needed the credibility, resources, and organizational ability of the NAACP but they did not get it.

Likewise, the newly formed Black Police for Positive Action (BPPA) also made their own demands to reform the NOPD. In a private meeting with Giarrusso and Philip Batiste, an administrative aide to Schiro, John C. Raphael, the senior African American in the NOPD, outlined an eight-point proposal that would effectively end racial discrimination within the department. The letter began by stating, "These are areas of grave concern to the black members of the police department": (1) do away with the systemic restriction of assignments to areas and bureaus relegated to a position based on race alone; (2) provide in-service-training; (3) establish a biracial group of academic professionals to objectively evaluate the police academy program; (4) allow black guest lecturers to more actively participate in the mainstream of the academy program; (5) assign black policemen as permanent academy instructors; (6) establish a biracial committee of police officers to interview applicants in order that personal bias or prejudices by an individual interviewer are eliminated; (7) establish a recruiting program that will include black members of the department in an effort to attract black applicants; (8) establish a biracial committee of police officers to hear grievances of officers. One officer insisted that the NOPD honor transfer requests to preferential assignments to show that race was not a factor in assignments. Further, black officers demanded that Giarrusso issue a clear statement to the rank-and-file of the NOPD "that policemen in all divisions be assigned on the basis of ability and departmental needs, not race." Remedies for the racially insensitive in-service training involved letting black officers attend seminars and workshops that dealt with the community relations side of policing and also allowing black officers to bring African American instructors into the police academy curriculum. The desire for a biracial committee to assist with hiring was clear. "This is to eliminate the objectionable bias, and gross misrepresentation of information relative to civil rights, black leaders, the current social movement and the federal government, by academy instructors." In conclusion, the BPPA acknowledged that although the department had a community relations division "to establish a good image" to the broader community, "the department is dangerously lagging behind in establishing a healthy and mature racial development within itself." The proposal closed by reminding Giarrusso of the challenges faced by officers within the NOPD. "You must also realize that the black officer is denied full and equal participation in the overall activities of the police department making them victims of racism and discrimination."[43]

One of the major sources of complaints from black officers concerned insensitive and derogatory instructors at the police academy. According to NOPD Sergeant Sam Reine, new officers were routinely told that African Americans could only be made to obey the law through fear. He further mentioned that one of the instructors at the academy, Captain Drake, told recruits that "Dr. Martin Luther King, Jr., was a communist, the Civil Rights movement is communistic, and that the social movement is communistic." Despite the protests of black officers, Giarrusso refused to make changes. The demands made by the BPPA showed that it was concerned with structural reform within the NOPD rather than tokenism. The recruitment, testing, appointment, and retention of African American police officers, along with drastic curricular reform in the police academy, they believed, would make the NOPD more responsive to the needs of the black community.[44]

The need for major reforms within the NOPD became more apparent in the aftermath of the Southern University–New Orleans (SUNO) Black Nationalist flag controversy in the spring of 1969. Like black college students across the country, students at the all-black SUNO were smitten by the black studies bug and they demanded wholesale changes in curriculum and faculty. After a demonstration on Wednesday, April 3, the Bad Niggers, a student group, removed the American flag and replaced it with the flag of black liberation. Although the demonstration ended peacefully, Dr. Emmett Bashful, the highest-ranking administrator at the university, warned the students that the university would not tolerate them disgracing the American flag. "We will not tolerate further tampering with the American flag which flies over our campus daily . . . It is our intention to use whatever resources necessary to insure that similar incidents do not occur again." Giarrusso concurred by stating that the black flag of liberation would not be allowed to fly over SUNO, and that it was a "shame" to remove the American flag. Mayor Schiro echoed these sentiments to a local reporter. "It is inconceivable that any American citizen would show this disrespect to this flag." Despite the threats and edicts from Giarrusso and Schiro, the students were not backing down. "Nobody is taking this flag down without a fight. I don't care if it's Dean Bashful, Mr. Perkins [a custodian], or the pigs from Downtown. It's going to be a fight." Another student from the grievance committee stated, "we are coming back mad as ever on Monday for our demands to be met."[45]

The following Monday six students "overpowered three campus security officers, hauled down the American flag," and once again replaced it with the flag of black liberation. According to one observer, "cheers went up from the estimated 200 students who watched." They then announced their demands: (1) the removal of Dean Bashful; (2) a tuition reduction; (3) a course in black liberation; (4) a degree-granting department of black studies; (5) more faculty; (6) a resumption of the school building plans; and (7) a black draft counseling center. Then a melee erupted when police officers put the American flag back on the pole and began to taunt the students. When an officer grabbed a student and dragged him into the police wagon, officers clubbed and sprayed the students with mace. The students, who objected to the mere presence of the officers on campus, were outraged: "We paid tuition to come to school here. What are you doing on our campus," one student yelled. Fourteen students were arrested in the disturbance. During the altercation, Dean Bashful was forced to lock himself in his office to avoid being rushed by students who wanted to meet with him. The students then took over the first floor of the administration building, but not before they kicked in a panel outside his office, threw rocks into the office, and thrust a fire hose through a ventilator opening and turned the water on. Police eventually forced the students out of the building.[46]

In the aftermath of the disturbance, Mayor Victor Schiro commended the actions of the NOPD in breaking up the demonstration. "There is no excuse for the actions of youthful college students in hurling bricks, rocks, glass, and other objects, as well as their obscenity." Schiro then went on to mention that all protestors would be dealt with harshly. "Desecration of the flag is not an act of social protest; it is pure and simple a defilement of our nation's standard, a slap at Americans who died in its service. We are going to arrest each and every person who commits or partakes in such an act." He then issued a strong warning: "The police department, in a trying situation, handled these incidents with restraint. But I want all potential troublemakers to know that the police department is prepared to use all necessary force to preserve the peace in New Orleans and that it has the mobility and manpower to do so effectively and thoroughly."[47]

Although the flag controversy at SUNO was of a nonviolent nature, the NOPD's violent response was becoming all too typical. Giarrusso was unable or unwilling to exercise any restraint and Schiro was his biggest booster. Once again, the NOPD saw the raising of the black liberation flag as an expression of black power and they considered it a personal affront to their identity, status, and hegemony, and community activists responded angrily. Local civil rights leaders blamed the disturbance on Giarrusso, who they believed was trying to earn his law-and-order stripes for greater political motives. In a joint statement released by the New Orleans NAACP and the New Orleans Urban League (NOUL), black leaders placed the blame at the feet of the superintendent of police. "Giarrusso, being unable to recognize the motive of the initial demonstration at Southern University, found it necessary to create a situation which would justify his intervention and force a confrontation between students and police officers, to wit, the dubious question of the flag. Such irresponsible action on the part of the Superintendent has made a very explosive situation on the Southern University Campus."[48]

The SUNO incident was part of a larger issue, and that issue was the way black people were treated by the city's finest. The newly formed black city council expressed its displeasure with the nature of police-community relations in a vicious open letter to the New Orleans city council. The black city council opened the letter by stating that the city was "on the verge of a major civil disorder." The two reasons for the "explosive situation" were racist police practices and ineffective leadership of the NOPD. Although the council mentioned two reasons, it chose to focus its comments on Giarrusso's lack of leadership. The council questioned why the NOPD continued to brutalize black people, particularly when another "long, hot summer" was fast approaching. It then questioned why Giarrusso instigated the brutality at SUNO. They concluded that Giarrusso, by tolerating misconduct and brutality, was planning to run in the 1969 mayor's race on a law and order platform. Giarrusso did not seek office.[49]

THE ELECTION OF MOON LANDRIEU

As tensions increased between the NOPD and the African American community in the late 1960s, some very important developments were taking place in the political realm that would have a profound impact on police-community relations. The first event came in 1967, when Ernest "Dutch" Morial was elected to the Louisiana state House of Representatives from uptown New Orleans. His election was historic in that he was the first black elected to the Louisiana state House since Reconstruction. In many ways Dutch used his presidency of the local NAACP to launch his political career by filing court cases to protest segregation, recruiting new members to the local chapter, and spearheading massive voter registration efforts. But it was actually the defeat of two other black candidates for state representative that year that would change the face of black politics in the Crescent City.[50]

In an effort to take advantage of expanded black voting power, two relatively political unknowns, Nils Douglas and Charles Elloie, made unsuccessful attempts at getting elected to the state House. In the aftermath of the election, both Douglas and Elloie sought to institutionalize the black vote by creating two major black political organizations. The Southern Organization for Unified Leadership (SOUL) was formed by Douglas, and the Community Organization for Urban Politics (COUP) was established by Elloie. Douglas, a former CORE worker, initially ran for the state House in 1963, but it was his defeat several years later that served as the impetus for SOUL. Although SOUL and COUP were both black political organizations, they catered to different constituencies. As a political offshoot of CORE, SOUL, in the words of historian Arnold Hirsch, "embodied the heightened racial consciousness and militance of the civil rights era." On the other hand, COUP "brought together young professionals who represented the assimilationist and conservative tendencies" of the black community. In spite of their avowed differences, both COUP and SOUL would hinder the development of black political power in New Orleans by assuming a powerless patron-client relationship with white politicians similar to the Orleans Parish Progressive Voters' League (OPPVL) of the 1950s. Quite simply, COUP and SOUL were established to deliver the black vote to the white politicians who would provide patronage benefits to their constituencies; they were not concerned with power.[51]

SOUL and COUP showed that they could deliver the black vote in the 1969 mayoral election when Moon Landrieu announced his candidacy for mayor. As a liberal and former state legislator who opposed the segregationists during the 1960 school crisis, Landrieu was sensitive to black concerns while serving on the New Orleans city council from 1965 to 1969. During the campaign Landrieu actively sought black support, and he was elected on the strength of the black vote. He received more than 90 percent of the black vote while just getting a fraction of the white vote. The biracial coalition of Landrieu represented the liberal impulse in the Crescent City and anti-brutality activists were hopeful that their support of Landrieu would result in a host of racial reforms, most notably, police reform, while black professionals were optimistic that Landrieu would serve as a conduit for black political and economic advancement. While SOUL and COUP emerged as major players in local politics and became respected power brokers, they would serve as an obstacle to black political power, as the years ahead would prove.

Shortly after Landrieu's election, the Round Table of the Human Relations Committee (HRC) suggested to the new mayor that a new police chief was in the best interest of the city. They proposed that the city conduct a nationwide search to find the best candidate. "We do not believe that you should be inhibited by recruiting leaders from within the police department," they wrote. They also recommended that citizens be allowed to interview candidates, so that the candidates could "interact with persons and groups outside the profession and the willingness of the candidates to do so." They further demanded that one of the top three positions in the police department be "a black appointee," and that the International Association of Police Chiefs set the standards for the new appointee.[52]

The Round Table then offered a specific set of criteria that the candidates should meet: (1) openness to major reforms within the police department, which included more extensive recruitment of black policemen; (2) the ability to deal with sensitive issues such as the "racial and social prejudice of police"; and (3) extensive training in human relations. Landrieu chose not to respond to the letter and he retained Giarrusso as his police chief.[53]

Landrieu came under criticism from the black community not only for reappointing Giarrusso but also for failing to make police brutality investigations public. Officials from both the NAACP and the HRC complained that the chief rarely notified them on the disposition of brutality cases. Part of the larger problem was that the NOPD did not have a fair mechanism in place for handling "grievance procedures," and the NAACP and the HRC attempted to act as an ad hoc police review board. When asked whether or not he made the results of investigations public, the chief stated that he had released results of specific cases but as a general rule he would not make investigations public.[54]

While Landrieu ignored the letter laying out the committee's recommendations, he could not ignore the report prepared by the community entitled "The Police and the Rest of Us." The well-written and well-documented report was unique in that it was arguably the only such citizens' report on police-community relations in the nation. Although the original focus of the Round Table HRC was to look at hiring practices, they decided to take "a total look at the Police Department in order to develop meaningful recommendations." Prior to the report being published, its findings were aired on a ninety-minute television show. Landrieu received a copy of the report, but he did not make any comments regarding its findings and recommendations.[55]

The recommendations set forth by the biracial Round Table HRC reveal that police violence against blacks had now become a problem that crossed racial lines. Further, the ninety-minute television special on the report was unprecedented. It appears that the city's business leaders recognized that a violent police force created a bad business environment for a city that was in the midst of building a domed stadium and skyscrapers and refashioning itself as a tourist attraction. The city's future could not afford a confrontation between the police and its African American citizens. This pressure forced Joseph Giarrusso into retirement in August 1970. Landrieu then appointed twenty-one-year veteran Clarence Giarrusso to succeed his younger brother. The new chief and his officers would immediately confront the local chapter of the Black Panther Party in a series of highly publicized racial encounters.

3 "WE WANT AN END TO POLICE BRUTALITY"
The Black Panthers, Desire, and Police Repression

Point Number Seven of the Black Panther Party (BPP) Platform and Program, "What We Want, What We Believe," spoke directly to the issue of police brutality and sexual violence against women. "We want an immediate end to POLICE BRUTALITY and MURDER of black people," read the statement. Founded in 1966 in Oakland, California, as a direct result of years of abuse toward black residents at the hands of the Oakland Police Department, the Black Panther Party was a strong advocate of armed self-defense "from racist police oppression and brutality." In Oakland, the Panthers defined the police as "pigs," did not differentiate between black police officers and their white counterparts, proclaimed themselves the protectors of the black community, accused law enforcement of using Gestapo-like tactics, and established a neighborhood patrol to monitor the police. As the party grew in popularity, local chapters sprang up across the country. Conflicts with local police would claim the lives of thirty-four Panthers and fifteen law enforcement officers in 1970 alone. Considering the problem of police brutality and sexual violence in New Orleans, the Crescent City was an ideal place for a local chapter of the Black Panther Party.

DESIRE
The New Orleans branch of the Black Panther Party was established in the summer of 1970, a full four years after its inception in Oakland, California. Because of the city's brutal history of police misconduct, the Panthers were warmly received by the black poor after setting up their headquarters near the St. Thomas Housing Projects. In fact, one charter member of the chapter, Timothy Pratt, remembered that the residents of the St. Thomas

welcomed them from the start: "When the brothers first got started in late May or early June, they had very little trouble in establishing themselves. People related to them." While in the St. Thomas, the young chapter sold newspapers, held political education classes, and was also accused of extortion as it sought funds for a number of survival programs.[1]

The city became aware of the chapter's existence when a Panther by the name of "Steve" called William Rouselle, the twenty-four-year-old African American deputy director of the city's Human Relations Committee and former WDSU-TV news reporter, to tell him that he had arrived from California to set up a local chapter of the Panthers. Steve then asked Rouselle for assistance in organizing a free breakfast program. While Steve was asking for governmental assistance, the other members were apparently demanding donations and food from local grocery stores. This intimidation made the police aware of their negative presence. Nonetheless, Rouselle still arranged for the Panther leadership to meet with Daniel Vincent, executive director of the multimillion-dollar Total Community Action (TCA), a federally funded antipoverty program with its ranks filled by members of the city's black political organizations with strong ties to Landrieu. The meeting with Vincent was arranged so that TCA could possibly co-opt the Panthers by providing them with federal money for a social program. However, the Panthers chose not to attend.[2]

The Panthers were soon evicted from their St. Thomas address and relocated to the Desire Projects, a sprawling public housing complex located in an isolated area of the city by railroad tracks, the Industrial Canal, and the Mississippi River. By every indication, life in the all-black projects was poor. Of its 10,591 residents, 8,312 were under the age of 21. High unemployment, high crime, and, of course, police brutality were stark realities. One resident of the Desire Projects vividly remembers how the police treated them. "As kids we learned not to trust the police. We rarely looked to the police for protection. Many times people just got their revenge, and didn't even involve the cops. The cops treated us badly; they had little respect for us. I remember times we would be outside talking or playing cards, and the cops would come looking for somebody, and they would harass whomever they came across. I was more afraid of the police than of the criminals 'cause I knew the criminals."

By all indicators the Desire Projects gave the Panthers their best shot for success. According to Robert H. Tucker, a young African American special assistant to Mayor Landrieu, Desire was a time bomb waiting to explode.

Based on a thorough investigation and a seventy-two-hour stint living in Desire, Tucker concluded that the two-story projects "was one of the most explosive areas in the city." Tucker acknowledged that low-income life was very difficult; however, the conditions at Desire were on a totally different level. "The Desire housing project is a classic study of the worst and a living demonstration of what can happen when deterioration and despair break the confines of mere rhetoric." The conditions were appalling: children swimming in sewers for lack of recreational facilities; families afraid to leave their homes at night because of rape, assault, and murder; uncollected garbage; geographical, physical, and cultural isolation; roach-infested apartments; and a 61 percent poverty rate. Tucker felt that the main source of the problems in Desire was an abandoned building that served as a refuge for illegal activity. Tucker proposed an eight-point program to alleviate some of the problems in the Desire Projects: (1) increased police patrols, particularly near the food stamp center and check-cashing businesses; (2) routine garbage pickup; (3) demolition of all abandoned buildings and replacement with recreational facilities; (4) regular metro bus service; (5) health inspections in neighborhood stores; (6) the construction of a swimming pool; (7) clearing of vacant lots and removal of abandoned automobiles; and (8) the installation of metal doors and alarms on the child development center.[3]

After moving to Desire, the Panthers conducted a survey of the dietary habits of the youth in the community and soon announced a free breakfast program for area kids. "We as revolutionaries see the necessity in our young children being healthy and strong for the youth of our future. They will carry on our people's struggle for liberation after we're gone. The Free Breakfast for Children program provides a nourishing hot meal each morning to children from elementary to junior high school ages. We see this as a necessity, because in the black community hunger is a reality." In addition to the breakfast program, local members launched a host of community survival initiatives in Desire, including political education classes, a security patrol, and an apartment-sitting service. While these community programs were somewhat small in scope, they were important because they were instrumental in gaining grassroots support. The Panthers were helping the people to survive by meeting bread-and-butter needs, and they quickly gained the support of the community. The survival programs gave the Panthers instant credibility as community leaders as opposed to loud-talking armchair revolutionaries since the programs grew out of a practical political agenda that combined self-help and education, while at the same time addressing a community need.[4]

Despite the apparent success of their survival programs, the Panthers were eager for some type of confrontation with the New Orleans Police Department (NOPD) for several reasons: it would aid recruitment, raise the consciousness level of Desire residents, send a message to the power structure that they were serious about defending themselves and the community, and give them an opportunity to display the bravado so many had come to associate with the Black Panther Party. Less than three months after moving to Desire, the Panthers staged a disturbance in order to confront police. After nearly losing several officers that night, the NOPD discontinued regular night patrols through Desire and instead assigned two black patrolmen to patrol the area. The officers, Raymond Reed and Ormond Orticke, were singled out as "uncle toms," although they had grown up in the Desire area. After the first incident in Desire, Giarrusso, Mayor Moon Landrieu, Administrative Officer Ben Levy, Executive Assistant Richard Kernion, City Attorney Blake Arata, Deputy Director Sherman Copelin of the city's model cities program, and Rouselle all met to discuss how to infiltrate the Panthers and get them out of town because the presence of the Panthers and their ability to arouse project residents over the issue of police brutality presented a serious threat to the authority of the NOPD.[5]

The visibility of Landrieu's African American appointees in the city's effort to neutralize the Panthers represented a bold new approach in the history of New Orleans race relations. Mayor Moon Landrieu was politically astute enough to understand that members of the Black Panther Party operated by a different set of rules. They were not interested in integration, preached violent self-defense, and hated the police. Despite their best efforts, Rouselle and Copelin had little success tempering the enthusiasm of the Panthers.

PANTHER-POLICE CONFRONTATION I

Out of that meeting Landrieu and Giarrusso decided to have two officers, Melvin Howard, twenty, and Israel Fields, twenty-one, infiltrate the Panthers. Throughout the summer Howard and Fields gained the confidence of the local chapter and regularly attended its meetings at the Desire headquarters. The two officers were the main intelligence contacts with the NOPD. Both men informed city officials that the Panthers were stockpiling weapons and ammunition in case of a police invasion.[6]

On the evening of September 15, 1970, the true identity of the two undercover officers was discovered during a Panther-led political education class. When word spread around the Panther headquarters that Fields and

Howard were agent provocateurs, the community was livid. Both men were made to stand before an assembly of more than a hundred people called "The people's court." The trial got underway when members began discussing what to do with the "pigs." When the undercover officers attempted to speak on their own behalf, they were hit in the heads with weapons and guns, with pistols being pointed at their heads. When one of the Panther interrogators asked the crowd, "Are these men guilty of being pigs?" the group yelled in unison, "Right on," followed by chants of "Off the pigs" and "Kill the fascist pigs." A Panther spokesman asked the crowd if the Panthers should deal with the agents or if the people should deal with them. "Let the people deal with them," they shouted. As the tribunal continued, Howard and Fields were pushed to the floor, and beaten and kicked at gunpoint. They were then forced to wipe up their blood with their clothes.[7]

The two officers were then led out of the building, where a large group of residents waited with guns, sticks, bottles, pipes, bricks, and chains, with hopes of killing the infiltrators. Desire resident Glenbell Gilmore wanted the two officers beaten. "They were dealt with by the community because they pretended to be working for the community. We have breakfast programs for our kids at the Panther headquarters. But those pigs didn't tell their bosses about that; they spoke about the weapons. We believed in them but they broke the faith." Panther member Henry Jerome echoed the same sentiments: "We found two pig infiltrators in our meeting. We held a trial with members of the committee. Our decision was to let the pigs go on their own and that the people would deal with them. And the people dealt with them. It was the decision of the people and not of any particular organization."[8]

As the residents waited to carry out their punishment, Howard and Fields "jumped from the stairway of the second floor" and began running for their lives. During their escape, they were still being beaten and were knocked to the ground several times. Fields found refuge in a nearby grocery store, while Howard managed to elude the crowd by jumping over a seven-foot fence. While running toward Broussard's grocery store, they were spotted by two other officers, Patrolmen Reed and Orticke, who had come into the area to investigate a burning car. Reed and Orticke soon came under heavy fire when bullets riddled their car.[9]

As they dodged bullets and passed Panther headquarters, they saw a rifle sticking out of a window. More shots were fired at them and they got out of the car under heavy gunfire. Reed was apparently a marked man because the Panthers had distributed a pamphlet that called for the "Death of Raymond Pig," and it mentioned that Reed had no other choice than to die with the rest of the pigs. The burning car, which the officers had been called to investigate, drew firefighters to the area, but the Panthers threw Molotov cocktails at them.[10]

Giarrusso then dispatched more than two hundred officers to Panther headquarters later that night. Shooting began when the NOPD tried to force its way into the two-story Panther headquarters. The NOPD justified its search on the grounds that police officers were there to serve search and arrest warrants against the Panthers. The Panthers were able to resist until they were overcome by tear gas. However, as the Panthers were being taken out of the building a crowd of residents protected them by pushing police officers and throwing rocks and bottles while raising clinched fists to show their respect for the Panthers. The crowd managed to force the NOPD contingent across a drainage bridge before withdrawing. A total of seven people were shot and sixteen arrests were made.[11]

When the officers and firefighters sent word that they had been attacked, Giarrusso ordered the area sealed off and barricades were set up to block all entrances into the area. The chief then encouraged all residents to vacate their homes because of the impending gun battle. As residents departed, the NOPD came into the area with two hundred officers with automatic rifles and armored cars. According to one eyewitness, some residents refused to leave and walked around with clinched fists chanting, "I don't know, but thus been said, Pig Giarrusso should be dead."[12]

The arrested Panthers were then marched out of their headquarters with arms raised and after walking across a narrow bridge they were told to lie on the ground, face down, while they were searched. In all, seven people were injured, including four police officers: Fields, Howard, Reed, and Orticke. Orticke was the only officer to suffer gunshot wounds. A total of fifteen Panther members were arrested. Police confiscated a number of weapons at the Panther headquarters, including eleven shotguns, two revolvers, one M1 Rifle, one training rifle, and a Bowie knife. NOPD ballistics found a total of 887 shotgun shells.[13]

Community involvement in the confrontation was a clear sign that the Panthers had the support of the people in Desire. Residents were active in the interrogation of Officers Howard and Fields; they were participants in the beating of the two officers; and they raised clinched fists as they assisted the Panthers in their confrontation with police. Although these residents were not necessarily card-carrying members of the Black Panthers, they represented the large number of supporters and sympathizers. The broad support for the Panthers among Desire residents made the efforts at neutralization difficult for the NOPD.

At a press conference later that day, Giarrusso announced that the gun battle was over and that the Desire area had seen a return to normalcy. He further remarked that the incident was an excellent example of teamwork, harmony, cooperation, and coordination among the various law enforcement agencies: NOPD, the state police, the Jefferson Parish sheriff's office, and the district attorney's office. Giarrusso also mentioned that approximately ten to fifteen Panthers were largely responsible for the shootings. Then, as expected, he attempted to place much of the blame on outside agitators by mentioning that those arrested were not from New Orleans but were outsiders who had come into the city to start trouble. When asked by a reporter about an intelligence report that more Panthers were coming into the city, Giarrusso stated that the NOPD was prepared to handle any situation. He also mentioned that he had already obtained information that the Panthers were going to set up a headquarters in another part of the city. "These people are not going to gain a foothold in this city," he said.[14]

Giarrusso closed the press conference by stressing that the NOPD was ready to respond to any situation. Mayor Landrieu praised Giarrusso for his handling of the crisis, particularly since no lives were lost. Landrieu stated that the Panthers had embarked on a "reign of terror, without provocation" and that the "worst is behind us." J. Gilbert Schieb, the executive director of the Housing Authority of New Orleans (HANO), also heaped praised on Giarrusso: "The Housing Authority of New Orleans commends the New Orleans Police Department for its prompt, efficient, and thorough procedures in speedily bringing to a halt the wanton savagery that erupted." He recognized that as usual "the victims and intended victims were innocent black citizens." He closed by stating, "We are happy, indeed, that no resident of the Desire Projects was seriously injured by the acts of criminals labeling themselves 'Black Panthers.'"[15]

Giarrusso's attempt to blame outsiders for the disturbances was strictly a public relations ploy. The chief wanted to minimize the incident by placing blame on a few isolated members of the Panthers. Omitted from Giarrusso's remarks was any mention of community support for the Panthers. The chief understood that the Panthers had generated a great deal of goodwill by providing the community with several community-based programs that met their daily needs. While some members of the chapter did have violent and criminal backgrounds, their behavior in Desire endeared them to the community.

When Gus Broussard, an African American owner of a Desire area grocery store and owner of the building that the Panthers were leasing, was threatened by the Panthers the following day, the NOPD placed four policemen in his grocery and at his residence. The police protection was certainly not unwarranted since Broussard's son had been shot twice the previous night protecting his father's store. Around 8:30 p.m. approximately fifty African American males gathered across the street from the grocery store and made repeated trips to a nearby bar for Molotov cocktails. At 10:00 p.m. the group then made its way to Broussard's grocery store and residence. They lit the wicks of the cocktails as they got closer to the store. At this point, according to police accounts, an officer stationed inside the grocery came out and told the angry crowd, "Police . . . Hold it. Don't shoot." When the leader of the group ignored the warning, officers shot and killed him instantly. Three others were shot as well; however, there were no other fatalities. Two of the wounded men were taken to Charity Hospital; a third escaped the scene and was transported to Charity by family; while the lone fatality, Kenneth Borden, age twenty-one, remained in the street because of sniper fire. After the shootings, two of the victims, Donald Sneed and Jefferson McCormick, who denied any involvement with the Panthers, gave a different version of events. McCormick told reporters that there was no warning of any type before the officers started firing. "Why didn't they say halt? Instead of just shooting. I didn't hear no one say anything. I would have stopped and threw up my hands." Sneed, a Vietnam veteran, stated that he and McCormick went to Desire just to see what had gone on the previous night. "I used to live there. I thought it was nothing to be afraid of." They were headed to Champ's Place to play pool and drink. Sneed stated that as he was coming down the driveway in the housing project, the shooting started. "Jeff got hit first," he said. When Sneed went to assist McCormick, he was then hit by a police bullet as well. "There was a whole lot of shooting going on. It was coming from all sides. I don't know who hit me." Both men emphatically denied their involvement with the Panthers or with the planned firebombing of Broussard's Grocery.[16]

Borden lay in a pool of blood for more than two hours while police waited for an armored car to retrieve his body. However, three black civilians picked up his body and carried it to police. Giarrusso told reporters

that the NOPD did not willfully neglect Borden. "When this person was lying in the street our radio monitoring will reflect we were interested in getting him to the scene and to a hospital." Then he argued that the armored
car malfunctioned as it was heading to Desire. "And it developed a short as
it was leaving and we couldn't get it. We thought about bringing in a car
with a loudspeaker and pleading with the people to allow us to remove this
man to the hospital."[17]

In the aftermath of the Broussard shootings, the city administration
quickly assigned blame. At a city hall press conference, Mayor Landrieu labeled the arrested Panthers "self-styled revolutionaries" and not civil rights
activists. To illustrate that they were revolutionaries, Landrieu reminded
reporters that the Broussards were the first people attacked during the disturbance, and the owners were African Americans. Further, Landrieu then
spoke about the people's court that almost cost Officers Howard and Fields
their lives. "No community can afford to have a small group of people assume the powers of the government and hold mock trials on people." Landrieu also acknowledged that Desire residents had been quite hesitant to
denounce the Panthers, but he was hopeful "that that attitude has changed
because of the way they have abused people of the neighborhood. I have
never seen that the Panthers had much community support. I'm just
pleased with the whole attitude of the Desire community." When reporters
questioned Landrieu about the living conditions in Desire, he stated that
the city would make the requisite property improvements as recommended
by Robert Tucker. When Chief Giarrusso was asked to respond to allegations that the NOPD had initiated the shootings, he stated, "The Black Panthers simply declared war." Giarrusso was equally confident that the NOPD
would respond in similar fashion if another conflict erupted. "We are going
to move against anybody who takes the law into his own hands and threat-
ens the citizens of the community. We are going to see that the people of the
community get police protection." Then in a statement that illustrated how
out of touch he was with the black community, Giarrusso remarked, "We've
enjoyed a fine relationship with the community leaders in that area."[18]

After hearing Giarrusso's statements, black community leaders held a
press conference to tell their side of the story. They argued that the real
reason for the shootings was the horrible conditions at the Desire Projects
rather than the Black Panthers. They termed Giarrusso's statement mini-
mizing living conditions at Desire "absolutely ridiculous." The black press

conference took place at the Total Community Action Center adjacent to the Desire Projects. At the podium were Johnny Jackson, director of the Desire Project Community Center; Sidney Duplesis of the Sons of Desire; Barbara Allen of TCA; Henry Fagan of the Concerned Residents of Desire; and Clara Porter, the mother of a sixteen-year-old boy wounded in the shootings. During the press conference, Duplesis argued that the Panther raid was "a racist move" and that the NOPD acted without any provocation. He then insinuated that the local media twisted the actual sequence of events in an effort to make the NOPD seem heroic. He also criticized the local media for interviewing black folk "off the street" but neglecting to interview community leaders who could better articulate the frustration of the black masses. Clara Porter told the assembly that her son was not armed when he was shot by the police and that he was only "out to get some beer" on the night he was shot. The entire group expressed its greatest criticisms against Broussard, the grocery owner. They claimed that by charging high prices, and even higher prices on the days welfare checks were issued, he was openly "exploiting the black community." If the police were going to arrest Panther members, then they should arrest Broussard and others who exploited the black community, the panelists argued.[19]

Black leaders called another meeting the following Monday to express concern about the police actions during the shootings. "After careful consideration a cross section of concerned black citizens feels that the time has come to speak out. We have allowed the news media, along with certain public officials, to distort the events which occurred in the Desire area on September 14 and 15." The trio of leaders at the press conference stated that the "resentment and hate" being directed at the Panthers from the white media centered on the ideology of the Panthers as opposed to "the substantive issues involved in the case." They then announced that the black community was "in the process of conducting its own investigation. We feel it is absolutely necessary that all sides of the story be told. It is our hope that objective consideration on the part of the entire community of all the facts in this case will clear the air of tensions and hatred that is strangling our city." They reminded Mayor Landrieu that although he was mayor of the city, he did not speak for black folks when he minimized the conditions in Desire and praised the police. In closing, they asked Landrieu to reduce the $100,000 bond for the Panthers arrested for attempted murder, since the average maximum bond set for attempted murder was $5,000. They then urged Landrieu to "conduct a personal investigation into the Desire area "in an effort to understand how supportive the Desire residents and black New Orleanians were to the Panthers."[20]

The absence of the new black leadership such as the Community Organization for Urban Politics (COUP) and the Southern Organization for United Leadership (SOUL) in the aftermath of the Desire shootings indicated that the black middle class and other moderate elements within the black community sided with the NOPD in this incident and did not consider the shootings to be racially motivated or without cause. In fact, a good portion of the black community believed that the NOPD showed amazing restraint in Desire and that it should have been thanked instead of criticized. For many black moderates the Panthers were a radical organization with a dubious program of race advancement. Further, they knew that Panther chapters across the country were made up of ex-cons, hustlers, and criminals, posing as black revolutionaries. But once again, the black middle class did not publicly express their support for the NOPD, but privately praised Giarrusso.

In all, fifteen Panthers, twelve men and three women, including Charles Scott of New Haven, Connecticut, who already had an outstanding FBI warrant against him, were arrested and charged with attempted murder. Criminal District Court Judge Bernard Bagert set bail at $100,000 for each of the defendants but then recused himself from the trial because the Panthers rented a house he owned for their headquarters before moving to Desire. Although Bagert recused himself in an effort to avoid conflict of interest charges, Ernest Jones, attorney for the arrested Panthers, claimed that Bagert had already showed "prejudice" by setting bail at $100,000 when the typical bail for attempted murder in Louisiana was $5,000. "The hostility of the atmosphere surrounding the eviction process demonstrates an incurable bias and prejudice against the defendants" since Bagert had a previous landlord-tenant relationship with the arrestees. Further, since the judge had issued the initial arrest warrants against the Panthers, Jones wanted to know how he could set bail. Bagert denied any prejudice or anything sinister in his setting of bail. Although the judge pretended not to know much about the Panthers, he did mention that "if they stand for what I saw in the news media I could have no regard for them. They are certainly anarchistic and revolutionary."[21]

Once the Panthers were taken to Orleans Parish Prison, prison officials received threatening phone calls from their supporters. One caller stated that if any of the prisoners were harmed, the jail would be blown up. Another called to state that the prisoners would be broken out of the jail. To prevent a prison uprising, the Panthers were quarantined inside the jail. Parish Prison Warden A. J. Falkenstein told a reporter: "We put them in a secure place. We located them in an area where it would be highly improbable that they could create any disturbance in the jail. They're all in an area where they can't possibly cause any havoc."[22]

In the wake of the Desire disturbances, the Human Relations Committee expressed frustration at the police intrusion but asked black residents to be patient. "The people of New Orleans should be reminded that the events in Desire are not isolated and local. They are part of a national crisis resulting from past inaction. Years of accumulated neglect will not be undone simply because we wish it so—but the work has begun. The HRC pledges its total support to this effort, and urges all citizens, black and white alike, to unite in building a New Orleans where the quality of life will so enrich all so that none will be tempted to use violence." By putting the disturbances into the larger context of police-community relations, the HRC was acknowledging the obvious. Years of unfair police protection at the hands of the NOPD had generated a great deal of generational rage and anger in the black community toward the police. Consequently, those that did not particularly approve of the Panthers methods were nonetheless glad to see the NOPD and its historic treatment of black people challenged.[23]

As the arrested Panthers sat in jail, Judge I. M. Augustine, the first black judge to serve in the criminal courts of New Orleans, ordered a reduction in bail. Nine of the twelve were eligible for bail reduction that was set at $5,000. The other three did not have their bail lowered because they were already wanted on outstanding federal warrants. For instance, Alton Alsworth was wanted on attempted murder charges in New Haven. As expected, the twelve defendants from the September incident pled not guilty in criminal district court. In an effort to bring about a peaceful solution to the disturbances, HANO agreed to let the Panthers stay in the apartment. "The board is aware that there is an unauthorized presence of the NCCF [National Committee to Combat Fascism] in one of the Desire project units, but we are not going to go in off the top of our heads and unnecessarily inflame the situation," said HANO official Thomas Heier.[24]

Republican State Legislator James Sutterfield reacted angrily to Heier's decision and requested that HANO remove the Panthers immediately because of a housing shortage and on the grounds that it could jeopardize future federal funding. "It is my understanding that there is a tremendous shortage of housing units in the area and that it violates all guidelines of HANO to allow an organization to occupy an HANO apartment." He further stated that "history has proven that appeasement is not the answer in dealing with radical, racist subversive groups such as the NCCF."[25]

Despite Heier's willingness to let the Panthers stay in the apartment, Jim Garrison, the Orleans Parish district attorney, repeatedly made known to the public that the Panthers were in violation of the state criminal trespassing law. But Giarrusso, despite knowing the grave danger of the situation, was still hesitant about using force. "Some people say, 'Just get in there,' but it isn't that easy. I think that it is something we should move into with human spirit." When it became apparent that the NOPD would respond to public pressure and go back into Desire, an interracial group of ministers attempted to convince the Panthers to leave voluntarily. They refused.[26]

PANTHER-POLICE CONFRONTATION II

Over the next two months, the remaining members of the Panther chapter ensconced themselves in an abandoned apartment in Desire. Despite rumors of intimidation and threats, the NOPD still had nothing concrete on the Panthers. When the NOPD could not find any open violation of the law, they decided to arrest them on charges of illegally occupying an apartment. Since October 25, 1970, the Panthers had occupied Apartment 3315-A without the permission of HANO. On the morning of November 19, Giarrusso told a group of reporters that the NOPD was about to make a "last-ditch effort to remove the Panthers from their headquarters." He was hopeful that he would get them out of the apartment without any violence because he did not want another confrontation.[27] When the Panthers got word that the NOPD was soon going to try and force them out of their apartment, they stated that they did not intend to leave and that they would resist any attempt by the police to remove them. "The pigs have threatened to use whatever force necessary to extract the National Committee to Combat Fascism from the Desire Housing Projects and our homes that were given to us by the people of Desire," said chapter leader Harold Holmes.[28]

In an effort to avoid a dangerous nighttime raid, the NOPD police caravan rolled into Desire at 11:30 a.m. on November 20, 1970. Over the armored car loudspeaker officers instructed project residents to stay in their apartments for their own protection. The residents ignored the appeal and instead came out of their apartments to observe the impending confrontation. Police, armed with riot gear and bullet-proof vests, marched into the projects behind the armored car and urged over a loudspeaker, "For your own safety, please move out of the area." The people replied in unison, "More power to the people." As the police convoy approached Panther headquarters, approximately two thousand Desire residents blocked the armored tank and the convoy by forming a human shield and throwing bottles and cursing at officers. At 12:20 p.m. the police convoy made its way to Panther headquarters, announced that the Panthers were in violation of the law, and gave them eight minutes to come out of the building. "Eight minutes came and went; but police did not advance on the building and the NCCF members did not exit," said one eyewitness. Another warning was issued at 1:45 p.m., with the same result. During the standoff, Giarrusso and Panther mediators met every fifteen minutes in hopes of coming to a truce. The Panther mediators were Jerome Ledoux and Reverend William London. At approximately 3:30 p.m. London told Giarrusso that the Desire residents had taken a vote and had "unanimously" decided to support the Panther holdout as long as the NOPD was occupying their community. London further mentioned to Giarrusso that he explained to the Panthers that if they gave themselves up they would only be charged with a misdemeanor. "It is surprising to note the number of people who are supporting this movement," London told reporters. He then told them that the Panthers were in for the long haul even if that meant violence. "They're not conscious of what the police have out here in the way of weapons, and I don't know what they have in there. But they are dedicated to their revolution and they would rather commit suicide (than surrender), and they would consider it suicide. They would rather die for the cause."[29]

Giarrusso then told the officers to leave the projects because an "agreement" had been reached. The NOPD agreed to give the Panthers twenty-four hours to obtain a federal temporary injunction against the NOPD to prevent them from carrying out the eviction order. As the police convoy rolled out of the projects, residents yelled "Death to the Pigs," while another was seen writing "power comes from the barrel of a gun" on the side of a wall. As expected, the officers who had been on the scene all day were livid because Giarrusso did not let them take the Panthers by force.[30]

As criticism mounted against Giarrusso, he took full blame for not letting his men shoot their way into Panther headquarters. He stated that he was concerned for the residents who were foolishly supporting the Panthers. "We went there to remove some people called Panthers. However, if the police hadn't left, the people who would have been hurt would have been the people that live in the Desire community and the total community. The Panthers would have been totally unaffected in their fortress." Other factors for withdrawing his men included the good faith negotiating and the oncoming nightfall. Giarrusso had also been told that an injunctive proceeding was in progress. "I talked with some of the community leaders and they talked in good faith. They had nothing but the interest of the community at heart. I was impressed with their sincerity." He then warned the Panthers that in the future his men would do whatever was necessary to get them out of the apartment. Giarrusso was asked if the NOPD had gotten intimidated by the Panthers. "Professionals do not lose face, my men are professional enough to recognize what was at stake. I don't believe anyone wanted the possibility of a bloodbath back there." Mayor Landrieu supported Giarrusso's decision to pull out and praised the courage of the rank-and-file police officers. "It was a difficult decision and I support it fully." He then emphasized that the recent confrontation was different from the September incident: "At that time the men being sought were being charged with very grave felonies; but today there was a principle of law being upheld." As expected, Federal District Judge Herbert Christenberry refused to issue a temporary restraining order sought by the Panthers and several Desire residents. Now that the Panthers could not lawfully stay in the apartment, another police-Panther confrontation was inevitable.[31]

Giarrusso's restraint in Desire showed tremendous courage. In a departmental culture that stressed group solidarity, a sense of loyalty, and limited interaction with others, Giarrusso went against the prevailing attitudes of his department when he would not use a show of force to get the Panthers out of the apartment. By challenging the authority of local law enforcement, the Panthers were in effect begging for a shootout. In fact, in many cities across the United States local police departments did not need any sort of provocation before using a show of force to deal with black revolutionary organizations. In retreating from Desire, Giarrusso probably prevented a race riot, since all of the necessary ingredients were there for an explosion, and he probably saved the lives of innocent Desire residents who supported the Panthers in an effort to protect themselves and their community.

The Panthers got an unlikely source of support when Jane Fonda, in town for a lecture at Loyola University, organized a protest demonstration in front of the HANO office. Prior to the demonstration, Fonda went into the HANO office to locate "the man in charge"; however, Thomas Heier, HANO chairman, was unavailable. Although the turnout was low, Fonda was convinced that the demonstration was a success. "Numbers are not that important, it's always minorities that change the world." Fonda then told reporters that the Desire community should be run by its tenants. "The Housing Authority should not, the mayor should not, the city council should not." After the march Panther spokesman Larry Johnson said, "The worst is yet to come," and warned that if the police attempted to remove them from the apartment a massacre would be inevitable.[32]

On the day of the HANO demonstration, Giarrusso learned that the Panthers were planning to leave for a Black Power Conference in Washington, D.C., on Wednesday, November 24, 1970. Police officials first learned of the trip when Fonda rented four vehicles on the day of the demonstration. Once the trip was confirmed, the NOPD set up surveillance and roadblocks. At about 4:05 p.m. the Panther caravan left the Desire Projects, but the four cars carrying the Panthers, approximately twenty-five of them, were stopped by police at the intersection of Interstate 10 and Paris Road. The NOPD knew it could not blow an opportunity to arrest twenty-five Panthers away from their headquarters. All of the Panthers were arrested on trespassing charges.[33]

Early the next morning, the NOPD conducted another raid on the Panther headquarters in an effort to arrest the remaining members of the chapter and in the process completely dismantle the Panther presence in New Orleans. At about 1:15 a.m., approximately twenty-five black NOPD officers, dressed in plainclothes, including two dressed as priests, stormed the Panther headquarters, and after a brief exchange of gunfire the Panthers were arrested on charges of criminal trespassing and an assortment of other charges, including attempted murder of a police officer. There were no fatalities, but Betty Powell, a Panther, was shot by police in the chest. After witnessing the mass of community support during the daytime raid days earlier, police officials decided to conduct a potentially dangerous nighttime raid, and it worked. "Most of the people in the projects did not even know that we were there. The watchword of the strike force was speed and silence," said Giarrusso. The superintendent was also happy that the Panthers had now committed more serious acts. "We don't have to worry about the trespass charge the court is considering, we're talking about attempted murder now." At a press conference later that day, a reporter asked Giarrusso if the strike force used in the Panther raid was entirely African American. His response, "No, they were Americans."[34]

During the raid, the NOPD seized an automatic rifle, five shotguns, two dismantled shotguns, hundreds of rounds of ammunition, tear gas grenades, and poisonous liquids. In summing up the raid, Giarrusso stated, "We cleaned out the headquarters, there's no one in there now." That evening approximately twenty-five students held a march in front of Mayor Landrieu's home to protest the caravan arrests and the early morning raid. They marched with signs reading, "Stop killing black people" and "This land belongs to the people." Landrieu came out and spoke to the demonstrators. In all, the protest lasted no more than fifteen minutes.[35]

Since the Panthers were considered heroes to many in the Desire Projects, the black community was outraged at the arrests and the raid. Johnny Jackson, Jr., director of the Desire Community Center, summed up the black community's frustration with the heavy-handed police tactics of the NOPD. "I am not a revolutionary and don't claim to be but I do consider myself concerned about my people and the injustices that have existed. I too like many others was thinking that things were bad but never have I conceded that we are living in a Nazi situation."[36] Despite Jackson's pronouncements, the confrontation in Desire convinced black residents that the NOPD had exercised restraint and that the future of police-community relations in New Orleans was going to change. "The one thing that is sure appears to be the fact that the problems of black folks will not be dealt with in the usual manner, the last say being held by white folks. We protected our brothers and sisters of the NCCF," said one Desire resident. Others, however, were upset that the NOPD came into their apartments during the standoff when officers used some buildings as a lookout point. In particular, some residents accused the NOPD of humiliation, intimidation, harassment, damage to furniture, and violation to the right to be secure from unreasonable search and seizure. In fact, three Desire residents filed a $25,000 damage suit against the NOPD along with a restraining order to keep the police out of their apartments.[37]

In the aftermath of the Thanksgiving Day raid, the district attorney filed charges of attempted murder, criminal anarchy, and criminal trespassing against eight Panthers, including Harold Holmes, chapter leader, and Larry Jackson, a fugitive from California who was wanted on seven counts of attempted murder in his home state following a gun battle in Oakland.[38] Although the Panther chapter was driven out of the city, all was still not well in Desire. In late December, police were called to Desire after a reported stabbing death. When they arrived, they were immediately showered with rocks and bottles. Things got heated as the crowd grew bigger. When residents began attacking motorists driving through the area, the NOPD cordoned off the area to avoid further injuries. Although there were broken windshields, dented cars, and vandalism at a nearby school, there were no injuries or arrests.[39]

The Panther presence in New Orleans came to an end during the early morning hours of January 12, 1971, when the two former Desire area headquarters of the Black Panther Party burned to the ground. The former Piety Street headquarters was ablaze at 8:00 p.m., while the Desire headquarters was set on fire at 12:30 a.m. "Police were called about 8:00 p.m. Monday evening and were told by the police operator that a report of the fire on Piety Street had been received but that the fire trucks could not get back to the area of the blaze and was awaiting a sufficient police escort," said America Davis, Desire resident. The firefighters did not get to the blaze until 9:30 p.m., when they were escorted by twenty heavily armed officers. But by then it was too late; the building had already burned to the ground. As the firemen fought what was left of the blaze, a crowd of onlookers shouted, "All power to the people" and "Death to the fascist pigs." Similarly, the New Orleans Fire Department did not report the other fire until 12:30 a.m. The second structure burned to the ground as well. The fires were set by an unknown source but perhaps by Panther sympathizers who were responding to the arraignment of three members of the now-defunct New Orleans chapter of the Black Panther Party.[40]

THE FELONY ACTION SQUAD

For many citizens, both black and white, the Panther-police showdown illustrated a complete breakdown of law and order in the city of New Orleans. Contributing to the notion that things in the black community were out of control was the city's escalating murder rate. In 1971, the city witnessed a record 106 murders. Although many of these murders occurred in the black community, white residents were alarmed. Many whites felt that the city was completely out of control and that the NOPD had lost its power when it retreated from a Panther showdown in November. Beginning in the spring of 1972, local civic organizations began to demand that the NOPD do something about the crime rate. George Singelmann, chairman of the local white citizens council, stated that the city had become a veritable "jungle" of crime and murder. He asked the business community to demand that the city council provide additional funding for the NOPD because "without restoration of law and order we are rapidly approaching a vigilante situation." He then remarked: "Day in and day out unbelievable, heinous crimes of murder, rape, and perhaps the most atrocious of crimes, the muggings and assaults on defenseless, elderly women" occur in the city. Singelmann blamed the state of Louisiana for some of the problems since in his eyes the state spent four times as much money on welfare as on both police and fire protection.[41]

In response to broad criticisms of the escalating lawlessness in New Orleans, Chief Giarrusso launched a multiphase plan "to make the streets and homes safe again" in the fall of 1972. At a council meeting in early September, he asked the city council for a larger 1973 appropriation to fight crime. Based upon the 1972 budget, the NOPD received $17.2 million of the city's $79.4 million. The all-white city council agreed to consider Giarrusso's request of an additional $1 million for the next fiscal year. Although the city was cutting funding for social welfare programs, council members expressed enthusiasm at giving the NOPD a larger share of the budget. "I have great confidence in Superintendent Giarrusso," said Council President Joseph DiRosa. "I am willing to provide whatever is necessary to make the streets of New Orleans safe again." DiRosa argued that the city's economy was taking a hit because people were afraid to go out at night. Likewise, Councilman Eddie Sapir added, "If money can assist in lowering the ever increasing crime rate in our city, I will give every consideration to increasing the police department's budget."[42]

In an effort to crack down on the city's crime rate and to prove to residents that he was serious about taking back the city from thugs, hoodlums, and lowlifes, Giarrusso announced the creation of the felony action squad (FAS), a select group of specially trained officers to attack murders, armed robberies, rapes, and aggravated burglaries. Giarrusso was also motivated by the unfortunate reality that by September 1972, the city had already chalked up 142 homicides for the year. Giarrusso was confident that the FAS would be successful: "The people who perpetuate these crimes are one degree above animals and we are not going to tolerate them. They're going to stop; you'll see." The editors at the *Times-Picayune* were elated. Under the headline, "Felony Action Squad—Good News Due," the city's most-read paper appeared confident that the FAS, modeled after similar units in New York

City and Detroit, would give New Orleans residents greater freedom from fear at home and on the city's streets.[43]

At a news conference on Monday, September 18, 1972, Giarrusso announced the new FAS concept to the public. FAS officers were to be semi-undercover, "Some of them will look like bank presidents and some like bums." The goal was for them to be in strategic places where crime might occur. Then, to the delight of some and to the despair of others, he told reporters that FAS members would have orders to "shoot to kill."[44]

Major Lloyd Poissemot was picked to head the unit and Sergeant Warren Woodfork, an African American, was named officer in direct charge of the FAS. "In a continuing effort to stop the recent trend of violent crimes in New Orleans, the police department is initiating a felony action squad which will operate in areas plagued by high crime." Giarrusso admitted that the highly select group of officers was hand-picked and that they had been undergoing "extensive training for several weeks in patrol and observation, narcotics activities and community relations." He conveyed that the main purpose of the FAS was to make the streets of New Orleans safe again. Consequently, the FAS was explicitly given "shoot to kill" orders. When FAS members closed in on a suspect and thought that person was armed, they were to give a three-word order, "Police, drop it!" If the suspect turned to face police with a weapon in hand, then the FAS was ordered to shoot to kill. Giarrusso also said that members of the FAS had undergone intensive training in night shooting since the majority of street crimes occurred at night. However, whenever possible, "the use of firearms by FAS will be avoided." But since the work of the FAS was "highly dangerous," the officers did have orders to kill suspects. Giarrusso asked his critics to remember the families of victims: "If we consider the picture of 116 black caskets lined up end to end in the past eight months, it is indeed terrifying. Then too, it must be remembered that these victims had families, children and loved ones who are suffering from the tragedies. We are determined to make this city safe." The *Louisiana Weekly* initially came out in support of the FAS since black New Orleanians were the city's biggest crime victims. Thus, the paper wrote, "the black community stands to gain the greater share of the benefits if the FAS operation is successful." Giarrusso acknowledged that black support for the FAS was critical. "Public support from the black community— or lack of it—can either make or break this program."[45]

The black poor and working class were outraged at the creation of the new unit while the black middle class remained quiet. First to respond was the New Orleans National Association for the Advancement of Colored People (NAACP), which was becoming increasingly more aggressive in its tactics. NAACP officials challenged Giarrusso to explain the "shoot to kill" order. "The consistent resorting to the 'might is right' tactic is only a temporary stopgap measure which will help produce more fear in the community," said one NAACP official. Daniel P. Vincent of TCA condemned the FAS "shoot to kill" order: "The shoot-to-kill order is in itself barbaric and will almost certainly lead to the accidental killing of a young black male. History tells us that the accident will occur to a young black male." Vincent further mentioned that the establishment of the FAS represented "opportunities for police abuse that are unprecedented in New Orleans." He also clearly laid out how black folk would be the victims of the FAS rage. "The potential for racism and police abuse of this kind of activity is enormous, with law-abiding citizens in black communities being the ones with the most to suffer." Despite Vincent's criticisms, he and other TCA leaders stated that they were not against the creation of the FAS, just "the creation of an environment that will legitimize killing." He then spoke to Giarrusso's plan of having some FAS officers dressed like hippies. "What's a cop dressed like a hippie going to do? Go up and show his identification before shouting, 'Police, drop it!'?" Vincent asked. The real solutions to the crime problem, according to Vincent, were increased employment and job opportunities and an end to racism. "Unless basic causes are attacked, no emergency police action can stop crime in this city." In response to the initial wave of criticism, Giarrusso felt compelled to modify the "shoot to kill" order. In giving the warning "Police, drop it!" Giarrusso stated that officers would not use force on anyone caught in the act of committing a crime of violence if the warning were heeded. "This is by far more of a warning than the victim of a crime gets."[46]

Noticeably absent during the debate on the controversial new police unit were members of COUP, SOUL, the Black Organization for Leadership Development (BOLD), and the New Orleans Urban League (NOUL). The NAACP voiced its displeasure, but it was no longer a major player in local politics after the new black political organizations siphoned off prospective members. Their silence during the debate was predictable for two reasons. First, like many members of the black middle class, they were in favor of legislation that would stop crime in the black community. Second, they were closely tied to the Landrieu administration and its multimillion-dollar antipoverty program. They were unwilling to cross him on the potentially divisive issue of police brutality and jeopardize their access to the city largesse. Again, their main concern was personal advancement as opposed to community uplift. The selfish motives of COUP and SOUL not only hindered the development of a strong black political culture in New Orleans, but they also left the black poor and working class without an effective institutional mechanism to challenge racism and discrimination. Prior to the creation of SOUL and COUP, the black middle class would have been active in the NAACP, but now, with young black professionals joining the ranks of SOUL and COUP, the local NAACP was decimated and as police-community tensions increased during the remainder of the decade, the black poor and working class would suffer from inexperienced and reactionary leadership from their spokespersons and would be left to fight police brutality without the help of their middle-class cousins who had hitched their wagons to Landrieu.

When Giarrusso learned that the FAS had a successful opening week with fifteen arrests and not a single use of force, he was elated. "The newly organized FAS of the NOPD could be called the first preventive crime squad in its first week of operation." After relating several cases of the FAS's first week in action, Woodfork, FAS director, mentioned that in two cases of "Police, drop it!" FAS officers arrested five people carrying guns as concealed weapons and ten who were carrying knives. Woodfork reiterated that "in all cases the arrests were made by FAS officers with the use of minimum force."[47]

Despite Woodfork's assertions, the black poor were still unhappy with the FAS. At an Orleans Black Legislative Caucus (OBLC) meeting, which consisted of five New Orleans area African American members of the Louisiana state House, held on Monday, October 2, 1972, they called for a "march on city hall" to protest the "shoot to kill" order by Giarrusso. State Representative Dorothy Mae Taylor told reporters that black community leaders met at the caucus headquarters to implement a plan to initiate a citywide march on the city council for the morning of the next city council meeting, which was going to be a public hearing on the FAS. In preparation for the protest, the OBLC urged citizens to join the march and to write letters to the mayor, the city council, and Giarrusso expressing their concerns about the FAS.[48]

On the morning of the special city council meeting, hundreds of African Americans marched to city hall from two locations to gain emotional momentum before the council meeting. Once council chambers opened, approximately five hundred black folk jammed the gallery to protest the

FAS. The tone of the meeting was set when the black crowd erupted in boos when the council attempted to carry out its customary pledge of allegiance. City Council President Joseph Dirosa then told the crowd: "Nobody in this council is going to stand this kind of conduct. If this kind of thing keeps up we will clear the council chambers and none of you will be allowed to stay." After the council dealt with two zoning changes, Councilman Eddie Sapir made a motion to alter the order of business so that the hearing on the FAS could begin.[49]

State Representative Louis Charbonnet opened up the heated session on behalf of the OBLC by calling for three major reforms: first, "immediate disbandment of the felony action squad," because it creates a situation that jeopardizes lives of "innocent individuals" and because it does not address organized crime; second, "rescinding the shoot to kill order because shooting to kill exceeds the policeman's authority" in light of the Supreme Court ruling and because "it is not the function of a policeman to act as an executioner"; third, "the creation of a police review board since the police department is a service agency, the community through its representatives has a right to be informed of police activities." Charbonnet called for action on the proposals by the end of the following week by arguing that "the absence of response by the NOPD and the city council to the concerns of our community will create an even more dangerous situation." Again, Charbonnet hit at what he felt was the true cause of lawlessness in the black community. "A more visible solution would be to attack the root causes of crime, institutional racism, which condones and supports both organized and spontaneous crime in the black community, poverty, housing conditions, unemployment and the general racist attitudes of individual policemen supported by the judicial system." Following Charbonnet, approximately twenty other speakers went to the podium to express their displeasure with the FAS. Edna Tickles of the Cooperative Voters League told the city council that "one of the things that troubles us is the order to shoot to kill. We are here to protect honorable people who may panic. What we want to do is straighten this out so a lot of innocent people will not get killed." Community Advancement Committee (CAC) member Reverend Jerome Owens stated, "We do not condone the action of the police chief. The police's job is to protect, not to murder." He continued by acknowledging that there was a crime wave in the community but insisted that "we can come up with some alternatives" to the FAS. Clothide Bernard, also of the CAC, stated that "it is the feeling of the association's [CAC] board that the superintendent's order was poorly worded and triggers fear in the black community." She added, "We realize there is a problem, but we should not support the superintendent, not in shoot-to-kill, but to investigate the cause of crimes." New Orleans Southern Christian Leadership Conference (SCLC) chair Avery Alexander stated that the order makes the police an "executioner," and that it was a case of "overreaction and we don't want to overreact and kill the innocent." State Representative Johnny Jackson told the council that there had been constant harassment and killing of black and innocent people and undercover and entrapment activities "since the Desire confrontation." State Representative Dorothy Taylor told the council that they needed to understand what a "shoot to kill" order meant to black folk. "To us it means the same thing just as you sent soldiers into Vietnam." She then reminded them that the Supreme Court had outlawed capital punishment, "but here we are giving an individual the right to act not only as judge, not only as the jury, but as the executioner." State Representative Conner told council that "on the one hand maybe I can understand Giarrusso's felony squad, since we have lost 122 blacks since the first of the year. There is a need for such action if we can reduce the amount of killings." However, he also asserted that the "shoot to kill" order was illegal and he urged the council "to use your influence to see that this order is rescinded."[50]

While some questioned the legality of the FAS, others made simple accusations of racism. Leroy Jones told the council that he wasn't surprised about the creation of the FAS since "they have been murdering black people for 400 years. We know we picked all the cotton and there's very little need for black folks in America anymore." He then argued that "there is no such thing as justice in America for black people," and that public officials were only out "to keep black people in their place." Jones closed by stating an undeniable fact: only 60 percent of all NOPD officers lived in the city of New Orleans. Val Ferdinand, III (who would later change his name to Kalamu ya Salaam), clinical director of the Ninth Ward Neighborhood Health Center, told the council that "we wouldn't even be here if slavery hadn't occurred. We will be heard whether or not we vote. The people are tired of oppression." He then made a strong appeal to the council: "Accept the inevitability of the rise of the black man no matter how distasteful it will be. We will not stop until we have complete control of ourselves. There are many people, including myself, who think that white people are devils. Prove you are not devils and sit down and discuss matters with black people." Dillard University Professor Addison Carey cut straight to the heart of the matter. "I am introducing a resolution directing Superintendent Giarrusso to abolish the FAS by 1:00 today. It's 12:35, so you don't have much time." One observer noted that throughout the two and a half hour council meeting white city hall employees seemed "jittery." It was also noted that an unusual number of police officers were inside city hall and that employees had been briefed on what to do "if something breaks out."[51]

Despite the council tensions at the hearings, Giarrusso stood by the FAS with the support of the city council and the mayor. The following week Councilman James Moreau introduced a resolution to retain the FAS. It read: "The council hereby concurs with the superintendent of police in the establishment and continuance of the FAS and congratulates the police department on its administration of this program. The council hereby requests that any person who believes his or her legal rights have been violated by FAS notify superintendent Giarrusso and the clerk of city council."[52]

Mayor Landrieu threw his support behind the FAS at the following week's council session and asked that the FAS be continued. "I approved the squad and I find that it is working excellently at this point." He then termed the squad "an innovating, imaginative, way to get at the crime problem in this city." However, Landrieu did admit that black people had a right to be concerned over the "rhetoric" that had developed around the "shoot to kill" issue. Landrieu also stated that force would be used only when necessary but that he would not permit police officers "to become a shooting gallery for every murderer and rapist." The mayor then suggested that he was opposed to the formation of a citizens review board as requested by the OBLC. Once Landrieu sat down, the crowd began to heckle and boo. One angry black resident yelled, "We didn't come here for no bullshit from Giarrusso. We came here to make an emphatic statement to this. We put you here. Our black folks are going to continue to be killed, murdered on the streets."[53] City council members retired to the clerk of council's office until order was restored and the booing stopped. After reentering the chambers, Charbonnet was allowed to speak again but he did not dwell on his previous requests. Further, he said, the council's inaction regarding the FAS "leads us to believe that we must get some black folk on the city council."[54]

Much of the black frustration toward the creation of the FAS came from Landrieu's supporters, who believed that he had betrayed them because it was their support that had put him in city hall. However, this frustration was class-based. Since the black middle class now had access to city employment and strong ties to potentially lucrative antipoverty programs, they were unwilling to challenge Landrieu about the controversial FAS. In fact, some members of the black professional class were in favor of the unit. The black poor could possibly understand tougher crime-fighting techniques, since they were the main victims of violent crime, but they could not understand an emphasis on "shoot to kill."

Although many African Americans came out against the FAS, there was considerable support for the FAS in the black community, although few would admit it. Isaac Green, who represented an unnamed group, told a reporter: "Many of the persons that will be represented have said that they have been afraid to make statements or give their true opinions for fear of being thought disloyal to black people." An anonymous black business owner stated that two months before the creation of the FAS, "Judge Augustine called a meeting of about one hundred black leaders to deal with the problem of crime among blacks, two months before the police and the FAS came out. Instead of the group getting larger it got smaller. No one wants to work; they want the TV and the newspapers with their names in it. A little cooperation with the judge and his program would have made the Superintendent of Police's action unnecessary. We need leadership to begin to act and not react." An unlikely supporter of the FAS was state NAACP leader Emmit Douglas, who stated that he supported Giarrusso's efforts to curb crime in the black community.[55]

With the jailing of the local Black Panther Party members and the subsequent formation of the felony action squad, the NOPD was certain that it had eliminated all elements of radicalism from the city. However, Mark Essex was on his way to New Orleans to finish what the Panthers had started.

4 THE POLITICS OF SELF-DEFENSE

Mark Essex, the Soul Patrol, and Black Vigilantism

With the popular radicalism of the Black Panther Party (BPP) and other organizations, such as the Revolutionary Action Movement (RAM), the Republic of New Afrika, the Liberators, the Defenders, and the Black Liberation Front, in the early 1970s, government authorities called for an increased police presence in urban communities, partly designed to neutralize radicals, maintain order, and get rid of troublemakers. Consequently, black activists had to contend with a climate that celebrated jailings, beatings, and constant harassment. But during this period some not only preached self-defense but also expressed themselves politically by going on the offensive against police officers. Yet others decided to protect their own community since the police were unwilling to do it.

JIMMY

Mark James Robert Essex was born to Mark and Nellie Essex on August 12, 1949, in Emporia, Kansas, a small college town home to Emporia State Teachers College. He was the second of five children. Life for black people in Emporia was not overly oppressive. Of the city's 28,000 people, less than 2 percent were African American and they lived alongside the city's small Mexican American population near the Sante Fe Railroad in small houses. Raymond Call, managing editor of the local Emporia newspaper, concluded this about African Americans in Emporia: "It's tough for them to get a house in a nice area of town, even if they can afford it, and they usually can't. When it does happen it's generally because the black family was there first and the white suburb wrapped around them. There are few of what you would call 'racial incidents' here. Racial prejudice is more subtle, nothing at all like the large cities." Reverend Chambers, former president of the Emporia National Association for the Advancement of Colored People (NAACP) and pastor of St. James Missionary Baptist Church, was a bit more frank about the racial situation in Emporia. "Most young blacks leave as soon as they can. They go to Kansas City, Topeka, or Colorado to find work. You can't blame them. There are few jobs for them in Emporia and those that are available don't pay much. There is a lot of unspoken prejudice here and if you look you can see it in jobs, in housing, in education. The discrimination may be quiet, but it's very real."[1]

Essex was born into a solidly working-class family. His father worked as foreman at the Fannestil Meat Packing Company and his mother counseled preschoolers at a local Head Start center. By all indications, Essex had a rather normal and traditional upbringing. His high school teachers and friends remembered him as being polite and friendly. Emporia High School counselor Robert Lodle recalled, "He was an average student—just like millions who go through here. We talked a lot about vocational goals. Essex was not the type of student who seemed interested in intellectual subjects. He wanted to go into auto mechanics and he worked as a mechanic on the weekend at Johnson's Garage, the only black business in the city. His achievement tests showed that he was most suited to this type of career." But, although Essex wasn't into academics, he wasn't a thug either. "Rather than being prone to getting into mischief, Essex was the type who worked hard and reached above his ability. Although he wasn't one to go out for extracurricular activities, he did enjoy playing in the band." Frank Nelson, his biology teacher, recalled that Essex was a student "who didn't make an A and didn't make a D. He was average." Lodle also recalled that Essex came from a "hardworking family," and that his parents were "good solid citizens."[2]

As a teenager, Essex had both black and white friends and on one or two occasions even dated white girls. His mother recalled that "he told me that he didn't know why blacks dated white girls, because they're no different than black girls and they're not as beautiful." As a youngster, he enjoyed playing saxophone in the high school band, but his true love was the ministry, according to his former high school girlfriend, Renee Greene. "He really didn't talk about anything else. I know his mother was really happy about him wanting to become a minister."[3]

After graduating from high school in May 1967, Essex attended Kansas State College in Pittsburgh, Kansas, during the fall semester. At Kansas

State Essex enrolled in business and education courses. One school admin-istrator remembered him as a quiet student. "An organization of black stu-dents was forming at the time, yet Essex, a black, was not known to have been a member of any campus group."[4]

For the spring semester of 1968, Essex transferred to Labette Commu-nity Junior College in Parson, Kansas. School officials stated that "he was an average student in both attendance and grades." He did not belong to any black organizations. During the summer of 1969, he reenrolled at Pitts-burgh as a guest student and returned to Labette in the fall before with-drawing halfway through the semester. His inconsistent college enrollment did not surprise his high school counselor. "I figured Jimmy would prob-ably start college, then fade, but get a job and go back to night school and finish up."[5]

Primarily based upon the advice of his father, Essex joined the U.S. Navy on January 13, 1969. His dad told him that since he would probably be drafted for Vietnam, he should consider the navy because it had a repu-tation for being the least racist. As a black World War II veteran, the elder Essex recalled his own experiences in the army. "In World War II they would send us down to Mississippi to train with wooden sticks. Now why would they send a black man from Kansas or anywhere in the Midwest to Missis-sippi without any way to protect himself? Some of us decided we needed the guns and ammo more there than we did when we got to Europe." Essex took the navy entrance exam and scored in the top 25 percent; because of his college background, he signed up for a four-year stint at advanced pay.[6]

Upon enlisting, Essex was assigned to the naval air station at Imperial Beach, California–San Diego. He was elated at going to California because the self-contained city had endless opportunities for sailors. He finished boot camp in April and subsequently enrolled in the naval dental center. After a three-month course in dental assisting, Essex was assigned to the dental clinic there on the base, the first black worker at the office. At the of-fice Essex quickly developed a strong relationship with Lieutenant Robert Hatcher, a young dentist. Hatcher remembered Essex quite well. "He was the kind of person I liked to have around, a happy-go-lucky kid who was very hard to get rattled. I'm very demanding, especially when it concerns den-tistry. I demanded a lot out of him and he delivered. I felt we worked best working as a team and that's the way we produced our dentistry." Hatcher also felt that Essex "may have had inklings at one time of going back to school and maybe even being a dentist." Paul Valdez was also a dental technician and he remembered Essex being an "easygoing guy. He'd sing to himself and be real friendly toward everyone. When I first got here, he took time out and helped me. He showed me how to work with the doctors."[7]

Despite his professional success (he climbed in rank from seaman recruit to seaman in less than a year), Essex began to realize that black sailors were subjected to overt and blatant racial discrimination. These were things he not merely heard about, but things he experienced. For instance, when he began working at the Jolly Rotor, the enlisted men's club, he quickly noticed how racist the base was. "A white boy showed him what to do, how they had to get ice in another room next to the bar. The white went in and got the ice without asking permission. But it didn't work that way for Jimmy. Every time he needed ice he had to ask permission to get it from a white sailor. It was hard for him to accept this," according to his mother. He soon quit working at the club. The car Essex purchased as a twenty-first birthday present to himself also brought a lot of racism his way. Whenever he and his friends left or entered the base, they were literally always stopped and pressed for license, registration, and insurance papers. His sister recalled that he was often ordered out of the car and had to watch as the guards opened the doors and trunk and searched inside; they worked slowly, frequently spending a half-hour checking the car from top to bottom, even going so far as to unscrew door panels. But the harassment didn't stop there. "Wisecracks, jibes, whispered curses, and a stream of petty orders often dropped on the spur of the moment by ranking enlisted men were Essex's lot in the mess halls, barracks, everywhere." His sister also recalled that the navy became "his own private hell."[8]

The breaking point for Essex came when he and other black sailors were put on report for "excessive noise in the barracks." Although they successfully fought the charges, he and his friends were separated and assigned to different barracks. On August 12, 1970, Essex decided to fight back. After being insulted by a white petty officer, Essex responded by giving the white sailor the beating of his life before he was restrained by superior officers. For the first time in his life he had hit a white man and it felt heroic. However, from that day on, Essex would be singled out and become a marked man because he had struck a white officer. But Essex was not worried. He told his friends, "You know what I say? I say if a black sailor can't get a fair shake when he's in the right, then to hell with the whole United States Navy."[9]

Essex's encounters with racism at the base coincided with the emerging black power movement. Huey Newton's trial, Bobby Seale's arrest in Chicago, and the prominence of the Black Panther Party along the West Coast were ripe conditions for Essex to become completely disillusioned with life in America. Once Essex purchased his automobile, a 1963 Chevrolet, he began spending more and more time off campus with local black power enthusiasts. He befriended several local Panthers and began to associate with a so-called militant group in the black community of San Diego. He also became good friends with a New Orleans enlistee, Rodney Frank, whom military officials labeled a "militant." It was at this point that his attitude completely changed. "I have a feeling that he got in with a group of blacks who really felt that they were being put down. And I don't think it was just base oriented. But then as he started listening to some of these hard-core militant types, I think he really got involved in the movement," said Hatcher.[10]

C. B. Wilson, a fellow enlistee and a friend of Essex, recalled how the young sailor from Kansas was treated. "All the young blacks around the base were being hassled. Essex felt that he was getting a particularly rough deal and that he wasn't going to take it lying down. White sailors in the enlisted men's club came down hard on Essex, regarding him as a 'cocky nigger.' They would sit, a group of Negroes at one table, Filipino-Chicano at another, and whites by themselves. Then, before you knew, it some white boy would call a black a spade and like a firecracker it would touch off an explosion." Fred Allen, who knew Essex from boot camp, summed up why Essex changed. "Essex came into the navy expecting to be treated in the same decent way he always had been treated back in Emporia, and he found it wasn't like that at all. It wasn't long before he wanted out of the navy, and most of us blacks did."[11]

In October 1970, Essex went AWOL (absent without leave) and left the base for twenty-eight days. He went home to Emporia "to think about what a black man has to do to survive." His mother remembered that Essex "told us he didn't see how he could go back to the navy and start it all over again." Nonetheless, his parents and pastor encouraged him to return to the navy and he did. Essex reported to the military police upon his return and pleaded guilty to the AWOL charge. At his court martial he explained why he took twenty-eight days of unapproved leave. "I had to talk to some black people because I had begun to hate all white people. I was tired of going to white people and telling them my problems and not getting anything done about it." Essex was fined, restricted to the base for thirty days, and received a pay grade reduction. He accepted the sentence and then requested and was granted an early discharge on February 11, 1971. Days before he left the base for good, he told a friend: "There is no place in the white man's navy for a self-respecting black man."[12]

After leaving San Diego, Essex spent the next three months in New York City, where he got loosely involved with the local Black Panther Party. His local connection was Bernice Jones, "one of the few free hard-core members who had not gone underground in the wake of the trials and inner-party warfare." She was eventually sentenced to forty years in prison for attempted bank robbery. He then returned to Emporia but had difficulty maintaining steady employment. He purchased a Ruger .44 caliber Magnum Deer Slayer rifle in October 1971 from Montgomery Ward. Ronald Lewis, the store employee who sold the weapon to Essex, stated that Essex specifically requested that model. After purchasing the weapon, Essex spent hours practicing in the Emporia countryside because he knew that in the near future he would go on a killing spree. By then his family noticed that their son and brother was slipping away and they petitioned the family pastor for help. "There is nothing I can do, the boy just hates white people. I'm sorry," said Reverend Chambers.[13]

In August 1972, Essex reconnected with his navy buddy, Rodney Frank, and relocated to New Orleans, where they shared an apartment. Upon his arrival, Essex had the Ruger rifle and a colt revolver. Both men enrolled in a Total Community Action (TCA) training school's concentrated employment program. Essex was in the program's vending machine mechanics school, where he received $50.50 a week. Classes were held at the TCA headquarters. Ivan Delpone, one of the instructors at the camp, vividly remembered Essex. "He was eager to learn, always asking questions about his schooling, never giving us any problems. I taught him and the rest of the class how to repair vending machines. But Mark was way above that, and I pushed him hard into reading electrical circuit diagrams, which I did for only bright kids. I was even trying to line up a job for him with South Central Bell. Of the twenty students I had in class, he was at the top."[14]

In the fall of 1972, two events caused Essex to prepare for an all-out attack on the New Orleans Police Department (NOPD): the formation of the felony action squad (FAS) and the slayings of Leonard Brown and Denver Smith, two Southern University–Baton Rouge students killed by state troopers during a student protest. Less than a month after the November 16 shootings in Baton Rouge, Essex decided to kill as many police officers as he could. Plus, Essex was certainly aware of how the NOPD had conducted a reign of terror in the black community throughout much of its history. He attended his last class on December 22 and on Christmas Day he spent time with a school classmate. Sometime between Christmas and New Year's Day, he wrote two prophetic letters. The first was to his parents: "Africa, this is it mom. It's even bigger than you and I, even bigger than God. I have now decided that the white man is my enemy. I will fight to gain my manhood or die trying." The second was a letter to WWL-TV, the New Orleans NBC affiliate: "The downtown New Orleans Police Department will be attacked. Reasons, many, but the deaths of two innocent brothers will be avenged and many others. P.S. Tell pig Giarrusso the Felony Action Squad ain't shit." It was signed "Maja," which in Swahili means "a weapon." Because of the holidays the letter would lie unopened until the first week in January.[15]

Late in the evening on New Year's Eve, Essex drove to the NOPD headquarters, locally referred to as central lock-up, and parked on the Perdido side of the building. He hid in a field, pulled out his rifle, and gunned down two police officers: nineteen-year-old Alfred Harrell, an African American, and Lieutenant Horace Perez. Perez was only grazed in the ankle but Harrell was killed instantly. Harrell, a graduate of St. Augustine High School, had been appointed to the department on September 8, 1971, and was a student at Loyola University. Both he and Perez were assigned to central lock-up for night duty in which they raised and lowered the gate for prisoners entering the facility. Bruce Weatherford was also assigned to the post. Perez recalled the incident: "Weatherford was running like a wild man. I thought that someone was trying to break into lock-up to free a prisoner. That's when Harrell ran into the sally port and headed toward the main entrance. At the last minute, though, he seemed to change his mind and turned around and ran back toward a patrol wagon that was parked by the gatehouse. He was about two steps from it when he went down."[16]

Once word reached Giarrusso that two men had been hit, the NOPD launched a vicious manhunt for Essex, whose identity was still unknown. Essex then fled on foot and broke into the Burkhart Manufacturing Company, 1065 S. Gayoso Street, for refuge, triggering an alarm. Patrolmen Edwin Hosli and Harold Blapport, K-9 officers, responded to the call since many of the other officers on duty that evening had converged on central lock-up. They had no idea that there was no burglary; it was simply Essex's hiding place. Essex, who was positioned inside the office leaning over a desk, caught Hosli in his aim and fired. Hosli was shot in the back and would die of his injuries two months later.[17]

At a press conference the following day, Giarrusso told reporters that the shootings seemed "well-planned," then added, "There are overtures of a militant group. The evidence would seem to indicate a sniper wanted to kill one or more policemen. There may be one or more snipers." Patrolmen's Association of New Orleans (PANO) President Irvin Magri called the shootings "ruthless, coldblooded murder." Magri also used the opportunity to demand an end to one-man patrol cars and he wanted all officers to be given carbines. Mayor Moon Landrieu called the shootings "an act of brutality and an affront to the good conscience of man." The following day Giarrusso tried to diffuse the race situation. "The executioner didn't care for Police Cadet Harrell's race or color of religious preference. The executioner's prejudices were of a higher order—against law and order, against authority in any form, against the dignity of man." Since the NOPD had no tips, it offered a $10,000 reward for information leading to the arrest of the sniper. Giarrusso labeled the investigation "a blind alley" and encouraged people to call with tips or any information on the case.[18]

After exiting the manufacturing company, Essex left a trail of blood inside the warehouse along with a gas mask, a flashlight, and a purse containing fifty .38 caliber bullets. Henry Morris, the investigative officer, remarked, "This is no amateur. He had enough stuff in there to take on an army." On January 1, 1973, Essex broke into the First New St. Mark Baptist Church at 1208 South Lopez on Girt Town, an all-black, low-income community not far from downtown. That evening Essex was startled when the pastor of the church, Sylvester Williams, returned and flicked on the lights to see him standing at the rear of the church. Essex froze and Williams quickly backed out the door and called police. Williams described Essex as a "young, Negro male, about five-seven and 150 pounds, wearing dark pants and a dark jacket, standing at the rear of the church." Essex then escaped through a rear door. But he returned and apparently spent two nights or more at the church. Two days later, police searched the church and were startled at what they found. NOPD Lieutenant Robert Motz said, "Hidden in the ladies' bathroom we found a cloth sack filled with .38 caliber rounds. We also found bloodstains on several doors and window sills. Outside there was more blood on one of the walls." But before Essex left the church, he wrote a letter of apology to Reverend Williams. It read, "I am sorry for breaking the lock on your church door but Pastor at two O'clock I felt I had to get right with the Lord. You see I was a sinner then walking past your church . . . I was drinking . . . I then broke the door and fell on my knees in prayer. Now I have managed to get it together. I will send you the money for the new lock. God bless you."[19]

Although Essex had managed to elude the police since the New Year's Eve shootings, he made a tragic mistake. In search of toiletries and bandages for his wounds he suffered breaking into the manufacturing company and the church, Essex went to Joe's Grocery Store at 4200 Erato in Girt Town dressed in fatigues, visibly disheveled and with bloody wounds on his hands. After purchasing several items, Essex once again retreated to his neighborhood hideaway. Joseph Perniciaro, the owner of the store, suspected Essex was the sniper so he went to police headquarters but he incorrectly identified Essex as Curtis Moss, a cabdriver. While police went looking for Moss, Essex remained in hiding.[20]

THE HOWARD JOHNSON SNIPER

On the morning of Sunday, January 7, 1973, Essex once again entered Joe's Grocery, but this time he had a rifle in hand with the intent of killing Perniciaro, whom Essex suspected of going to the police. Perhaps Essex saw the store owner abruptly drive down to the station or he saw officers come to the store to further question Perniciaro. Or perhaps nearby residents told Essex that Perniciaro had gone to the police. When Essex entered the store, he shouted at Perniciaro, "You! You're the one I want. Come here!" and then he shot him. Essex then ran through some backyards with rifle in hand and carjacked Marvin Albert, an African American, for his 1968 Chevelle. According to Albert, Essex struck his rifle through the window and told him to get out. When Albert refused, Essex then calmly mentioned to him, "I don't want to kill you, but I'll kill you, too." Essex then got in the car, took Broad Street to Earhart to Loyola, and turned into the parking garage of the eighteen-story Howard Johnson's Motor Lodge. He parked on the fourth floor and took the stairs, and his rifle, to the eighth floor. After several attempts to enter the hotel, Essex was finally let in by a maid who didn't notice the rifle until he was running down the hallway. Three housekeepers at the hotel, Delores Arnold, Eva Mae Washington, and Atwood Wright, saw Essex running toward them. He attempted to put them at ease by saying, "Don't worry, I'm not going to hurt you black people, I want the whites."[21]

As Essex headed for the elevators, he spotted Robert Steagell, who was standing in front of his room. When Steagell saw Essex and the weapon he yelled, "What are you doing?" The young physician then made the mistake of trying to disarm Essex. Miraculously the small and lightweight Essex held on to the rifle and struck Steagell in the shoulder with the end of the gun. When Steagell tried to get up, Essex shot him fatally in the arm and the chest. Steagell's wife then yelled, "Please don't kill my husband," but it was too late. As she knelt and lay beside her dying husband, "cradling his head in her arms," Essex shot her in the back of the head, killing her within seconds. Essex then prepared to riddle their bodies with more bullets but he was distracted by a cracked door. Instead, he went to the Steagells' room and set the drapes on fire before heading out of their room.[22]

After killing the Steagells, Essex ran to the eleventh floor and, since the door was locked, shot the locking mechanism off the door to gain entry. Upon entering the hallway, he noticed Frank Schneider and Don Roberts, two motel employees. Essex chased them down the hallway firing his rifle. Roberts vividly recalled the tense moments: "We heard one shot and that was the one that went over my head as I was running low. Then the second shot apparently got Frank who was running behind me, and I kept running. Then just as I pulled the door open, the third shot was fired and I jumped down about eight steps and ran to the second floor." Schneider was struck in the face and killed. Before leaving the eleventh floor, Essex set several more fires. He then confronted Walter Collins, motel manager, on the tenth floor and immediately shot him in the back. Collins would die of those injuries on January 26.[23]

Essex then climbed from the tenth-floor balcony to the eighth-floor patio and shot Robert Beamish, a motel guest, just as he was about to enter the swimming pool. "I had slipped into a pair of slacks and a raincoat and I then opened the patio door . . . when a man stepped out from the bushes at the end of the swimming pool. As I was about to tell him 'Hi' he raised his rifle and I felt something hit me in the stomach." The force of the shot sent Beamish into the swimming pool, where he stayed for several hours until rescued by police. Next, Essex walked into a hotel room and began shooting at firefighters on extension ladders who were trying to extinguish one of the many fires he had started. Lieutenant Tim Ursin was shot in the arm while on the ladder. After shooting Ursin, Essex next targeted Officer Charles Arnold, who was stationed on the tenth floor directly above Essex. Patrolman Bill Trepagnier witnessed Ursin coming under heavy fire. "I had gone about twenty steps or so when I saw this guy come out on one of the balconies and lift up a rifle. He aimed at Ursin. I started screaming but with all the sirens going Ursin couldn't hear me. Then there was a shot and Ursin was hit good, and the blood just poured down. It was like rain." Ursin would have to get the arm amputated.[24]

Essex then went back to the balcony of a room on the eighth floor and shot and wounded Officer Kenneth Solis, who was standing near a tree down the street. The distance of Essex's shot was 217 feet. When Sergeant Emanuel Pelmisano went to aid Solis, he was shot too. "I had just stopped three yards or so onto the plaza and I was hit in the right shoulder. The bullet felt like a two-by-four. It came out under my ribcage," he recalled. As Officer Philip Coleman drove his car onto Duncan Plaza to rescue Solis and Pelmisano, an Essex bullet struck him in the head. He died within seconds.[25]

About noon Essex left the eighth floor and went to the fourth-floor parking garage to retrieve the carjacked vehicle and make an escape. Upon arriving at the fourth floor, Essex fired several shots at officers who were guarding the stolen car. Next, he headed back to the balcony of a room on the sixteenth floor and targeted Officer Paul Persigo, who was standing behind a police car at the intersection of Loyola and Gravier. He was shot in the head from a distance of 239 feet. He was pronounced dead at the scene. Essex kept shooting from the same position, wounding others with his pinpoint accuracy.[26]

Essex then went to the seventeenth floor, setting fires, and after he was unable to get access to the roof, he started for the stairs but stopped when he saw a group of officers, led by Deputy Superintendent Louis Sirgo, headed up the stairs. As soon as Essex spotted the group, he shot and killed Sirgo with a shot to the back. The other officers quickly retreated down the stairs. Essex then fled to the roof of the motel and took cover in a rooftop cubicle. From about 3:00 p.m. until approximately 8:30 p.m. Essex and the authorities would exchange gunfire. Periodically Essex would yell "Power to the people" from inside the rooftop cubicle. NOPD officials attempted to get Essex to surrender; one appeal went like this: "This is Father Rogers, my son. I'm a Catholic priest. God loves you. He doesn't want you to die. For the love of Jesus, surrender." Then someone yelled from, "Don't you believe him, nigger. We ain't taking you alive, Leroy. You hear that? We gonna blow you away." Another appeal was made: "Come on down, man. Don't die. Don't make us kill you." Meanwhile, during the standoff a local disc jockey made an appeal over the airwaves, asking citizens with "large-caliber rifles" to come assist the police at the Howard Johnson's. Another radio personality told listeners, in error, that large groups of black men with guns were headed to the hotel to assist Essex. As a result of these appeals, the white community responded. One witness described that "a large number of morons, marginal types, all of them armed to the teeth," came to the hotel to get Essex. Some wore gun club patches on their jackets and cowboy hats, many of them carried their rifles in "finely tooled leather cases." A few even had elephant guns. One white citizen pulled up to the police blockade and asked for instructions. "You want us to fan out on the Rault Center and the BNO [a downtown building adjacent to the hotel]? We got armor-piercing ammo. A few of us even got infrared scopes. We'll go anywhere you want." Although the rank-and-file of the NOPD wanted this assistance, Giarrusso politely told them that they didn't need any help from civilians. "I really don't know what you heard. But I believe we already have more weapons here than we need." Unable to get Essex out of the cubicle, the NOPD summoned a marine helicopter. On the helicopter's second and third passes over the cubicle, Essex fired at it. Periodically Essex would yell, "Come on up, you Honky pigs! You afraid to fight like a black man! Come on out you, Honky motherfuckers. What's the matter. You afraid, pigs? Die, you fucking pigs." At 8:51 p.m. Essex came out of the cubicle firing at the helicopter. Sergeant Saacks of the NOPD remembered when Essex came storming out of the cubicle. "He came out, running toward the helicopter, firing as he came. He was looking straight at us, holding the gun at the waist and firing. He took two or three steps before we opened up. I hit him a whole clip from the thighs to the neck. He was running at full tilt and his momentum carried him another five or ten feet." Detective Gus Krinke also recalled the last minutes of the standoff. "When he came out of the cubicle the second time, all of us started cranking away. There's no telling how many times he must have been hit. Guys were screaming, 'Die, you sonofabitch.' You could feel the release. After all those cops had been killed, now we finally had a chance to do something, to fight back." He was then shot more than two hundred times by police officers and "there was cheering when he went down" from the officers of the New Orleans Police Department. One police official predicted that Essex probably faced more than five thousand shots that evening in the cubicle. "Why did he come running out? He wanted to be a martyr."[27]

Because of continued gunfire from the roof, police officials assumed that Essex had not acted alone. They were certain that a sniper attack such as this could not have been carried out by one person. With six people dead, including three white police officers, officers were in a state of uproar

and they were determined to kill Essex. The shots officers heard coming
from the roof were in fact coming from the weapons of fellow police officers. The tense and tireless situation made some feel as if other black snipers were firing at them. Although Essex was killed shortly before 9:00 p.m.,
officers maintained their positions until 2:00 p.m. the next day. It was then
discovered that there were no additional snipers. After a complete search
of the hotel, room by room, Giarrusso dismissed his men and sealed off the
hotel for physical evidence. Despite not finding evidence for an additional
sniper or snipers, police officials and citizens would debate for months over
whether or not Essex had acted alone. Some hotel guests would later argue
that the man they had seen in the hotel with a gun was taller than Essex
and that the gunman had a goatee, while Essex was clean shaven. Some also
said that the gunman had a bolt-action rifle and not a semiautomatic carbine. Then an elderly black man told reporters that Essex had given him a
ride to church at the same time the first fires were being reported. Then
New Orleans Fire Chief Louis San Salvador was virtually certain that Essex
had help since, in his opinion, it was virtually impossible for one man to set
the hotel fires. Finally, some were convinced of a second sniper because of
the presence of a "shadowy figure" seen on the roof after Essex had been
killed. "Many, many shots were fired at this ghost while he moved, and furthermore, the men who were there near the roof heard conversation after
the first sniper was shot. I can't believe all of those men were hallucinat-
ing," said Giarrusso.[28]

On Tuesday, January 9, at a news conference with more than 150 reporters, Giarrusso identified the sniper as Mark Essex. Police learned his
name by tracing the registration of Essex's .44-caliber carbine and they confirmed his identity by matching fingerprints on the weapon with his military fingerprint card. At the news conference Giarrusso was bombarded
with questions regarding whether or not the Essex shootings were part of a
broader, Black Nationalist conspiracy to kill white police officers. Although
Giarrusso was uncertain, Louisiana Governor Edwin Edwards told reporters that the shootings had "to be a conspiracy or the product of a diseased
criminal mind. I can think of no other motive." Similarly, State Attorney
General William Guste, Jr., told reporters that the sniper was a member
of a local radical group. Both Edwards and Guste immediately made appeals for the reinstatement of the death penalty. New Orleans City Council President James A. Moreau was clear that Essex was operating as part
of a broader network. "I think this is just typical of the unrest that mili-

tants, regardless of creed or color, are trying to stir up in this country. Until people realize that when they violate the law they are going to pay the penalty will continue." Senator James O. Eastland was convinced that there was "ample evidence that a nationwide conspiracy exists to kill policemen." He told reporters that the evidence at New Orleans "is unmistakable that this is a war on policemen." He then made a strong appeal for a reinstatement of the death penalty. "The time has passed for hearings and investigations, we must move immediately," he said. Eastland then announced that he would introduce a federal bill making it a capital offense to kill police officers. "These men are putting their lives on the line day after day. This nation owes them a debt of gratitude. We must take whatever steps are necessary to protect them from these attacks," said the senator from Mississippi. Senator Richard Schweiker agreed. "Continued attacks on policemen necessitate immediate passage by Congress of legislation to make the killing of policemen a federal crime." Louisiana did not wait for Congress to act. In June 1973 the state of Louisiana reinstated the death penalty for crimes that involved the killing of law enforcement officers.[29]

In the days following the crisis, the city was filled with rumors and innuendo about roving bands of militant Negroes hunting down whites across the city. Tensions increased when the *States-Item* ran a front-page story on four so-called militant black groups that were operating in New Orleans and under FBI and Secret Service surveillance. The groups were Republic of New Afrika; New Orleans Urban Guerilla Group; National Committee to Combat Fascism; and the Maitryean Temple, a pseudo-religious group. As tensions remained high, local civil rights leaders were asked to condemn the shootings directly and black militancy in general. Louis Charbonnet told reporters that influential whites expected him to apologize for Essex's actions. "Now, let me say that it was not the white people who I consider to be community leaders or highly responsible who called me to shout insults. I think it was those people who wanted to hear the black community of New Orleans apologize for Mark Essex. What did we have to apologize for? Here was a boy from Kansas who had come here to vent his frustration in a suicide mission. What could I say about him? The black community in New Orleans did not invite him here nor did we send him up to that rooftop. Had he been white, I would not have called upon Mayor Landrieu to make an apology on behalf of the white community." While Charbonnet came under pressure from the white community to apologize for the killings, other black leaders such as local NOUL Director Clarence Barney and NAACP head Dr. Guy Gipson were warned by black activists not to demonize Essex. "We were going to appear on a television interview a few days after the sniping," Gipson told a reporter. "Before we went on, we were intimidated a bit by some men who wanted us to tell them in advance how we were going to answer certain questions. They didn't want us to condemn Essex." Despite the threats, Gipson issued a statement condemning the shootings. "The general black community was as shocked by this senseless act as the whites . . . we do not believe this incident should be construed as indicative of the mood of the black community." When asked about the death threats upon his life, he responded, "We feel these threats are just as deplorable as any act that the sniper performed." Likewise, Barney asked the black community "to exercise restraint and to rededicate itself to the goals of justice, brotherhood, and community unity." He then condemned "this senseless violence which took the lives of our police officers as well as private citizens. And we feel this tragedy is neither black nor white. It is human." Dr. J. D. Grey of First Baptist Church told reporters that the shootings did not represent the masses of black folk and he asked residents not to "condemn blacks wholesale just because this man [Essex] was black." Robert Tucker, the mayor's assistant, sympathized with Essex to some degree. While it was clear that Essex was dealing with some serious psychological issues and that the majority of African Americans did not condone the shootings, the incident revealed that the relationship between the NOPD and the black community needed to be addressed.[30]

After confirming the identity of Essex, police then searched his car and home. What they found was that Essex's intentions were clear. In the vehicle they found a half-ounce of marijuana and two partially smoked joints along with an army duffel bag with the name "Warrier" hand-printed in two places. They then went to Essex's last known residence, which was at 2619 1/2 Dryades Street in New Orleans. Detectives found his place of residence by checking the records of New Orleans Public Service, the local electric company. The filthy apartment was filled with trash, debris, and handwriting on the walls. The writings on the wall "in thick, crude strokes" were described as "anti-white slogans, anti-establishment slogans, anti-police slogans, and various combinations of what appeared to be African dialogue." Written in red and black paint, some of the slogans read: "AFRICA"; "my destiny lies in the bloody death of the racist pigs"; "destiny"; "death"; "Revolutionary justice is black justice"; "blood"; "KKK"; "blond hair, blue eyes"; "hate"; "kill"; "The quest for freedom is death—then by death shall I escape to freedom"; "The Third World—Kill Pig Nixon and all of his running dogs"; "Only a pig would read shit on the ceiling." The slogans painted in red related to killings and whites, while the slogans painted in black related to black revolution. Detectives also noticed that Essex had a copy of *Muhammad Speaks* and a copy of the popular *Black Rage*. The slogans and reading material convinced many white residents that Essex had prepared for his showdown with the police and that it was not just a spontaneous act.[31]

After being notified by detectives that their son had been killed in New Orleans, the parents of Mark Essex gave CBS an exclusive interview just days before the funeral. When asked by reporters why her son did the shootings, his mother immediately blamed the racist conditions Essex confronted in the navy. "He was mistreated in the navy. It was prejudice, I don't know if the navy is doing it deliberately, but they are doing it. I have talked to other young men, white men, and they confirm what Jimmy told me. Young blacks are not going to accept the white racist society." Mr. Essex echoed many of those comments. "If he had not been mistreated in the navy, he wouldn't have been gullible or easily influenced by outside influences and he'd be here now." Essex's sister then explained in more detail about the consequences of Essex's military experience. "When Jimmy went into the navy he really saw what life, the world, was all about. He saw that white people control the world, and blacks were being oppressed by the white man. He didn't like society the way it was. He wanted to change things. The navy to Jimmy was his own private hell." Mrs. Essex then added that the shootings were a "clear signal for white America to get off the seat of its pants and do something. I don't want my son to have died in vain. If this terrible thing will awaken white America to the injustices that blacks suffer, then some good will come of it." Mrs. Essex then told reporters that she had spoken to her son on Christmas day and that he seemed fine. "He said he had found himself in the South and planned to stay there." After the funeral, Mrs. Essex told a reporter that racism would cause other young African Americans to duplicate her son's actions. "I'll tell you this, though; they're going to remember him. The same old discrimination that made my son do what he did is just as strong as it ever was, and it will drive others to violence just like it did Jimmy. It can't be helped. I'm sorry. Jimmy wasn't doing this to be a martyr. He didn't want to be a hero. He just wanted to change things. Jimmy wanted to be a man."[32]

The body of Mark James Robert Essex was flown from New Orleans to Wichita Municipal Airport on a commercial plane and was then driven to

Emporia in a hearse. No members of the family accompanied the hearse on the seventy-five-mile trip to Emporia. The funeral was held at 11:30 a.m. at St. James Baptist Church. On the afternoon of the funeral the Eldridge Cleaver faction of the Black Panther Party sent a telegram to the Essex family. It read: "We the Black Panther Party take this opportunity to extend our profound condolences. The loss of your son was a loss to the revolutionary ranks and the black revolutionary struggle as a whole. Mark Essex was a black man, warrior, and revolutionary. He will never really die as long as the will to struggle is alive in the hearts and souls of Black Americans. All power to the people." Since the Panthers did not have the funds to send representatives to the funeral, they held a memorial for Essex at the Mount Morris Park Amphitheater in the Bronx. Only a few people attended. Back in Emporia the black coffin was covered with red roses and wreaths. "Power to the People," was written on a banner on one side of the coffin as more than two hundred friends, family members, and onlookers attended the service. According to one *New York Times* reporter, the funeral was filled with "mixed appeals for nonviolence with the militant symbols of black nationalism." Reverend W. A. Chambers told the mourners that he had a message for young people. He said, "Don't listen to them who seek to persuade you that the world's ills can be cured with their philosophy. It can't be done, particularly when these men try to teach you violence and hatred. The God I know teaches love." He then acknowledged, "I know our patience has worn thin but he will guide us and protect us. Trust in the Lord and wait patiently for him." Before the black coffin was lowered into the ground at Maple Woods Cemetery, several pallbearers placed their red, black, and green scarves through the handles of the coffin. As the body was being lowered a few short prayers were made and the Black National anthem was sung. Finally, one pallbearer raised his arm in the black power salute and shouted: "Up goes my arm, for today we have freedom from our bonds."[33]

While it would be easy to dismiss Essex as a lunatic, a fatalist, or a psychotic mad man, that is too simple an interpretation for several reasons. First, one must remember that his initial targets were police officers. The attacks at central lock-up were premeditated and well planned. He wanted to kill police officers. Only when he was eluding authorities did he begin to shoot civilians. Second, the graffiti in his apartment showed his frustration with local law enforcement, in particular the slogan that read, "my destiny lies in the bloody death of the racist pigs." Third, his knowledge of local political developments is another reason why Essex cannot be dismissed as

just "crazy." In the New Year's Eve letter to WWL his postscript—"Tell Pig
Giarrusso that the Felony Action Squad ain't shit!"—illustrates that Essex
was aware of the controversial unit and the great deal of angst it caused
among activists in the fight against police brutality. Finally, while there is
no evidence that he was ever a formal member of the Black Panther Party,
he embraced its doctrine, ideology, and philosophy, particularly its critique
of local law enforcement. Mark Essex genuinely believed that his community was under attack.

THE SOUL PATROL

In the immediate post-Essex period, a group of African Americans in the
city decided to take the law into their own hands to enforce the law, to stop
police brutality, and to fight crime. The Soul Patrol, under the leadership of
Eddie Sims, was a group of young Ninth Ward residents who were committed to keeping the streets safe even if it meant beating up other black residents. At a heated community meeting designed to introduce themselves
to the community, Sims was clear about their motives after a man going by
the name of Kuumba, age twenty-four, complained of the Soul Patrol beating up a man and breaking five of his ribs when he could not explain what he
was doing walking down the street with a television set. "Look, what we're
trying to tell you is that we're not going to sit by and let you shoot the little
boy on the street going to the grocery just for a nickel. And we're not going
to let you steal from hardworking people." Another Soul Patrol member was
even more blunt: "You may not like what I am going to say, but if I see one
of you out there stealing from somebody that's working hard for a living or
if I catch you trying to rape a sister out here, I'm going to get my rod and try
to blow your brains out. I'll try to pop your head open if I catch you." Nonetheless, some residents still had criticisms. Floyd Goyen, in his twenties, felt
that the methods used by the Soul Patrol were wrong. "You have to get out
here and talk with the little dudes and be a big brother to some of them if
you want to keep them off dope or out of crime." J. D. Commodore, another
youngster, also complained as he interrupted Sims. "Man, don't give me all
that shit. We've got enough pressure on us now. We've got the urban squad,
the felony action squad, tactical squad, plus the police. You can't even walk
out your door now before somebody stops you." In closing, Sims told the
young men, "Listen, if you don't like what the Soul Patrol is trying to do;
if you don't agree with what we're going to do, just get out. If you brothers are out here to help us, then we want your help." He then admitted that

there were some weaknesses to the program of the Soul Patrol. "We're not trying to say we have the best program, or that our program will lead to a Utopia, but at least it is something, and we need something badly." He then mentioned that they would pay close attention to police brutality in the area. "We're going to be the watchdogs over the watchdogs. All we're trying to tell you, man, is that we'll die for you or against you—take your pick."[34]

After reading of the activities of the Soul Patrol, Police Superintendent Clarence Giarrusso labeled the organization a "vigilante group" and stated that while their motives might be good, they could not operate in place of the law. "Under proposed vigilante programs, who determines if a citizen is guilty of a criminal act? The members of the Soul Patrol, it appeared, would have acted as policeman, judge, jury and even executioner. Constitutional rights of our citizens cannot and must not be so arbitrarily breached." He further mentioned that although community groups did have an obligation to fight crime, "the ultimate responsibility for these programs is in the New Orleans Police Department. We do not intend to abdicate this responsibility or subordinate it to any self-appointed group." Giarrusso then admitted that while the use of force against criminal elements "is frequently tempting, it is not a feasible or desirable alternative to professional law enforcement." The police superintendent closed by arguing that "if one group of citizens decides to take up arms for any reason—other groups of citizens have the same rights. The inevitable result would be armed warfare in this community."[35]

The emergence of the Soul Patrol was a loud indication that African Americans wanted the NOPD to enforce the law in black communities. Despite a legacy of police brutality in black neighborhoods, the Soul Patrol apparently felt that the community needed more police protection. Their promotion of vigilantism was in many ways a desperate call for the NOPD to enforce the law and stop police brutality, and for black criminals to stop their reign of terror in black communities. While the ideas of the Soul Patrol appeared outrageous, it was just one consequence of the NOPD's failure to provide equitable law enforcement and police protection to the city's poorest residents.[36]

NOPD officers approach the flagpole at SUNO to remove the black liberation flag and replace it with the American flag. A melee would erupt just minutes later between students and police officers. April 10, 1969. Photo © 2009 The Times-Picayune Publishing Co., all rights reserved. Used with permission of *The Times-Picayune*.

Officers of the NOPD occupy the headquarters of the local Black Panther Party after an exchange of gunfire. September 16, 1970. Photo © 2009 The Times-Picayune Publishing Co., all rights reserved. Used with permission of *The Times-Picayune*.

Members of the Black Panther Party and the NOPD engage in a heated argument inside the Desire Projects. September 20, 1970. Photo © 2009 The Times-Picayune Publishing Co., all rights reserved. Used with permission of *The Times-Picayune*.

Defiant police officers burn uniform shirts on the steps of police headquarters during a strike. February 9, 1979. Photo © 2009 The Times-Picayune Publishing Co., all
rights reserved. Used with permission of *The Times-Picayune*.

A young child displays the frustration of many in the aftermath of the Algiers killings. Photo © 2009 The Times-Picayune Publishing Co., all rights reserved. Used
with permission of *The Times-Picayune*.

Kalamu ya Salaam leading a group of protestors out of city hall after a sit-in in the mayor's office. June 21, 1981. Photo © 2009 The Times-Picayune Publishing Co., all rights reserved. Used with permission of *The Times-Picayune*.

Don't Shop on Canal Street. June 21, 1981. Photo © 2009 The Times-Picayune Publishing Co., all rights reserved. Used with permission of *The Times-Picayune*.

Valiant officers patrolling the streets during the chaotic days after Hurricane Katrina. September 1, 2005. Photo © 2009 The Times-Picayune Publishing Co., all rights reserved. Used with permission of *The Times-Picayune*.

5 THE RIGHT TO ORGANIZE
The Black Organization of Police, Mass Protest,
and the City Council Hearings

In the immediate post-Essex period, the New Orleans Police Department (NOPD) and other urban police departments adopted aggressive policing techniques as they increased their presence in black neighborhoods. Responding in part to escalating national crime rates, local law enforcement officials doubled police expenditures between 1971 and 1977 and launched law-and-order campaigns to keep the streets safe from thugs, criminals, and radicals. In 1972, 70 percent of Americans said that the U.S. justice system did not deal harshly enough with criminals. Six years later, that number increased to 90 percent. These conservative responses were not completely unwarranted, considering the trends. Between 1965 and 1972, the national murder rate doubled, per capita rape incidents per 100,000 increased from 12 to 26, and aggravated assaults rose from 111 to 127. Ironically, most of the victims of violent crime were African American. Nonetheless, conservatives demanded an aggressive police presence, longer jail sentences, and a crackdown on radical activity.[1]

THE BLACK ORGANIZATION OF POLICE
In this climate African American police officers took bold steps to improve their conditions within the NOPD and enhance the relationship between the black community and the police department by forming the Black Organization of Police (BOP). The BOP wanted to get more blacks on the force, to stop police brutality, and to bring about better working conditions for blacks already on the force. Detective Gustave Thomas told reporters and interested citizens the impetus behind the organization. "Because the

alarming rate of crime continues to plague the black community, because
the relationship between the community is very poor, black police in New
Orleans and the state of Louisiana have formed the Black Organization of
Police, Inc., to deal with these problems." Thomas stated that in the past
"black police have been used against the black community. We will no longer be used in this manner." When Thomas was asked whether or not the
BOP's objectives fit those of the department, he stated that he did not believe Giarrusso was in favor of the organization, but that his support didn't
matter because they were "prepared to go all the way because it was the
right thing to do." Thomas mentioned that the BOP had four main goals: (1)
to improve the relationship between black police and the black community;
(2) to improve police services in the black community; (3) to institute police
reform; and (4) to encourage more blacks to go into law enforcement. Of
course, stopping police brutality was high on their agenda. "We want to see
an end to police abuse and brutality and at long last see an effective program against crime in the black community." Asked what he meant by police brutality, Thomas stated, "We're talking about not beating people; not
harassing people; not pushing women up against cars and feeling on their
bodies." Thomas also told those gathered that the BOP would work within
the system and provide some "black input" into the NOPD. Of the eighty-
eight African Americans on the force at the time, twenty-eight joined the
Black Organization of Police.[2]

The formation of the BOP was important for two reasons. First, since
the all-white and discriminatory Patrolmen's Association of New Orleans
(PANO) had literally excluded African Americans from their group, or at
best, gave them no say in the affairs of the organization, black officers
needed an organization to address their issues. A large segment of rank-and-
file PANO members were racist, Negrophobic, and eager to see black officers
not make any advances within the system. At times they also acted as a sort
of defense against racial progress throughout the city. For instance, in 1973,
PANO reacted angrily against a $15,000 grant the city council gave the Free
Southern Theater, a black arts organization they labeled anti-police and
un-American. At a press conference called by PANO head Irvin Magri, Jr.,
he stated that the theater was responsible for "actions, policies, copyrighted
poems, and short stories that clearly advocate the killing of citizens and
police officers." Magri then went on to argue that the source of the funds
came from the general fund of the city, which was customarily used to pay
police and fire overtime. In response to Magri's grandstanding, BOP Presi-

dent Larry Williams praised "the action of the New Orleans city council in awarding funds" to the theater. Magri countered by telling the public that the BOP's support for the theater was "well beyond any logical person's imagination." Magri's accusations and allegations were just one part of a larger problem between black and white officers on the force and between the black community and the nearly all-white NOPD.[3]

Second, the formation of the BOP also represented a heightened sense of racial awareness by black officers. Although they were police officers, they were making a statement to their white brothers in blue and to the community in general that they were black police officers, and not officers who just happened to be black. Although the formation of the BOP would cause fissures between black and white officers, they were steadfast in their commitment. The creation of the BOP was actually part of a broader trend in which black police officers in Chicago, Atlanta, Los Angeles, St. Louis, and in other major cities were organizing themselves.

Third, the formation was also critical because in the post-Essex climate of law enforcement black officers were becoming more and more isolated within the department and they needed an institutional mechanism to protect one another. Some were labeled black power sympathizers, others were considered "weak" because they refused to take part in the departmental

TABLE 2.

Black Police Organizations in Select Cities and Year Established

CITY	ASSOCIATION	YEAR
Houston	Texas Police Officers Association	1935
Miami	Colored Police Benevolent Association	1946
Cleveland	Shield Club	1946
New York City	Guardians Association	1949
Philadelphia	Guardians Civic League	1956
Detroit	The Guardians of Michigan	1963
Chicago	Afro-Patrolmen's League	1967
St. Louis	Ethical Police Society	1968
Los Angeles	Oscar Joel Bryant Association	1968
Atlanta	Afro-American Patrolmen/s League	1969
New Orleans	**Black Organization of Police**	**1973**

Source: Dunlaney, *Black Police in America,* p. 121.

culture of brutality, and a segment of the black police population was considered unqualified by their white counterparts. High tensions throughout
the city in the weeks and months after the Essex shootings filtered into
precincts across the city and black officers bore the brunt of those feelings.

One month after the formation of the BOP, five African American police
officers filed a discrimination lawsuit in federal court against the NOPD. Officers Larry Williams, Gustave Thomas, Willie Carter, Jr., Edgar Morgan, Jr.,
and Ronald Bechet argued that the NOPD was replete with racism in the
appointment of officers to the force, in the assignment and promotion of
existing officers, and in the disciplining of officers. The suit asked the court
to promote black officers on an equal basis with white officers and to implement an "affirmative recruitment, hiring, and promotion program to eliminate the effects of past racially discriminatory practices." The petition further noted that although the city of New Orleans was 46 percent African
American, the NOPD was less than 7 percent black. Of the 1,400 officers on
the NOPD, less than 90 were African American. The lack of advancement
for black officers was clear. "In the twenty three years since the first black
male was hired as a patrolmen with NOPD, blacks have, at best, been to-
kenly included and promoted within its employment ranks," read the suit.
There were no black majors or captains; only one of the 65 lieutenants was
black and only 7 of the 115 sergeants were black. Thus, the prospects for
promotion for African American officers were low.[4]

In response to the lawsuit and general public dialogue about the lack
of black officers on the force, Jim Wayne, deputy director of the federally funded Louisiana Commission on Law Enforcement, argued that the
NOPD needed to be at least 37 percent African American. Wayne told reporters during an interview in Baton Rouge that he was scheduled to spend
six weeks in New Orleans monitoring the NOPD. Wayne felt that the NOPD
needed to establish some programs immediately in order to attract more
African Americans to the force. He did mention that the situation in New
Orleans was part of a larger problem. "It's not a situation found only in
New Orleans," he said, "This is true all over." He continued, "I was reading
the other day that in Detroit, Michigan, before the riots there, the police
force was only 3 percent black. Now it is 18 percent and the police chief
wants to increase that to 47 percent. It is a big problem everywhere. The
only way to solve it is for someone to sit down and map out some type of
construction program." Wayne was hoping that during his visit to New Orleans he would be able to meet with the black community. "What I see is a

series of meetings in the black community. We would want input from the whole community—even from the so-called militant organizations."[5]

At a Sixth District neighborhood meeting held at St. John Institutional Baptist Church "designed to foster police-community relations," it became apparent to all that there were some serious problems between the black community and the NOPD. Detective Gustave Thomas, one of the founding members of the BOP, said the root of the problem was the lack of communication between citizens and police. Although the meeting turned into a question-and-answer session concerning police procedure and citizen responses, it was a constructive meeting because the group planned to hold two more meetings at the church to build dialogue and answer questions.[6]

Despite the token efforts of the NOPD to reach out to the black community, police brutality was still a daily reality, and in mid-September a group of black citizens asked for Giarrusso's resignation. During a meeting with State Representative Louis Charbonnet at St. Augustine Church, citizens also demanded a police review board and the reinstatement of truancy officers. Charbonnet argued that such a meeting was necessary because "the police situation in our community is at a very high level of explosiveness as far as the relationship of police and the community." Charbonnet stated emphatically that he was not against the police; "what I object to is the methods they employ to do their job." Several members of the BOP were there and they confirmed that police brutality was a serious problem in the city. Giarrusso refused to resign.[7]

In 1974, the NOPD decided to make a special effort to recruit African Americans to the force. Giarrusso formed the four-person Citizens Advisory Committee on Police Recruitment with the overall goal of increasing the number of African Americans to the ranks. The committee members were Carl D. Mullican, Jr.; Aaron X. Gilyard; Ricardo Pardo; and C. C. Dejoie, editor of the *Louisiana Weekly*. "I have requested the Committee to develop a program designed to assist us in attracting qualified personnel to the Department with primary emphasis to recruitment of personnel from the community's minority groups," Giarrusso stated. "A major objective of the Committee's program will be to attract a minimum of one hundred qualified candidates from the minority groups in the immediate future." Giarrusso was hopeful that a solid recruiting campaign in the black community would achieve beneficial results. However, Giarrusso made it clear that the NOPD would not lower its standards in an effort to diversify. "We will not compromise the high standards for police personnel, but we will adapt promising

improvements." In order to become a member of the department, an appli-
cant was to have high moral character, a high school diploma, be between
the ages of twenty and thirty-five, and be a registered voter. The beginning
monthly salary was $584 a month.[8]

The Citizens Advisory Committee on Police Recruitment did not waste
any time in getting the word out to the black community that a special
drive was underway to get more African Americans on the force. In the May
25, 1974, edition of the *Louisiana Weekly*, the NOPD ran an ad for potential black applicants under the heading, "Your Community Needs Men and
Women to Serve as Police Officers." Below the title was a picture of a black
police officer talking to a group of black teenagers with a basketball goal in
the foreground. The caption read: "If you are looking for a satisfying career
with many benefits and if you have the desire to contribute to the community in which you live you should apply for a position as a Police Officer."
The requirements and benefits were listed.[9]

The recruiting efforts yielded immediate benefits. Of the forty gradu-
ates in the March 1975 police academy, nineteen were African American.
Gilyard, a member of the committee, stated that "this is the first time in
the history of New Orleans that we have had a high percentage of blacks
and females." Carol Dumas, a writer for the *Louisiana Weekly*, commented
that New Orleans should be proud "of the fact that they have taken steps to
do voluntarily what Cleveland, a northern city, was forced to do by a Federal Court order." In Cleveland, a federal judge ruled that the police department had to reconstruct its civil service examination to lessen the cultural
bias, to recruit more African Americans, and to integrate all units within
the department.[10]

Later that fall, twenty-six-year-old Stephanie Duplechain, an African
American woman, finished first in her co-ed police recruit class. She was
not only the first African American to achieve the honor but also the first
woman. Captain Elmon Randolph, director of education and training at the
police academy, was elated. "I think it is an outstanding achievement for
anyone to finish first in a class that comes and goes through the same training and receives the same attention, but I think it is a bit of a distinction for
a female to finish first in this class. It is my first time in my twenty year history as far as I can remember that a female has finished first in her class."
Ms. Duplechain was just as excited. "It is a great honor to win this award,
and one of the main purposes for joining the department is to help eliminate crime, especially by juveniles."[11]

As the repeated acts of brutality continued, the Black Organization of Police came out once again against the hiring and promotional practices of the NOPD. Gustave Thomas, president of the BOP, told the New Orleans city council that his organization had filed complaints with the federal government accusing the department of racially motivated "discriminatory practices." In the complaint Thomas told the council members that the BOP asked the Justice Department to withhold all federal monies to New Orleans until "such discriminatory practices and their effects are eliminated." Speaking on behalf of the mostly black Pontchartrain Park area residents who were demanding more police protection, Thomas stated that "we must report that Pontchartrain Park is an example of the failure of the City of New Orleans and the NOPD to provide equal protection and service to the black community in the entire city." He continued, "Black police are endeavoring to improve the relationship between the Police Department and the community. However, our efforts are being stymied by a worsening of the relationship between black and white police officers." In an interview with local reporters after the council meeting, Thomas stated that he was motivated in part by other black police organizations across the country that had brought similar charges to the federal government about their local police forces. Thomas was hopeful that the federal suit would "speed up relief" in addressing the charges of institutional racism with the NOPD. "When we look at the situation nationally, we feel that there is a conspiracy against the black community by the police departments across the country." Mayor Landrieu quickly denied the accusations by stating that a "staggering number of blacks" had joined the NOPD during his administration and thus there was no "justification for the charges of racial discrimination against the NOPD." Then the mayor cited the appointment of Sidney Cates and Louis Turner as black deputy superintendents. Thomas respectfully challenged the mayor's comments by revealing some glaring statistics. "I challenge that by giving you the actual numbers: there are 1,507 commissioned police officers in the NOPD, only 177 are black. We're supposed to have 750," he said, referring to the fact that the population of New Orleans was more than 50 percent African American. Thomas also mentioned that only 5 of the 177 black officers held rank—one lieutenant and 4 sergeants out of a total ranking corps of 255. In an effort to diminish the significance of the statistics, Acting Police Superintendent Tony Duke stated that 60 percent of the last graduating class from the police academy were black and that things were changing, albeit slowly. Thomas acknowledged Duke's statement, but he went on to suggest that before the situation between the black community and the NOPD could improve, "our city fathers must recognize and admit that a problem does exist." Thomas, a veteran officer, knew that would never happen.[12]

Months later, Thomas was elected president of the National Black Police Association at its annual meeting in New Orleans. Upon taking office, Thomas demanded that President Jimmy Carter institute an affirmative action program in law enforcement. Using the NOPD as an example, Thomas told reporters at the conference that the problem of police brutality was critical and urgent and that local police departments would not police themselves.[13]

Despite genuine and sincere efforts to attract more African Americans to the force, the increasing numbers of blacks within the NOPD did nothing to curb police brutality or police homicides. Between 1974 and 1975, the NOPD continued to kill black civilians at a higher rate than any other police department in the country. In December 1974, eighteen-year-old Edward Lee was killed by police after he allegedly pulled out a .22 caliber revolver after being told that he was under arrest. But witnesses stated that he was set up. "My son was set up to be killed," said the teen's father. According to the father and several witnesses, Lee and a female companion were eating at a shopping center when he was asked by someone to come outside to settle an altercation. "As soon as he went outside a shot was heard. Everyone rushed to the door. They saw my son run toward the alley and fall. Friends say that the police stood over him and shot him while he lay on the ground." Lee's girlfriend confirmed that he was unarmed. "He had spent the previous night at my house and we left my house and came straight to the bar. I know he didn't have a gun." Fueling suspicion that police misconduct was responsible for Lee's death was that neither his girlfriend nor his father was allowed to see the body at the scene of the crime. Mr. Lee vividly remembered that exchange. "When I got there they wouldn't let anybody get close to him or see him. They said he was involved in some kind of robbery, but wouldn't say what kind." Lee died from a gunshot wound to the chest.[14]

THE KILLING OF CHARLES CHEATHAM

The most troubling incident of police homicide during the period was the killing of twenty-seven-year-old Charles Cheatham of Algiers at the hands of a twenty-one-year-old off-duty police officer in April 1975 on Bourbon

Street. As expected, there were two drastically different accounts of what led to the shooting. According to police officials, Cheatham attacked off-duty Officers Daniel Renoux and Steve Reboul and, in the process of the altercation, Cheatham took Reboul's service revolver and aimed it at De-noux. Denoux then fired one shot at Cheatham, killing him instantly. Even the most pro-police person found this chain of events somewhat question-able. According to one eyewitness who chose not to be identified, the off-duty officers were harassing a young black shoeshine boy on Toulouse. "A man, I later learned his name was Charles Cheatham, walked up and inter-vened. They told him to stay out of it, it was none of his business. They still never said they were police officers. Cheatham told them that he was going to make it his business. He took the shoeshine boy by the arm and walked around to Bourbon Street, a few steps away." Then the off-duty officers walked to Bourbon and attacked Cheatham, who did fight back. "Shortly afterward I heard one shot fired. Then I saw one of the whites jump up wav-ing a badge in one hand and a pistol in the other as he ordered everybody to 'get the hell away,' to get back." Cheatham was then taken to the hospi-tal while the shoeshine boy fled. To make matters worse, a full forty-eight hours after the shooting, the Cheatham family still had received no official word from the NOPD that Charles was deceased. Cheatham, a Vietnam vet-eran, was a salesman for Pitney-Bowes and an upstanding and prosperous member of the Algiers community.[15]

The shooting triggered an immediate wave of protest from the New Or-leans National Association for the Advancement of Colored People (NAACP) youth council, while the parent organization requested a grand jury inves-tigation. Norbert Rome, youth council president, issued a statement that opened with the simple question, "How can this happen in our commu-nity?" The statement further blamed the Times-Picayune for not giving the Cheatham death or other incidents of police brutality adequate press cover-age. "The police in New Orleans feel no restraint. The responsibility belongs at the top. The Superintendent, the Mayor and the District Attorney all have the power to act. They must take steps to clean house in the New Or-leans Police Department. We want no more excuses. We want action now." The youth council then went on to label the NOPD's review procedures "a sham." It further stated that "we do not trust them. This death must not be brushed under the rug and ignored." The youth council concluded their statement by letting police officials know that they would be watching the investigation. "The NAACP will monitor this case from the beginning to the end. The police, the lawyers, and public officials will all be under scrutiny. We promise to keep the community informed, and we especially pledge to Mr. Cheatham's family and friends we will not allow public officials to over-look this outrage." Weeks later, the youth council demanded that the investigation of Cheatham's death go beyond the internal affairs division (IAD) of the NOPD and that District Attorney Harry Connick start a full grand jury probe into the murder. "Only then can the investigation gain some measure of confidence in the community." In response to this request and persistent outrage from the black community, the district attorney agreed to investigate.[16]

As city officials continued investigating the Cheatham murder, his wife filed suit in Orleans Parish civil district court for $1.4 million for wrongful death. Unfortunately, the lawsuit had no bearing on the grand jury's findings. The grand jury ruled the shooting a justifiable homicide after interviewing thirteen witnesses, including a cab driver who witnessed the entire altercation and testified that the officers never identified themselves as police officers.[17]

The central question that emerged after the Cheatham death centered around the interactions between off-duty plainclothes officers and the black community. The issue raised more concern during the months after the Cheatham murder when off-duty NOPD plainclothes officers killed two African American men during a three-week span. In June 1975, twenty-one-year-old Leo Brady was shot in the head and killed by Officer Mark Osborne during an altercation, and weeks later MacArthur Jones was killed by an off-duty officer after a dispute at a motorcycle shop on Broad Street. The deaths of Cheatham, Brady, and Jones were similar in that all three were engaged in altercations with officers who had not identified themselves as policemen.[18]

In an effort to quell complaints of police brutality and illustrate to the black community that the NOPD had a fair and unbiased internal affairs division, Landrieu and police officials pushed Office Edward Morgan, the lone African American in the department, into the spotlight. Morgan told reporters of the *Louisiana Weekly* that as a special investigator his responsibility was to listen, record complaints, and advise the complainants to write a letter to the superintendent of police. Then the IAD would conduct a thorough investigation into the complaint. When asked about the countless complaints brought by black citizens against the NOPD, Morgan refused to comment other than stating that the NOPD's system of "checks of balances" was pretty good despite the reality that not even one officer had been prosecuted for police brutality in years. Morgan made it clear that the IAD had no authority to determine if someone was innocent or guilty, but rather its responsibility was to conduct an investigation, compile evidence, and recommend action against the officer. Although Morgan was the second highest-ranking black police officer within the NOPD, he was not a member of the Black Organization of Police.[19]

The inaction by the IAD led community leaders to demand that the division restructure. At a city council meeting in October 1976 State Representative Johnny Jackson stated that "the problem lies in the fact that the police have been hearing the complaints lodged against them. If we are going to have good law enforcement this council will have to make an earnest effort to study the way the police handle complaints." Fellow State Representative Diana Bajoie told the council, "I receive calls about police brutality almost on a daily basis. People who file complaints feel they don't get any results in internal affairs." She then told the council that they should look into the possibility of a civilian review board or some other type of system to ensure that citizens got adequate redress on their complaints against the police. Several council members responded to her suggestion. While Councilman Frank Friedler stated that he would start "some sort of public forum or open discussion on police brutality," Councilman Philip Ciaccio promised to meet with Ninth Ward community leaders to discuss the issue. "We've come a long, long way in establishing a climate of trust." He then urged a complete review of how the NOPD handled complaints. Councilman Joseph Giarrusso, the former head of the NOPD, remained quiet during the debate but did state after the meeting that "I feel that police brutality incidents are not condoned by the department. Every case should rest on its own merits."[20]

THE CITY COUNCIL HEARINGS ON POLICE BRUTALITY

In November 1976, the grassroots-oriented People's Defense Coalition (PDC) ushered in a new era of anti-brutality protest and leadership when it called for public hearings on police brutality. "The PDC joins with several concerned organizations and individuals in demanding that the New Orleans City Council hold public hearings on police policy and practices. The PDC believes that police just like all other city servants, should be accountable to the citizens they are supposed to protect and serve." This was important because the mainstream media throughout the city still continued to ignore police brutality cases. Public hearings in the city council would expose the problem of police brutality for the entire metro area to see. During a subsequent city council meeting, council members agreed to the hearings. Community leaders were elated that the city council finally acknowledged that police brutality against African Americans was a serious issue. Civil rights groups were excited about finally being able to voice their concerns openly about a systemic pattern of discrimination, abuse, and brutality. In the days leading up to the hearings, the Ad Hoc Committee for Accountable Police (AHC) told reporters that they would produce at least thirty-five police brutality victims at the hearings. But some black leaders were not overly optimistic. Many responded with the sentiment, "Let's wait and see what happens."[21]

Spearheading the drive against police brutality in the mid-1970s was William Rouselle and Kalamu ya Salaam, who would emerge as spokespersons for the black poor and working class in its fight against police brutality. Although Rouselle had become the city's first African American news reporter in 1968 at the age of twenty-four, and had served with Landrieu as deputy director of the Human Relations Committee, he left city hall in 1972 to focus on grassroots organizing through the Free Southern Theater. While at the theater he worked closely with Salaam, who was well known across the city for his poetry. Born in 1947 as Val Ferdinand, III, in New Orleans, Salaam served in Korea after high school and during the black arts movement he established BLACKARTSOUTH before assuming the editorship of *Black Collegian Magazine*. Both Rouselle and Salaam emerged as leaders in the anti-brutality fight by using the rhetoric of racial militance and confrontational protest, and in the process they would keep the issue of police brutality in the spotlight.

At a panel sponsored by the Militant Forum in December 1976, State Representative Johnny Jackson submitted a proposal for a civilian review board to hear cases of alleged police brutality. Jackson stated that "there is too much of a possibility of fraternalism" under the present inner-department investigation system. He suggested that "with the use of an impartial third party to hear cases, police brutality could be curtailed." He told the audience that before he presented it to the city council police reform advocates had to build a strong case for it. He further suggested that the city create a system of monitoring corrupt officers and that all prospective officers undergo a thorough psychological evaluation. He mentioned that he would present his proposal at the special council hearings on police brutality.[22]

In response to Jackson's proposal, Councilman Giarrusso not only came out against the idea of a civilian review board, but he even rallied support from other police organizations and law enforcement agencies in an effort to defeat Jackson's proposal if it was ever brought to the council floor as a piece of legislation. "Civilian review boards have been a failure wherever they have been tried. I am unalterably opposed to such a board. The police department is best qualified to take proper administrative and disciplinary action against any officer who has infringed on the rights of any individual." Giarrusso was also confident that the NOPD's current system was effective. As evidence, he noted that between 1970 and 1977, 191 police officers had been dismissed or forced to resign because of disciplinary reasons. "This is not a record we take pride in reporting. However, decisive action is taken when warranted." Giarrusso's opinion was important since he was the former police chief and brother to the current police chief, Clarence B. Giarrusso. Further, the newly elected councilman was to be in charge of the hearings. The fact that Giarrusso would be chairing the hearings did not sit well with William Rouselle and the AHC. "It is our view that the council should appoint Councilman A. L. Davis or one of the other district councilmen to preside at these hearings," said Rouselle. When asked why his group recommended Davis, Rouselle simply responded, "Because he is black." The former newscaster and city hall deputy director left the Human Relations Committee and started working on grassroots organizing in the mid-1970s, and now he was leading a movement against police brutality. He further stated that that the hearings would be fair as long as Councilmen Giarrusso and Dirosa were not chairing the meeting. Rouselle was then asked why the hearings were so important. He responded, "At this point in our investigations we have generally concluded that police brutality is directly related to racism, to improper screening, to the poor training policemen receive, to the faulty operational policy of the police department, and to the absence of an effective redress mechanism for people who are brutalized."[23]

At a "jampacked" city council meeting that was described as "lengthy and boisterous," thousands of African Americans showed up to voice their opinions on police brutality. During the hearing, black leaders aired their complaints while city officials tried to minimize or diminish the reality of police brutality. Bill Rouselle of the Ad Hoc Committee for Accountable Police told the council that NOPD officers were being trained to act in a "brutal" and "insensitive manner" toward the city's black community. He further made it clear to the audience that despite repeated attempts to deny it, "there is police brutality in this city." Gustave Thomas, president of the BOP and newly elected local NAACP president, told the council that the fact that the hearing was scheduled indicated to him that police brutality existed in New Orleans and that in order to effectively fight the problem the NOPD and the community "must work together." Thomas also said that since the NOPD had "alienated" the black community tensions between the police and the community were at an all-time high. Kalamu ya Salaam, chairman of the People's Defense Coalition, told the council that "progressive thinking people" would continue to struggle for a better society. Cyril Davallier, a member of the BOP, called on the NOPD to hire more black officers and to promote more blacks into supervisory positions as one means of deterring police brutality. In contrast to the complaints aired by black leaders, Chief Clarence Giarrusso told the council and the audience that police brutality incidents were at a minimum when compared to the amount of arrests. He stated that during 1976 the NOPD arrested roughly 47,000 people and that they only received 92 complaints of excessive force. Councilman DiRosa told the audience that he did not think a change in procedure for investigating complaints was necessary and that under no circumstances would he favor a police review board. Similarly, John Harrington of the Fraternal Order of Police, who also served in Philadelphia, Pennsylvania, on the nation's first civilian review board, told the council that it was an ineffective way to curb police brutality. Despite all of the "emotional displays" at the hearing, "not one solution or answer emerged to combat police brutality."[24]

In response to the hearings, the New Orleans chamber of commerce issued a statement stating that a civilian review board for the NOPD was not an appropriate mechanism for stopping police brutality. Rather, the chamber recommended that the police department strengthen its internal affairs division and increase the salaries of police officers to attract more qualified candidates. "It is the feeling of the chamber that with initial salary level increases, better employees will be attracted to the jobs in law enforcement. Thus, with better employees, many of the problems being raised now concerning brutality, in many cases, would be answered by a superior grade of people in responsible positions," said chamber President F. Poche Waguespack.[25]

At the next week council session, several resolutions were introduced to address the problem of police brutality. Councilmen Giarrusso and Ciaccio's resolution called for a "beefing up" of the NOPD's internal affairs division through hiring more staff to investigate complaints. The resolution introduced by Councilmen Brod Bagert, Mike Early, and Frank Friedler called for the abolishment of the IAD, establishing a police bureau of investigation (PBI), and that the police superintendent and the city council work on ways to improve the overall operation of the NOPD. Rouselle and Salaam hit hard at the councilmen's proposals. Rouselle labeled the PBI "a political publicity stunt aimed at confusing the public into believing that an independent agency will investigate police brutality complaints. The fact is the PBI is no more than a glorified, dressed-up version of the beefed-up IAD as proposed by Councilmen Ciaccio and Giarrusso." Salaam concurred. He stated that the PBI proposal was no different from the current system of investigating complaints. "I respect Giarrusso's position more; at least he is being straightforward with the people, but Bagert is trying to give the impression that he is a liberal councilman with his PBI proposal, but we know better."[26]

A third resolution sponsored by Councilman A. L. Davis, the first black councilman in the city, with the help of Rouselle and Salaam, was also presented. Davis proposed a citizens committee with the power to investigate police practices, which including training and operational procedures. The committee would then make specific recommendations within a four-month period on key changes needed in the overall operation of the NOPD. Rouselle suggested that the committee be made up of eleven people and that it should be representative of the racial makeup of New Orleans. Davis was confident that his resolution met the demands of the hundreds who came to the special hearing on police brutality weeks earlier.[27]

During the meeting, a related issue was raised by Rouselle concerning the claim by city council members that they as a body did not have the authority to change the policies of the NOPD and that under the city charter the superintendent of police was given sole authority to set police policy, including disciplining those found guilty of police misconduct. In an effort to make council aware of their jurisdiction, Rouselle read a portion of the city charter that gave clear authority to the council to oversee police matters. "The Council shall have the power to conduct investigations of: The operation of any officer, department or board administering the affairs of the city." Rouselle then asked the council, "What is the council and the police department trying to hide from the public?"[28]

After debate on the three proposals, the city council delayed voting on either plan for two weeks. In the midst of the stalemate, Councilmen Ciaccio and Giarrusso introduced a compromise resolution that involved designating the internal affairs division as the sole responsible agency for

receiving and investigating citizens' complaints. Ciaccio said that this proposal would centralize the authority of the IAD and eliminate the involvement of other officers in the investigation process. He further believed that
this resolution was a "reasonable response" to the police brutality controversy without the formation of a civilian review board. In laymen's terms,
Ciaccio and Giarrusso were calling for a beefed-up IAD.[29]

State Senator Sidney Barthelemy of the Community Organization for
Urban Politics (COUP) came out against the proposal to prove that he was
concerned about community problems. "The committee feels that the reality of brutal and abusive police in New Orleans cannot be dealt with by su-
perficial changes or by beefing up the same old internal affairs agencies." In
opposing the resolution Barthelemy stated clearly that "the problem goes
to the heart of the police department recruiting, training and operational
policy." He then made an appeal that the council accept Councilman Davis's
proposal. "We therefore recommend that the city of New Orleans appoint
a citizens committee to do a thorough investigation of police practices,
including training, operational policies and procedures." Ironically, Barthelemy, like many of his COUP and SOUL cohorts, had been virtually silent on police brutality throughout his public career but since Landrieu was
now in his final year in office he stepped out of the shadows in hopes of
fulfilling greater political motives.[30]

After postponing the vote on the proposals twice, the city council passed
the Ciaccio–Giarrusso-sponsored resolution with one major revision. At
the request of Mayor Landrieu, the resolution called for the abolishment
of the IAD and the establishment of a new investigative unit that would report directly to the chief of police. The measure, which was greeted with anger by black activists, passed 6–1, with Councilman Davis casting the lone
dissenting vote. Police reform activists were upset because it left the police
chief with the final authority on police brutality cases. The plan also mentioned two other important components: the new unit must have its offices
away from police headquarters; and complaints against the police could be
lodged orally or in writing, formally or informally. In a strong editorial supporting the plan, the *Times-Picayune*, cautioned supporters of a civilian review board that although their displeasure was understandable, "the harsh
fact is that this is the best plan the council of mayor was likely to draft.
Critics would be wise to accept this improvement, voice their reservations,
and give it a chance to work."[31]

Despite the limitations of his resolution, Landrieu's plan was rather progressive for its time. Knowing that a civilian review board had little chance of passing, and that the establishment of a civilian review agency would have the adverse effect of unifying already resistant police forces, Landrieu was aware of the new investigative unit's shortcomings but he was optimistic that it would provide a more adequate means of redress than the historically ineffective and inept IAD.

In the midst of public debate and discussion concerning a civilian review board, black New Orleans was once again mobilized to fight against police brutality after learning of the violent death of Wayne Smith, who died in police custody during the city's Mardi Gras festivities. According to witnesses, Smith, a Kansas City native, was standing in front of Woolworth's watching a parade when he got into a fight with Robert Harper, a white man, "over some beads and trinkets." After exchanging blows, both men stood about five feet away from each other arguing. At that point three NOPD officers intervened and one hit Smith in the head with his blackjack. One eyewitness stated that the blow Smith received from Officer Richard Hoselle sounded like "pool balls breaking on the table." The others then congratulated the officer who hit Smith. The blow knocked Smith unconscious and then police dragged him down the street while they "escorted" Harper down the street. Bernard Causey, who was with Smith, told reporters that the last time he saw Smith alive was when he was being dragged down the street. He next saw him in a bed at Charity Hospital suffering from a blood clot of the brain just days before he died. While laying in a coma Smith was booked in absentia in municipal courts on a charge of simple battery against Harper. When word reached the black community of the incident, the Ad Hoc Committee for Accountable Police went into action by stating that it appeared as though Smith had been "kidnapped" and "beaten" by police.[32]

The Ad Hoc Committee called for a "full-scale investigation of the police and an end to police brutality" after the Orleans Parish coroner ruled that Smith died as a result of a skull fracture and ultimate blood clot "from one side of the top of the head to the other." Although the coroner did determine that Smith died from head injuries, he could not say whether or not Smith was hit with a blunt instrument or was pushed down and hit the side of his head on the pavement, as police had suggested. The committee then asked the U.S. Justice Department to conduct an investigation "of our police department in view of the repeated cases of police brutality and the failure of our mayor, city council, police chief and district attorney to address a solution to a widespread, extremely explosive community problem."

The Ad Hoc Committee and black residents were certain that Smith had died from the blow.[33]

Black political leaders also demanded that the Justice Department conduct an investigation into Smith's death. State Representative Johnny Jackson said that the incidents of police brutality in New Orleans had reached a "critical level." He further stated that the "killing of Wayne Smith is the straw that breaks the Camel's back and therefore, I have no other positive alternative but to call upon the Justice Department." Jackson also called for a full federal investigation of the entire NOPD "as it relates to police brutality, misconduct, and other procedures and practices that have been and still are violating basic Constitutional and Human Rights."[34]

In response to the public outrage, Superintendent Clarence Giarrusso announced an investigation and suspended Hoselle from active duty. Giarrusso then stated that Harper received so many injuries from Smith that he had to have surgery. Giarrusso recalled seeing Harper's face bloodied. "I just happened to be walking by. It looked like a train hit him or Muhammad Ali." However, community leaders could not find any record of Harper having surgery and police officials refused to say what hospital performed the operation. District Attorney Harry Connick took heat from both sides when he launched an investigation into Smith's murder. Police officers attacked him for "playing politics" with the grand jury to appease black voters, while black voters attacked him for predicting that the investigation would be a "whitewash" like all other police brutality incidents.[35]

In an effort to bring mass media attention to the death of Smith, approximately fifty to sixty protestors, many of whom were members of the Ad Hoc Committee, staged a funeral procession and march from Orleans and Broad avenues to police headquarters downtown. Bill Rouselle led the crowd, who carried signs reading, "Dead, but not forgotten," "End to police brutality," "The police killed Wayne Smith," and "Fight police brutality." After arriving at police headquarters, the marchers announced that they wanted to meet with Giarrusso in the lobby to discuss police abuse, but Giarrusso refused to meet with them there. Instead, he invited three committee members to meet with him in his office but they refused, stating that they wanted to confront him as a group. Giarrusso refused to meet their demands and they eventually left the building after vowing to be back.[36]

They were. While the Smith case was still under "investigation," the Ad Hoc Committee for Accountable Police urged all concerned citizens to attend a mass demonstration against police abuse and brutality. In making its appeal for support, the committee called for an investigation of the NOPD and the creation of neighborhood organizations to supervise police activity. Since city officials were unwilling to adequately address the problem of police abuse, "the responsibility falls on the citizens of this city to organize and build the fight against police brutality." The planned demonstration was designed to gather citywide momentum behind major police reforms and to protest the death of Wayne Smith. "We have no illusions. We recognize that the problem of police abuse and brutality along with crime will not significantly change until the more fundamental, explosive nature of this society changes, but we also recognize the need for people to organize to defend and support their own interest. It is our interest to fight police brutality," said a committee spokesperson.[37]

Approximately five hundred people participated in the march and the rally. March organizers, participants, and sympathizers were even more motivated to join in after the Orleans Parish grand jury found no cause to indict Officer Hoselle in the beating death of Wayne Smith. The protestors started their separate marches from different areas of the city. One group was led by Salaam, while Rouselle headed the other. Once they reached city hall, Salaam gave an energetic address to the crowd. "We are here today to talk about the serious matter of police brutality," he stated "It's roll call time." He called out the names of BOLD (Black Organization for Leadership Development), SOUL (Southern Organization for United Leadership), COUP, OPPVL (Orleans Parish Progressive Voters' League), NOUL (the New Orleans Urban League), other local groups that appealed to the black professional class, and individuals who should have been present. Many of the groups and individuals he called out were not in attendance. Rather, most of the protestors "consisted of every-day black people," students, rank-and-file members of the NAACP, the Southern Christian Leadership Convention (SCLC), the Citywide Housing Coalition, and the People's Defense Coalition.[38]

Bill Rouselle then took center stage to energize the crowd a bit more. He told the protestors that "we cannot depend on the police to fight crime in our community. In many cases, the police are the criminals; they act like rabid dogs!" Rouselle then moved to the Smith murder and put his death in the broader context of American history. "Police brutality is not a new thing in the black community, but has existed since blacks first step foot on the shores of the North American continent." Rouselle then went on to mention that the Smith murder was part of a larger conspiracy that existed between the police, certain elected officials, physicians, and the white press to protect police officers who were charged with abusing the black community. In closing, the Ad Hoc Committee spokesman called for the creation of a committee mechanism outside of the NOPD with the power to hear complaints against the police and to recommend penalties against officers found guilty of committing brutal and aggressive acts. He then gave some practical advice to the protestors. "Return to your neighborhoods and organize against police brutality. We've got to start looking out for each other, and stop walking away when we see a 'brother' or 'sister' being abused by police." Southern University at New Orleans (SUNO) SGA President Michael Williams told the protestors that asking the "police to police the police, is like asking Dracula to guard a blood bank." After the last speaker, the protestors marched from city hall down Loyola Avenue to Canal Street, down Canal to the Rivergate building before dispersing. While marching down Canal, they urged shoppers "to get out the stores and get in the streets and fight police brutality." They then would occasionally chant, "It could be you; it could be me, we got to fight police brutality." Although the protest was largely symbolic, the black community was now mobilized to fight police brutality.[39]

Weeks after the grand jury failed to indict Officer Hoselle for Wayne Smith's death, Gustave Thomas, president of both the BOP and NAACP as well as an investigator in the district attorney's office, went after Harry Connick, Jr., the district attorney, for his constant refusal to indict police officers. Thomas released a statement to the press stating that Connick's investigation into the 1975 Charles Cheatham murder was a "mockery of the public trust" and that the investigation should be reopened. The Ad Hoc Committee, State Representative Dorothy Taylor, and Councilman A. L. Davis supported Thomas. Connick denied the allegations and was angry at Thomas. "I find it inconceivable that you, in your capacity as president of the NAACP, and as a police officer assigned to my office and as the lead investigator in this case, would choose a press release as the method of criticizing your own investigation, the grand jury and this office!" Superintendent Giarrusso then accused Thomas of "wearing two hats—one as a police officer and the other as president of the NAACP." Predicting that a complaint would be filed against Thomas, Giarrusso stated that when a formal complaint was received, "I'll deal with it." Thomas, who did not respond to Connick's letter, did make a statement. "I would like to inform Superintendent Giarrusso that there is an increasing number of black police officers across the country who feel they have a contribution to make to their community other than just putting someone in jail." He continued, "A long time ago, blacks wanted more black police officers on the force because they felt by having them they would be of some assistance. In as much as the white police officer has not served the black community as the white police officer serves the white community, we feel it is a continuing injustice that in a city whose population of blacks is in excess of 50 percent, there still exists only 15 percent blacks on the NOPD force."[40]

Former New Orleans NAACP head Gyan Cole attacked Thomas and questioned his motives for criticizing Connick. She accused Thomas of making false statements. "I could see the community rallying around him then, had he done so. But it looks mighty shady now. It makes me sad if Gus Thomas is willing to come forward now and jeopardize his job, why didn't he come forward back then. I think it's a personal problem dealing with his job. Or could it be because Mrs. Cheatham got $654,000?" Although the local NAACP executive committee issued a statement supporting Thomas, Cole felt that it was "not the general consensus of our [NAACP] membership."[41]

As expected, Giarrusso suspended Thomas but not before he was transferred from the district attorney's office to the NOPD urban squad. Connick stated that Thomas had "an obvious conflict of interest" and that it was "impossible, under these circumstances, for this office to productively utilize" his efforts. In suspending Thomas, Giarrusso charged him with unauthorized leave and for failure to give his department adequate notice of his leave. "The day he was to report for work—30 or 40 minutes before he was supposed to go on duty—he called and asked for emergency furlough." The request was denied. Although this privilege was afforded all officers, except rookies, Giarrusso charged that he could not let officers take off whenever they wanted to regardless of the nature of the function. When asked whether or not Thomas's trip to San Francisco was police-related, Giarrusso said it didn't matter. "If he been there to see President Carter, does it make any difference? We can't have officers calling in saying when they want to come in." Renault Robinson of the National Black Police Association came to Thomas's defense by revealing that Thomas had fifty days of leave time and had never been denied a leave request until he criticized Connick. Ironically, Thomas took the trip to San Francisco to make arrangements for the black police convention, which was to be held in New Orleans later that summer. Kalamu ya Salaam called for Thomas's immediate reinstatement. "Gustave Thomas should be reinstated, but to put him back on his job without reopening the Cheatham case and investigating the District Attorney's role in that cover-up will not settle the problem of police abuse and law enforcement accountability." Robinson was equally upset but vowed to take action. "The tip of the iceberg was the attack on our chairman [Thomas]. There have been plans to file suit against the New Orleans Police Department in the past, but the action taken against Thomas pushed us over the top."[42]

FEDERAL INTERVENTION

In late 1977, Thomas and the Black Organization of Police got a bit of a reprieve when the U.S. Office of Revenue Sharing (ORS) accused the police department of discrimination in the hiring of women and minorities. In a letter to city officials, the ORS informed city officials that if the NOPD did not come up with a plan to hire more women and minorities, they would lose $21 million in revenue sharing payments. Thomas and the BOP, which filed the complaint, were elated while city officials were upset because of the potential loss of $40 million in federal revenue. "It is one of the most idiotic letters I have ever seen a federal agency write. I don't have anything to straighten out," said Mayor Landrieu. Landrieu also stated that the complaint filed by Thomas was "unfounded. There is no discrimination in that department which they have allegedly found. That letter is an absolute absurdity. We embarked on one of the most aggressive affirmative action programs of any U.S. city." As a result of an investigation of the NOPD's hiring practices in July 1977, Bernadine Denning, director of the ORS, said in a letter to the mayor, "I find New Orleans is in violation of the State and local Fiscal Assistance Act of 1972." Denning wrote that the investigation revealed a "stark" contrast in the percentage of women and minorities in the NOPD as compared to the city's overall labor force, a guideline the ORS encouraged all municipalities to comply with. According to the federal agency, 43.6 percent of the New Orleans labor force was minorities while the police department was only 26.8 percent minority. Terrence Duvernay, chief administrative officer for the city, was appalled at the action. He stated that the city followed the suggested guidelines but if they followed it to the measure then only 13.5 percent of the jobs would go to white males. But Duvernay was open to hiring more minorities. "The Office of Revenue Sharing is going to have to tell us how to get more women and minorities into the department rather than just tell us, 'get more.'" In addition to adding more women and minorities to the force, the order also asked the NOPD to look at the written exam so that African Americans could have a better chance of passing the test.[43]

In anticipation of a "face-to-face" meeting with federal officials, Duvernay released some NOPD hiring statistics to illustrate that the police department had done a good job of hiring African Americans and women. According to Duvernay, since 1970 the city had annually averaged adding nineteen black police officers for every three white officers. In a letter to the Office of Revenue Sharing, Duvernay wrote that it would be unrealistic "and in many contexts undesirable to assume that the NOPD should have parallel representation of females in each of the job classifications in the department." He then made a broader point. "The arbitrary assignment of minorities and females to operational units where alleged underrepresentation exists, solely to reach parity with the composition of the labor market, may not be in the best interests of the individuals nor the citizens of this city." The federal directive was particularly upsetting to Duvernay because the city's equal employment opportunity and affirmative action plans had already been approved by the Department of Housing and Urban Development (HUD), the Department of Justice, and the Department of Labor, and they were in accordance with the Equal Employment Opportunity Commission Guidelines.[44]

Despite Duvernay's rebuttal to the federal directive, federal officials "didn't budge" from their claim that the NOPD was discriminating against minorities and women. Duvernay, who was "downright" mad, labeled the charge "ludicrous" since the city had made sincere efforts to redress past discrimination. Duvernay was told that the city needed to submit an outline of how it would reflect the makeup of the city's labor force. Duvernay was hopeful that the city could get an extension until they worked out the problem of how to hire more women and minorities. "They want me to admit guilt. They want me to make changes. But they don't give me the tools to do it," he said.[45]

One of the problems in complying with the federal order was that the NOPD was confused over the percentage of black officers on the force in 1977. Although this appeared rather easy to determine, NOPD officials issued two reports at different times of the year and they were trying to figure out just who was classified as a commissioned officer. Consequently, the Office of Revenue Sharing was even more disgusted with the NOPD's lack of accurate personnel data. Nonetheless, a group of white officers filed suit in federal court seeking to nullify the threatened suspension of federal revenue sharing funds.[46]

As the threatened loss of funds continued to hover over the NOPD, Mayor Landrieu invited the director of the office to come to New Orleans for an inspection. He noted, "I am convinced that such an inspection will result in a favorable determination to the city of New Orleans." Office of Revenue Sharing Director Bernadine Denning declined the invitation. But two weeks later, the ORS backed off its discrimination claim after it discovered that the NOPD had made some progress in the hiring of women and minorities and agreed to restructure some of its units to reflect the city's racial makeup. In a letter to city officials, Denning wrote that her office "certainly recognizes and commends the city's past efforts to eradicate discrimination and to afford equal employment opportunity to minorities and women." Gustave Thomas and members of the Black Organization of Police were not pleased with the decision by the ORS. They felt that Landrieu and Duvernay "tricked Revenue Sharing into an agreement." In a press release Thomas stated that reducing black representation on the urban squad would not add more African Americans to the force. After mentioning that there were only 211 black officers out of 1,500 on the NOPD, he concluded by stating that "until these conditions are changed, discrimination still lives with us." In reaching the agreement with the city, the ORS was also convinced that Ernest "Dutch" Morial, the city's first black mayor, would institute major reforms within the NOPD once he took office on May 1, 1978.[47]

For anti-brutality activists the Landrieu era was one of mixed results. As the beginning of his tenure in 1969, they were hopeful that the liberal coalition that elected him would be able to implement major reforms and usher in a new era of policing in New Orleans. While Landrieu and Giarrusso, his police chief, exercised remarkable restraint in confrontations with the Black Panther Party and in the aftermath of the Mark Essex shootings, implemented an aggressive recruiting drive to get more African Americans on the force, and established a new internal investigative unit for police misconduct, many activists felt that Landrieu still did not do enough in the era of police reform. The creation of the felony action squad and its "shoot to kill" order; his refusal to support a civilian review board; his manipulation of personnel statistics to avoid federal intervention; and his failure to press for an indictment for officers involved in the deaths of Charles Cheatham and Wayne Smith convinced activists to hold mass protests and public hearings in the city council. Thus, what began as a mayoral tenure of great promise for police reform ended with great disappointment to some. When Landrieu exited city hall in 1977, the more moderate and sensible elements of the black community knew that they were losing a friend and supporter. Even anti-brutality activists such as Rouselle and Salaam realized that although there were serious issues within the NOPD, those problems were not created by Landrieu; in fact, many were institutional and cultural. With the election of Dutch Morial as the first black mayor of New Orleans in 1977, anti-brutality activists raised their expectations for police reform and wanted immediate changes within the NOPD.

6 BLACK POWER POLITICS

Ernest "Dutch" Morial and the Limits of Police Reform

One of the greatest accomplishments of the postwar period was the transition from protest to political power. Beginning with Cleveland's election of Carl Stokes in 1967, virtually every major city in America would elect an African American as mayor by the mid-1980s. As expected, black mayors launched an impressive array of programs and services out of a need to address African American concerns that had been neglected for decades. Although black mayors were given the keys to the kingdom when they entered office, many encountered unrealistic expectations from the black electorate, who were eager to see the municipal apparatus provide them with jobs, better schools, improved housing, and a reformed police department. But when they attempted to implement major reforms in city government, they met a hostile reaction from white conservatives, business leaders, city council members, city workers, and insular police departments. At times they also received a hostile reception from fellow African Americans, who were expecting an immediate redistribution of city services. Dutch Morial would receive the full brunt of this criticism when he became New Orleans's first black mayor because black voters wanted to see wholesale changes in the operations of the New Orleans Police Department (NOPD).[1]

DUTCH MORIAL AND THE EVOLUTION OF BLACK POLITICAL POWER

The election of Ernest "Dutch" Morial in 1977 as the first black mayor of New Orleans represented an opportunity to redress black grievances against the New Orleans Police Department. With an impressive list of civil rights accomplishments that included president of the New Orleans National Association for the Advancement of Colored People (NAACP), the first black to graduate from Louisiana State University (LSU) law school, the first black elected to the Louisiana House of Representatives since Reconstruction, the first black juvenile court judge, and the first black circuit court judge, Morial had an impressive resume. But his dark horse candidacy was not greeted with unanimous applause in black political circles. Most notably, although the Southern Organization for United Leadership (SOUL), the Community Organization for Urban Politics (COUP), and the Orleans Parish Progressive Voters' League (OPPVL) considered themselves black political organizations, Morial's candidacy threatened their strategic plan. When SOUL refused to support Johnny Jackson's state representative race in 1972 in favor of a white candidate, and when both SOUL and COUP supported a white candidate with money for a judgeship in favor of a more qualified black candidate, Morial and others were convinced that SOUL and COUP were sellouts. As brokers of the black vote, SOUL, COUP, and the OPPVL could only maximize their potential when a particular candidate needed their support. Then, they could exchange black votes for money and patronage. However, since Morial did not need their support and would not even ask for their assistance, SOUL and the OPPVL quickly threw their support around white candidates. COUP only supported Morial since one of its own members, Barthelemy, was running for city councilman-at-large and it concluded that his candidacy could not afford any loss of credibility or support because of COUP's nonsupport of Morial. The city's two black newspapers, the *Louisiana Weekly* and *Data*, also supported white candidates.[2]

Some of the concerns regarding Morial had less to do with his refusal to get involved with the city's black political organizations, and more to do with the fact that he was fair-skinned and could pass for white if he chose to. Others felt that despite his track record as an attorney, civil rights leader, and politician, he had not paid enough dues. Others believed that he was not black enough and did not represent the interests of the New Orleans black community by emerging from a creole tradition that tried to remove racial barriers, while the livelihood of civil rights professionals depended upon maintaining racial barriers and tensions. Even with these concerns expressed by members of SOUL, COUP, and the OPPVL, Morial became the first black mayor of New Orleans by capturing more than 97 percent of the black vote with the help of sixty-odd grassroots black political organizations in the city. After his election, the black poor and working class were eager to see the NOPD reformed from top to bottom and they were confident that now with political power they would be able to transform the NOPD. Throughout the campaign Morial stressed that, if elected, he would begin the search for a new police chief immediately.

If Morial needed a blueprint for how a black mayor should reform a police department with a culture of police brutality, other black mayors such as Cleveland's Carl B. Stokes and Atlanta's Maynard Jackson provided excellent examples. As the first black mayor of a major city, Stokes made police reform a central component of his agenda after his historic election in 1967. Although he did not appoint a black police chief, Stokes launched an aggressive recruitment campaign for black officers; changed the nature of the civil service commission, the city agency in charge of all police testing; and empowered the city's black police organizations. Jackson followed Stokes's blueprint, with one exception: he appointed a black police chief upon entering office in 1973. Despite the examples of Stokes and Jackson, Morial would take a more conservative but more practical approach to police reform, causing anti-brutality activists to intensify their protests.

Shortly after his election, the question of who Morial would select to lead the city's police forces occupied the mind of everyone. While Morial was also expected to pay close attention to employment, housing, education, and urban redevelopment, his black supporters were largely concerned about police reform. While attending a seminar at Harvard on leadership and transition for newly elected mayors, Morial was asked if a black police chief would deal more effectively with brutality and crime. "I don't want to comment on that; it will inhibit the selection process. I don't care if he's black, white, red, pink, gray, or green as long as he is qualified." Morial told the reporter that he was looking for a candidate who had a good crime-fighting background and also possessed "management skills." Morial also said that he would appoint a citizens committee to help him pick Giarrusso's successor. "It is something that will be done rationally and with reason. I am not going to be pushed into it immediately."[3]

In February 1978, Morial announced the search committee that would help him select the next head of the New Orleans Police Department. The co-chairs of the committee were Xavier University President Norman Francis and prominent businessman Harry England. The committee was interracial and interdenominational in makeup. The committee began taking applications in late February and they expected to submit a list of names to Morial by April 1. During the search process, members of the black community made it clear that they wanted a black police chief. At a public hearing called by Morial's task force to recommend a police chief, community activists made their positions clear. Kalamu ya Salaam was not convinced that the committee was a good idea; he felt that Morial should take more daring measures to find a police chief and bring about serious reform. "You want to take a half a step forward when two giant steps are necessary." Salaam argued that Morial needed to conduct a thorough citizens' investigation of the NOPD prior to the selection of a new police chief. Otherwise the new chief would merely serve as a façade covering up the problems within the NOPD. Bill Rouselle stated that Morial's approach ran the risk of "having another Joe Giarrusso or Clarence Giarrusso as police chief—a risk blacks can't afford." James Tucker of the Treme community stated that "whoever takes charge has to make a very sincere effort to do away with the insensitivity that exists in the police department." He added that the new police chief should be black with "grassroots" in the black community. Rouselle, a spokesperson for the Ad Hoc Committee for Accountable Police (AHC), which now referred to itself as the Committee for Accountable Police (CAP), called the public hearing an "insult" to those present. He said that the meeting was a cover-up by the committee, "which doesn't know how the police department works." Rouselle then mentioned that the meeting was called on such short notice that it precluded a large turnout (less than a hundred people were in attendance). Further, the choice of a small auditorium was indicative that a large turnout was not expected. The conspiracy theory was further proved when it was revealed that the three hundred-seat city council chamber was available, yet the meeting was moved to the third floor of the public library, which had a capacity of less than a hundred. Francis responded by stating that the citizens committee was a good way to get community input since Morial could have appointed a police chief without their help. In response to that statement, one woman in the audience labeled the committee "bourgeois" in character and argued that they did not know how to relate to the problems of poor people.[4]

Activists paid close attention to the search process because they wanted a black police chief who would come in and bring the NOPD under control. A black chief would add an important dimension—administrative reform— to the police brutality fight. While activists had used grassroots protest for decades, it rarely resulted in institutional reform. A black police chief, they hoped, would come in and immediately change the culture of the NOPD.

In April, Morial released the names of the four finalists: James Parsons, police chief of Birmingham; Joseph T. Rouzan, police chief of Compton, California; Joseph Ball, police chief of Charleston, South Carolina; and Daniel

Guido of Nassau County, New York. Rouzan, a native of New Orleans and a former LAPD police captain, was the only African American among the group of finalists. When the finalists were announced, Morial took heat for not considering an internal appointment. Frank Minyard, the Orleans Parish coroner, was highly disappointed. "The committee goes out of the city to find the most sensitive appointment. We're not good enough to supply a police chief? Baloney! It makes us all in the city of New Orleans look like, you know, second-class citizens." Minyard then argued that appointing an outsider would be detrimental to good law enforcement. "A police chief has to know the people, know the good cops from the bad cops . . . has to have the feeling that this is the only city in the world to live in. These guys are coming in for a job. You've got to understand the philosophy of New Orleans. You've got to be one of us."[5]

Morial made it clear as he appointed his administrative team that he would not select black people for the sake of appeasing the black community. He sought to appoint people on the basis of merit. In essence, Morial was assuring white New Orleans that he was not about to usher in a black power government. According to Arnold Hirsch, Morial promised that his new appointments would be made "by the yardstick of intellect and public dedication, regardless of race, creed, or national origin. I have no intention of politicizing the incoming administration on the narrow grounds of reverse prejudice." Despite the obvious reality that Morial only received 10 percent of the white vote in the general election, he was still seeking to make appointments that would appease that 10 percent.[6]

In May, Morial announced the appointment of James Parsons as superintendent of the New Orleans Police Department. It appears that Morial did not want to appoint a black chief and upset the predominantly white NOPD, nor did he want to alienate white residents. Parsons, who succeeded Bull Connor, had gained national notoriety for modernizing and professionalizing the notorious Birmingham Police Department (BPD). The Birmingham native joined the BPD in 1954 as a patrolman and from 1972 to 1978 he served as police chief of that department. According to some experts, Parsons turned the BPD into one of the top ten departments in the country. During his years in Birmingham, Parsons completed his bachelor's and master's degrees and he had begun working on his doctorate in educational administration from the University of Alabama in Birmingham. He had also published several articles in national and international police journals. Birmingham Mayor David Vann gave Parsons a high recommendation.

"I have known Chief Parsons for nearly twenty years, having first become acquainted with him during the struggle to change the form of government of Birmingham during the racial strife of Birmingham." That is precisely why he was brought to New Orleans. Morial was confident that Parsons could establish credibility with the white rank-and-file and that the black community would support him because of his track record in reforming the BPD. For Morial, the Parsons appointment was a way to appease both his black and white critics. Although community activists wanted a black police chief, Morial understood that a black appointee would have trouble implementing many major reforms in a department that was openly hostile to black concerns.[7]

The appointment of Parsons came as a surprise to the black community. During his campaign Morial had made it clear that Sydney Cates, the highest-ranking African American on the NOPD, would be his police chief. But as Carl Galmon of the Citizens For Action League stated, "After he got elected, seem like he got a bad case of amnesia. Forgot what he told the folks that supported him in the grass roots areas." Galmon was also suspicious of the so-called committee "that was put together by the mayor to seek

TABLE 3.

Police Chiefs of the New Orleans Police Department, 1946–2005

NAME	TENURE IN OFFICE
Adair Watters	1946–1949
Joseph Scheuring	1949–1955
Provosty Dayries	1955–1960
Joseph Giarrusso	1960–1970
Clarence Giarrusso	1970–1978
James Parsons	1978–1980
Henry Morris	1980–1984
Warren Woodfork*	1984–1991
Arnesta Taylor*	1991–1993
Joseph Orticke*	1993–1994
Richard Pennington*	1994–2001
Eddie Compass*	2001–2005
Warren Riley*	2005–

* African American

out and find a police chief. I'm totally convinced that the committee was a smokescreen to fool the public. It's very obvious when a person usurps his own power and gives this power to someone else to carry out his duties." Galmon's criticism of the mayor and the establishment in general would continue throughout Morial's tenure and he later would gain national notoriety for leading a campaign to change the names of schools in New Orleans that were named in honor of slaveholders.[8]

At a news conference announcing his appointment, Parsons promised to reform the NOPD without any problems. "I will say to all of you in the police department that reform does not necessarily mean turmoil and strife. It means communication with one another, getting some idea on what has to be done in the police agency, and working very closely with one another to accomplish goals." Morial then took the podium and effectively discouraged questions from the press by stating, "He is not going to tell you here today what plans he has for reforming the police department. That would certainly be unwise on his part." However, Ben Young, associate editor of the *Louisiana Weekly,* asked Parsons his specific plans for curbing police brutality. Parsons attempted to answer the question, but then Morial interjected by stating that neither he nor Parsons would give the press any specific information concerning police policies. At the conclusion of the press conference, Morial went after Young and asked him, "Why didn't you ask me that question?" Young responded, "You're not the police chief and that is why I didn't ask you." At that point Morial started cussing out Young and the young editor was soon escorted out of city hall by Morial's bodyguards.[9]

Later that afternoon, Parsons addressed about seventy high-ranking officers within the NOPD. He told the officers that "if you are uneasy about me, don't be. I'm one of the easiest people to get along with." In the event of possible conflicts, Parsons told them that "you and I will talk about it face to face. Saying things about me or rumoring things about me would not make me a better man." He then stated that his philosophy of minority recruiting was to get more African Americans on the force. "They in turn are your best recruiters." He closed by expressing his desire to see rank-and-file officers receive better pay and working conditions. However, Parsons did not mention a single word about police brutality.[10]

Shortly after Parsons's appointment, Morial received a flood of calls, letters, and telegrams from concerned people in Birmingham. One major area of concern was that although Birmingham was 45 percent African American, there were only 64 black officers on the force of 800. In an *Ebony* Magazine article, Dr. Richard Arrington, former mayor of Birmingham, talked about his failure to reform the Birmingham Police Department under Parsons's leadership. One citizen of Birmingham sent Morial a telegram concerning his new appointee. "I would like to urge the rejection of James Parsons currently Chief of Police in Birmingham, Alabama. His record indicates he has no concern for controlling the use of deadly force nor removing the stigma of corruption from police agencies." This citizen perhaps had no idea how prophetic she was. In response to allegations from the black community in Birmingham that Parsons had been soft on police brutality, Morial felt the need to address it. During a city hall press conference, the mayor stated that "there was a field check on Chief Parsons before we decided on him. We are satisfied that he can do the job." The mayor then announced some of his ideas about handling police brutality. "It is not important how large a problem police brutality is. It is important that it exists, regardless of the quantum of it. If there is one case of police brutality, that is one case too many." Morial mentioned that he had not decided on whether to form a citizens committee to handle police complaints but he did state that there would be a change in the mechanism for handling those complaints.[11]

After securing a significant, yet difficult, pay increase for Parsons through the city council, the mayor was eager for Parsons to get to work. And he did. After being sworn in on June 12, Parsons immediately tackled the issue of police brutality and corruption at a news conference. On the subject of police brutality, he noted that "complaints about this are not unique to New Orleans. That's common across the nation." He then argued: "What you have to do is find out if the complaints are real or imagined. Either way they have the same consequence—people don't like the police; they don't support them; they don't vote for convictions in court. It is very important citizens think their police are great." He then mentioned the importance of perception versus reality. "If it is imagined, we have a problem of convincing them if it is not true. The only way to do that is be above reproach and provide excellent service. If it is real, you have to deal with that on a hard ball basis. I know that with my background of social behavioral sciences, some people think at times I can't play hard ball. But I can make those decisions—the editorial when I left Birmingham said I was the only chief in Alabama who could fire people and make it stick." Shockingly, while Parsons was given his remarks on police brutality, Mayor Morial appeared uncomfortable and uneasy during the entire session. Parsons went on to

state that he encouraged citizen complaints but that he did not favor a civilian review board. "Citizen complaints are a sensing mechanism that tells
me the problems the department is having interfacing with the citizens. I
always take them very seriously, it doesn't mean everybody is guilty every
time a complaint comes in. Many times you find it is a procedural problem." With regards to citizen review boards, Parsons argued that they had
a tendency to frustrate everyone involved—police officers, the chief, board
members, and citizens. For Parsons, it was simply an issue of due process.
He felt that there were more effective ways of disciplining officers. "There
are ways of doing that and I know how to do it. It is what you do when you
catch him, if you handle it properly you won't need a board."[12]

Shortly after his swearing-in, Parsons reorganized the NOPD with the
overall goal of making it more efficient, more successful at curbing violent
crime, more accountable, and more lean. "I found the organization was
blind. It's not aware of what the community thinks about it. It's not aware
of the attitudes of the public. It's not aware of the attitudes of policemen on
the lower ranks." He wanted to make the NOPD more human: "You think
of a police organization as a kind of a human being; if it doesn't see or hear
or feel, it dies. The police organization if it doesn't perform those functions,
then the policemen will get in trouble. They're out of touch with the community and management is out of touch with the policemen and things get
out of control." With this in mind Parsons created a professional standards
bureau to ensure that departmental standards were being met; an administrative services bureau that would "look inward at the way the department does its job," which would be staffed by civilians who would set strict
standards for the department; and a major offenders bureau that would locate and arrest career criminals. Parsons announced that Edgar Morris, Jr.,
an African American, would head the internal affairs division (IAD), which
was in charge of handling civilian complaints and police discipline. He was
hopeful that these minor administrative reforms would change the overall
character of the NOPD.[13]

THE COMMITTEE FOR ACCOUNTABLE POLICE

A major part of Parsons's efforts to reach out to the black community was
a series of town hall meetings where he would meet with black residents
to discuss the issue of police brutality in hopes of lessening some of the
criticism of him and Morial. Arranged with the help of Bill Rouselle and
the Committee for Accountable Police, the first meeting was held at the

Treme Community Center and sponsored by the NAACP. Parsons was "grilled and literally taken to task" by more than three hundred angry attendees over the issue of police brutality. Rouselle opened the meeting by stating that the objective was to "get a clear record of what the new police chief proposes to do about police brutality so we will know what to expect." The crowd, many of whom were direct victims of police brutality, then started chanting along with Kalamu ya Salaam: "We want some police off the force and into the jail." Salaam repeated the chant on several occasions and then he handed Parsons a list of sixteen police officers the CAP wanted "put off of the police force and into jail." The sixteen officers, identified as repeat "citizen beaters," included Officers Steven Rebould, Daniel Denoux, Richard Hoselle, Reginald Williams, Kenneth Harrison, the Canatella Brothers, and Stanley Burkhart. "This chant isn't rhetoric. I agree with Harry Connick that career criminals ought to be put in jail, so then why aren't these policemen in jail?" Salaam asked. Throughout the five-hour session Parsons was questioned by rank-and-file citizens who wanted to know what he would do about police brutality. One victim, who attended the hearing with a broken foot she had received at the hands of the NOPD, told Parsons that he needed to understand the long-standing tensions between the department and the black community. "You don't know because you haven't been around us. You haven't been treated like a dog. I'm willing to live with you, man, just give me some room. Treat me as a human being. You just don't know what it's like to be stepped on and treated like an animal." Parsons responded by asking, "What more can you promise somebody than to be fair" in handling complaints. "You can promise to make them stop beating us," someone shouted from the audience. "I'll stop them," the chief replied. At one point during the hearing, Parsons angered those in attendance by attempting to make a connection between police brutality and black-on-black crime. "This produced extreme displeasure from the audience," who accused Parsons of not answering their questions and not giving a damn about them. Parsons then talked about his experiences in Birmingham. "You can question any black citizen in Birmingham and find that not one says he was mistreated by me. I enjoyed a good reputation in Birmingham's black community and will enjoy one here before it is all over." Parsons assured the crowd that the entire department needed reform from top-to-bottom. "You can't take a broken-down '53 Studebaker, take Giarrusso out of the driver's seat—put Parsons in and expect it to run. If it's broken down, it's broken down and nobody can drive it."[14]

At the close of the hearing, Parsons told the crowd that "criticizing the police and jumping up and down" wouldn't solve the problem of police brutality. Those in the audience disagreed. They felt that if Parsons provided solutions to ending police brutality, the hearing could have been instrumental in bringing about reform. However, although the hearing did allow black people to vent their concerns, the meeting "did not afford the black community the opportunity of understanding Parsons's plans to deal with and end police brutality in our communities since he did not specifically answer none of the questions," said one CAP member.[15]

In September, Parsons and NOPD officials held another town hall meeting at the Desire Community Center. The meeting began on a "hot note" when Sydney Duplesis, director of the Desire Community Center, asked all police officers that were present and were not participating in the forum to leave the gym. "So far there are six or more policemen here that weren't invited. I am asking them to leave or we will call off the meeting. It seems that these officers are here just to protect the NOPD and are not that concerned with the people residing in the Desire Housing Project." Parsons then explained that he had asked the officers to come out of respect for the community and not to intimidate the residents. Duplesis was not swayed and Parsons asked the officers to leave. Once the meeting began, citizens told Parsons about various incidents of police brutality. One resident told Parsons that he was stopped on suspicion of drug possession and that the police went through his car and ripped up his upholstery without a warrant. "That just shouldn't happen," Parsons responded. "And in that case the officers shouldn't have gone that far without a warrant. We hope to stop such things from occurring in the future. We are putting together a book that will let you know exactly what an officer can, and cannot do. This should be a great guide for the black community and all citizens as well." Parsons also mentioned that it was his plan to implement sensitivity sessions at the police academy so that all new officers could understand the diverse community of New Orleans. For example, rookies would learn "what it is like to live in a project apartment without air conditioning . . . to be without a job. We want the patrolman to have a better understanding of some of the problems you face."[16]

The town hall meetings on police brutality were important for several reasons. First, they gave the black community a public venue where they could voice long-standing complaints. Second, they opened up much-needed dialogue between the primary victims of police brutality and police officials. Third, they gave ordinary citizens a voice in city affairs. While these meetings did not necessarily result in immediate reforms, they represented a good first step in the early days of the Morial administration. Finally, the meetings gave activists the feeling that Morial was serious about reforming the NOPD since his selection of Parsons caused some to question that commitment.

Despite Parsons's efforts to reach out to the black community, CAP was not convinced that the chief was serious about reform. "After hot sessions with members of the black community, New Orleans Police Superintendent James Parsons, generally speaking, has done a poor job responding to questions relating to the pressing issue of police brutality," said Rouselle in an letter to Parsons after CAP made a list of demands at the Treme town hall meeting in early August. The demands were: (1) immediately removal of sixteen officers; (2) remove the IAD from the jurisdiction of the NOPD; (3) implement a citizens review committee; (4) support a policy that required officers to "call in the time and location of an arrest"; (5) stop "pedestrian identification checks," which were akin to those found in South Africa; and (6) explain his decentralization plan to the black community. Rouselle was further critical of Parsons because since his arrival in New Orleans he had not seriously addressed "himself to the issue of police brutality."[17]

In response to Parsons's refusal to meet their demands, CAP called a press conference and demanded "the immediate firing and for the criminal charges of assault and battery against several New Orleans Police Officers," and a rally at the Lakefront to protest an assault against two black families by several police officers. During the annual company picnic of the Monteleone Hotel, the Montrells and the Johnsons "were peacefully picnicking when they were viciously beaten with baseball bats, guns, and tent poles by these police." The problem occurred when the off-duty officers told them to go back to the black side of the beach. They stayed, were beaten, and were arrested. At the press conference, Rouselle remarked that the "overwhelming evidence against the police officers involved dictate that they be charged and removed from the force, but instead," he emphasized, "they are still with the NOPD." Rouselle then announced that the CAP would hold a demonstration and a picnic at the Lakefront site to highlight the "right of all people, black and white, to picnic on the lakefront without fear of racist brutal police attacks and to demand that these criminal cops be immediately fired and charged with this crime."[18]

At the demonstration approximately a hundred or more persons gathered and Rouselle told them the purpose for the protest. "On the one hand we are interested in seeing the policemen named fired and prosecuted to the fullest extent of the law for their crimes against these two black families." Second, "we want to prove to everybody, the police, the police chief, the Klan, everybody, that black people have the right as everybody else to congregate peacefully in public places and areas." The demonstrators chanted and shouted freedom slogans and carried protest signs reading: "Stop National Oppression"; "Stop Police Brutality"; "Lakefront Belongs to the People"; "Mayor Dutch Morial and Chief Parsons Must Be Held Responsible." Before dismissing the crowd, Rouselle stated that they were planning another demonstration to counter a planned Ku Klux Klan march that same day. "CAP as well as other concerned groups will rally to keep the Klan out of this city. We believe the Klan does not have a right to be here and we are asking all freedom loving people to join in with us against these racists." In planning to confront the Klan, Rouselle wondered why Morial would even issue them a permit. But he noted that CAP's protest "will also focus on continued instances of police abuse and brutality in the city, which is rooted in the same ideology the Klan represents."[19]

The CAP–Klan showdown never occurred because Parsons encouraged the Klan to move up their protest by two hours to avoid a confrontation. At the CAP rally, which occurred at the controversial Liberty Place Monument, Rouselle and Kalamu ya Salaam took aim at Morial and the NOPD. Morial "should have been out here with us. If a Jew was mayor of New Orleans, no permit would have been issued to the KKK to have any type of demonstration, because the Jewish people got a Jewish Defense League and they know how to deal with a situation like this." He then shouted, "Black people better wake up." Although the CAP-planned confrontation was successful, Rouselle reminded the demonstrators of CAP's purpose and encouraged them to continue "in the fight against police brutality."[20]

CAP's criticism of Morial showed its commitment to fair police protection and it proved that it was not going to go easy on Morial just because he was black. CAP was unwilling to be patient with Morial. They wanted Morial to show some grit and bring the department under his control. The appointment of Parsons, the chief's inability to answer direct questions at the town hall meetings, and Morial's approval of the Klan march led activists to one conclusion: Morial was more interested in maintaining the status quo than in taking drastic measures to change the police culture. This was disappointing to activists who had hoped that the battle against police brutality would be fought from city hall and police headquarters. But with Morial's apparent indifference activists had little choice but to denounce the mayor.

Morial was confronted with his first major NOPD crisis when officers went on strike in February 1979 over salary and benefits. Although Morial promised the officers a 15 percent pay increase, officers were told that they would have their sick leave reduced from twenty-four to thirteen days a year, and their annual leave or vacation days reduced from eighteen to thirteen a year. "After consideration of the proposed pay plan I come to only one conclusion—if the city decides to diminish our benefits we have no alternative but to take strike action," said Vincent Bruno, president of the Patrolmen's Association of New Orleans (PANO). The police union began threatening a strike in November 1978, but Morial refused to give in. As the strike date neared, Morial told officers that any police officer who went on strike would be fired since the city did not have a collective bargaining agreement with any police organization. But he did vow to protect citizens in the event of a police strike. "We will take whatever steps are necessary to assure that the people have adequate protection and we will take disciplinary action against any officer who refuses to obey a legitimate order from his superior." Morial then came down hard on Bruno. "We are not going to allow a rabble rouser leader of someone who is not recognized as the collective bargaining agent with the city to panic the people of New Orleans." Despite Morial's threats, many residents were convinced that an agreement would be reached before Mardi Gras, the economic engine of the New Orleans tourism industry.[21]

On January 17, the police union voted unanimously to strike before Mardi Gras. "We'll be on strike before Rex toasts his queen at the Boston Club," Bruno remarked. He then mentioned that his organization did speak with authority. "Morial thinks we only have two hundred to three members in our organization, but I can show you figures which will prove that we have nearly a thousand members. The city administration has put us in a position where we either have to put up or shut up. We're going to put up," Bruno declared. But Parsons was confident that in the event of a strike, there would be sufficient police protection to protect residents and tourists.[22]

In an effort to divide the rank-and-file of the NOPD, Morial announced that he would recognize the Fraternal Order of Police (FOP) as the exclusive bargaining agent for police officers. NOPD officers were divided into two organizations, PANO and FOP. FOP had a much better relationship with Morial and both the mayor and the FOP leadership were confident that they could reach a settlement. Days later R. Pat Stark, national president of the Fraternal Order of Police, came to New Orleans and urged its 647 members not to strike. "We don't believe in strikes . . . we think that there is no problem so insurmountable that it can't be solved." Instead of striking, he stated, "we prefer to go through the courts. We hire the best lawyers available."[23]

Morial's hard line forced PANO to strike on Thursday, February 8, 1979. "We have been forced to strike by the mayor's refusal to negotiate," said Bruno. "The policemen feel that they can no longer let the mayor take advantage of them." Bruno then stated that the next move was up to Mayor Morial. "We are throwing the ball to the mayor. He said all along we don't represent a majority and have only a hundred members. I think we have shown him otherwise." With the strike less than two hours old, approximately a hundred officers gathered at the front of police headquarters and burned their uniforms while shouting, "Strike, strike, strike," "Down with the FOP," and "Crime doesn't pay, and neither does police work." At the demonstration black officers were highly visible, leading chants and carrying signs. On the second day of the strike it was learned that Parsons and Morial disagreed over what police organization should be the chief bargaining unit. Parsons was aware that more than 50 percent of the department were members of PANO and that unless Morial recognized PANO the strike would continue. As the strike continued, Morial reversed his earlier decision and announced that he would negotiate with PANO after FOP officers withdrew as the bargaining unit. After that announcement, the striking officers agreed to return to work for a week until a deal could be reached. Morial was also forced to change course because on the second evening of the strike there were only 18 officers on duty, and only one policeman protecting 60,000 residents in Algiers.[24]

Despite the brief settlement, the officers went on strike again a week later after Morial rejected the union's offer of binding arbitration. With that announcement Morial cancelled Mardi Gras for lack of police protection. As the officers stayed off the job, the Black Organization of Police (BOP) urged its members to go back to work for the welfare of the black community. At a heated discussion that involved Councilmen Jim Singleton and Sidney Barthelemy, Joseph Orticke, BOP president, and a spokesperson for PANO, the BOP decided to ask its officers not to strike. "We are encouraging the local to support the mayor's efforts," said National President Patrolman's Association President Howard Saffold. "We feel that a police strike adversely affects the black community more than any other community. We feel first policemen should be dedicated to public safety and should worry about working conditions second." Gustave Thomas, the local BOP vice-president, and Orticke then went throughout the city trying to persuade black officers to get back on the job. They circulated a flyer to black officers that read, "The BOP has sided with Mayor Ernest N. Morial because many issues are clouded by misunderstanding and confusion. Historically, black officers have been fighting for equality and justice and have found themselves behind the proverbial eight ball. Our support of your position, Mr. Mayor, not withstanding, will subject our members to blatant repercussions on the part of our brothers in blue." Two black officers who were interviewed just after talking to Orticke and Thomas stated that the two BOP officers were trying to turn the strike into a race issue. "This is not a blue issue to them, it's a black and white issue," one officer remarked. Despite the efforts of Thomas and Orticke, their racial appeals did not convince the striking officers to return to their jobs.[25]

On a related matter, CAP sent letters to the Justice Department and the United Nations Security Council urging that they send investigators to look into the threats made by the Klan that they would patrol the city with forty men armed with shotguns to keep order in the black community. "We've learned of a few instances of KKK cross burnings particularly in the New Orleans East area. We feel there's great potential for a race war if this kind of thing keeps up and we want federal and international officials to look into it," stated Rouselle. He then added that when the police strike was over CAP still wanted federal agents to investigate the entire NOPD.[26]

As the strike entered its second week, CAP called upon all black residents to stay off the streets and be prepared to defend themselves in an effort to counter possible Klan activity. In its letter to the United Nations Security Council CAP wrote: "The Committee for Accountable Police representing poor and black people of New Orleans are requesting the immediate dispatch of a U.N. peacekeeping mission to New Orleans."[27]

After sixteen days, the city and PANO settled on an agreement and the officers went back to work. Although PANO got many of its demands met, Morial emerged as a hard-line mayor who had taken on the NOPD. Now, black residents wanted to see Morial take a similar stance against police brutality and unfair police protection.[28]

A VOLCANO THAT COULD ERUPT AT ANY TIME

A horrific incident of police brutality took place in May 1979 that illustrated to black residents that the presence of a black mayor did not necessarily translate into fair police protection. On the evening of April 30, 1979, twenty-eight-year-old Lyle Allen was shot three times by Charles Bretz, an off-duty officer, for no apparent reason. The incident began when Allen was about to enter the Dixie Package Liquor Store. Bretz, who came out of the Tasty Donut Shop, called Allen and "immediately" started kicking and beating him at gunpoint. Allen then broke free and ran into the liquor store for help, but as he entered the store he was shot twice in the back. Bretz then followed Allen into the store and fired another shot. As a result of the gunshots, Allen was paralyzed from the waist down and hospitalized. After Allen filed a $7 million lawsuit and community concern grew over the shooting, Bretz was placed on administrative leave while the district attorney's office looked into the case. While the city council and the district attorney's office investigated the case, the Committee for Accountable Police demanded an indictment on attempted murder charges. "Harry Connick should prosecute police officers without grand jury probes. By asking the grand jury to charge the police, Connick is merely passing the buck and attempting to fool the black community." Rouselle then added, "Very few policemen guilty of abuse on citizens have been charged by the grand jury or by Connick."[29]

On June 14, 1979, Bretz was indicted by the Orleans Parish grand jury of attempted first-degree murder charges. Bretz immediately resigned from the police force, which caused many black observers to wonder "if deals were being made to get Bretz off" since the twenty-two-year-old officer should have been fired and not allowed to resign. Allen's lawyer, Joseph Thomas, thought that Morial was a part of the assumed cover-up. In a letter to the mayor, Thomas mentioned, "When you became Mayor of the City it was my hope that some of the abuse of authority that had become the trademark of the New Orleans Police Department would come to an end. You, after all, had spent a good portion of your life voicing protest of abusive police conduct. Apparently however, this is no longer a concern of yours." Thomas closed the letter by stating: "I will let you judge how it becomes the City's chief law enforcement officer to cover up any misconduct, but especially police misconduct. Be assured however, that, while your voice has been lost in the struggle against abusive conduct, mine has grown stronger." Morial refused to respond to Thomas's letter because the case was still in litigation.

But he was also convicted by Thomas's words. Yes, Morial wanted to do more in the area of police reform but he was well aware of the political realities and that reforming the NOPD would take years and not months. Parsons's continued ineffectiveness made him a liability for Morial instead of an asset. After a brief three-day trial, Bretz was found guilty on the lesser charge of attempted manslaughter. The black community was ecstatic since this was one of the first times that a police officer in New Orleans had actually been convicted for brutalizing black residents. Bretz was sentenced to three years in prison; Allen was permanently paralyzed from the neck down.[30]

While the black community was no doubt happy that Bretz was convicted, community residents were largely unaware of the serious racial tensions within the NOPD. One high-ranking officer referred to the racial situation as a "volcano that could erupt any time." In October 1979, a group of black officers met with Morial, Parsons, and several other city officials "for more than four hours." Although Parsons tried to deny that racism was the central topic, Morial confirmed that the meeting centered around the pervasive racism and discrimination that black officers received at the hands of white officers. "We've got a lot of problems and we feel something has to be done. It's just getting to the point where it's reaching a crisis stage," said one black officer. Apparently, the BOP's decision not to support the strike and its efforts to get black officers to return to work intensified the racism they received, from their white counterparts. "We feel the strike was directed against a black mayor. This would have never happened when Landrieu was in office. And now the blacks who didn't join the strike are being harassed on the job," said the same officer. At the meeting black officers submitted a list of complaints that included harsher discipline for black officers, discriminatory assignments on special units, lack of black officers in supervisory positions, indiscriminate transfers of black officers, and racist civil service exams. "Blacks constitute 10 percent to 12 percent of the force. But when it comes to discipline it seems like we make up 99 percent." One officer recalled how they "interrogated one officer for seven straight hours over a minor violation. That just seems racist. I'm in the system, but I don't want to be a part of it. It's time someone who's been there screams for a change."[31]

The lack of black officers on special units was a major problem. Of the 186 blacks on the force, 4 were on the vice squad, 4 in internal affairs, 3 in the crime lab, 4 in special assignments, 5 in the auto pound, one in narcotics, and 43 on the urban squad. The urban squad was home to the majority of black officers and that is the only unit where they felt comfortable.

When BOP President Sandy Gavin was asked to comment on the meeting, he was blunt. "We, black policemen, are having serious problems within the department. The situations are departmental problems and they are being handled departmentally. We are working on the problems along with the administration and we will have a report later on the outcome." Many BOP officers were confident that Morial would tackle the issue of racism within the NOPD because "it was alive and well."[32]

The case of Officer Randolph Thomas was particularly illustrative of the problems black officers had to confront. Thomas was dismissed from the force on July 6, 1979, after he refused to sign an arrest warrant for Gary Honore, who was apprehended by police after a domestic dispute. Thomas refused to participate in the arrest because his partner, Norman Ceaser, fractured Honore's skull, punctured his eardrum, and did not inform him of his rights upon arrest. "Under no circumstances will I sign this report. I will not support Officer Ceaser or any other officer who over reacts and makes mistakes regarding the rights of citizens, and who refuses to correct their mistakes." After several hearings with Parsons, Thomas was dismissed from the force. Parsons's decision to fire him was partly made because of the officer's reputation as a "firebrand," a rebel police officer who would not go along with the system. "They wanted Thomas and they would do anything they could to get him off the force," said one officer. After a civil service hearing that made headlines in the city papers, Thomas was reinstated to the force.[33]

The poverty-stricken Desire Projects was the scene of a showdown between the NOPD and three hundred to four hundred black residents in September 1980. The disturbance began on a Monday afternoon when Lawrence Louis was killed by police in Desire as they were attempting to arrest him. At a "hastily called press conference," Officers Albert Spies and Michael Addison gave their version of the incident. The officers stated that Louis attracted their attention because he was carrying a .25 caliber automatic pistol. After stopping and disarming him, Louis allegedly turned on them and grabbed Addison's weapon. "They both had their hands on it," said Lieutenant Steve London to reporters. "But if you were going to say either one had possession of it, it would be Mr. Louis. And this weapon was being turned and directed at Officer Addison." Fearing for his life, Spiess fired the fatal shot that killed Louis. Witnesses to the shooting recalled a different version of events. "It was cold-blooded murder. The black guy was sitting on top of him while the white guy had a pistol in his neck," said one eyewitness. One woman told reporters that "the black cop held him and told the white cop to hit him." The following day the Liberation League held a protest march in front of the Fifth District police station, despite the fact that the officers involved did not work there. After a brief investigation, the two officers were suspended by Parsons. "A departmental investigation was launched as soon as I became aware of the situation. When all the facts are gathered, they will be submitted to the district attorney to be considered for presentation to the grand jury. The mayor and I have requested the FBI to conduct an independent, concurrent investigation of the incident." Under pressure, Morial attempted to assure the black community that he would see that the officers were investigated. "I want to assure the public that this matter will be handled properly and thoroughly investigated."[34]

The next evening tensions erupted in Desire after urban squad Officers Byron Adams and Roy Humphrey chased a suspected hit-and-run driver into the projects. The suspect, Gregory Nunnery, was apprehended at the crowded intersection of Pleasure and Piety, when a crowd of young people surrounded the squad car. After Nunnery was put in the car, an altercation broke out between the officers and several witnesses who protested the way that Nunnery was being handled. After a crowd of several hundred young people surrounded the squad car, they pelted it with rocks and bottles. As other squad cars responded to the call for backup, they all were forced to leave the scene when the crowd became unruly. In an effort to quell the tensions, city, parish, and federal officials, residents of the projects, and community leaders from Desire gathered to talk about the incident. During the ninety-minute meeting at the Desire Community Center, officials attempted to satisfy community concerns that the shooting was being thoroughly investigated. Lieutenant Rinal Martin said that the residents were shown that "anything they could have demanded and traditionally would ask for in a police shooting was being done already. Once you get the district attorney involved, and the U.S. attorney involved, and then you get the FBI and an outside impartial investigation, you can't do anything more." Although Martin felt that his assurance of an impartial investigation was warmly received, he acknowledged that some people were certain that it was a cold-blooded murder and that the police were not acting in self-defense.[35]

While the shooting was under investigation, a group of Desire residents formed Community Action Now (CAN), and called for the dismissal of the two officers involved in the shootings. Members of CAN later interrupted a city council meeting to protest the killing and the pattern of brutality and clear-cut harassment in the black community. At the council meeting approximately thirty-five to forty demonstrators marched into the chambers chanting, "We want justice, we want justice." CAN Spokesperson Jesse Turner then took over the microphone and demanded that the city council address the long-standing issue of police brutality. "We're tired of always being killed and abused and beaten time and time again." Council President Sydney Barthelemy told Turner that he was out of order, but Turner continued to speak. "We'll be organizing We'll be back next week—stronger. Next time, we'll bring the citizens from all of the communities that realize the need for a new system of police investigation." When Turner finished his oration, CAN members marched out of the chamber "clapping hands and shouting slogans." Councilman Giarrusso felt disrespected. "Putting up with their conduct is really a direct insult to us and shows nothing but weakness on our part. It weakens our entire government when anyone can come in here, regardless of what they call it—black, white, pink, or yellow—and interrupt a legal proceeding and decide that they're going to do what they want to do." Giarrusso then threatened that order would be kept even if it meant a violent confrontation. "I think it's high time we take a tough stand. If it takes a physical confrontation of some kind, which I hope we can avoid, well by God, if that's what it takes, we ought to do it." Barthelemy told Giarrusso that "to have a confrontation would have given them exactly what they needed." However, Councilmen Ciaccio and Bagert wanted the protestors arrested. Ciaccio stated, "There are laws on the books and we ought to arrest and charge the ringleaders and see that they are prosecuted."[36]

Days later, the Liberation League organized about twenty Desire residents and marched on police headquarters in an effort to have Officers Speiss and Addison fired from the force. Malcolm Suber, a spokesman for the group, stated that the purpose of the demonstration was to "keep alive" the issue. "What we're attempting to do is bring attention to a police murder. We think the city is trying to stall it, trying to let it die. It is very important that there be some form of punishment for these two officers." He added, "It is a critical issue." Although the Liberation League was not affiliated with CAN, Suber supported CAN's disruption of the city council meeting. "We support that group's activity. That action was called for." As the protestors chanted, "One, two, three, four—police terror has got to go!" the police offered no response.[37]

At the next city council meeting members of CAN appeared again, but this time they were included on the council agenda to discuss police brutality. Michael Williams, a CAN member, told the council that the NOPD had no legitimate desire to enforce the law in the black community. "The murder rate is on steep increase, and it's mostly blacks killing blacks. It is clear that the police cannot rid the ghetto of crime, nor can they significantly alter its proportions. Why are they there?" Williams then called for the elimination of the urban squad from the city's public housing units and the creation of a civilian review board to investigate police brutality. To ease tensions the city council passed a resolution sponsored by Councilman Jim Singleton stating that the council would accept proposals from the public on how to improve the handling of brutality complaints. It was merely symbolic since the jurisdiction of the NOPD fell under the mayor's office. Councilman Brod Bagert voted for the measure but told the council the resolution had no teeth. "This is a sham. If anybody here today thinks that what we're doing carries the slightest weight of legal authority or has the slightest ability to effect a change, don't let anybody deceive you. The authority to make a decision in this matter and effectuate a change lies in the mayor's office." Singleton responded by stating that his resolution was simply "a mechanism to put things in place" so that city officials could "hopefully" come up with a solution to the problem. He then added, "My hope is that the resolution will not lead to a whole new set of public hearings on police brutality complaints. I hope it will lead to getting some proposals, recommendations, or suggestions for changes on how to handle complaints of abuse and mistreatment against police."[38]

Despite community efforts to see that the officers who killed Lawrence Louis were brought to justice, the Orleans Parish grand jury found the officers not guilty of any wrongdoing. After hearing thirty-five witnesses, the grand jury agreed with the NOPD internal affairs report that concluded that the officers had acted in self-defense. After the grand jury found the officers not guilty, there was little response from the black community. Perhaps they concluded that unless there was some other mechanism for investigating complaints, beatings, and killings by the police, they could never expect justice. The involvement of Officer Michael Addison, an African American, in the killing of Lawrence Louis represented a watershed period in the relationship between African Americans and the New Orleans Police Department. In the decades-long struggle for fair police protection, many of the complaints were targeted toward white police officers. But as black officers increased their visibility within the NOPD, many of the police brutality complaints were now aimed at black cops, and particularly those on the urban squad.[39]

THE URBAN SQUAD

The issue of black officers and the urban squad came up for discussion as the number of police complaints against the urban squad increased. Established in the mid-1970s, the urban squad was a group of mostly black officers who were trained to handle the vicious environment within two of the city's notorious housing projects, Desire and St. Bernard. When Parsons became chief, he immediately instituted several changes within the unit. He first integrated the unit and he eliminated its all-volunteer and overtime status He then made the squad a regular beat, much like a district assignment. In making the changes Parsons noted that "it was not a good way to address the problem. Living in the projects was considered special because blacks were living there. Special because you have to put a lot of police there. Special because they're government owned and it's ostensibly cheap to live there."[40]

Project residents had complained for years about brutality, harassment, and inadequate police protection on the part of the urban squad. "The only time you see a police car around here is when someone is getting shot up," said a Housing Authority of New Orleans (HANO) employee. One resident remarked similarly, "You won't see a police car around here until someone is dead. If you call and say it's an emergency, they'll take an hour to get here." She continued, "If someone breaks into your home and you say you know who has your property the police will tell you, 'Go get the receipt.'" The officers on the urban squad had a different perspective. They argued that they were not allowed to enforce the law because residents were uncooperative. One officer recalled his experience in trying to solve homicides that occurred in the projects. "I have handled several murders in this very courtyard and whenever I ask someone if they have seen or heard anything the answer is always, 'No.' Now you tell me how me, how can a murder happen in broad daylight and not anybody know anything about it?" He also mentioned that this did not only occur with homicides. "You can have a group of people standing in front of a grocery store and an armed robber can be right there in the middle. He knows no one is going to mess with him with all those people around."[41]

Community leaders were disappointed that the relationship with the urban squad and the black community had deteriorated because the original intent of the squad was for it to be staffed by black officers who were sensitive to the community. "The police officer who works in the Desire, or any other project, has to adjust from handling a lot of crimes to handling a lot of social problems. And when that officer is not able to handle it, then people resent it." Chief Parsons agreed that black officers on the squad were having a tough time dealing with their assignments, but he offered a different explanation. "I think there is an inclination on the part of the white police officer to go a little light because of possible misconduct and being called racist. The black policeman doesn't have that to worry about," he said. Stevens Moore, director of the Desire-Florida Community Anti-Crime Program, echoed Parsons's sentiments. "The white officer has to be careful mainly because of the race thing. If the police officer is not afraid when he comes in the project then he comes in with the attitude right away of, 'I have to show these people who is in control.'" But Moore understood that this relationship didn't just develop overnight. "We've had our history of skull-crackers," he said.[42]

The involvement of black officers in the beating of black civilians represented a new phenomenon in the history of police-community relations in New Orleans. Throughout much of the twentieth century, black activists argued that the presence of black officers would diminish police brutality. However, once on the force some black officers no longer thought of themselves as black; they considered themselves a part of the fraternity of the brothers in blue. Now, black residents could not necessarily be convinced that the mere presence of black police officers did not mean an encounter with police brutality. In fact, by the end of the century, more police brutality complaints would be lodged against black police officers than white officers.

7 "WE ARE LIVING IN A POLICE STATE"
The Algiers Tragedy, the Maturation of Community Protest, and the Politics of a Civilian Review Board

Between 1976 and 1982, the United States experienced an unprecedented crime wave as rape and violent crimes continued to escalate. Trapped in enclaves of high unemployment, poor housing, bad schools, and inadequate social services, blacks turned their frustration inward as American's inner cities became sites of general despair. In particular, black-on-black homicide rates were at unprecedented and unheard of levels. In 1980, 50 percent of all murders in the country involved black males killing other black males. As murder rates increased, per capita police expenditures jumped nearly 50 percent from those of the previous decade as politicians made crime reduction a national priority. As historian Manning Marable notes, "white Americans of all classes became terrified of the omnipresent specter of the 'black criminal, rapist and burglar.'" Supported by community mandates, local police departments went on the offensive in black neighborhoods, applying a variety of extralegal techniques, including excessive force.[1]

THE MURDER OF OFFICER GREGORY NEUPERT
A new era of tensions between African Americans and the police department erupted in the aftermath of the murder of Officer Gregory Neupert, who was found shot to death in a ditch in the early morning hours of November 9, 1980, in Algiers, a community on the West Bank of New Orleans. Officer Charles Moreau spotted Neupert's squad car running with the headlights on and the door open. He then saw Neupert lying alongside the car in a ditch with his police radio clutched in his left hand and a flashlight in his right. His gun was still in its holster. "He made no radio transmissions that

he was having problems," said police spokesman Don Joly. "He must have stumbled across something." Joly stated that one of the chief difficulties in solving his murder would be the absence of any radio activities from Neupert during those last moments. Neupert was last seen around 12:40 a.m. at police headquarters on S. Broad Street, just thirty-five minutes before he was killed.[2]

In an effort to warn vengeful officers that misconduct would not be tolerated in the search for Neupert's killer, Morial issued a statement. "We are all shocked and outraged by the tragic shooting of Officer Gregory Neupert. We must respond calmly, professionally, and quickly to apprehend the perpetrator of this crime." Morial then stated that he, too, was "grieved by this outrageous act." Morial knew that the murder of the twenty-three-year-old white officer in an all-black neighborhood would bring revenge, harassment, and perhaps murder, but he was completely powerless to control the terror that white officers were about to unleash on the black community of Algiers.[3]

When no new details emerged in Neupert's death within twenty-four hours of the murder, the felony action squad (FAS) and other officers came out in force to find the murderer. "Everybody's working on it," said one detective. The night after the murder approximately twenty officers went into the Fischer Projects, "wearing jeans and blue windbreakers with the police emblem on the back," without warning. They parked their cars in the back of the projects and proceeded to harass residents. "You niggers know who killed that policeman. You all know everything in here and you all know who shot him," one tenant recalled the police saying. The officers then kicked down doors, grabbed young men, and with guns drawn marched the twenty youths "like soldiers" through the housing development. They threw the boys against the wall and interrogated them about the murder. "Y'all niggers back here know everything and y'all know who killed that policeman," said one officer. When several parents asked the officers why they were interrogating their boys, many of the officers replied, "Get your asses back." One officer told Dorothy Mitchell, "Lady, I'm telling you for the last time, go back or I'll put you in jail or shoot you." Six of the young men were taken to police headquarters for further questioning and two of them were beaten while in police custody. Eighteen-year-old Louis Thornton said the officers took him to the police station and beat him in an effort to get him to talk. "They were trying to get me to talk, but I didn't know anything," he recalled. His mother stated that the police apprehended him by kicking in her front door, with guns drawn, and dragging him out of his room. The officers did not produce a search warrant or explain what they were looking for.[4]

After the initial invasion of the New Orleans Police Department (NOPD) into the Fischer Projects, black residents were livid, as expected, but Parsons failed to acknowledge the possibility that his men did terrorize innocent citizens in their search for Neupert's killer. Parsons stated clearly that he did not believe that members of the FAS had been roughing up residents. "I really don't have that kind of problem with those guys," he said. When he was asked what precautions he had taken to make sure that officers would not seek revenge, he told a reporter that he "instructed the commanders at the very outset to take control over their men." But he did mention that he knew how emotional his men were to catch the killer, adding, "I don't think anyone is going to take any off days until they catch this killer." However, the FAS did kill a man in their search for the suspect that night. As the "swarms" of police continued to harass Fischer Project residents throughout the week, Raymond Ferdinand, thirty-eight, was killed by officers when he allegedly pulled a knife on them. However, his fiancé recalled that Ferdinand did have a knife but that it was inside a small bag he was carrying and not in his sleeve as police stated. He was shot twice, once in the neck and once in the back of the head. The local paper made sure to mention that Ferdinand was a drug addict.[5]

During the week-long manhunt for Neupert's killer, FAS officers beat and tortured Algiers residents Johnnie Brownlee and Robert Davis in an effort to get them to tell what they knew about the murder. Although there was some discussion in Algiers that the murdered officer was killed by a fellow officer over drug money, both were taken into the woods and, Davis recalled, "they said they was 'gonna waste my black ass' so nobody couldn't find me. I really thought I wasn't gonna make it back." Brownlee was taken to the woods and blindfolded. "They made me get on my knees first". A shotgun was placed at the back of his head, and later a round was fired off next to his ear. Brownlee remembered one officer stating to another, "You this close and you missed this nigger?" Brownlee then began to pray in preparation for his execution. However, both men were taken back to the station and they were coerced into stating that James Billy killed Neupert. The officers insisted that both men saw Neupert stop Billy and Reginald Miles and order one of them to place his hands on the patrol car and the other to place his hands over his head. When Neupert looked to his left at a house number so he could radio his location to police dispatchers, Billy shot and killed Neupert. Both informants were threatened with death if they did not sign a statement stating that they had indeed seen Billy. At the end of the hours' long interrogation, they were subject to more beatings, and both men were given $1,000 by the police and "advised to leave the city of New Orleans." The Liberation League publicized the forced confession and Davis and Brownlee immediately went into hiding. They had no idea that their forced statements would lead to the deaths of three innocent civilians.[6]

THE ALGIERS TRAGEDY

Several days later, at around 2:45 a.m., sixteen white police officers converged on the Algiers neighborhood where Billy and Miles lived with no intent of serving warrants, making arrests, or bringing any of the suspects into police custody. They were looking for revenge. Ironically, all of the black officers who were assigned to the Neupert investigation were excluded from the raid. Eight officers went to Billy's house and, after pulling a woman and an infant out of the house, killed Billy in cold blood. However, police officials claimed that Billy came up firing. "Right from the get go he came up smoking. It all went down in milliseconds. As soon as they got near his door, muzzle flashes were popping." Kim Landry, who was in the house with Billy, said he did not make an attempt to escape nor did he have a weapon when police started firing. Ten blocks away, a similar raid took place at 1133 Teche Street, where Reginald Miles, twenty-eight, and Sherry Lyn Singleton, twenty-six, were killed after allegedly pulling guns on officers— Miles after he allegedly went for a gun and Singleton after her gun allegedly misfired. But a woman next door vividly remembered Singleton yelling, "Please, don't shoot. Please, don't shoot." NOPD Deputy Chief Dave Kent was clear about what happened, "You're talking about two situations where the people just came up smoking, firing their guns."[7]

Although the police version of events was questionable, Kent was confident that his men had acted in self-defense. "I think the officers used a lot of self-control. All the evidence indicates that the suspects fired first. I'm convinced the police officers did not fabricate any of this," he said. Kent's defense of the officers was predictable, yet disturbing at the same time. Fellow police officers, politicians, anti-brutality activists, and common citizens knew that Neupert's death would be avenged by rogue cops. The raid was unsupervised and unauthorized and black officers were deliberately left out of the planning. Nonetheless, NOPD brass shielded the killer cops from criticism. Parsons refused to identify the officers involved in the shooting, saying it would bring unjustified harassment, and police officials made sure that the public knew that Billy and Miles were drug users and that all three victims had criminal records. The urban guerilla tactics of the thug cops put the city on the verge of a race riot.[8]

The night of the killings twenty-nine residents from three of the city's largest housing projects, Desire, St. Bernard, and Fischer, met to discuss the shootings. Sidney Duplesis of CAN warned city officials that something had to be done. "Either you do something now or get out. This is the situation we're in now. We need something to be done now, not one or two years later." Michael Williams, a representative from the St. Bernard Project, echoed Duplesis's feelings. "We're past the talking stage. We don't need talkers, we need warriors. It has to be something bold. We don't need any more 'We Shall Overcome' crap." As expected, black residents did not believe the police version of the shootings, but many were afraid to speak out for fear of police reprisals. "The mood among many black persons is that of being afraid," said Rose Loving, executive director of the Algiers-Fischer Community Organization. "This is an extremely serious situation and it's going to be with us for a while. It's not going to be buried in the graves with those people," she said. Prior to the shootings, Loving was among a number of community leaders calling for a Friday meeting with police over the week-long harassment. But after the shootings, she called the meeting off for fear of a riot. The meeting was to be held at a church directly across the street from Billy's residence. "That's too close to the residence involved. When it's the right time in terms of not inflaming the community we'll have the meeting. But right now we're looking at the pulse of the community."[9]

Approximately 250 Fischer Housing Projects residents protested the killings the next day and demanded the removal of Parsons as police chief at an afternoon rally in the "sprawling low-income housing complex" in Algiers. During a news conference that preceded the rally, Attorney Mary Howell, who often represented police brutality victims in civil lawsuits against the city, said that a coalition of organizations, including the Equal Rights Congress, the Free Southern Theater, The Southern Prisoners Defense Committee, and others throughout the New Orleans area, were calling on police to make a complete disclosure about the shootings. "This is not an investigation of a killing of black people over there. This is a cover-up of those killings. The police investigation into the Neupert slaying was shoddy at best. They just gunned down Sherry Singleton in cold blood. They did not choose to let her live to tell her story. What we have is a situation where the police department is setting itself up as judge, jury, and executioner," Howell stated. Malcolm Suber of the Liberation League said Morial and Parsons must share the blame. He then called on Morial to fire his police chief. During the rally, Fischer resident Reverend Donald Crockett, pastor of the New St. Martin Baptist Church, called the killings "a senseless, barbaric, and savage thing to do." He continued, "We still don't know who killed the policeman." That statement was in reference to Parsons's announcement that the Neupert murder was solved with the killing of Billy and Miles. Crockett then stressed the need for black unity and for Morial to act. "We have to stand together, we must move as a group of people. We must tell the mayor we want an investigation into these police shootings. He's the mayor of the people in the projects. We know we are poor, but we are people." The group then chanted, "Police terror must go. Police terror must go. Now, now."[10]

Among those absent in the fight for justice in Algiers were members of the Southern Organization for United Leadership (SOUL), the Community Organization for Urban Politics (COUP), and the Black Organization for Leadership Development (BOLD). But their absence did not come as a surprise to anti-brutality activists. First, they knew that black moderates did not want to align themselves with the more radical elements in the community, such as the Liberation League, and they realized that the black middle class also did not wish to confront Morial, the city's first black mayor. More important, however, anti-brutality activists also realized that the black middle class did not wish to engage in a protest over the deaths of people with criminal and drug-addicted backgrounds.

As black citizens continued to demand justice for the killings, the Liberty City riots in Miami were in the back of everyone's mind. In May 1980, the black communities of Liberty City, Brownsville, Overton, and Coconut Grove exploded after an all-white jury returned a not guilty verdict on white police officers who had killed a thirty-three-year-old African American insurance executive. The evening of the verdict, black residents damaged over $250 million in property; several blacks died; and approximately 400 people were injured and 1,250 arrested. Local leaders were praying and hoping that New Orleans would not explode. But all of the ingredients for a disturbance were there: a police department with a reputation for brutality, an ineffective police chief, a mayor unwilling to assert control over the city's police force, and black rage.

The Algiers–Fischer Housing Projects board of directors responded to the shootings by calling for the city council to create a civilian review board. Reading from a prepared statement at the offices of Total Community Action, Melvin Bush, president of the board, praised the conduct of project residents while deploring the actions of the NOPD. "We are extremely proud of the residents in our community for the way they have conducted themselves during the past week of harassment, tragedy, and loss of life." He then took aim at the NOPD. "While we are in no way questioning the right of law enforcement officers to seek out those suspected of breaking the law, we do take strong exception to the conduct of the New Orleans police and the resulting actions that led to intimidation, harassment, and the eventual death of four residents of our community." Bush then spoke of the need for a civilian review board. "It is clear that the time for such a body has finally come." Bush then enthusiastically announced that the FBI had opened an investigation into the shootings, which was confirmed by Cliff Anderson, FBI spokesman in New Orleans. "I'm not sure just what the scope of the investigation will be. At the same time, we're perceptive; we read the papers, we have heard the television reports, and we're all aware of the allegations made in those reports," Anderson said.[11]

After the emotional funeral of Sherry Singleton, approximately a hundred protestors led by Attorney Mary Howell marched from Canal and Broad streets to police headquarters. Once there, they went up to the fifth floor, claiming that the victims were "executed at the hands of murderous police officers," and they demanded to see Parsons. They were told that he was not in. Howell told reporters that an examination of Singleton's death revealed that she "was either lying down or in a fetal position" when she was gunned down. The demonstrators then reassembled in front of the monument to police officers killed in the line of duty. "We're gathered here in front of the monument to their dead, and we bring our dead here today." The protestors carried a green coffin adorned with pictures of Singleton in her graduation robe. The posters said, "Sherry Singleton, murdered by New Orleans police November 13, 1980." Many protestors also wore black armbands and said they were "badges of defiance against police terror." Malcolm Suber of the Liberation League told the group that there would be "no peace, no harmony, and no safety until justice is done." He then promised that the League would try to disrupt the economy of the city in order to focus attention on the killings. The protestors carried signs reading, "End Police Terror," "End Police Murder," "Prosecute All Murderers," "Fire Parsons," and "End Police Brutality."[12]

"DO SOMETHING, MAYOR"

Morial made his first public statement on the Algiers tragedy several days after the shootings and announced that he had ordered a full investigation into the shootings. But he was careful not to take any side in the dispute. "It is a tragic and outrageous act for a police officer, a servant of the people, to be gunned down in cold blood while performing his duty. But no crime, no matter how much it offends our sensibilities, should give rise to the violation of anyone's rights in the pursuit of the person who committed the crime." The mayor then attempted to put residents at ease by stating, "I intend to see that illegal tactics are not employed under the guise of law enforcement to suppress the alleged criminal misconduct, regardless of how reprehensible the criminal behavior." Morial was now facing the biggest crisis of his historic administration.[13]

Once the FBI began interviewing Algiers residents, community leaders were confident that a riot could be avoided. "As long as the people know the murders are going to be investigated, I think things will be all right. The FBI is in it. The people have faith in them. They liked the mayor's statement. I think they're satisfied that something is going to happen. Unless something else happens to upset it, I think we're out of the woods," said Loving. Loving then thought about how close the city had come to a full-fledged race riot. "You know, we've been sitting on a powder keg since the first officer was killed here in Fischer, and that did not end in the killing of any people here. You know, we had a resident shot by police in Desire. It probably would have sparked there, and I think it would have been citywide. But we're just so thankful for the people over here, that they did not immediately react." Loving credited the relative stability of the Algiers–Fischer Projects to open communication with the police.[14]

At a meeting sponsored by the Alliance for Good Government, the Liberation League, headed by Malcolm Suber, a local activist in the Rouselle–Salaam tradition, picketed before the meeting and interrupted the meeting when Parsons rose to speak. The meeting, which was not called in connection with the Algiers shootings, included Parsons and Connick along with other law enforcement officers. Members of the League remained quiet and calm until Parsons spoke. Then a yell of "He's a murderer and everybody knows he's a murderer" was heard from the demonstrators, while some chanted, "Parsons has got to go." Parsons began leading the chant himself in an effort to mock the demonstrators before sitting down and "nervously" lighting a cigar. After repeated attempts to quiet the demonstrators, the meeting was adjourned, to the delight of the Liberation League.[15]

In its fight to keep the Algiers murders in the spotlight, the Liberation League received help from the three hundred-member Concerned Citizens of Algiers, who threatened an economic boycott if four demands were not met: the firing of Parsons, the immediate dismissal of the officers involved in the shootings, the release of all information pertaining to the case, and an immediate halt to police patrols in Algiers. If these demands were not met, they planned to call a boycott of all stores in the central business district and perhaps a boycott of all white-owned stores. Leaders of the group said that their boycott would coincide with the enormous national exposure the city would receive from the Sugar Ray Leonard–Roberto Duran championship boxing match at the Superdome, the Bayou Classic, and the Christmas shopping season. Organizers were also hopeful that the boycott would affect the attendance at the Sugar and Super Bowls in January. Arthur Bush stated that many Algiers residents were being harassed and that some officers were shouting obscenities at motorists. He then mentioned that Algiers residents would not sit back and forget the killings of Billy, Singleton, and Miles. One day later Bush told reporters that his group would try and meet with Morial. "I think it's his duty to meet the demands. I don't think we're asking anything unreasonable. It's going to jeopardize the whole relationship between the community and the administration if he [Morial] decides not to deal with it."[16]

After the killings, a group of moderate community organizations, such as the local New Orleans Urban League (NOUL) and the National Association for the Advancement of Colored People (NAACP), asked Morial to appoint a special citizens panel that would "seriously address the issue of police use of excessive and deadly force." They made specific recommendations to the mayor. First, they wanted civilians appointed "immediately" to the internal affairs division of the New Orleans Police Department. Second, they wanted all of the facts "that are presently known" about the Algiers killings to be made public. Third, they wanted a grassroots attack on black-on-black crime. Finally, they asked the city to host a conference on police-community relations. Morial took the matter under advisement.[17]

Morial's reluctance to take a more active role in reforming the NOPD can partly be attributed to the tightrope he had to walk. He was smart enough to understand that the police department was perhaps the most difficult city agency to reform. The NOPD had a unique culture; officers could not be fired without sufficient cause, since they were protected by civil service rules; and broader public opinion also favored aggressive policing. Further, Morial did not want to move too quickly in the area of police reform because he did not want to give the appearance that his administration represented a black power takeover of the city's police forces. With constant white flight, Morial had to be careful not to alienate the whites who still remained in the city. Also, Morial had other important issues to focus on even though the issue of police brutality occupied much of his time. Parsons did not make Morial's job any easier; in fact, he made it extremely difficult. The chief's ineffectiveness seemingly kept Morial in the middle of controversy.

Amid "the groundswell of protests" in the aftermath of the Algiers killings, New Orleans Police Superintendent James C. Parsons resigned. Contacted back at his home in Birmingham, Parsons was frank about the reason for his leaving. "They were hollering for some heads down there. They were wanting something done to the police before the investigation had been completed, and I couldn't in good conscience do that, so I just resigned myself." Parsons denied having any problems with Morial; in fact, he acknowledged that his departure would probably save Morial's political career. "He was in a bind. The people were demanding he do something. We talked about it, and I thought it would be best if I resigned." Although Parsons did not mention the killings as the sole reason for his departure, he made reference to it in his resignation letter. "The deaths of Officer Neupert and the Algiers Citizens have caused the entire community much distress. I support your efforts to have the incident thoroughly investigated and will aid in that endeavor any way I can." But Parsons felt that he had done a good job during his two-year stay in New Orleans. "I came to this city to build an effective police department. In my opinion, I have accomplished that mission. Our programs are functioning and police personnel are working steadily to improve them. A cadre of young leaders has been developed, and I am sure they will continue to improve the department." Community leaders were elated. Arthur Bush of the Concerned Citizens group was satisfied enough to call off the boycott. "We are thus far satisfied with the way the mayor has handled these items. Whichever way it happened, he's no longer with the department. We will not be conducting the boycott." Malcolm Suber of the Liberation League was not impressed with Parsons's resignation, and his group was still planning to demonstrate in front of the Superdome on the night of the fight because they knew that despite a change at the top the culture of brutality was rampant within the NOPD. The League had previously demanded that all of the officers involved in the shootings be placed in a lineup to be identified by Algiers residents. In a more moderate tone, Clarence Barney of the Urban League stated that the resignation of Parsons was "an important first step to relieve tensions in the community as well as restoring confidence of the police department in the black community." Barney then asked Morial to establish a civilian review board. Rose Loving simply responded to the chief's resignation by stating, "Thank God. It's a relief."[18]

Morial replaced Parsons with thirty-four-year NOPD veteran Henry Morris, a white officer who was described as a "cop's cop" because of his traditional approach to law enforcement and his strong administrative background. The decision to promote from within was a goodwill gesture to the rank-and-file of the NOPD. By selecting Morris, Morial figured that the long-time cop could deal with the rogue element within his ranks, maintain the status quo, and guide the department and the city through the Algiers episode. Morris was named permanent chief in April 1981 and Warren Woodfork, an African American, was named deputy chief.

Morial then announced that he would appoint a special investigator to look into the shootings. That person would determine if the police had committed any wrongdoing in the shootings. The investigator would then turn over any information to the district attorney's office and federal authorities. The announcement of a special investigator was a bold step in Morial's efforts to recapture his black support for his reelection. It was an acknowledgment that the existing judicial apparatus was virtually useless when it dealt with allegations of police misconduct. Since the special investigator would be outside the official investigative channels, it would "have the flavor of a citizens review board." Morial knew that if he did not act quickly, the Algiers killings could lead to a riot, cause a complete breakdown in law enforcement in New Orleans, and ruin his political career.[19]

Orleans Parish District Attorney Harry Connick was not happy about the idea of a special prosecutor. Although Connick asked Morial to delay his request for a special prosecutor so that existing investigations could conclude, the district attorney privately felt that Morial was undermining his authority and questioning his competence. He was right. Morial and even the more moderate elements in the black community had no faith in Connick because the district attorney's office had historically been complicit in exonerating officers of even the most obvious violations. In response to Connick's request, Morial agreed to postpone the appointment of a special prosecutor. The mayor told the press that he did not wish to "impede or improvidently interfere with the existing ongoing investigation." He then told reporters that he was assured that the Justice Department and the district attorney's office would conduct a thorough investigation. "I have concluded after very serious and agonizing consideration, that the initiation at this time of an independent investigation may be counterproductive to swiftly obtaining all of the facts involved in the incidents."[20]

PICKETS, PROTESTS, AND ECONOMIC BOYCOTTS

At the following city council meeting, about fifty protestors presented a proposal that would establish a civilian review board to govern the police department. The protestors addressed the council for more than an hour with threats of racial strife. "If something isn't done about police brutality, there will be no more Super Bowls in New Orleans," said one unidentified protestor. Michael Williams, chairman of Community Action Now (CAN), said black residents were tired of coming to city council meetings without any results. "We are coming to the council for the one-thousandth time to express concern about police brutality." He continued, "We feel the council has dealt only in rhetoric. The resignation of Chief Parsons was only a ploy to dilute the anger of the community about the problems of police brutality." William Quigley, an attorney, outlined the proposed civilian-run police department. "The Police Administration Commission is a citizens board, with representatives elected from each neighborhood in New Orleans." Quigley felt that a civilian-controlled department was an absolutely "necessity because the present system is obviously not working. Police brutality has been an issue for years, yet no real changes have taken place within the present police structure to combat police brutality."[21]

The threat of an economic boycott reemerged after a mass meeting at St. Mark's Community Center, where several hundred persons participated in the People's Conference on Police Brutality. The demonstrators called for a citizens board to administer the NOPD and it demanded that Morial fire acting Police Superintendent Henry Morris. Although the earlier threat of a boycott was called off, Bush stated that the boycott was back on since "Morial hasn't done anything since Parsons's resignation." Bush announced that the boycott would begin on Saturday, December 20, and continue until the Super Bowl on January 25. The boycott plans were finalized and announced days later by Kalamu Ya Salaam, head of the Police Brutality Committee (PBC), at a press conference at the Liberty Monument. Salaam predicted that a 5 percent loss in profits would stir merchants to get involved in the fight for equal police protection. "Canal Street is the economic backbone of this city and black folks keep it going," he said. "It's time to send the police a message. It's time to tell the people with money that there will be no peace and no profits for the rich while there is police brutality for the poor." He then called upon the black community "to double your money this Christmas by folding it over and keeping it in your pocket. Call the stores and tell them that you're not shopping because of police brutality. We're going to put some pain on them."[22]

On Saturday, December 26, 1980, approximately a hundred picketers marched in front of Canal Street stores to protest police brutality. "We're asking people not to go in these stores, and the weather is helping us keep people away," said Salaam. "These businesses exert power over the police department and the city council. If we can just cause a 5 percent decrease we can do something." Local merchants, however, did not understand why they were being picketed. "I don't understand what they're doing. They should be in front of the police station, or they should picket Algiers businesses," said one store manager. Despite the presence of picketers, the first day of boycotting appeared not to have much effect on business. The picketers were out once again a week later, but once again the protest appeared to have little impact on business. However, Salaam was still confident that they would be successful. "The thing the store owners have to contend with is that they're saying it's not hurting. But they're saying that believing that we're going to leave after the first of the year, when in fact we'll be here through Easter if necessary." Ironically, many of the big chain stores on Canal reported no loss of business while black street vendors reported a serious loss of business. The picketing continued into the new year.[23]

While the Police Brutality Committee continued its selective buying campaign, it came under attack as a communist-front organization. Matt Miller of the Citizen's Committee on Crime and Communism distributed leaflets, arguing that the PBC "is doing the work of communists." Miller argued that the Canal Street boycott and other efforts of the PBC were laying the foundation or a communist takeover, "whether they know it or not." Miller went on to state that "in every country that falls to communism, agitators have destroyed the effectiveness of the local police by accusing the police of brutality, and because of this, demanding a civilian review board." Salaam found Miller's remarks quite humorous.[24]

The ineffectiveness of the economic boycott did not temper the enthusiasm of anti-brutality activists. In February 1981, the Liberation League held a picket outside the home of Morial to protest comments the mayor made during a speech at the University of New Orleans claiming that the League was trying to ruin his administration and using the poor people of New Or-

leans in a sinister manner. "To the contrary, we say it is Morial and his political cronies, along with District Attorney Harry Connick and the NOPD
who are the sinister elements in the community," stated Malcolm Suber.
The League wanted Morial to fire the officers and release the names of the
officers involved and stop an alleged "cover up of the facts about the execu-
tions and beatings in Algiers." Morial had previously refused to do so by
claiming that it would violate the rights of police officers. But, as Suber suggested, Morial feared alienating the NOPD. "He just will not do this because
he weighs it as a political risk among his white supporters. Well, the Liberation League is not concerned about the mayor's race, what we are concerned
about is justice—we want to see those killer cops indicted and the families
of the victims compensated for their losses."[25] The Police Brutality Committee echoed many of the League's sentiments and started a petition in an
effort to get Morial to release the names, badge numbers, and photographs
of the officers involved. The committee also wanted Morial to use his "powers to appoint, remove, and reorganize the department to immediately deal
with the problem of police brutality." When Morial still refused to release
the names or take action against the officers, he was labeled an "Uncle Tom"
and a "yellow bastard." Morial's refusal to deal strongly with the NOPD convinced many African Americans that even as they gained political power
they were yet powerless to reform the city's police department.[26]

The race-based attacks upon Morial by activists such as Galmon, Rouselle, and Salaam illustrated the class divisions with the New Orleans
black community. The black middle class did not engage in protest during
the Morial era for several reasons. First, they had confidence that Morial
would exercise the power of his office to reform the NOPD. Second, many
of them were in favor of tough law enforcement to protect themselves and
their property from black criminals. Finally, the black middle class did not
have the same experience with the NOPD as members of the black poor.
While activists such as Salaam and others were considered a "nuisance" to
the more respectable elements in the black community, they nonetheless
stayed the course in the fight for fair police protection.

As the grand jury prepared to release its findings on the Algiers incident,
the Police Brutality Committee made it clear that anything less than felony
indictments for the officers involved would be a "total travesty of justice." It
was prepared for mass demonstrations if the officers were cleared. "Let me
make this clear now," said Bill Rouselle. "We're not calling for a riot. We're
only calling for organized protest for justice." Rouselle then mentioned that

the "riot drills" the NOPD had begun would not keep them from protesting. "The police seem to be preparing for a riot with their apparent riot drills. With this preparation they are trying to intimidate the community. It is not our objective to riot and be violent. Our objective is to see that justice is done and part of that objective is to protest and demonstrate." The NOPD's riot preparations indicated to Rouselle and others that the grand jury would find the officers innocent.[27]

On Monday, May 11, 1981, the Orleans Parish grand jury cleared thirteen members of the NOPD in the Algiers shootings and related acts of brutality. But Harry Connick, the district attorney, knew that the officers had engaged in brutal misconduct. "It is my conviction that fundamental constitutional rights were violated and that some members of the police department were responsible for them. It is regrettable that the investigation and protracted grand jury hearings failed to turn up sufficient evidence to justify criminal prosecution of these violations." The grand jury, composed of seven whites and five blacks, met twenty-three times and questioned eighty-eight witnesses throughout the five-month long investigation. The black community responded with disgust and outrage at the decision. Reverend Donald Crockett of Algiers stated that he was not satisfied with the lack of indictments, but he and other community leaders urged calm. "I, as a leader and pastor, want to say to the people in Algiers we want to stay calm. We don't want another Miami, Detroit, or Los Angeles." He then implored the community to "please be calm and live by the decision." Shirley Porter of the New Orleans NAACP stated, "We are hoping that the people will stay calm and bear with us." Morial echoed similar sentiments. "Regardless of what one's personal opinions may be on the outcome of the Orleans Parish Grand Jury investigation, we must respect our system of law. While no system can be perfect, our system has proven to be one of the strongest and most important elements of the foundation upon which our nation has been built."[28]

The Concerned Citizens of Algiers sent a strong letter of protest to Morial, Connick, and U.S. Attorney John Volz. The letter opened by stating that they were extremely dissatisfied with results of the investigation. "We know that the Administrations of the City of New Orleans and the New Orleans Police Department are primarily responsible for the evidence submitted to the State Grand Jury. Therefore, we hold the City Administration directly responsible for the faulty findings of the State Grand Jury." It further argued that the killings committed by the officers in Algiers were "premeditated murder," and that Chief Parsons allowed police officers to act as a police assassination squad. The letter closed by blaming Connick, Morial, and Parsons for the tragedy.[29]

Kalamu ya Salaam and members of the PBC responded by assembling the next day at police headquarters and demanding justice. "The reason the police have locked doors is because they don't have an explanation about what's going on. They don't feel they have to give us an explanation. We did not intend to be out here a long time. The only reason we came is to make sure that the city understands that we are displeased with the so-called findings of the grand jury." He then mentioned that Connick was "derelict in his duty" if he knew some misconduct occurred but failed to take action. He then warned NOPD officials about what was to come. "What we want to make clear is that this is the last time that we're going to come to Connick and the police in this manner. You will see us on other occasions or you will see the worst that we do. There will be no more dialogue. It is over. It is over. There will be no more peace and this we promise you. Goodbye." The crowd of about fifty demonstrators yelled. The meeting closed with Salaam calling for a mass demonstration in Algiers later that week.[30]

Although Rose Loving and the Algiers–Fischer Community Organizations board of directors came out against the PBC-sponsored rally, it was nonetheless a success. Loving did not support the rally because she felt, along with many others, that Salaam was just an opportunist and that he did not represent the best interests of the black community. "This rally is being organized by persons who do not live in our community and by persons who did not contact anyone in our community on planning the rally," said Charles Rice, vice-president. "We see no real purpose of holding a rally near the Fischer high-rise where our senior citizens are trying to live a peaceful life." More than two hundred demonstrators participated in the march through Algiers, chanting, "We're fired up—we won't take no more." The marchers stopped in front of the small white cottage where James Billy had been killed and Salaam told the crowd, "This was the house where an assassination squad came in and knocked the door down and murdered three people." In addition to making chants against the NOPD, Connick, and Morial, the marchers also chanted, "Down with the police and down with Rose Loving." However, march leaders said that they would take their demonstrations to area churches and "meet Rose Loving in church."[31]

Later that week the Police Brutality Committee held a "Unity Banquet" to ease the tensions between the Algiers–Fischer Community Organization and the more militant Police Brutality Committee. Reverend Benjamin Chavis was the keynote speaker and he talked about the need for unity to effectively fight police brutality. Chavis stated that the "black response to police brutality must not be divided" along class lines, "with one person saying one thing, another saying something else." Chavis's comments were appropriate in the context of the Loving–Salaam feud. Loving believed that Salaam had no right to come into their community and launch a protest without their approval. Conversely, Salaam did not respect Loving's leadership and he was certain that she was too moderate to spearhead the drive for justice in Algiers. Chavis then spoke of the need for the black middle class to get involved with the grassroots movement across the city of New Orleans. Chavis energized the crowd to such an extent that evening that weeks later, Michael Williams of Community Action Now (CAN) padlocked the front door of the Patrolmen's Association of New Orleans (PANO) meeting hall where more than two hundred officers were meeting inside. Williams was soon roughed up and arrested.[32]

In mid-June members of the PBC took their protest to city hall, where they staged a fifty-six-hour sit-in in the mayor's office. The siege began at 11:00 a.m. on Thursday, June 18, 1981, when Salaam and eight others attempted to meet with Morial. Wearing signs around their necks, the protestors entered the waiting area next to the mayor's office and told the receptionist they were there to see the mayor. When the receptionist activated the security door to tell a mayor's aide that the demonstrators were waiting, "the protestors rushed the door and before she could do anything they were headed to the mayor's office." Morial told reporters that the group "forcibly pushed their way" into his office and assaulted the receptionist on duty. While Salaam and the others were inside occupying the mayor's office, Tayari Salaam, his wife, was outside with a megaphone shouting, "This is a blow the whistle on Dutch Morial campaign." She then stated that the action was taken against the mayor because he had not taken the moral responsibility and authority to deal with the problem of police brutality. She then made three demands of the mayor: (1) that he fire all of the officers involved in the Algiers shootings; (2) that he release the photographs and names of the officers involved in the Algiers killings; (3) and that he require all officers involved in the shootings to take lie detector tests. For the most part the sit-in was peaceful and quiet throughout the day, although city officials shut off the air-conditioning and locked the bathroom door. The door was later opened when protestors starting using a garbage can as a toilet.[33]

Later that evening, Morial gave his first remarks on the sit-in. He stated that the demonstrators were looking for a violent confrontation. "They clearly seek a confrontation. We will not accommodate them. They may stay in the office as long as they cause no threat to any other person or endanger the safety of any other persons." The mayor also noted that "if they are truly interested in meeting for a discussion, they can simply make a request. Rather, they want to create divisiveness in our community and obviously they have a strong desire to discredit our great city and all of its fine citizens of all races."[34]

On the second day of the protest, a group of black ministers attempted to persuade the protestors to leave the mayor's office. However, only one protestor, Troy Abery, left after his mother saw him on television, went to city hall, and told him to "Get your ass back home." Morial finally responded to the three demands point by point. He stated that he could not fire any member of the police department without a hearing and that he could not release photographs of the officers because of the threat of harassment and possible retaliation. He then went on to mention that he did not know the legality of a lie detector test.[35]

On Saturday the protestors left city hall during a CAN-PBC sponsored rally attended by more than two hundred people. Once the march reached city hall, the marchers positioned themselves where the protestors could see them. The protestors then emerged from the mayor's office. "Do not misunderstand us. We have achieved our primary objective of dramatizing the issue of police brutality in New Orleans. However, we are not leaving the struggle. We will continue to disrupt the status quo until justice is done. There will be no peace until there is justice and an end to police brutality. We are not afraid. We will continue to struggle. You may think it's the end, but it's just the beginning," the protestors said in a prepared statement. Morial was gloating at the end of the protest. "None of the demands were met. My reply speaks for itself." Morial then mentioned that the protestors had "no interest" in meaningful reforms within the NOPD." Morial's middle-class black supporters were elated that the sit-in was over. One of the ministers who attempted to end the protest on the second day stated that his group "did not agree with the method used, the sit-in. We question the judgment. We stand by the mayor all the way but we admit there is police brutality."[36]

Days later the United Front for Justice (UFJ) held a mass rally in memory of those killed in the Algiers massacre. The rally was held in response to a Dutch Morial fundraising affair being held that same evening. Flyers read, "Will You Take Part In the 'Dutch Fun Affair'? Or Will You Take Part In The Struggle For Justice?" The mailing then asked "decent people" not to attend the mayor's event, because the nights in Algiers were not "nights of enjoyment; they were nights that the victims would have preferred to miss." The appeal closed by stating that for people concerned about racial justice it "is a time of rededication, commitment and resolve, not a time for political fun."[37]

Because the various anti-brutality organizations kept the Algiers tragedy in the spotlight through a series of organized protests, marches, and sit-ins, a federal grand jury indicted seven police officers for their involvement in the shootings: John Mckenzie, Stephen Reboul, Dale Bonura, Stephen Farrar, Ronald Brink, Thomas Woodall, and Richard LeBlanc. They were not indicted for murder but for civil rights violations. Each officer faced a maximum prison time of ten years. Rose Loving summed up the feelings of many in the black community when she remarked: "I am relieved. I think the indictment will bring a sigh of relief to the Algiers–Fischer community." Salaam was happy but not satisfied. He stated once again that Connick should bring state charges against the officers. The indicted officers were immediately removed from their regular assignments, but they remained on active duty. As expected, all seven officers pled not guilty and a trial date was set for September 8.[38]

However, U.S. District Judge Adrian Duplantier threw out the indictments, alleging that the prosecution was overzealous in its investigation into the shootings. In blunt language, the judge ruled that the prosecutors had pressured the grand jury into a decision. Melvin Bush was disappointed that "one man can make such a far-reaching decision in such a short time, where the Justice Department took months of research to prepare the case." The following day the Liberation League held a midday protest at the federal courthouse, which drew jeers from passing motorists. League spokesman Malcolm Suber was angry at the decision. "This court system is completely rotten just like the rest of the politicians and everything in this society. Working-class people and poor people have to organize themselves so we can become power brokers in this society so that killer cops and corrupt politicians like Duplantier won't be able to render these decisions that affect our well-being." Days later Duplantier received a death threat. Rouselle was equally angry. "The system ain't working for us. We're going after Connick and that's the bottom line. This stuff has just gotten to the point where we certainly can't expect the courts to do it through any reasonable, traditional means." Rouselle stated that the group would seek Connick's and Morial's recall as a way to hold them accountable for the police killings in Algiers.[39]

The officers were later re-indicted and in 1984 three of them were found guilty of civil rights violations. Officers John Mckenzie, Dale Bonura, and Stephen Farrar were sentenced to mandatory five year-prison terms. In 1986, the city of New Orleans paid out more than $2.8 million in lawsuit settlements to the victims of the Algiers shootings.[40]

The protests launched by anti-brutality activists in the aftermath of the Algiers shootings helped secure passage of several important reforms within the NOPD. The resignation of Parsons and the conviction of the officers involved in the Algiers incident gave anti-brutality activists and their organizations a degree of credibility in the eyes of the black middle class. While the conservative elements in the black community frowned upon their methods of protest, they could not argue with the results. After a hostile first term that included marches, sit-ins, economic boycotts, and volatile town hall meetings from his main constituency, black voters, Morial was looking forward to a more peaceful second term in office.

THE REELECTION OF DUTCH MORIAL
In the spring of 1981, Morial coasted to reelection with 53 percent of the vote as he defeated Ron Faucheux, a white candidate. In the primary both SOUL and COUP supported State Senator William Jefferson, who received an embarrassingly low 7 percent of the vote. Once Morial was reelected, both SOUL and COUP would see their influence in local politics decline. With the election now behind him, Morial decided to address the long-standing concerns of black officers within the NOPD.[41]

Shortly after his reelection, Morial attempted to negotiate a settlement in the eight-year-old police discrimination lawsuit filed by the Black Organization of Police in 1973. Although Morial had been in office since 1978, there had been virtually no change in the makeup of NOPD supervisors. Only 5 of the department's 198 sergeants were black and only 2 of its 66 lieutenants. Among the city's 23 police captains, none were African American. Among non-ranking officers, approximately 230 of the city's 1,000 officers were black. These figures were very disturbing in a city that was roughly 60 percent African American. In a settlement between the city's Chief Administrative Officer Reynard Rochon, Civil Service Commission Chairman Wood Brown, III, and O. Peter Sherwood, who was representing the black officers, they agreed that forty-four black officers would be promoted. Thirty would be promoted to the rank of sergeant, twelve to the rank of lieutenant, and two to the rank of captain. The agreement also proposed to accelerate black promotions until they reached "a significant percentage throughout each rank." The agreement would mean that no white officer could expect a promotion for years. The city would also pay $150,000 to black officers in back pay. The agreement was tentative because Brown was not completely sold on the settlement. When word reached the white rank-and-file of the proposed agreement, they immediately claimed reverse discrimination. Officer Richard Cassanova, who represented seventeen white officers in line for a promotion, stated that "discrimination is wrong—period. But you don't resolve an injustice against one person by an injustice against another." PANO attorney Sidney Bach remarked that the settlement would bypass white officers on the promotion list although they scored highest on the latest promotion test.[42]

When the settlement was announced, city leaders agreed to promote the forty-four black officers but they also agreed to promote eight white officers whose promotions to sergeant had been frozen for a year. "We were trying to keep this suit from resulting in reverse discrimination," Brown said. "This agreement does not take anything away from white officers. Police union President Ronald Cannatella claimed that the settlement was made to enhance Morial's support among black voters. "This case has been pending since 1973. Now, on the eve of an election, it surfaces again with a settlement . . . what do you think?" Cannatella also argued that the settlement would place unqualified police officers on the city streets and in supervisory positions. He then got to his real issue. "From listening to the proposals I heard in court, we won't be seeing any whites promoted for a long time." Dozens of black and white officers heard the terms of the settlement in court and their reactions were predictable. Blacks filed out of the courtroom smiling and saying, "amen," while white officers left bitterly. As expected, the settlement created more friction within the NOPD and Chief Morris was being blamed for assisting the city in drafting the settlement. However, he told officers that he had nothing to do with the agreement. "I would like to take this opportunity to advise each and every one of you that the Police Department did not in any way participate in negotiations leading to this proposed settlement."[43]

The settlement also included other provisions, sixteen in all, such as revising the test for promotions; recruiting more intensely in the black community, removing the IQ test as a condition for employment, placing at least four black officers on the academy staff as instructors, establishing a biracial panel of officers to help cadets having problems in the academy, and reducing the amount of experience necessary to be promoted. However, to the surprise of city officials, some black officers who initially filed the suit found the settlement unsatisfactory because it created too many loopholes. Stanley Hayes stated that the settlement called for the city to promote black officers "in a timely manner. What is a 'timely manner' it could be years before this is done." He also stated that the compensation package was not enough to pay back those officers who, because of racism, did not receive higher wages. However, for the majority of black officers on the force the settlement was adequate. Officer Israel Fields was confident that with more blacks in supervisory positions, "black officers will enhance the understanding or sensitivity between the whole police department and the common man on the street."[44]

Predictably, three white officers filed suit the next day in civil district court to stop the settlement on the grounds that the Civil Service Commission did not adequately represent them. Judge Revius Ortique, the only black judge on the bench, issued a temporary restraining order preventing the settlement from becoming law. Days later, Ortique dismissed the order after the white officers took their suit to the U.S. 5th circuit court of appeals.[45]

After a year-long legal circus that included numerous appeals, motions, and restraining orders, the city and the black officers who initially filed the suit reached an agreement that was strikingly similar to the original 1981 agreement. The only difference was that the consent decree included a one-to-one promotional scheme that called for the promotion of one black policeman for every white officer until blacks made up one-half of all upper ranks in the department. At a ceremony to promote the officers after the agreement was signed, Morial stated that the city "should have a department that's reflective of the community." Twenty-six-year NOPD veteran Rinal Martin was appointed to captain under the agreement and he understood the obligation he and other top-ranking black officers had to the black community. "I think the black sergeants to a certain extent will be more responsive to the community, just through their innate empathy with them."[46]

Expectedly, white officers were angry over the NOPD affirmative action mandate and the legislation made some feel as if they had no future within the NOPD. Consequently, many officers began to look for jobs either in the surrounding suburbs, with the Orleans Parish sheriff's office, or with the Louisiana state police. In their eyes the NOPD was increasingly becoming a place where white police officers were not wanted. The creation of the city's first civilian review agency served as further proof, to them, that they needed to look elsewhere for work.

THE OFFICE OF MUNICIPAL INVESTIGATION

In the aftermath of the Algiers tragedy, the New Orleans city council decided to hold public hearings on the proposal for civilian review of the NOPD. Prior to the hearing, Bill Rouselle stated that the PBC would not compromise the proposal for community control. The much anticipated meeting quickly turned unruly. The meeting began with a shouting match between Councilman Giarrusso, who presided over the hearing, and Salaam and other PBC members. After Giarrusso opened the session, laid the ground rules, and read the list of speakers, he was interrupted by Salaam, who yelled, "Point of order." Although Giarrusso recognized him, the councilman also told several other PBC members to sit down. "I am recognizing you, Mr. Salaam. You can make your point of order at this time, but I must ask that those other people sit down. You have no point of order at this time, but I'm recognizing you as a courtesy," Giarrusso stated. Salaam shouted back as he walked toward the exit of council chambers, "You're a city councilman and you're telling me, a citizen, that I have no right to speak and that you've recognized me as a courtesy. Man, you're no dictator. I'm trying to make a point of order, so that we can have a meaningful dialogue and you tell me I have no right to speak." Giarrusso gaveled the crowd to order and told Salaam and other members of the PBC who remained standing that if they did not "behave yourself," they would be ejected from the meeting by the scores of police officers that were in attendance. Michael Williams, a PBC member, was angered by Giarrusso's words, "behave yourself." He walked up to the podium and yelled, "You behave yourself. I'm a man and you don't tell me what to do. I'm not afraid of you or any of those policemen. Where do you come from, telling us to behave." After a few minutes of verbal exchanges, Giarrusso called for a ten-minute recess. The hearings resumed with members of the PBC outlining their proposal and members of the Fraternal Order of Police stating why they opposed the formation of a civilian-run department. The meeting ended abruptly when Williams denounced the newly freed American hostages in Iran by saying, "They should have stayed there forever." As a result of the volatile hearings,

Council President Giarrusso stated that there would not be any more hearings on police brutality. "I am utterly opposed to any type of civilian review board and I'm not going to have any more hearings on police brutality." Giarrusso mentioned that since 1979 the council had three public hearings and all of them were abusive toward city officials. "After three times of getting your head kicked in, it should be enough to prevent it from getting kicked in a fourth time," he said.[47]

Morial soon introduced legislation calling for the creation of the office of municipal investigation (OMI), which would investigate misconduct within city government, including the NOPD. Morial stated that it was important that an investigative office be set up "to give citizens a place where they can go, free and unfettered, with the belief that their complaints are going to be heard fairly." He acknowledged that there had been a decline of confidence in the NOPD and that it was imperative that the city do something to restore that confidence. The OMI would investigate alleged misconduct but it would not have the authority to arrest people. It would be established within the chief administrative office and would be composed of civil service workers. "We are determined to stamp out misconduct in the New Orleans Police Department," Morial said. Community leaders embraced the proposal and city council passed the legislation to create the OMI.[48]

If Morial needed any evidence to justify the creation of the OMI, then the involvement of Officer Stephen Reboul in the Algiers shootings exposed the limitations and ineffectiveness of the IAD in handling complaints against officers. Prior to the Algiers killings, Reboul had been the subject of thirteen complaints regarding unnecessary use of force from citizens between 1975 and 1980. Reboul had also been the subject of a number of civil lawsuits that forced the city to pay out $814,000 in civil damages to his victims. His remaining on the force in the face of such a long record of complaints and jury damages testifies to the IAD's inability to properly police its officers.[49]

Like other similar police review bodies throughout the country, the OMI was to be staffed by full-time civilians, who would investigate complaints against all city employees, not just police officers. The OMI would review complaints and reports, and make recommendations to the chief administrative officer. The New Orleans OMI was one of the most independent citizen review boards in the country upon its creation and this was perhaps Morial's greatest accomplishment in the area of police reform.

In November 1981, thirty-two-year-old Morris Reed, an African American, was selected by Morial to head the newly created office of municipal investigation. The New Orleans native was well equipped to handle the demanding responsibilities of the position since he had been a former police officer and then a Drug Enforcement Agency agent while pursuing a law degree at Loyola University. Upon graduating, he became an assistant U.S. attorney, spearheading the investigation and subsequent indictment and conviction of the officers involved in the Algiers shootings. Although Morial conducted a national search for the position, everyone in Morial's inner circle knew that Reed was the person for the job. His experience as a former officer and his ability to go after the officers in the Algiers incident gave him a set of unique qualifications. In an effort to make the job more appealing to Reed, Morial convinced the city council to raise the starting salary of the unit's first director from $28,000 to $38,000 so that the young attorney would not have to absorb a pay cut in his new position.[50]

Raymond Reed, no relation to Morris, was selected for the number two position in the OMI. The fourteen-year NOPD veteran and president of the Black Organization of Police was attractive to the mayor because of his extensive network of street contacts. "I've been around a while, and I know a lot of people. People call me all the time. I don't call them informers. I call them concerned citizens," he said. With an external review agency staffed by former police officers Morial was certain that OMI would effectively crack down and thoroughly investigate brutality complaints since they were familiar with the culture, habits, and practices of the NOPD.[51]

Armed with solid reputations and a much-needed degree of credibility, Morris Reed and Raymond Reed were ready to provide a degree of oversight never seen before within the halls of the NOPD. But the rank-and-file who opposed the creation of the OMI raised their level of indignation at the unit when they learned that Morris Reed would be running the unit with the assistance of Raymond Reed. Both Reeds were considered sellouts to the masses within the NOPD—Morris because he led the investigation after the Algiers killings, and Raymond because he convinced black officers to cooperate with the same federal investigation. Thus, at its inception the OMI was considered an anti-police organization and a struggle between the NOPD and the new unit began immediately.

Less than three months into his new position, Raymond Reed was illegally arrested on drunken driving charges and also charged with reckless driving and attempting to intimidate a police officer. According to police reports Reed was stopped on Interstate 10 and after being issued several traffic citations, he told the arresting officers that they could not arrest him because of his position with the OMI. Reed was later cleared of all charges when it was revealed that his blood alcohol level was .024 percent, far below the legal limit of .100 percent. Nonetheless, the NOPD had made a statement in their unlawful arrest of Raymond Reed.[52]

During OMI's first year in operation, Morris Reed set up a twenty-four-hour telephone complaint line, distributed brochures across the city about the new agency, and made numerous radio and television appearances to acquaint citizens with the functions of his office. These steps were important because in other cities that had similar review bodies citizens were not even aware of the agency while some were unsure how to file complaints. The telephone hotline was also a progressive step since citizens often felt threatened walking into an office and filing a complaint against a police officer.[53]

Although the majority of police officers fought hard against the OMI, the agency was not as powerful as they had believed. It had no arrest or subpoena powers, had no power to enforce its own conclusions or to recommend disciplinary action, and was understaffed and lacking in basic equipment such as automobiles and a radio communications system. However, several policies and procedures of the OMI did feed the perception that

TABLE 4.

Civilian Review Board Type Agencies in Selected Cities and the Year Established

CITY	AGENCY	YEAR ESTABLISHED
Atlanta	Civilian Review Board	1996
Boston	Community Affairs Board	1997
Chicago	Office of Professional Standards	1974
Indianapolis	Citizens Police Complaint Office	1989
Minneapolis	Civilian Police Review Authority	1990
New Orleans	**Office of Municipal Investigation**	**1981**
New York*	Civilian Complaint Review Board	1992
Philadelphia	Police Advisory Commission	1993
Portland	Police Internal Investigations Auditing Committee	1982
San Francisco	Office of Citizen Complaints	1982
Washington, D.C.	Civilian Complaint Review Board	1982

* The New York Police Department had several internal review boards but they were still under the authority of police officers.

they were anti-police. The first controversial policy dealt with the agency's role in investigating police shootings. Morris Reed told homicide detectives to wait for OMI agents before interviewing police officers involved in fatal shootings or whenever police officers discharged their weapons. Once OMI agents arrived at the scene, they would then monitor and record the police interrogation. Officers resisted this intrusion into their territory and one officer believed that it created a morale problem for detectives. "I guess I can explain it to you like this. A feeling of respectability is important to a detective, and if you do something to them that leaves them feeling you don't trust them, then it ruins the whole squad, and makes them lose their drive and incentive," said one detective. Other officers wanted to know, "From where do they get the authority to investigate police shootings. Are they law enforcement officers?" Another source of frustration regarding the OMI was its reopening of completed internal police investigations in which officers had been cleared. This policy fed the idea that the OMI was on a witch hunt to discipline police officers.[54]

The debate over OMI'S involvement in shooting investigations and reopening internal investigations was an important one. Knowing the history of the NOPD and the shameful ranking of New Orleans as the number one place in the country for police killings, Morris Reed was adamant about investigating shootings involving a police officer. But because of constant pressure from officers, Morial later revised the controversial investigation policy by only allowing OMI agents to observe the preliminary investigation by the IAD.[55]

One particular case involving two white police officers was often mentioned as evidence of the anti-police nature of the OMI. On the night of September 10, 1982, Officer Robert Hecker and his partner Joe Maumus were arrested and booked with possession of cocaine on the words of two women who said they had sex and cocaine with the officers. Maumus was arrested while having sex with one of the women in a downtown hotel during his break and Hecker was arrested a block from the hotel by Raymond Reed. Hecker alleged that after Reed ordered him off his horse while he was on mounted patrol, he and two other OMI agents detained him and searched his horse trailer and later his apartment, where they eventually found a vial of cocaine. Hecker claimed that when he was taken to central lock-up he was not allowed to call an attorney and was forced—under the threat of losing his job—to give a statement to OMI investigators. Maumus told authorities that when he was arrested at the hotel he was handcuffed and left sitting nude in a chair for several hours. Both officers were later cleared of any wrongdoing by the district attorney and in a strange turn of events the district attorney launched an investigation against the OMI for false imprisonment of Hecker. In a letter sent to the city council, police officers expressed their displeasure with the OMI. The letter accused OMI and its investigators of having "misrepresented themselves and their intentions, used arrest powers they don't possess, intimidated officers, civilians and even lied." In response to the complaints about his agency, Morris Reed said that "some of the investigative techniques used by our office are foreign to members of the NOPD."[56]

Statistics from its first year show that despite its anti-police reputation, the OMI conducted its business in a fair and impartial fashion. Of the 449 investigated complaints, 439 were made against police officers. From that number Reed recommended suspension for twenty-six officers and termination for twelve. Sixty-eight percent of all officers investigated were exonerated while the majority of those found guilty were only lightly reprimanded or warned.[57]

When the OMI came up for refunding, black officers were initially hesitant about supporting the temporary agency because many of them felt that it singled out police misconduct and not wrongdoing on the part of other city workers. "We support OMI as long as it's an investigative unit. We realize it does not mete out justice or disciplinary action. We also feel the office has functioned within its guidelines and has been fair and impartial in its investigation," said the BOP's Acting President Yvonne Bechet. Other black officers felt that the OMI was fair. "If you did it, they got you. If you didn't you'll be cleared."[58]

During the city council hearings on whether or not to continue OMI, black citizens packed the council chambers to argue on behalf of the OMI. For many anti-brutality activists and concerned black citizens, the OMI was seen as a continuation of the civil rights movement. After suffering from years of unfair police protection and brutality, they viewed the OMI as an agency that would protect them from rogue cops and they were not about to tolerate the discontinuation of a unit that had been created in the aftermath of the Algiers killings. During the hearings, many supporters mentioned that OMI had saved the city millions in lawsuits because the incidents of police brutality were decreasing. Louisiana Service Coalition President Ted Quant summed up the feelings of many when he remarked, "Before OMI came into existence, New Orleans had the highest number of police brutality complaints in the country."[59]

Despite its apparent success as an oversight unit, OMI came under

attack in March 1983 when white police officers created an uproar by arguing that investigators overstepped their authority and created mis-
trust and hostility between some officers and police officials. Councilman
Bryan Wagner stated that OMI should be disbanded because it duplicated
the work that could be done by the NOPD's internal affairs division. "All
we've done is add another bureaucratic layer at city hall." Chief Administrative Officer Reynard Rochon was clear why OMI needed to become permanent. "We don't feel that a department, be it the police department, streets,
sanitation—whatever—can objectively investigate complaints against its
own employees." He then went on to mention the fear many citizens had
of reporting police brutality under the old system. "They also felt an intimidation when they went into a police department unit to lodge a complaint
about a policeman to a guy who came with a badge on and a uniform and
a big old pistol saying, 'Can I help you?'" Rochon said that he was "bewildered" by the uproar over OMI. "We have received essentially no citizen
complaints." OMI Director Morris Reed argued that OMI kept city employees honest and that it helped reduce the number of lawsuits against the
NOPD. The debate over the future of OMI was brought upon by a June 1,
1983, deadline whereby the unit would be either disbanded or continued on
a temporary basis.[60]

Tempers flared in April at a special city council hearing over whether or
not to continue funding the two-year-old OMI. "The police department has
always cleaned its own house. Look at the records, look at the facts and abolish OMI," said Cannatella, head of PANO. Then, another PANO leader got to
the real reason why they wanted to disband OMI. "What we're looking at is a
political animal. We feel OMI is a strong arm of the mayor's office," said Officer John Marie. Vincent Brown of the NAACP stated that the original reason "for OMI is still valid, to make city government accountable to the people." More than 325 people, including dozens of uniformed police, filled the
chambers. Stephen Reboul, one of the acquitted defendants in the Algiers
killings, told the council that "OMI takes the complainant over the police officer so many times that policemen don't trust OMI as an investigative out-
let." As Reboul got up to speak, the crowd chanted, "Murderer, murderer."
Throughout the evening more than a hundred speakers took the podium to
express their opinion. The meeting did not end until after 1:00 a.m. The city
council later voted to continue funding the OMI on a temporary basis.[61]

After the city council voted to extend the life of the OMI until the end of
1983, Morris Reed made an appeal for OMI investigators to carry weapons

since their job exposed them to danger. "Agents must go into high-crime areas at all hours of the day and night to conduct interviews and they need guns for their protection," he said. Although Reed did not mention it at the city council meeting, he also wanted guns so that his agents could protect themselves from vengeful cops. Reed also asked the city council for a special badge since NOPD officers often harassed OMI agents for wearing a badge similar to the department's crescent and star badge.[62]

During the city council hearings in the fall of 1983 over whether to make OMI a permanent agency, Mayor Morial established a thirty-four-person OMI rewrite committee to make recommendations about the controversial agency. Among its many recommendations included an OMI policies and procedures manual so that everyone would be clear about their rights and the rights of the OMI. Part of the problem between the OMI and the NOPD was that officers and OMI agents were not clear on jurisdictional issues. This manual would establish guidelines, procedures, and rights. OMI regulations were further tightened after the city council voted six to one to make it a permanent city agency. The new rules called for OMI agents to investigate all police shootings, allow OMI investigators to carry guns, give the OMI seven months to solve a case, and give city department heads thirty days to take action on OMI recommendations; and publish monthly reports. Morris Reed had no problem with the guidelines. "We can operate under the standards set by council," he explained.[63]

The resistance by white officers toward the continuation of the OMI means that the agency was somewhat effective in providing oversight. If it was simply a departmental rubber-stamping unit, like the historic internal affairs division, then there would have been little outrage over its existence. Interestingly, although the OMI exonerated 68 percent of all officers during its first year, there was still considerable outrage from the rank-and-file. Much of the criticism toward the OMI was rooted in the culture of big-city police departments that feel that ordinary citizens are incapable of understanding the unique mission of the police.

The OMI and Mayor Dutch Morial were soon thrust into a major police scandal when police officers killed eighteen-year-old Gerrard Glover in August 1983. Around 12:45 a.m. on Wednesday, August 31, 1983, Glover was shot and killed by Officer Stephen Rosiere while he was riding on the back of his cousin's motorcycle as police were chasing them for a traffic violation on the Palmetto overpass. During the two-mile chase that reached speeds of ninety miles per hour at some points, Rosiere fired several shots at the

motorcycle, killing Glover. Immediately after the shooting, Officers Rosiere and Fred McFarlane told authorities that the motorist fired shots at
them during the chase. As evidence, they claimed to have found a 9 milli-
meter automatic weapon in the street next to the body of Glover. Glover's
cousin, Rayney Brooks, the operator of the motorcycle, was arrested on two
counts of attempted murder of a police officer. After the shooting, Glover's
mother, Catherine Peacock, a fellow NOPD officer, was not notified about
her son's death until the following day even though his driver's license was
in his pocket. NOPD officials stated that Glover had no identification.[64]

Once NOPD and OMI officials began investigating the shootings, they
discovered that the alleged gun found in the street was a "rusty .25 caliber automatic with no bullet clip." When questioned about this, the officers
changed their story to say that they heard pops and saw flashes of light
they thought to be bullets. They then admitted that the gun they planted in
the street belonged to Rosiere and was put there by him after they saw that
Glover was unarmed. Brooks was immediately released from prison. The officers were suspended immediately for lying; the black community wanted
them arrested and indicted for murder. At a Liberation League–sponsored
rally, days after the story broke, two dozen demonstrators carried signs in
front of Connick's office. "We're saying there's enough information that
Connick should arrest them for murder. I'm sure we're not going to be satisfied with the grand jury." Throughout the protest demonstrators chanted,
"Killer cops, must go. Harry Connick must go. Police terror must go. Whitewash must go. Dutch Morial must go. Henry Morris must go." Theron
Glover was at the rally with a photograph of his dead brother. "We only
have one goal, and that's to get justice," he said. Brooks was also at the rally
and, while he admitted eluding the police, he "didn't see any reason for anyone to get killed." He then recalled what happened. "I didn't know he was
shot. I thought he got scared or fell off."[65]

Unlike his deafening silence after the Algiers shootings, Morial quickly
responded to the Glover killing by issuing a strong statement. He labeled
the actions of the two officers "unpardonable and reprehensible." Days
later, the Orleans Parish grand jury indicted Rosiere on second-degree murder charges and on charges of malfeasance in office. He pled not guilty.
Glover's mother was relieved. "We're relieved that the indictment is finally
handed down." She then filed a $10 million lawsuit against the city. Council-
man Sydney Barthelemy called for the immediate resignation of the police
chief. "We have to do something," he said. But he made it clear that Morris

was not the only impediment to serious reform. "I'm not talking about us-ing a scapegoat. I'm talking about some serious changes within the police department." However, on the day after the indictment was issued, Con-nick told reporters that OMI investigators interfered with the investigation in order to help secure a quick indictment. Connick charged OMI investiga-tors with "malfeasance in office," and accused them of "manufacturing and embellishing evidence." Much of Connick's disgust focused on the fact that OMI did not notify him every time it interviewed witnesses. Nonetheless, the district attorney launched a formal investigation into OMI's activities during the Glover investigation.[66]

OMI Director Morris Reed told reporters that Connick perceived the OMI as a threat since its inception and that he wanted it disbanded. "We have reliable information, as far back as a year ago, that Harry Connick has been lobbying certain members of the city council to terminate the Office of Municipal Investigations or to limit its authority to the point that it would be ineffective." Reed was even more direct. "He has been working behind the scenes against the OMI, but the Glover case, and our performance in that case, has caused him to come out in the open." Reed then mentioned that he considered Connick's investigation into the OMI "a concerted effort to chip at the base of the existence since city council made OMI permanent two weeks ago."[67]

Black moderates did not appreciate the attack upon OMI by Connick. Clarence Barney of the NOUL stated that "the attack on the agency un-dermines the credibility of the agency. The OMI is important to all of our progress and development. It affords people who feel they have been ex-cluded from the criminal justice system a credible agency they can turn to. We worked too hard to bring this agency about." Connick's investigation of the OMI ended without any findings and in February 1984 Rosiere was con-victed of murder and sentenced to life in prison with no possibility of pa-role. However, the conviction was later overturned and when he was retried two years later he was found not guilty.[68]

The repeated jurisdictional issues between the OMI, the NOPD, and the district attorney's office enticed Morris Reed to resign in hopes of challeng-ing Connick for his long-held reign as the city's district attorney. Raymond Reed took over as acting director for one year until he was replaced by Peter Munster, an appointee of the newly elected mayor Sydney Barthelemy and a fifteen-year veteran of the Justice Department's Drug Enforcement Asso-ciation in New Orleans. His leadership of the OMI would be drastically dif-

ferent from that of the confrontational Morris Reed. While Reed was quick
to exercise the authority of his office to investigate police violence and misconduct, under Munster's leadership the agency would have an unusually
low profile because of Barthelemy's conservative style of governance. Consequently, black residents would once again complain about the need for an
effective watchdog agency over the NOPD throughout the remainder of the
decade.[69]

While OMI added an external check on the NOPD, it was unsuccessful for several reasons. Its initial problems were structural because it was
understaffed; had a limited budget; and, after its initial creation, suffered
from a woeful lack of visibility. It was also undermined by members of
the NOPD who often refused to cooperate with OMI investigators and by
PANO, which constantly undermined the agency in the local press. Another
reason OMI did not reach its potential is because it often failed to produce
public reports and the reports it did make public were often incomplete.
However, the primary reason the OMI failed was because of the existing
culture within the NOPD that stressed an "us versus them" mentality that
made it suspicious of outsiders.[70]

Civilian review agencies like the OMI have historically been hard to
evaluate due to a lack of published reports detailing complaints, recommendations, and dispositions. However, even if reliable data and statistics
are available, a drop in police complaints or a rise in complaints could be
interpreted in different ways. For example, a drop in complaints is not necessarily an indication of success because the community could possibly be
discouraged by the agency's limitations, its lengthy investigative process,
or citizens' belief that filing a complaint is a complete waste of time. Conversely, a rise in complaints many mean a jump in police abuses but it may
also mean that the community has faith in the agency.[71]

THE CITY'S FIRST BLACK POLICE CHIEF

When Chief Henry Morris retired in December 1984, Morial took the opportunity to appoint the city's first African American police chief, Warren Woodfork, a twenty-year veteran. After a brief internal search, Morial
appointed Woodfork over three other candidates. Woodfork was a forty-
seven-year-old native of Opelousas, Louisiana, who had moved to New Orleans during his teenage years. After attending Joseph Clark High School
and Xavier University for a year, he joined the air force. After returning to
New Orleans, he joined the NOPD in 1964 during its early years of integra-

tion. He admitted that "as a kid I never had a latent desire to be a police-man. But I took the job and fell in love with it." Like all black officers during that time period, Woodfork was assigned to an all-black housing project. He remembered that "blacks worked with blacks and were assigned to the projects." He then moved to the vice crimes unit, then to intelligence. In 1970, he served briefly as assistant commander of community relations. He then organized the controversial felony action squad, which he commanded from 1972 to 1980. In 1980, he moved into administration.[72]

Woodfork's appointment was a godsend for Morial. He needed to appoint an African American to appease his black constituency, but he also needed to appoint a rank-and-file officer, someone who had moved up the ranks but who had credibility in both black and white circles. For instance, although Woodfork commanded the FAS, he was still a charter member of the Black Organization of Police (BOP).

In announcing Woodfork's appointment, Morial made it clear that his selection had nothing to do with race. "I view Warren Woodfork as a police officer first; I view him as a man who has served well and admirably. We didn't look at the issue of color as much as we looked at the issue of qualifi-cations." Following a standing ovation at a his swearing-in, Woodfork said, "I am going to be dedicated to bringing the police department and commu-nity together to deal with the problems as they are allied to crime in this city. The police department itself is not a panacea for the problems we have today, as far as public safety is concerned and particularly street crime. I'm looking forward to help from my friends in the police department, and all of my friends within the community." The new chief mentioned that he would emphasize "old-fashioned, neighborhood policing."[73]

Community leaders applauded the appointment. Yvonne Bechet of the BOP stated that "the city has been needing someone who grew up in the city and knows the city, since the city is predominantly black." Further, a black police chief could relate to the problems of the black community. She then stated that a black police chief "could encourage more community par-ticipation in police activities and more grassroots input, by instilling trust and confidence in the police department. Attorney Ronald Wilson, who represented the black officers in the discrimination suit, felt that a "black police chief can reverse the image of the department and the historic con-flict between black and white police officers." Others, such as former Chief Jim Parsons, felt that Woodfork's race would not play a major role in his duties. "I don't think his race will be a factor at all," he said. Likewise, former Chief Clarence Giarrusso believed that Woodfork would be colorblind. "Woody is down the middle. He is not a coward, and he will not be bullshitted. He knows this is a community city, an American city, not a black city or a white city. He is an American." However, NOPD Captain Charles LaDell knew it would make a difference. "No matter how you cut it, it's going to be a difference in how the public perceives the department and how the men perceive the leadership." Another black officer noted, "I don't think people are going to be looking at the chief in terms of his color. I think people will realize we have a black chief, and expect more from him in terms of fair treatment of black citizens." One Hispanic officer stated that he did not have any objections to working for a black superintendent "as long as he doesn't mind having an Hispanic working for him." Even Ron Cannatella, the head of PANO, praised Woodfork as "a street cop who came up through the ranks."[74]

Just weeks after his appointment, Woodfork appointed Yvonne Bechet, an African American, as deputy superintendent of police. She became the highest-ranking female police officer in the city's history. The appointment of the fifty-one-year-old veteran and former president of the BOP made headlines throughout the city. Prior to her appointment, Bechet had been working as Woodfork's executive assistant in the detective bureau. When it appeared as if she was in line for the promotion, she resigned her position in the BOP. She was elated. "I feel great joy, great humility, and I also feel great steadfastness, and we are going to progress in this department." For Woodfork the appointment was exciting. "I thought it was a bold step. We wanted someone who would be reflective of the community and the populace of the police department. Traditionally, blacks and females have not been represented, particularly in high positions." Woodfork agreed that a key element of reform was "bringing in more minorities and females in the rank-and-file and into higher positions in the department."[75]

Born in the historic Treme area and raised in the Lafitte housing project, Bechet was praised by her fellow officers as articulate, fair, progressive but conservative, and determined more than openly aggressive. After she left the police academy, she and the other five recruits were sent to central lock-up. "We spent three months there to toughen us up. They wanted to let us know there was such a thing as criminals. As if I wouldn't know growing up in the projects." She was then confined to the newly created women's division, "where we had to hunt down our own assignments." While in the women's division she and the other women were told that "we would be on call in case we were needed for investigative assistance to other units. Needless to say, the phone never rang." She then worked in the crime prevention bureau, the juvenile division, and as head of community relations in the 1970s, "when everyone was concerned about the poor relations between the community and the police. There was fear of violence." She became a "welfare sergeant" in 1983, which referred to her being promoted as a result of the discrimination suit. When Bechet reflected upon her rise through the ranks of the NOPD, she recalled that "there weren't as many roadblocks as one might believe. I learned to accept things I can't change. But I do change those things I can." She did admit "that being a woman could be a hindrance to me in the minds of others. I know it's no hindrance to me. But I wasn't sure other people knew." Prior to accepting the appointment, she was president of the BOP and she acted as a liaison between the New York attorneys and black officers in the discrimination lawsuit. However, her tenure did not last long. When Morial left office in 1986 because of term limits, she was replaced.[76]

While Woodfork and Bechet were excited about the opportunity to lead the NOPD, they knew that they were inheriting a department with some major problems. Among them were police pay, morale, racial division, poor equipment, a hiring freeze, and a city infested with high crime, caused by the rampant drug culture in the city. Plus, as recreational drug use took off in New Orleans, the NOPD had a tough time recruiting young officers because many potential recruits could not pass the departmental drug test. At a speech at the Press Club of New Orleans Woodfork mentioned that "youngsters pass the test and other aspects of their application and fail when it comes to the question about using narcotics." Of eight hundred police applications the NOPD received in 1984, only eighty were recruited. Of those rejected, 75 percent were because of drug usage. But Woodfork's biggest problem was dealing with the reality that New Orleans had the fourth highest murder rate among the nation's cities in 1984. But on the positive side, Woodfork did take the helm of a department that was increasingly more African American.[77]

Of the approximately 1,030 officers on the police force in 1985, roughly 350 were black. That included 16 sergeants, one captain, one lieutenant, and one major. But although black officers now represented one-third of the department, there were still issues. Bechet told reporters that "there is still discrimination in hiring, promotions, and disciplinary actions, but it is not as blatant as it was in the early 1970s." For instance, despite the consent de-

cree, black officers still only made up less than 2 percent of the top management jobs.[78]

Once in office, Woodfork restructured the NOPD by putting more officers on the street and emphasizing old-fashioned neighborhood policing.
"I want to create an atmosphere where we can disrupt the opportunity for
certain people who commit crimes and the citizens feel confident because
we are there, they have met us, and they have the confidence to call and tell
us about suspicious activity," he said. During his first year in office, Woodfork put police officers in "baseball caps and running shoes" and some on
bicycles, established a central traffic division to handle all accident investigations, added thirty-one detectives to the criminal investigation bureau so that patrol districts could strictly focus on patrolling the streets,
and had the department start taking more crime reports over the phone.
Plus, Woodfork placed a strong emphasis on community participation in
neighborhood crime-watch groups. As a result of his reforms, there was a
drastic reduction in major crimes for the first half of 1985. Compared to
the same period in 1984, rape was down 16 percent, armed robbery 19 percent, and homicide 40 percent. While a small segment of the force resented
Woodfork, the rank-and-file embraced his reforms. "I really feel like the
department is going forward now," said Russell Vappie, a longtime NOPD
veteran.[79]

Woodfork's harshest critics were members of the BOP. Although Woodfork was a chapter member, one-time vice-president, and still a dues-paying
member, they were highly critical of him. BOP President Jeanne McGlory
was blunt. "We have problems with this administration." She then went on
to cite the disproportionate number of black officers who were still being
denied promotions. She argued that most black officers were relegated to
district patrol work and were skipped over when positions in other divisions became available. Randolph Thomas reacted similarly. "The emotional
high of his appointment is over with and now we're faced with the reality.
Blacks still come out on the short end of the stick." Woodfork was not surprised by the accusations. "When I joined this department in 1964, there
were thirty-three blacks, 5 percent of the department." He then mentioned
that the most recent graduating class from the police academy was one-
third African American. "I have been making efforts to attract more blacks
to this job since I became assistant to the superintendent in 1971," he said.
Some of his critics stated that Woodfork benefited from "luck and good
timing," since morale was already creeping up and crime down. However,

the chief wanted some credit. "If things were turned around and morale was low, crime was up and murder and everything else was up, who would you be blaming?"[80]

THE ELECTION OF MAYOR SYDNEY BARTHELEMY

As Morial approached the end of his second term, he attempted to change the city charter, which limited a mayor to two successive four-year terms in office. The measure was defeated at the polls because of low turnout in the black community although over 85 percent of blacks voted to change the charter. Ninety-five percent of white voters rejected Morial, signaling that they had grown tired of the Morial administration. That did not come as a surprise to Morial, considering that while he enjoyed moderate white support during his early years, that support had waned and was virtually invisible during his final years in office. Much of the criticism toward Morial from white voters stemmed from his perceived arrogance. While Morial could be abrasive and confrontational at times, arrogant he was not. White New Orleans was not accustomed to dealing with someone of Morial's stature. His personal, professional, and political pedigree were intimidating to many whites and when he repeatedly did things his own way it created the image of an arrogant and divisive man.[81]

When Morial's bid to succeed himself failed miserably, local black political organizations were jockeying to get their candidate into city hall. Councilman-at-Large Sidney Barthelemy emerged as the early frontrunner since he had wide name recognition across the city, he had the support of COUP, and his conservative non-confrontational posture was easy for whites to accept. But getting black votes would not be easy for the councilman for two reasons. First, like Morial, Barthelemy was a light-skinned creole who had to defend himself against charges that he wasn't black enough. Second, during his time on the New Orleans city council he often blocked many of Morial's initiatives, including his campaign to change the city charter. On the campaign trail Barthelemy made overt appeals to the black community in an effort to prove that he was concerned about the black masses and their problems. In the general election Barthelemy faced William Jefferson from SOUL and the councilman mounted an aggressive campaign on black radio stations in hopes of getting the black vote. Jefferson responded to Barthelemy's appeals by accusing him of "passing for white," and by stating that Barthelemy "would not be a mayor for the black community." Jefferson's strategy worked, but it was still not enough to keep Barthelemy out of city hall. He became the second black mayor in the city of New Orleans by receiving 85 percent of the white vote and less than 25 percent of the black vote. As one writer has mentioned, "New Orleans had now found itself a white mayor." Since Barthelemy was put into office on the strength of the black vote, black expectations for the new mayor were not high concerning his ability to deal with black grievances, especially police brutality. Barthelemy could not have chosen a worst time to become mayor of New Orleans. He would encounter structural problems that weakened the city's economic base, an out-of-control crack epidemic, and a police department that became arguably the most corrupt in the United States.[82]

8 BLACK-ON-BLACK CRIME
The Consequences of White Flight, the War on Drugs, and Political Indifference

After a decade of economic decline, white flight, and urban disinvestment, along with six years of Reaganomics and an oil bust that cost more than 60,000 residents their jobs, New Orleans was struggling to survive as Sydney Barthelemy took office. Like many of the nation's urban centers, New Orleans suffered from federal and state indifference. Although suburbanization came to New Orleans late because of the city's unique topography, by the mid-1980s, a good portion of the white middle class had left the city and settled into Slidell to the east and St. Tammany Parish to the north. Because of its weak economic tax base, the city could not afford to maintain even the bare minimum of city services. With astounding rates of poverty, high unemployment, and meteoric rises in homicides and violent crimes in New Orleans proper, the New Orleans Police Department (NOPD) would fall even farther into an abyss of corruption, brutality, unprofessionalism, and gangsterism.

THE ECONOMIC CONSEQUENCES OF WHITE FLIGHT
Just months after taking office, Barthelemy had to confront a $30 million budget shortage. To address the deficit, the mayor laid off police officers and cut the city work week down to four days. In particular, the NOPD lost 184 of its 1,700 employees but no uniformed officers. But the mayor openly acknowledged that when the layoffs took effect it would have an immediate impact on the department's ability to deliver services. When the layoffs hit, Woodfork announced that the traffic, mounted, and K-9 units would be disbanded. He then recommended the closure of the police academy, lim-

ited investigations of traffic accidents (only those that involved a death or a drunken motorist), and reduction of the number of officers available to investigate property crimes. The four-day work week was the equivalent of losing 266 officers. Woodfork made it clear that he wasn't trying to frighten anyone, but "I've got to let the public know what we can and can't do."[1]

During the budget hearings later that fall, Woodfork made an impassioned plea for reopening the police academy. "We've got a lot of catching up to do in 1987," he said. He wanted money for three classes of recruits in 1987 to offset the losses that had reduced the number of uniformed officers from 1,500 to 1,300 over the previous two years. "I'm thirsty and this plan offers me some drinking water, but it doesn't quench my thirst." At a minimum Woodfork needed two hundred more cops. He also asked the city council for money to rehire non-uniformed personnel so that they could free up uniformed officers for regular police duties. Part of the fiscal crisis came when voters rejected a $195 property service charge proposal in September 1986 that would have gone into the city's general fund. Now, however, with police services on the decline and crime high, voters indicated a willingness to pay a tax if it went directly to police services. But the city charter did not allow dedicating city funds to any specific department. Barthelemy told voters that he would "take an oath if the voters approve any revenue-raising issue dedicated to police and fire services, and that the designated funds will be spent only for those services." But Councilman Giarrusso was opposed to any and all proposed tax increases. "As an ex-cop and an ex-superintendent of police, I'm certainly sympathetic to the needs of the police and fire departments. But I think it is a poor idea to take care of two city departments at the expense of the other ten departments. I'd be opposed to it." Barthelemy then proposed a twelve mill property tax increase to improve public safety that would provide about $14 million a year in additional revenue and would mean a police force of about 1,400. Owners of homes valued at less than $75,000 would not pay the tax increase because of the state's homestead exemption, but taxes on a $100,000 home would increase by approximately $30 a year. The vote was scheduled for January 17, 1987.[2]

The Black Organization of Police (BOP) immediately came out against the property tax increase. Instead of the property tax increase, they asked Barthelemy to promote a service charge to raise police salaries rather than use the money to add a hundred new officers and rehire a hundred civilians laid off in 1986. Members of the BOP wanted salary raises for existing officers first, and an enlarged police force second. Jeanne McGlory argued that in order to stop the trend of approximately a hundred officers leaving the force every year for better-paying jobs, better working conditions, and early retirement, the pay raises were a priority. She also argued that increased pay would improve morale and productivity. However, some members of the BOP did favor the tax and insisted that the BOP resolution was not legitimate since less than 50 of the organization's 125 members showed up at the meeting. The Patrolmen's Association of New Orleans's (PANO) members narrowly approved the property tax increase although it was a close vote. Cannatella agreed that the tax increase did not do much for existing officers, but "we look at this as a beginning. Down the line we want some pay raises," he said.[3]

Despite an aggressive push from city hall, the city council, and the NOPD, the property tax increase failed by a 2-to-1 margin. Of the 65,000 voters who participated, only 20,000, or 31 percent, voted for the increase. Barthelemy conceded defeat around 9:00 p.m. on the night of the election. "We think the public did not understand and made a mistake. But we are going to try to do everything we can to still provide adequate services to the community." He then mentioned that "we are going to have to regroup and look at what other alternatives we can come up with in the future." For Woodfork the defeat meant that he could only add a hundred police recruits in 1987, far short of the number he needed to adequately protect the city. Giarrusso didn't gloat after the defeat. "This election was no victory for anyone. It just wasn't the right time or the right idea. We have to do a little more homework before we come up with any more proposals." Councilman Lambert Bossiere, a leading supporter of the increase, stated that council would not approve of a monthly service charge to raise additional revenue. "The message is loud and clear—no more tax increases. We've just got to go back and do the best we can with what we have to work with." The proposal failed for several reasons: first, the soaring unemployment rate in New Orleans, which hovered around 11 percent; second, the aggressive opposition by Councilman Giarrusso; and third, a slow get-out-the-vote campaign by Barthelemy because the election came so close to the holiday season.[4]

Because of the fiscal shortage that meant no new officers, no pay raises, and no money for physical improvements, the morale within the NOPD quickly veered low. "We're on a treadmill," said Woodfork to the city council in a one-hour emotional appeal for more police expenditures. "We are doing a lot of walking and we're not getting anywhere." He then told the council that while he appreciated the ability to hire sixty officers and rehire twenty-five civilians for the year, it was still not enough to adequately meet the needs of the city. "We have worked smart. We have bit the bullet. We have tightened the belt. With all rhetoric aside, this department needs funding that restores it to a level that allows us to adequately meet the demands for service required of us and provides the protection our citizens and guests deserve." Woodfork then went on to list how budget cuts had affected every aspect of the department, including a loss of 84 officers; a loss of 179 civilians, including jail guards; and a reduction of police cars from more than 900 to 670. He then mentioned the various physical plant problems that made it difficult for office personnel to do their jobs effectively.[5]

Because of the NOPD's financial crisis, the department could not adequately serve all of the city's neighborhoods. As a result, the city's ten housing projects became emporiums for crime because the NOPD just did not make it a priority. For instance, it generally took the police more time on average to respond to calls from the projects as opposed to white areas. In the upscale garden district, it took the police an average of fifteen minutes to respond, while the response time to Desire was an unbelievable thirty-two minutes. The lack of police protection in the projects was of significant concern because 10 percent of the city's entire population resided in public housing. A 1985 Loyola University study concluded that 66 percent of all public housing residents felt very unsafe at night. "I think about it all the time. I'm worried at night, but I try not to let it show. I don't like to have to think this way. I don't believe in living in fear, but where do I go,"

TABLE 5.

NOPD Response Time to Various Parts of New Orleans, 1986

AREA	TIME (IN MINUTES)
Garden District	15.6
Algiers area	2.1
Uptown area	21.3
Carrolton area	23.3
Fischer Housing Project	24.5
St. Thomas Housing Project	26.2
Desire Housing Project	32.5

Source: Times-Picayune, March 8, 1987.

said St. Thomas Housing resident Michelle Crockett. Statistics compiled by the NOPD showed that in the three most dangerous housing projects—Desire, St. Thomas, and Fischer—residents called the police more than in any other area. NOPD officials justified their slow response time to the projects by arguing that most of the calls were domestic in nature and that those disturbances could be dangerous. "If it's a domestic disturbance, a lot of policemen don't like to have anything to do with that call. That's also the scene which most police would get hurt," said Sergeant Bruce Adams. "One of the basic problems is extreme density—so many people living so close together. We'd need a police force half the size of the Fifth District to adequately patrol the Desire housing project. We just don't have the manpower." Plus the maze-like layout of the projects made it easy for criminals to elude the police.[6]

As the budget crunch shrank the number of police officers, routine patrol became a thing of the past as most officers went from call to call. "We never see the police in here unless they're chasing somebody, and even then they disappear pretty quick," said Paul Tramontano, director of the St. Thomas. "Even if they were just more visible, I think it would help." Adding to the problem of police protection in the housing projects was the bad relationship between project residents and the police. Project residents stated that the police never showed them respect. "They talk to you any kind of way, like you're nobody. They come in here with the wrong attitude," said Barbara Jackson of the St. Thomas tenant council. Conversely, the police felt as if project residents were often hostile and uncooperative. Bruce Adams remembered the trend. "It's funny. In a regular neighborhood, if someone gets shot, then everyone will run away from it. And when you ask around, you get a few witnesses. But if the same thing happens in the project, people run toward the shooting. And if you ask around, nobody saw anything." The desire not to help the police was because the witness identified more with the criminal than with the police.[7]

Because of the persistent lack of police protection, crime flourished in the projects. "The situation here has totally changed from what it was fifteen years ago. We didn't have half the problems we have now. Rape, murder, drugs—they are everywhere," said Sydney Duplesis of the Desire Community Center. Many of the crimes in the projects grew out of the drug trade. "The permutations are endless—they rape, rob, and pillage each other for stuff."[8] In an effort to heal the fragile relationship between the NOPD and public housing tenants, Woodfork set up two officers to spe-

TABLE 6.

Average Quarterly Police Complaints Received by the New Orleans
Office of Municipal Investigation, 1988–1993

YEAR	AVERAGE COMPLAINTS PER QUARTER
1988	67
1989	67
1990	76
1991	81
1992	70
1993	101

Source: Times-Picayune, April 30, 1993.

cifically deal with the problems in the projects. Officers Julian Debeau and
Norman Taylor were assigned to the Housing Authority of New Orleans's
(HANO) police liaison office. The officers spent most of their time working
cases the people had called in. "They decided in dealing with crime in public
housing it would be better if policemen talked to residents about the problem than for HANO security to do it."[9]

THE WAR ON DRUGS

Much of the crime problem in the projects was crack related. Of the city's
hottest crack spots, the majority of them were located in the projects and
the NOPD was at a terrible disadvantage in trying to defeat the drug dealers. With the city's fiscal crisis leading to a decline in officers, members of
the narcotics unit were pessimistic about winning the war on drugs. "It's a
nightmare, it is always a nightmare," said Lieutenant Carol Hewitt, commander of the NOPD's narcotics unit. "I don't think they [drug dealers] can
be stopped entirely. What you can hope to do is thwart as many of them
as possible." Because of the shortage in manpower, narcotics officers were
overworked and only spent half of their time fighting drugs. In a city with
a high drug rate, the NOPD had only 16 investigators dedicated to narcotics
in 1987. That year they made 718 arrests. By comparison, the Atlanta police
narcotics squad, with about 30 officers, made roughly 2,000 arrests. Similarly, the Jackson, Mississippi, narcotics unit made about 1,000 arrests with
10 investigators. Although the NOPD began doing a better job of cracking
down on drug dealers, Woodfork still felt defeated. "You know what gets me

sometimes? We get real excited over here when we get $350,000 or so for enforcement. And you bust a cocaine pusher and he puts up $350,000 for bail like it wasn't nothing. So you can see what we're fighting." Woodfork then wondered how a smaller police force could be expected to handle a growing drug problem, particularly as the unemployment rate rose throughout the city.[10]

In an effort to balance the equation, Woodfork merged the fourteen-member vice squad with narcotics. The merged unit would attack an area of heavy drug trafficking and clear the streets. When the drug dealers moved to another area, so would the police. This game of cat-and-mouse was ongoing. "Every time we come up with a plan, they come up with a plan," said Sergeant David Peralta of the narcotics unit. Nonetheless, Woodfork was hopeful that by going after the street pusher and the user, they would be able to have a degree of success. But the NOPD was not only outmanned but outgunned as well. While drug dealers routinely carried machine guns and uzis, officers were carrying .38 specials. "We're the front line guys. We're the ones going through those doors. I'm worried when we're kicking in the door and they're firing 30 rounds before we can fire one," said Peralta. In their frustration, members of the narcotics unit often took out their bitterness against innocent black civilians. For instance, officers from the Sixth District were accused of robbing drug dealers (but not taking them to jail); illegal search and seizure; and arresting residents on false drug charges, or "police planting" as it was called. Consequently, although black residents wanted the drugs out of their community, they wanted the police out as well. Reverend Gregory Hill, pastor of Greater Mount Pilgrim Church, understood the dilemma. "We want the drugs out of here, but we want people treated rightly," he said.[11]

While the NOPD would often assault drug dealers and innocent citizens, at times black residents fought back. In November 1988, as two officers searched a vehicle for drugs in the Fischer Housing Projects, they were immediately greeted by a noisy crowd that began taunting and throwing bottles at them. Although they found the driver of the automobile in possession of drugs, they let him go because they feared for their lives. A week prior, two other officers were hit by rocks, bottles, and sticks while subduing an armed suspect in the St. Bernard Projects. Although the suspect was taken into custody, the officers went to the hospital for cuts and bruises. Lieutenant Dan Bell was familiar with the hostility. "We've lived with it for some years down here. You always draw a crowd when you make an arrest in the projects. Sometimes the crowds are not hostile, sometimes they are. I'd say we run into it at least once a week. Maybe two or three times a week." Because of the hostility, NOPD officers were trained to "stick and move," to grab a suspect and get out. Officers were warned not to retaliate. "The officer will be at a disadvantage if he stands out there and battles. The main thing is to just get the individual and get the hell out of there. If you go in there and try to battle them, you're creating a problem that's long term." One evening in the Desire Projects, Officer Howard Robertson was fired upon by bystanders while he and his partner were chasing two suspected drug dealers. Although Robertson avoided getting shot, it seemed like a frequent occurrence. "That happens all the time in the project. Why they do it or what causes it, I can't tell you. But, we definitely feel like a target," he said.[12]

As the drug epidemic worsened, HANO officials asked the NOPD to provide a twenty-four-hour police presence in the projects. Larry Jones, executive director of HANO, was not wasting time. "It is an urgent situation that we get police protection in these developments," he said. He wanted the NOPD to reinstate its urban squad. However, the NOPD did not have the money to reinstate the special unit and the state legislature was not eager to provide the funds. Although Representative Sherman Copelin of New Orleans made a commitment to the urban squad in the state budget, the House Appropriations Committee took the money out on the House floor. Jones felt that state politicians were out of touch with the severity of the problem. "I don't think they understand how bad things are. You have people hitting the floor at 2:00 a.m. because of bullets." NOPD officials stated that twenty-four-hour protection would cost about $500,000 a year for each housing project. If funded, squads would be initially placed at the Fischer and St. Thomas projects. Jones was eager to see the urban squad reinstated because squad members became trusted authorities. "By being there every day, tenants developed some trust of the officers." Now, because of misconduct, project residents did not trust the police.[13]

Rinal Martin, founder of the urban squad, remembered how effective it was and thought it ironic that roughly twenty years after its founding "the people still remember it and want to bring it back." Larry Jones agreed. "I see a clear difference in the amount of police protection and the quality of police protection under the urban squad." Jones remembered that the urban squad could respond in minutes. "Most important was the trust that was developed in the community." But although Martin wanted to see it on the streets again, he noted that the unit would not work if it was a promise of overtime. He believed that the urban squad needed to be a separate unit with its own equipment and personnel. "Sure, it costs a little bit more," he said, "but when you think about what it saves in terms of lives and vandalism it saves ten times what it costs."[14]

But some residents did not want to see the urban squad or any other unit established for the sole purpose of fighting crime in the projects. Thirty-year-old Sydney Rayfield, a resident of the Iberville Projects, told reporters that "people need to know that police are their friends. The people here need help, not busted heads." His views were echoed by his neighbors. "The police commit just as much crime as the people. They need to clean up their own house first," stated Harold Herbert. Other residents believed that since the police did not live in the housing project, they had no clue how to help solve the crime problem. "They [city officials] can't understand what's going on here because they don't live here, they don't come here. How are they going to solve our problems sitting in their offices in their suits and ties?" one resident asked.[15]

In an effort to handle the high crime rate in the projects, Woodfork announced plans to set up a police substation in the Magnolia Housing Projects and increase patrols at five other projects. The plan was made possible by a $1.3 million grant HANO received from the Department of Housing and Urban Development (HUD). "Obviously a $1.3 million grant won't provide all the protection we need, but we think it's a step in the right direction," Larry Jones said. Jones wanted to model the patrols after the urban squad. "We know that relations are strained in the black community in general with the police. Once they trust the police they'll tell them where the drugs will be hidden. With different people the residents don't get to know them," Jones argued. But Jones also made it clear that the program would focus on much more than just law enforcement. "We're also trying to highlight the social services component. We don't want to give the impression that just more police protection is the solution. People need hope, education, counseling."[16]

As the NOPD continued to lose the war on drugs, the city's murder rate reached unprecedented levels. In 1990, the city of New Orleans had a record number of murders. If that wasn't enough pressure on Woodfork, he also had to deal with in-house corruption. In 1988, Officers Mark Washington and Tyrone Smith were convicted on charges of a conspiracy to distribute cocaine. In March of that year, an additional eleven officers were called in for questioning by a federal grand jury concerning corruption in the French Quarter that included police involvement in burglaries, cocaine distribution, credit card fraud, and possession of stolen property. Officer Thaddeus Petit, twenty-nine, a seven-year veteran of the NOPD, was indicted on charges of protecting shipments of cocaine and two months later four additional officers were convicted on charges that they kept cocaine and money seized in drug raids. Officer Darrell Hughes was arrested and booked on charges of armed robbery after he and his wife lured a man to the lakefront. In November 1989, Officer Eric Berger was booked on charges of attempted murder after he fired his weapon in a nightclub. One year later, David Fisher and Ralph Jones, two officers of the NOPD's elite special operations division, were indicted on charges of taking cash to protect a cocaine dealer in the city.[17]

The most controversial case of police misconduct was the beating death of Adolph Archie in March 1990. On the afternoon of Thursday, March 22, Archie, a prison escapee, attempted to steal a car in the Superdome parking lot. When a security officer spotted him, Archie punched her in the face, took her gun, and proceeded to run through rush hour traffic downtown. Officer Earl Hauck was directing traffic at the time, but he joined the chase when he saw Archie running. Hauck drew his gun and told Archie to get on the ground. Then, for whatever reason, Hauck put his gun away. "I can't believe he put his gun back in his holster," said one eyewitness. Then Archie fired four shots at Hauck. Hauck was killed instantly and Archie was found minutes later hiding under a car. What happened in the next forty minutes is still unknown.[18]

TABLE 7.

Complaints Received by the NOPD Internal Affairs Department, 1986–1990

YEAR	NUMBER OF COMPLAINTS
1986	518
1987	400
1988	421
1989	490
1990	462

Source: Compiled by the author.

When he was captured, Archie was taken to the door of Charity Hospital's emergency room but they did not let him out of the car because a group of officers had gathered there eager to avenge Hauck's death. Instead, they took him to the First District police station, where Archie allegedly tried to take an officer's gun. In the struggle that followed Archie was knocked unconscious and was bleeding from the face and head. He was then taken to Charity Hospital, where he died of those injuries thirteen hours later. After a six-month investigation, the Orleans Parish grand jury cleared the officers in Archie's death, although the Archie family would receive a settlement years later from the NOPD.[19]

POLITICAL INDIFFERENCE

Because of the ever-increasing police corruption and the escalating crime rate, which toward the end of 1990 was 25 percent ahead of 1989 statistics, some residents began calling for Woodfork's resignation. Rafael Goyneche, III, of the Metropolitan Crime Commission said, "A lot of people have been telling Sidney [Barthelemy] about Woodfork. I think he's lost control of his department. There are a lot of good cops who are embarrassed by what's going on." He then mentioned the ongoing federal corruption probe. "With the feds rooting around here in the department, I think Woodfork's becoming more of a liability every day. This could be the thing that sends Woodfork to greener pastures." In December 1990, Woodfork announced his decision to retire in April 1991. "I think the timing is right," he said. "It's time to make room for new leadership and I'm ready to seek new endeavors." Weeks later, Barthelemy appointed Arnesta Taylor, a low-key African American deputy superintendent, to be his police chief.[20]

The choice of Taylor, a father of six and native New Orleanian, was safe for Barthelemy, who did not wish to go outside the department and find another chief, but it would prove disastrous for black residents as Taylor was simply unqualified for the job. Taylor was a relatively unknown officer who had spent much of his twenty-five years on the force in a variety of administrative positions. He had very few enemies and his laid-back approach to law enforcement complemented Barthelemy's leadership style. Although Taylor was an African American, he was low-key and would not make changes too fast, if at all. In many respects the selection of Taylor meant that there would be no major reforms in a department that was quickly spiraling out of control. This was a dangerous situation, considering that the city was plagued with a runaway murder rate fueled by crack cocaine.

When Taylor entered office, he confronted five major issues: a record murder rate that continued to escalate, federal investigations of corrupt officers involved in selling drugs or protecting drug shipments, a lack of public confidence in the police in the aftermath of the Rodney King beating, an alienated community that was distrustful of police officers, and low morale. When Taylor entered office on April 1, 1991, the city had recorded its ninety-first murder in ninety-one days, keeping the homicide rate ahead of the pace set in 1990. This situation would have been difficult for an experienced chief to tackle, but for Taylor it was insurmountable. However, Taylor was optimistic that he could get a handle on the issues. "If anything is wrong, it can be corrected," he said. "Of course I know everything is not fine." Taylor admitted that the federal investigation made the department look bad, but he was still confident that "for the most part we have an honest police department." At least Taylor did have one thing in his favor: an infusion of $7 million annually from a 1990 tax increase that would provide money for cars, equipment, and additional officers.[21]

Taylor promised "to take the streets back from criminals" by having door-to-door patrols, something that Woodfork was unable to implement because of budget shortages. "We're going to give the city back to the citizens." Taylor favored aggressive policing even if it meant stopping innocent civilians. "I would rather receive complaints from mothers saying my officers stopped their sons without adequate cause than calls from the same mothers complaining that their sons had been shot to death because police didn't patrol aggressively enough."[22]

In an effort to beef up the police presence in the city, Taylor formed a special task force just days after his inauguration. On their first night, the unit made sixty-four arrests, including twenty for felonies, and they interviewed and questioned thirty people. Taylor also placed more officers in the internal affairs division as a precaution to prevent what had happened in Los Angeles with Rodney King. "We do not want a Los Angeles. Our citizens will not tolerate brutality," he said. And he placed full-time officers in the Desire Projects while the Iberville Housing Projects was home to a new NOPD substation.[23]

The killing of Corey Horton, age sixteen, was an injustice just like the Rodney King beating. Horton, who was wanted by police for his involvement in a shooting and for a variety of other charges, was shot by police four times (in the back, neck, ear, and chest) after being pulled over in a stolen car. Although witnesses stated that Horton was unarmed, officers claimed that they shot him when he attempted to grab an officer's gun. Eyewitnesses could not believe the police version. "His hands were up. His hands were up when he left the van and they were up near his face when he was on the ground. There's no way he reached for a gun. I could sleep for a hundred years and I wouldn't forget what I saw," said one eyewitness who had been seated in his truck less than twenty feet from the scene. As the investigation into the murder commenced, residents of the St. Bernard Projects held a march through the complex. "Our message to the police is this: you come into the black community and take one more black life and we're going to pound you into the ground," march organizer Randy Mitchell yelled. Malcolm Suber of the Afro-American Liberation League said that mere talk would no longer make a difference. "There are differences of opinion within the movement, but some are at the point that they think a violent attack needs a violent response." A similar march was held the following day as protestors carried a sign reading, "Charge killer cops."[24]

While the case was under investigation, the officers involved in the shooting, Christie Williams, Robert Canedo, and Frank Polito, were reassigned. In the meantime it was discovered that at the time of his death Horton had cocaine in his system. At a city council meeting weeks after his death, concerned citizens sounded off about his murder. "This was an execution, not a murder. This is not the time to be backing down and pretending that the wheels of justice are going to roll," said Suber. Rudy Mills, Sr., of the United Front to Stop Black Genocide argued that the NOPD had a different standard for black murder victims than white victims. "A white person was killed so someone had to pay immediately," he said referring to the murder investigation of a young white pharmacist, Pamela Block, "but when a young black man dies at the hands of the police, we have to investigate. There should have been an immediate arrest. There were enough eyewitnesses to know exactly what happened. The investigation comes after," he said.[25]

But not all black people were protesting his death. Some believed he got what he deserved since he lived a life of crime. Sixty-nine-year-old Herman Taitt did not condemn the shooting. "So you live, so you die. If you're a criminal, and you're stealing, you die. I'm black myself, but I believe in justice, I believe in living right." Taitt, in speaking for the silent majority, was right. The Horton case did not arouse much community outrage because he was a criminal. The cops were eventually cleared in the killing of Horton.[26]

The Fischer Projects was the site of another confrontation between police and about two hundred residents in May 1992 after three hours of violence involving unrelated incidents. Around 8:30 p.m. one evening, police officers went to the housing complex to investigate complaints about boys fighting in the complex. When the police arrived to break up the fight, eye-witnesses said they beat the boys with batons. The crowd started throwing rocks and bottles at the officers. Hours later, a carload full of young men arrived at the Fourth District police station in Algiers. "They were shouting things about police terror and Rodney King. They were in the parking lot shouting that they were not going to stand for this anymore," according to Captain Anthony Genovese. One month later, tensions flared between po-lice and Fischer residents again when officers arrested a man they said fired a stolen gun at them. While the officers were arresting the man, residents threw bottles and other objects at them. Luckily, no one was hurt. Later in the St. Thomas Projects, an anonymous police officer was shot while trying to arrest a suspect on drug charges. The suspect grabbed the officer's gun and wounded him.[27]

As a string of police corruption cases hit the news, it soon became clear that Taylor was not the right person for the job. He was ineffective on many levels. In 1991, the International Association of Police Chiefs found that the NOPD "suffered from an abundance of organizational and staffing flaws. A number of fundamental principles of organization have not been observed." One year later, New Orleans earned the dubious distinction of leading the nation in police brutality complaints. When the Justice Depart-ment released the findings of its national survey of police complaints filed by citizens against local law enforcement agencies, New Orleans ranked at the top of the list, followed by Los Angeles County, San Antonio, El Paso, Houston, Chicago, and St. Louis. The report found that between 1984 and 1990 the NOPD averaged thirty-five complaints a year, or one complaint for every 1,305 arrests. In comparison, the New York Police Department aver-aged only 14 complaints a year, or one complaint for every 15,393 arrests. Also that year the city recorded 352 murders, making it the murder capi-tal of the country. Similarly, in the first three months of 1993, the office of municipal investigation (OMI) had 101 complaints lodged against the po-lice. In the previous five years the OMI had about 72 police complaints a quarter. "Last year we didn't get where we are now until June," said OMI Director Peter Munster. "It kind of bothers me." Munster stated that the increase was led by allegations of excessive force. In the first three months of the year, the NOPD received a wave of bad publicity. In February, Officer

Edward Messina was indicted for allegedly forcing a prostitute to have sex with him. In March, Officers Jimmie Turner, Jr., and Warren Walker, Jr., of the Sixth District were booked on charges of raping a female in police custody. Later that month, members of the NOPD beat up eighty-two-year-old Avery Alexander, a longtime civil rights activist, during a demonstration at the Liberty Place Monument, an obelisk that honored the White League's militia victory during a Reconstruction-era battle. In April, Sergeant Ronald Johnson was indicted by an Orleans Parish grand jury on charges related to receiving stolen property. And weeks later Officer Michael Thames was charged with two counts of armed robbery. In fact, Thames had robbed the same bank a year prior.[28]

As criticism mounted, Taylor came under considerable heat to do something. He initially moved some of his top brass to other positions. But these administrative moves had little effect on the corruption that was woven into the fabric of the department. In late April, the nonprofit Metropolitan Crime Commission asked for a special investigation of the NOPD. Rafael Goyenche, director, stated that "there is a disease within the department. It's obvious." In a letter to Barthelemy and the city council Goyenche wrote, "Public confidence in the NOPD has now diminished to the point where it is no longer possible for our own police to credibly conduct such an investigation." Although Goyenche appreciated the district attorney's office filing criminal charges, he was certain that more needed to be done. "We need to go beyond that and look at internal violations and ethical laxity. We're asking the council to act aggressively. Don't wait for the next occurrence." Taylor was not in favor of a special investigation into his department. "We have a human relations commission, we have the FBI, we have OMI, we have the DA's office, we have the U.S. Attorney's office. And we do investigate ourselves. We have better success investigating ourselves than any other agency." But Taylor did admit that the department did have some rogue cops. At a city council meeting Taylor told the council that during his two-year tenure he had fired forty-eight officers. "That is a large amount of people. Do we have bad apples on the New Orleans Police Department? Do we have bad apples in any other profession? Yes we do. Do we do something about it? Yes we do. We clean our own house," he said as officers applauded. But Malcolm Suber, who was also in the audience was not among those applauding the chief's remarks. In fact, he was mad at the council for going easy on the NOPD. "This police department has murdered its citizens and they are the criminals," he said. "They steal money from people all the time and we all know it. Not one of you have mentioned about these people taking people's lives. It's not just the vice squad, it's all of them."[29]

Despite the scrutiny and the numerous ongoing investigations into the department, the corruption continued unabated. On May 2, 1993, former members of the vice squad were indicted for pocketing money seized in an illegal gambling house. The following week, Officer Kenneth Taylor was booked with kidnapping and aggravated battery charges in the beating of his girlfriend. During the kidnapping, Glenda Richard was held hostage in his apartment and beaten with a metal flashlight over the course of three hours. It was also learned that a number of police officers had their pick of stolen cars. Although they were supposed to notify the owners of the cars, officers instead appropriated the cars for personal use.[30]

In an attempt to change the culture of the NOPD during his last year in office, Barthelemy asked the city's Advisory Committee on Human Relations to study the excessive force problems within the NOPD and submit a list of recommendations. Its most important recommendation concerned the ineffectiveness of the internal affairs division and the office of municipal investigation. The thirty-four-person committee recommended the replacement of the OMI with a stronger unit consisting of both police officers and civilians. The new office would hear evidence about police misconduct and then make binding disciplinary decisions with the advice of the police chief and the mayor's office. Rabbi Edward P. Cohn talked about the necessity of this new unit. "The police department itself helps to cover up such people through the code of silence, and anyone who rats on another guy will find himself never promoted. Those signals come from the top and work their way down." The committee also suggested that the NOPD make quarterly reports to the public detailing the number, type, and resolution of citizen complaints about misconduct; the number of excessive force lawsuits filed against the city and individual officers; and the amount of money the city paid to settle such cases. Arnesta Taylor dismissed the report and got himself fired after making the following comment concerning excessive force: "Use of force, as unpleasant as it may be, will unfortunately always be part and parcel of police work. There will be those who speak only the language of violence and understand only the language of force."[31]

When Taylor announced his retirement that summer, Barthelemy made another safe appointment by picking another African American in-house candidate, forty-five-year-old Joseph Orticke, Jr., to be the new chief. Orticke was excited about the opportunity: "We're starting today with a new police department, a new front, and a new attack on crime." The twenty-five-year veteran was certainly optimistic, but he did not have a clue as to how to reform the corrupt department. Less than three weeks after he took office, the NOPD was forced to lay off 120 officers despite a soaring murder rate. As Barthelemy's two terms came to an end, police reform activists were elated. During his eight years in office, the mayor did not attempt or accomplish anything in the area of police reform. His inability to tackle the corruption within the NOPD proved that black leadership did not necessarily mean black concerns would get addressed. Despite confronting a host of structural issues during his tenure, Barthelemy could have paid more attention to law enforcement considering the city's escalating crime rate and a string of police scandals. As a black moderate who maintained close ties with the city's economic elite, Barthelemy preferred the status quo to real change in the area of law enforcement. His appointments of Taylor and Orticke were clear signs that he was not interested in using his office as an agent of change and it was also a sign to black residents that black mayors did not have the same philosophy of governance.[32]

The wanton corruption and brutality by black officers during the Barthelemy regime quieted the anti-brutality activists who had been so visible during Morial's tenure. Since much of the protest during Morial's years as mayor focused on the racism of the white police officer, activists were unable to adjust their protest to deal with corrupt black officers. They failed to understand that although police brutality had historically been a black and white issue, there was a distinct institutional culture within police departments that transcended race. Thus, activists were beginning to realize that the problem of police brutality could no longer be attributed to white racism when black officers were committing outrageous and unthinkable acts of violence toward black civilians. This culture would become more apparent during the early years of Marc Morial's administration and anti-brutality activism would virtually disappear as Dutch's son embarked upon an ambitious plan to professionalize the NOPD.[33]

9 "A NEW DAY IN BABYLON"
The Professionalization of the New Orleans Police Department and the Claiming of Urban Public Space

SIMPLY THE BEST PERSON FOR THE JOB

In 1993, Marc H. Morial captured the mayor's office largely on a platform to completely overhaul the New Orleans Police Department (NOPD) and stamp out corruption and brutality. The thirty-six-year-old attorney and alumnus of the University of Pennsylvania and Georgetown Law School ran an unsuccessful race for Congress in 1990, and between 1992 and 1994 he earned a great deal of political experience while serving in the Louisiana state Senate. After defeating Donald Mintz, a white candidate in the 1994 mayor's race, Morial was eager to change the perception that New Orleans was a dangerous city with an even more dangerous police force. While his father had to confront white racism on the police force during his tenure as mayor, the younger Morial would confront a group of rogue black cops who preyed upon black citizens. Morial would witness the NOPD sink to an all-time low, but he would also be instrumental in its transformation.

Shortly after taking office, Morial received a rather thorough transition report on the NOPD. The *NOPD Revisited* by the International Association of Chiefs of Police examined every area of the department and provided the young mayor with specific instructions on how to reform the troubled police force. Community-based policing was the association's primary recommendation. While the report admitted that this required training, planning, retraining, public education, and, most important, a change in the departmental culture, the consultants were confident that it could be achieved. More specifically, the report also recommended raising the standards for new recruits, limits on paid details and outside employment, public housing policing, integrity training, separate office space for the internal affairs division, and a national search for a new police chief.[1]

After his election, Morial received a $1.26 million federal grant to hire more officers and for other innovative programs. He then announced a major crime initiative to add police, training, citywide curfews, and more recreational programs. In the plan labeled "New Sheriff in Town," Morial promised a hundred more police officers added to street patrols, mobile NOPD stations to target high-crime areas, a gun buy-back program, and conflict resolution training for NOPD officers. While these were excellent ideas, Morial's supporters and existing officers were more concerned with the choice of a new superintendent.[2]

The formation of a Police Superintendent Search Committee was launched by Morial shortly after taking office. Reverend Harold Mayberry, pastor of Payne Memorial African Methodist Episcopal Church, and business leader Ralph Brennan chaired the committee. The committee was assisted by the Police Executive Research Forum, a Washington think tank on the "leading edge of modern police management research." After a grueling six-month-long search to find a new chief, the young Morial settled on an outsider from Washington, D.C., forty-seven-year-old Richard Pennington, a native of Little Rock, Arkansas. The twenty-six-year veteran and deputy chief of the Washington Police Department assumed control of the 1,475-member NOPD on October 14, 1994, at a salary of $92,000, approximately $30,000 more than that of his predecessor. "Superintendent Pennington was simply the best. Insider, outsider, male, female, black white, Northerner, Southerner. He was the best because he combined the qualities that I saw in a variety of individuals in one package." Morial was particularly impressed with the breadth of Pennington's experience. While in Washington Pennington worked in almost every aspect of policing, including stints as a patrol officer, head of homicide, district commander, robbery detective, recruiter, and budget director. Morial stated that his experience in the nation's capital "represents know-how, it represents ability, it represents command performance." Pennington fit the profile that Morial was looking for in a chief: an experienced African American from the outside with a solid track record. But Pennington was not Morial's first choice. Both Joseph Leake, head of New York City's Housing Authority, and Clarence Bradford, an assistant chief with the Houston Police Department, turned him down. In addition to the Pennington appointment, Morial also named former Chief Joseph Giarrusso as commissioner of criminal justice for the city of New Orleans.[3]

As expected, rank-and-file officers of the NOPD greeted Pennington with both optimism and apprehension. One officer, who could not give his or her name because of the department's policy against speaking to the media, stated, "I think it's great. We finally have a chance to get this department moving." But another added, "There's a lot of apprehension. I think he really needs to come in and take control to gain the confidence of the upper management." One officer felt that Pennington's record in the nation's capital was all hype. "If he was coming in on a wave of crime reduction in D.C. that would be different. Remember, Washington was the first city to ask for help from the National Guard."[4]

Regardless of how he was greeted by the officers, Pennington knew that he had a tough job ahead of him. Since 1992, the department had been under a U.S. Justice Department investigation for civil rights violations in brutality cases. He was taking charge of a department riddled with corruption and a city that was on pace to set a record high for murders. The rest of the country knew that Pennington's job would not be easy as well when 60 *Minutes* did a segment called "NOPD Blue" that examined the corruption, brutality, and incompetence of the NOPD. At his first city council meeting, Pennington told council members that he had plans to make a number of "very controversial" changes in his first year on the job. He spoke briefly about putting more officers on the street, limiting overtime details, and bringing professionalism to the department as part of council's budget hearings. When Councilwoman Suzanne Terrell mentioned that the NOPD received money to hire two hundred civilians to take over jobs being performed by officers but that one year later only seventy-seven civilians had been hired, Pennington had a wonderful response. "It might have happened last time, but it won't happen next time," he said. At the close of the session, Terrell told Pennington that he had "restored some faith" in the department."[5]

KILLER COPS

On the day of Pennington's inauguration, federal officials arrested nine officers under allegations of contract murder and protecting cocaine dealers. In addition, they arrested Officer Len Davis, along with two civilians, Paul Hardy and Damon Causey, in the contract murder of Kim Groves, who had filed a police brutality complaint against Davis a day earlier. On the day of the murder, Davis plotted the killing over phone lines tapped by the FBI, which was concluding a ten-month probe into a large-scale cocaine operation that was being protected by Davis and other officers. On the day Davis found out that Groves had filed a complaint against him, he dialed Hardy, who had been arrested but cleared in two previous murders. As he dialed Hardy's number, he said to himself, "I can get P [Hardy] to come and do that whore now and then we can handle the 30." In police code, 30 is the signal for a homicide. That evening he and Hardy spoke several times over cellular phones that were tapped. Davis described Groves in great detail to Hardy and told him where she lived. In a conversation recorded at 10:43 p.m., Davis told Hardy, "I got the phone on and the radio. After it's done, go straight uptown and call me." Groves was shot in the back of the head and killed just minutes later. Police officially lodged her death at 11:22 p.m. The following transcript reveals how Davis and his partner, Sammie Williams, reacted:

DAVIS: Yes!
WILLIAMS: It's the whore!
DAVIS: Yes!
WILLIAMS: Hello.
HARDY: Yeah, what's happening?
WILLIAMS: (Laughing) It's confirmed, daddy.

Davis, Hardy, and Causey, who hid the murder weapon, were charged with conspiring to violate the civil rights of Groves by killing her, a capital offense.[6]

In addition to the murder, eight other officers were arrested as a result of the federal probe, which was so secretive that former Chief Joseph Orticke was not even told about the investigation. The officers were indicted on charges of conspiring to distribute large amounts of cocaine. The investigation ended a bit prematurely after the Groves killing because they had to get Davis, who recruited the other officers into the drug protection scheme, off the street. Once Pennington got word of the arrests, he called the NOPD top brass and scores of other officers to the municipal training academy and each was given a subpoena to testify before a federal grand jury.[7]

The city was even more outraged when residents learned that Davis had a long history of complaints. "He's got an internal affairs jacket so thick as a telephone book. But supervisors have swept his dirt under the rug for so long that it's coming back to haunt them." Since Davis joined the force in 1987, he had been suspended four times and reprimanded twice, including a five-day suspension for striking a woman in the head with a flashlight. Further, Davis had twenty complaints against him that were never acted upon. The complaints included brutality, physical intimidation, and theft.

Mary Howell, a local attorney who specialized in police cases, stated that "Davis is an example of the complete dysfunction of the department and the inability of internal affairs to police itself." Davis, whose patrol included the Desire Projects, was known as the "Desire Terrorist." According to Reverend Raymond Brown, Davis was "very brutal." Although project residents and Councilman Johnny Jackson attempted to get Davis transferred to another neighborhood, the transfer never happened.[8]

In an effort to root out all corruption, Pennington and Morial asked the FBI to join forces with them. The FBI agreed to work with the NOPD and Pennington assigned them to work with the newly formed public integrity division. This arrangement was the only one of its kind in the country. FBI Director Louis Freeh stated that "it's obviously in response to very serious problems that both the FBI and the chief and the mayor recognize." The joint effort also meant that the NOPD would be able to capitalize on the up-to-date technology of the FBI. Lieutenant Sam Fradelia of the NOPD stated that "this will give us the opportunity to be very creative in our investigations." Although the indictments were the catalyst for the partnership, Freeh told reporters that his office had planned to work more closely with the NOPD once they discovered how involved the officers were in protecting the drug warehouse.[9]

Davis's mastermind behind the killing of Groves cemented the idea into the minds of everyone that the Fifth District was far and away the worst precinct in the city. This perception was partly because the city's worst officers were sent there to work. The district included the Desire and Florida housing projects, and it had the city's highest murder rate. Of the city's 421 murders in 1994, 145 occurred in the Fifth District and 26 occurred in the Florida Housing Projects. "There's no question the exposure to temptation is greater here than elsewhere," said Captain Lonnie Swain, the district's commanding officer. According to rank-and-file officers, the Fifth District was a cesspool of bad and corrupt police officers, given room to mix with the worst element of street people. But while Swain acknowledged that there were some problems, he argued that they were in the process of changing the reputation. "It's true the Fifth has been utilized as a dumping ground by the department in the past, but it's also in the process of change." The Fifth District was no stranger to the worst kind of police corruption. In 1985, Officer Lloyd Dickerson was arrested for a string of armed robberies he pulled while in uniform. U.S. Attorney Eddie Jordan stated that while the Fifth District was bad, it was not the only spot of corruption in the NOPD. "The

Fifth District is just one cell of corruption, and it is not far-fetched to assume there are other cells with just as many corrupt officers as the Fifth
District; I wouldn't be shocked if that were the case," he said.[10]

What made Davis such an interesting figure is that in 1993 he was presented the NOPD's second highest honor, the Medal of Merit. He was one
of only fifteen officers to receive the medal. One of the others was his partner Sammie Williams.[11]

The only reason Groves filed a complaint against Davis was because the
brutality "was getting close to home," said Groves's great-grandmother.
"You're wondering who might have killed her and when you find out it was
the police, suddenly it's not just the people on the street causing all this
murder," said Francine Green, a friend of Groves, who was with her just
minutes before she was killed. Reverend Brown put it simply, "The black
community here is under attack from the police department. Our complaints have gone nowhere for years because the police have covered them
up." One of Groves's neighbors, Lorraine Ford, stated that she was scared.
"I'm afraid to call the police department and say anything."[12]

On December 14, 1994, Davis and eight others were arraigned in federal court on charges related to guarding a Franklin Avenue warehouse
where cocaine was stored. They were paid about $100,000 during the investigation. All of the officers were suspended and detained after two days
of hearings. Assistant U.S. Attorney Mike McMahon told the court, "It is
the position of the court that each one of these so-called cops is a disgrace
and a menace and should be detained without bond." One week later, Davis was arraigned on the murder charges in federal court where he, Davis,
and Causey pled not guilty. However, after a week-long trial, Davis was convicted of conspiring to violate Groves's civil rights and he was sentenced to
death; he was later sentenced to life for his involvement as ringleader of the
cocaine operation.[13]

While the city and Pennington were shocked by the actions of Davis
and the other officers, Pennington was convinced that he had to reform the
NOPD quickly and in the process bring down the city's murder rate. Pennington perhaps found it ironic that on the day of his swearing-in, Davis
was orchestrating the cold-blooded execution of Groves. Pennington recalled that when local FBI Chief Neil Gallagher confronted him about the
killing, he was blown away. "I was devastated. I didn't show any emotion
on the outside, but inside, I felt like everything was dropped on me at one
time." He then recalled being warned about the challenges the NOPD pre-

sented to any new chief: a runaway murder rate, low morale, and rampant corruption. Despite the challenges he faced in his first few months on the job, Pennington told a reporter, "I'm enjoying it. We have a lot of work to do, but I wouldn't want to be anywhere else." Although the public was eager to see the new chief's reorganization plans, Pennington was playing it close to the vest until he learned about all the inner-workings of the NOPD. However, Pennington did warn residents that "it took a long time for the department to deteriorate. It will take a long time to make the organization outstanding."[14]

As Pennington was putting his plans into effect, he was hit with another hideous and barbaric form of police corruption. In the early morning hours of March 4, 1995, Officer Antoinette Frank, twenty-three, and a friend, Roger Lacaze, eighteen, entered the Kim Anh Restaurant in New Orleans East at approximately 1:50 a.m. Frank, who moonlighted there as a means of earning extra income, knew that the Vietnamese family-owned restaurant often had large sums of money on hand. The restaurant was also the moonlighting detail of her partner Ronald Williams, II, a white officer. Frank arrived at the restaurant knowing that the robbery attempt she was planning hinged upon executing all witnesses. Frank ate there earlier that night but came back less than an hour later with Lacaze. "When Antoinette came to the door the first time, Ha cooked her dinner, when she came in the second time she shot her," said Chau Vu, who hid in a cooler during the shootings. "I had a bad feeling about it. I told Ronnie not to open the door." Once Frank entered the restaurant, she "walked up to me real fast and say, 'Chau, Chau, I have to talk to you,' and she's pushing me back in the kitchen. I hear boom, boom, boom and she run back to the front." Lacaze shot Williams and then Frank stood over her partner and shot him in the head. Cuong Vu, seventeen, and Ha Vu, twenty-four, then fell to their knees in prayer, but they were shot in the back of the head and killed.[15]

Frank and Lacaze then left the restaurant in an old Toyota. But as word spread throughout the city that an officer had been killed and as other officers arrived on the scene, Frank showed up at the scene of the crime behind the wheel of a Seventh District patrol car. Her arrival aroused immediate suspicion because she was under suspension at the time. "She had left the scene and returned under the guise of bringing help," said Detective Sergeant Eddie Rantz. Nonetheless, Frank asked Chau Vu what happened. "You saw what happened you killed my brother and sister," he said. When questioned by police at the scene, Frank told a story that seemed inconsistent and she and Lacaze later confessed to the killings. At a press conference the next morning, Mayor Morial was at a loss for words. "The superintendent contacted me at 3:00 a.m. with this shocking and disappointing news, I was left somewhat speechless," he said. Pennington used the tragedy to stress his commitment to clean up the department. "The time where things like this would happen and nothing would occur—those days are gone. It's evident and apparent that when we get complaints about police officers, we're going to act." Fellow officers of the Seventh District spoke highly of Williams. "Ronald was an excellent police officer, you can't imagine anyone wanting to kill him. And for what? Ten thousand dollars?" said one officer, stating the amount taken in the robbery. Others could not believe Frank's involvement. "Everybody's shocked, she was one of the best people in her graduating class, she was soft spoken, and not very aggressive. It's like a different person," the officer said. Frank's neighbors recalled that they were excited when she moved next door. "My husband and I were excited knowing we had a police officer next door. And she always had a lot of cops over there, which made us feel even safer," said Diance Mason.[16]

The Williams family was in total shock. Williams's wife had just given birth to a boy earlier that week. "To think we started our week celebrating a birth and now . . . It's the most terrifying thing to have people come to your door at that hour to tell you your child is dead. You try to close your eyes and think it's not reality. And you close your eyes and hope and pray it's not true," said his mother. Although his mom did not want him to become a police officer, he joined the force in 1992, and he worked at the restaurant to earn extra money. "That child worked this night detail just to make a living for his family. My heart goes out to all the police officers that have to work details to survive," she stated.[17]

As the authorities attempted to sort out the crime, the relationship between Frank and Lacaze came under scrutiny. It was first reported that Lacaze was her nephew but then it was learned that there was no relation between the two assailants. Frank befriended Lacaze while he was recovering from gunshot wounds he had sustained in a November 1994 shootout. Lacaze's mother told reporters that Frank visited her son the night he was released from the hospital. "He got out of the hospital on a Tuesday. She came to my house that night," she said. About two weeks later, Lacaze began telling his mother that Frank was "crazy," because she kept following him. Lacaze's girlfriend stated that right around Christmas Frank bought him a cellular phone, a pager, and nice clothes. She even rented him cars from a local Avis dealership. Then Frank apparently started stalking him. "She started meeting with him often, said there was information she wanted to give him."[18]

As investigators, officers, and friends attempted to make sense of the killings, a background check into Frank made it clear she had no business being a member of the NOPD. Although she failed two psychological exams in the fall of 1992, she was admitted to the police academy anyway on the basis of a favorable examination from a doctor and a city psychiatrist. To further bolster her application, she managed to get endorsements from city officials, including former Mayor Sidney Barthelemy. When she hit the streets of the Seventh District, her supervisor recommended that she be returned to the academy for further training. "She really didn't seem to have a grasp on what she needed to be a policeman," stated one officer. Even some of her fellow officers wondered about her bizarre behavior. In recent months, they argued, she had begun to lead the life of a gangster in a police uniform. A February 1995 arrest raised several eyebrows about her behavior. In that report Lacaze was portrayed as a victim of a robbery, when witnesses stated that Lacaze was the robber. "It's looking like the persons that Lacaze and her were fingering were actually victims of the crime. They were actually perpetrators of something Lacaze was trying to pull and was using her to help," one Seventh District officer recalled. As a result of that discovery the arrested man was freed after the fictitious robbery charge was dropped. "There was no credibility on the part of the arresting officer or the alleged victim," according to the district attorney's office. Some Seventh District officers stated that Frank and Lacaze were partners in crime, drug-selling, and terrorizing New Orleans East through robberies and shake-downs. In September 1995, Frank was found guilty and sentenced to death.[19]

Of all the police scandals in New Orleans, the Frank case was perhaps the most unbelievable. Frank was the fourth NOPD officer charged with murder in less than a year. In April 1994, Officer Weldon Williams was charged with first-degree murder, attempted murder, and kidnapping in connection with the killing of one man and the shooting of another in retaliation for a burglary. In September, Officer Lynelda Sylve, a thirteen-year veteran, was charged with second-degree murder after she shot an unarmed man inside a lounge. And in December, Len Davis was charged in the killing of Kim Groves. Others were charged with rape, theft, extortion, brutality, and intimidation. For the city of New Orleans, the week of the Frank killings was the bloodiest in the city's history. That week twenty-one people were killed and nine were wounded in the city. Mayor Morial stated that after a bloody week and being notified of the Frank killings he wondered if the city was under some sort of voodoo spell. "I had the feeling that events were beyond our control. I had the feeling that this community has been cursed."[20]

THE REMAKING OF THE NOPD

Pennington did not waste any time in his efforts to reform the NOPD. In a letter to citizens of New Orleans, the new chief stated the reform of the NOPD was "a battle for the soul of the city." The chief reiterated to residents his commitment to "reforming and reorganizing the department, curtailing our crime epidemic, restoring public confidence and bringing dignity, integrity and respect back to the NOPD." He was hopeful that his reforms would ensure that the city's finest no longer be identified as "corrupt, brutal, or ineffective in carrying out their law enforcement duties."[21]

One of Pennington's major initiatives was new hiring rules to screen out undesirable recruits. This was a major problem Pennington had inherited from the Barthelemy regime. Under Barthelemy, the NOPD was so desperate for new recruits that they all but suspended background checks. Thus, the ranks of the NOPD were quickly filled with those having criminal records, questionable employment records, drunken driving arrests, dishonorable discharges from the military, and financial problems. Pennington told city council members one evening that the city's screening policy was vague and ambiguous. "There is no rule that says a fired officer can't come back to the force. We need specific guidelines so there are no ambiguities." He appeared before the council because he fired an officer who was dismissed from the force in 1983 for his involvement in stealing another officer's paycheck, but who was rehired by then-Chief Joseph Orticke. Although the officer in question followed proper procedures for reinstatement, Pennington's new guidelines disqualified someone with a history of drug use or a felony conviction.[22]

Much of Pennington's plans centered around the idea of community policing, a national movement that involved getting officers out of patrol cars and using foot and bicycle patrols as a method of fighting crime. The concept of community policing was based upon the idea that police officers needed to form a partnership with the community they served. In many ways it was a social work approach that suggested that police officers should be mobile social service agencies that looked to meet the needs of people instead of focusing strictly on fighting crime and emergencies. As community policing was implemented in other parts of the country, its critics argued that the police had no business getting involved in the affairs of its citizens except when it related to law enforcement. Despite the criticism from criminal justice experts, Pennington moved ahead with his community policing initiative because it had been successful during his time in Washington, D.C. The Pennington philosophy of community policing integrated the five major types of community policing: problem-oriented policing, the establishment of mini-police departments in low-income communities, community foot patrols, neighborhood-oriented policing, and foot patrol and fear reduction. Pennington knew that in order for him to be successful, the NOPD had to take an entirely different approach.[23]

When Pennington entered office, the city was on its way to a record-high 426 murders in one year. He was also high on the idea of putting mini-police stations in the public housing projects as a way of getting officers in the heart of crime-ridden neighborhoods. Although these proposals were very expensive and labor-intensive, Pennington was confident that he could start it in a small area, as opposed to citywide. "You experiment in those areas that are causing you the greatest concern. You put people on foot patrols, bicycles, motor scooters, even horseback. You can't do problem-solving in a car. You have to be out in the street making one-on-one contact with people," he said.[24]

The name of the unit that patrolled the projects was the community-oriented policing squad, or COPS. Morial praised the new program as a "commitment from the NOPD to stop the cycle of violence in our public housing developments. Officers will be working closely with residents, experiencing life within the developments and finding new ways to solve crime problems together." For the most part, project residents were optimistic. "We need this. We need to give these kids a chance to live," said one resident. But some residents were wary. "A lot of people are afraid of the police because of the problems that we've had with them in the past. Everybody here knows someone who's been harassed by a cop," said another resident. Pennington tried to allay fears by stressing the cooperative nature of the initiative. "This is a positive thing, not an aggressive initiative. I've seen this work in other cities. People just have to remember that it's a partnership."[25]

The new plans called for officers to move away from the desks and other assignments and patrol the complexes in cars, on foot, and on bicycles. "I think it does entail that all the agencies in city government work together to help solve problems. It entails taking abandoned cars off the street, making sure there's good street lighting. It entails making sure police officers are here for the citizen to provide quality service—all of those things. Not just one component," Pennington stated. Prior to the announcement, a hundred NOPD officers had just completed community policing training at the police training academy. Forty-five of the officers were immediately assigned to the city's most violent housing projects: Desire, Florida, B. W. Cooper, and Fischer. The substations opened in February.[26]

In addition to community policing, Pennington also outlined plans for limiting detail work, the number of hours per week officers could work outside jobs; making all officers report to the station in uniform, unless working undercover; and placing more officers in homicide and district division, by trimming other units. But his entire philosophy centered around community policing. "My goal is to put together a team together that will carry out my philosophy of community policing."[27]

When Pennington announced his reform plan at a special city council meeting, he began his talk by stating that he was beginning a battle "for the soul of New Orleans." In addition to his community policing idea, Pennington also announced the creation of the public integrity division, to replace the internal affairs division, with offices outside NOPD headquarters so that citizens would feel comfortable filing complaints. The new unit would be responsible for investigating allegations of corrupt and criminal behavior by officers, with a strong emphasis on criminal, as opposed to administrative, investigations. Another initiative was an internal "early warning" system to monitor the conduct of officers by tracking citizens' complaints and counseling or disciplining officers who violated departmental rules. A third major initiative limited detail work for officers to twenty hours a week, and it prohibited detail work in nightclubs and bars. All details now needed Pennington's permission. When council members mentioned that he was cutting off a major source of income for some officers, he responded that many officers were making "outside employment primary and police employment secondary." Also, Pennington implemented a police warning system to track citizen complaints against officers and a professional performance enhancement program that "also identifies and monitors police conduct so that corrective action can be taken before an incident of abuse occurs."[28] The mayor was ecstatic about the plans. "The reorganization and major reform of the NOPD will be tough, but with the leadership of Chief Pennington we can rebuild the department and continue our comprehensive efforts to fight crime in our city." Ironically, Pennington had said nothing yet of increased pay for officers. But he wanted to clean up the department first, restore public confidence by rooting out corruption, and then seek pay hikes.[29]

The Patrolmen's Association of New Orleans (PANO) immediately went to court to fight the twenty-hour detail limit and the outright ban on bars. "If an officer wants to work twenty-five hours a week as a carpenter or in a bookstore, then the city shouldn't be able to restrict that without showing it would affect the officer's police work." Lieutenant David Benelli of PANO stated that "the officers are ready for change and they're looking forward to working with the new chief, but they're aggravated that they have to reach into their pockets to do it." Also, alcohol store managers and club owners were outraged at Pennington's edict. But Morial informed reporters that the new detail rules were partly put in place as a key element of reform. "I want to let you know," he said, "that the International Association of Chiefs of Police, the National Guard, and the FBI said if we do not come up with a fair set of rules for details, we'll never change this department." Other officers were upset about the new uniforms Pennington unveiled. "A lot of the guys are disappointed about the uniforms. Mostly because it's tradition. It's a very historic uniform." Another officer added that the uniform was "sacred" to her. "I've seen officers get killed wearing this uniform. If it's good enough for guys to die in, it's good enough for me to wear." But most officers felt that Pennington was not allowing them input. "Once again, our input was neglected. How can an outsider come in and change our uniforms? It's like changing Mardi Gras colors or changing the Saints emblem."[30]

If officers thought that Pennington was not serious about curbing misconduct, they got a rude awakening when Pennington dismissed two officers, one for hitting a man with a police radio and the other for falsifying a police report. He later fired six new police recruits for a variety of reasons, including prior arrests, unfavorable military records, and shaky employment histories. The new chief even fired one officer on the eve of his graduation from the academy for financial problems. "He's saying that if you can't fit through the eye of this needle, you can't become a cop," said one officer. Another added, "It's unflattering, but it's something that needs to be done. This is the kind of change he wants."[31]

With a police force in the midst of a major crisis, Pennington was forced to reexamine a city ordinance that stated that city employees had to live in New Orleans in order to get a promotion. Although the ordinance was designed to curb white flight to the suburbs, it had the opposite effect of keeping potential good officers off the force because they did not want to live in the city. Morial was in support of the residency law because it kept a portion of the city's tax base from leaving. But with a police department staffed by unqualified officers and torn by low morale, understaffing, corruption, division, and brutality, Morial and Pennington realized that the residency requirement was having an adverse effect. When asked about the residency requirement, Pennington attempted to avoid the issue by stating, "The number one priority right now is crime and violence in this community. I don't want to get distracted by the domicile issue." When pressed for a comment, Pennington told a reporter that "as chief law enforcement officer I have to obey the ordinance." Although Pennington did not come out and call for the repeal of the ordinance, because Morial liked it, he did suggest that officers living outside of the parish be grandfathered onto the list of those eligible for promotion. The residency law was repealed in federal court when a judge ruled that the law did not apply to police officers. Many officers, including black officers, felt that the residency law was irrelevant. "You can live anywhere you want to live. I don't care. You can live in California as long as you come to work. If I could, I'd live in Mandeville or Covington, but it's just too far." But although the court ruled against the city and white officers were promoted, some white officers were still leaving the NOPD and going to nearby Jefferson Parish to work for the sheriff's department.[32]

Despite the controversies and scandals that Pennington confronted in his first ten months as chief, he still believed that his reforms were working and that a new professionalism had begun to emerge. There had been 366 murders (compared to 425 the previous year) and police brutality complaints had dropped as well. In his "state of the department" speech to the Metropolitan Crime Commission, Pennington spoke of the progress the department had made under his leadership. Among his accomplishments were a drop in the murder rate, greater visibility of officers in public housing complexes; a boost in the number of homicide detectives by 40 percent; stricter admission requirements for the police academy, more rigorous background checks, and tougher training; an increase in regulations such as prohibiting detail work in bars and a uniform dress policy; and the creation of the public integrity division headquartered away from other NOPD offices and assisted by the FBI. "We're going to continue to strive to continue to restore the public's confidence in this department, and these moves have made a difference as far as I'm concerned," Pennington said. He acknowledged that during his brief tenure the department had its fair share of scandal and shame. However, many of the officers involved in the corruption were on the NOPD payroll long before he became chief and it would take time before he could get rid of them. "I can't just walk up to a guy who was hired inappropriately ten years ago and say, 'I'm going to dismiss you,'" he said. He then mentioned that other problems needed to be addressed. "We've had individuals out sick for two to three years. I don't know what they do. They just sit at home. They're certainly of no service to me." But then Pennington acknowledged the most pressing concern: low pay. "I could go out tomorrow and hire 150 officers, but would they be the kind of officers you want to hire? I have to say no, because you have to address the pay issue. We've been very fortunate to have people apply based upon our pay scale." Although officers were to receive a 5 percent pay increase in July, Pennington stated that was just a start. He found it appalling that "officers in Kenner make more money" than the cops in New Orleans, whom he felt should be the highest paid in the state. "We should never be second to anyone."[33]

Pennington was particularly pleased that the NOPD had more of a presence in high-crime areas. In fact, the increased presence in the projects was such a success that the Housing Authority of New Orleans (HANO) considered letting the officers who patrolled the projects live in the complex rent-free. Pennington urged HANO to consider the proposal and they jumped at the idea. Officer Del Castillo, twenty-seven, planned to get an apartment in Desire because he enjoyed the people there and "my wife grew up in Desire." Similarly, Fannie Mae Mortgage Company announced that it would make available a $10,000 home-purchase subsidy if officers moved into

TABLE 8.

Complaints Received by the NOPD Public Integrity Division, 1995–2004

Year	1995	1996	1997	1998	1999	2000	2001	2002	2003	2004
CC	661	341	435	440	352	297	320	299	267	180
SI	233	294	231	272	291	268	203	194	180	187
Total	894	635	666	712	643	565	523	493	447	367

CC = Citizen Complaints

SI = Supervisor-Initiated Complaints

Source: Compiled by the author.

high-crime areas. Further, the chief was also elated that his initiative to put more marked cars on the road had been a deterrent to crime as well. Pennington even rode in a marked car that read "superintendent. If I can deter one crime driving from here to City Hall, then that justifies doing this," he said. Previously, special unit cars were unmarked, but Pennington marked all cars except the narcotics and homicide division pool cars. He also purchased twenty-six mountain bicycles, bringing the departmental total to thirty-eight, to help police patrol areas where cars had trouble maneuvering. Officers Michael Reily and Scott Monaco enjoyed the bike patrol. "It keeps us in shape," Monaco said.[34]

Pennington's reform efforts received assistance from a blue-ribbon panel commission that recommended the city boost police salaries by 40 percent to attract better officers and build a more professional force. "A culture develops where if you don't pay a lot, you don't expect much," said Xavier University President Norman Francis, the commission chairman. "This isn't anything magical, it's just you won't have a competitive environment." Francis stated that the increased salaries would cost the city $7 million a year and he believed that the money could be found by streamlining existing city expenditures. "There are no other choices. New Orleans cannot afford the luxury of waiting to start the development of an improved police force," the report read. Specifically, the report suggested raising entry-level pay from $16,334 to $22,885; paying bonuses to officers with a college education, $1,200 a year for an associate's degree and $2,400 a year for a bachelor's degree; and establishing a police foundation to raise money for specific programs such as tuition support for continuing education. The salary issue was of serious concern because Dallas was offering a starting salary of $24,618, a full $8,000 more than New Orleans. Because of the low pay, many highly qualified officers were leaving the state and Pennington was not able to attract quality men and women to the force. But the committee felt that the city had to act soon because of the high attrition rate and the plethora of convictions and indictments against officers. To meet its target of 1,500 officers, the NOPD needed to recruit approximately 135 new officers to the force every year. But Sandy Krasnoff, president of Victims and Citizens Against Crime, felt that the proposed salary increase was not big enough. "It's too little money," he said. "Base salary is the most important component of integrity."[35]

The chief's efforts received another show of support when the Metropolitan Area Committee argued that PANO was the main obstacle to Pennington's reforms. "The only consistently negative response to the reform effort comes from PANO," stated committee member Daniel Kelly. "Unfortunately, even though it claims an extensive membership in the ranks of black and white officers, PANO can arguably be considered among those who are not allies in reform."[36]

Just days before he delivered his annual progress report on the NOPD, Pennington launched "the department's largest overhaul in three decades" by announcing the transfers and promotions of more than two hundred police officers. "Restructuring the command staff in the police department gives these qualified officers the opportunity for career development that will ultimately benefit the entire department, as well as the citizens of New Orleans," he said. "This is a happy occasion for the officers and their families. They've been waiting a long time for this opportunity." Pennington appointed three new district commanders and a host of other positions got new leaders as well. Pennington was now confident that with the right people in place it was only a matter of time before the NOPD was completely reformed.[37]

During his annual address, Pennington rattled off a set of statistics to illustrate the positive effect of his reforms in such a short period of time. Among them were an 18 percent decrease in the city's murder rate, including an 83 percent decrease in the Desire, B. W. Cooper, and Florida public housing complexes; a 28 percent decrease in civil rights complaints to the FBI and a 23 percent drop in complaints against officers for illegal activity; more than $4 million in federal grants for community policing; new equipment for the city's crime lab; and a housecleaning of corrupt officers investigated by the public integrity division, which included thirty-eight arrests or indictments, eighty-nine suspensions, eighteen dismissals, and twenty-four resignations or retirements from officers under investigation. "The New Orleans Police Department is changing," he stated cheerfully. "We are becoming more professional. It's being done because the public supports it and demands it. It's happening because the rank-and-file of this department want it." But despite his success, and even though veteran officers agreed that he had earned the respect of most of the force and that officers were more disciplined because supervisors had become less tolerant, Pennington still had his fair share of enemies. One high-ranking officer was openly critical of Pennington. "He's done a poor job. He's driven a lot of good people off the department, both black and white. He doesn't run the police department; city hall does." Mayor Morial responded that politics had nothing to do with his initiatives. "These changes are real, and these changes will last because the people who oppose them have had their legs chopped off. This reform is coming because the people want it, and the people aren't going to tolerate anything less."[38]

Despite his success Morial did not include a pay raise for officers in his proposed 1996 budget. "That's something the mayor and city council have to decide," Pennington stated when he was asked how he felt about the budget. Morial argued that he was waiting to hear more from the blue-ribbon commission and that on principle he did not want to give police a pay raise unless other city workers received an increase as well. The budget called for $87.2 million for police, a $970,000 decrease from the department's 1995 budget. Consequently, the department was scheduled to lose eighty-nine officers from the force. Councilwoman Suzanne Terrell argued, "At some point, sooner rather than later, there needs to be a pay raise for police." She was right.[39]

THE PROFESSIONALIZATION OF THE NOPD

In March 1996, Pennington and the NOPD received a big boost in their fight against corruption and crime in New Orleans when forty business and civic leaders formed the New Orleans Police Foundation. "We want to enhance the capability of the individual police officer, out there, 24 hours a day doing his job," said Executive Director Terry Ebbert. The foundation's goals were to raise money for continuing education for officers, upgrade equipment, assist the families of officers, and provide in-service training and support for community policing. But Ebbert was also clear about what the foundation would not do. "We are not an oversight committee. We're not here to critique the police department or tell the chief how to run the department. We're not operational and we aren't replacing taxpayer funding. We're enhancing that base." Ebbert made it clear that "the end result we're after is to show a reduction in crime." Pennington embraced the idea. "This is what helped turn the crime situation in New York around—a similar police foundation there that channeled money to the police department to enable it to improve itself." Morial was equally elated and he called the foundation "a vote of confidence from the business people, for the recognition of what we've done so far, and the realization of how we have a long way to go to make the department what we all want it to be."[40]

If poor pay, low morale, corruption, and police murder were not enough issues to deal with, Pennington also had to confront a department that was way behind in information technology. The chief noticed the problem the first time he entered his office. "I wanted to know where my computer terminal was. I couldn't believe it when they told me there was no computers," he said. The lack of technology left the department with an outdated crime lab, a primitive crime analysis system to track crime trends, no computers to write reports on, and poor communication between the different divisions. This meant that a good number of officers spent way too much time handling paperwork and not fighting crime. Pennington wanted to see the NOPD move to an online system. "We have done things manually for too long. The proper way is to log things into a computer. Most police departments are getting away from paper trails. They don't have the voluminous amounts of records like we do." Although the department did have up-to-date forensic materials, that division was understaffed. "We have only three or four crime lab specialists who are running around the whole city. They have their hands full trying to process murder scenes."[41]

As a result of the manpower shortage, Pennington announced several changes: detectives would work in district stations instead of headquarters, officers assigned to headquarters would pull patrol duty once a week, officers on patrol would work twelve-hour shifts, there would be a large-scale recruitment drive, and there would be a limit to the number of 911 calls answered. Pennington acknowledged that his plans were not going to sit well with the rank-and-file. "I can't worry about that because I have to think about safety. That's my number one concern, and that's why I'm taking this approach." His administrative moves put sixty more officers on the street immediately.[42]

Spurred by the death of three restaurant workers in the French Quarter, the city council gave Pennington an additional $4 million to implement his initiatives, which included hiring an additional two hundred officers. But he told the city council that he would need additional dollars in order to cut the city's murder rate in half. The city council also approved pay raises for all NOPD officers after it enacted a service franchise fee for Entergy New Orleans. Pennington was hopeful that the increased wages could beef up the strength of the department to 1,700 officers. The increased pay gave recruits an additional $2,376 a year; sergeants $8,036; lieutenants $7,140; and captains $9,516. The pay increases went into effect in February 1997.[43]

Once the officers received their increased pay, morale rose quickly. Officer Robert Stoltz probably spoke for a lot of officers when he remarked, "Now I can start looking at buying a house. The raise has definitely made a lot of people happy." The pay increase also generated a flood of interests from officers from across the state. "I think that's why it is important to push for a pay increase, to keep good, quality police officers, but also to go out and hire good ones as well. You have something now to offer them," Pennington stated. Now with the pay increase many officers were now looking for the NOPD to deliver on other promises, particularly in the area of new equipment and up-to-date technology. "The bottom line is a lot of guys decided to stay because of all the reforms taking place, not just the pay raise. The department is definitely on the rise," remarked Sergeant Marlon Defillo.[44]

In an effort to handle the increase interest in working for the NOPD, Pennington set up a toll-free number, 1-888-NOPD-YES, which attracted 773 calls after the pay increases were approved. Each caller received a signed letter and an application from Pennington. Also, the Civil Service Commissions received 356 completed applications. Because of the incredible interest in working for the NOPD, Pennington was working to streamline the recruiting process and get officers through the academy and onto the street in a few months. However, because of the new standards, which included a thorough psychological evaluation and a battery of other tests, it would still take some time to get the recruits into uniform. One group of people looking for work with the NOPD were existing law enforcement officers from neighboring suburbs and parishes. Recruited by Pennington largely because they were experienced, they were able to bypass some of the academy training and get on the streets in a matter of weeks. But NOPD officials made it clear that they would not ease the process in an effort to get more officers on the street. "We need to work on as timely a basis as possible, but we're not trading quantity for quality. We're not going to skimp. We recognize that we have to be quite strict in our background investigations. If not, you only bear the fruits of such a problem three or four years down the road," stated Major James Treadaway, head of management and administration.[45]

In addition to the pay increase, another major initiative that was working to reform the department were "integrity checks" that involved various temptations, such as leaving a wallet around a police station and arranging for the confiscation of a bogus drug dealer's money to see if the money would be returned. "We began running them about three months ago," Pennington said. "In fact, we ran one against an officer four weeks ago and he failed. We fired him last week." Although Pennington did not go into detail about the tests, he did mention that when officers did pass a test their supervisors would be notified. Although the integrity checks were only done after a complaint had been filed against an officer, the chief was employing them randomly. "We want the whole department to know that we're going to check and see if everyone is following our rules and regulations. I mean, you hear it all the time: dirty cops in the department, dirty cops shaking down drug dealers, cops taking money. We just want to make sure that our officers are out there doing their job and not violating the law."[46]

With two years in office focused primarily on "bringing credibility back to the organization," Pennington now turned his attention to fighting crime in a major way. With the help of the New Orleans Police Foundation he hired corporate consultant John Linder and police strategist Jack Maple from New York City to help him with everything from recruit training to crime-fighting tactics. His major crime-fighting weapon was a computer program recommended by the consultants called COMSTAT, a program that analyzed criminal activity by showing the location of every reported crime. It also measured response times to arrest rates. District commanders analyzed and discussed the COMSTAT maps every week, focusing on crime trends and how to solve them. The district commanders embraced the program. "You don't want to be embarrassed. It forces the captains to be on top of everything in their territory. It really helps to see the trends and hear what's happening in other districts," said one officer. But it was also a nerve-wracking experience. Second District Captain Linda Buczek agreed: "It's a rigorous exercise. It's a very high-pressure environment. Every week you stand in front of your boss and you're held accountable for every-

TABLE 9.

Breakdown of Disciplinary Action Taken against Officers by PID, 1995–2004

Year	1995	1996	1997	1998	1999	2000	2001	2002	2003	2004
Fired	24	17	13	19	11	10	25	9	18	7
Suspended	79	97	135	100	89	104	82	71	117	109
RSUI/RTI	28	22	23	24	27	30	40	18	21	14
Arrested	36	23	20	26	24	19	28	26	11	24
Totals	167	159	191	169	151	163	175	124	166	154

RSUI = Resigned Under Investigation
RTI = Retired Under Investigation

Source: Compiled by the author.

thing that happened that week." As COMSTAT produced more results, it was embraced department-wide. "There's no more passing the buck. In the past, officers would be blockaded by territorial claims and red tape. A lot of things would fall by the wayside. Now, there is accountability." Another officer stated that "when I went to my first COMSTAT meeting it was the most professional display I've ever seen in this police department."[47]

COMSTAT was a major component of Pennington's efforts to "secure every street, every block, and every neighborhood in New Orleans." He told the city council that if they gave him the resources, he would cut the murder rate in half. That was impressive to many of his officers. One officer remarked, "How many police chiefs other than Pennington would go before city council and say, "Give me X, Y, Z and I'm going to knock down crime?"" But as usual there were detractors. "They're stat happy," one patrol officer said. "The game is to look good. It's generating paperwork galore." Despite this officer's statement, COMSTAT and other technology, such as patrol cars being equipped with laptop computers and a device that matched guns used in crimes by identifying the microscopic markings left on bullet castings, helped the NOPD fight crime. In the midst of the reforms, morale was at an all-time high. "This organization is becoming professional again. It's becoming proud. It's becoming successful. This is the greatest time in the world to be here," stated Assistant Superintendent Ronald Serpas.[48]

In the first full quarter of 1997, after the reforms were put into place, overall crime was down 23 percent, the murder rate down 22 percent, rape down 23 percent, and armed robbery down 31 percent. On the murder front between January 1 and March 31, there were 64 murders, compared with 113 for the same period in 1994, the year the city gained the reputation for being the murder capital of the country. Morial was delighted by the statistics. "Today marks an important step in our collective drive to rebuild the body, heart, the mind and the soul of our city." Pennington credited the crime decrease with three of his major reforms: the transfer of detectives to the districts, more accountability, and higher morale sparked by the pay increase. These reforms, he said, had allowed the department to concentrate on its primary mission: fighting crime. "I think the most important factor is that men and women have redirected their energies toward fighting crime," Pennington said.[49]

But in spite of the reforms Pennington still needed an additional two hundred officers, minimum, and he would have preferred an additional four hundred officers. But Pennington was clear what type of officer he was looking for. "We're looking for a higher caliber of officer. We're looking for people who want to be good public servants. Before we were just looking for bodies," he said. He preferred older and more mature officers. "We want them to make a difference." That October the NOPD had its largest class of recruits in its history when 67 people began training at the police academy; 6 months later, 100 new police recruits were in uniform. At the end of 1998, the NOPD had 1,670 officers on the streets with roughly 49 percent of those African American. As a result of the increased strength, the NOPD ended its 12-hour shifts for officers, which had begun in September 1996.[50]

As Pennington's stature grew as an excellent police administrator, he was asked to go back to the nation's capital and lead the police department. But Morial made it clear that he would do whatever was necessary to keep Pennington in New Orleans. "Because I believe that the retention of Chief Pennington is important to our continuing reform efforts, I am prepared to recommend that we meet or exceed any reasonable offer of compensation made by Washington." Pennington's $100,000 salary was among the lowest of all big city police chiefs and he looked at the Washington job as an opportunity to get a hefty pay increase. Terry Ebert of the New Orleans Police Foundation stated that his organization had begun a campaign to raise his salary to $175,000. "He is one of the lowest-paid police chiefs in America and is also one of the few truly successful ones." And Ebbert was prepared to use private funds if the city was unwilling to raise his pay through a mixture of funds from consulting agreements and university teaching contracts. As expected, Washington, D.C., offered Pennington a salary of $165,000 to become their top cop. Pennington told reporters that he was not interested in the Washington job because of its salary, but because of the huge retirement package it would give him. "If I went back to D.C., whatever my base salary would be, my retirement would be recomputed on that. If the base salary is substantial, my retirement would go up."[51]

Morial acted quickly to counter the Washington offer. He offered Pennington a base salary of $150,000 and $50,000 a year in pension benefits upon retirement. The proposed pay increase would make him the second highest-paid chief in the country, behind that of the Los Angeles police chief, whose salary was $207,130. Morial admitted that although money was tight, the city should not rely upon the private sector to pay the chief. "This is a governmental responsibility and we just need to face up to it. Money is always tight, and we have to find a way to do it." Morial then explained the economics of having a high crime rate and a corrupt police department.

"What did all of this corruption cost us in lost business? What have all these dead bodies cost us? What did the image of rampant crime cost us in terms of real estate values? If you subject this to a cost benefit analysis, it's an easy decision." John Casbon of the New Orleans Police Foundation stated that people should not get concerned about the chief's salary. "Whether it's $1 million or $10 million, that to me is a drop in the bucket compared to what the return is. You have to think more about that, rather than getting hung up on an amount. Three or four years from now, we'll be saying, 'Thank God we did that.'" Morial presented the proposed pay increase to city council in August and in October the city council approved the pay raise for Pennington.[52]

At the end of 2000, Pennington had achieved several major victories in his efforts to reform the embattled NOPD. The murder rate was down to 203 from its 1994 all-time high of 425, and the overall number of violent crimes had shrunk to 5,153 from the 1996 high of 11,115. Cases of police brutality were at an all-time low and the NOPD was more than 50 percent African American, with blacks represented at all ranks. The reform of the NOPD gave Pennington the reputation of being the nation's top law enforcement administrator. In fact, Pennington would serve as mentor for other mayors and police chiefs who came to New Orleans to learn how to implement similar strategies in their cities. At the United States Conference of Mayors Annual Meeting in Seattle, the city received the prestigious City Livability Award for police reform. Pennington and the NOPD were transforming the streets of New Orleans from "the city that care forgot into a city of hope and promise."[53]

PENNINGTON AND THE 2002 MAYORAL ELECTION

With Pennington's success in reforming the NOPD, he announced his candidacy for mayor of New Orleans in November 2001 when Morial failed in his bid to change the city charter and seek a third term. When it became clear that the chief was planning to make a run for city hall, several other mayoral candidates called upon him to resign his position. State Senator Paulette Irons, whom many considered the front-runner prior to Pennington, entering the race, stated, "Running for mayor takes up all of your time. Mr. Pennington should not put our citizens at risk, he should resign once he qualifies for this race." Irons, like the other candidates, knew that Pennington's level of success reforming the troubled NOPD made him an odd-son early favorite to win and Councilman Troy Carter made it clear that if Pennington entered the race it should not be as chief. "For the chief to throw his hat in the ring is one thing, but not his badge and the NOPD as well." Pennington did not understand calls for his resignation. "Nobody else is resigning, nobody else is stepping down, why would I have to step down when other people aren't stepping down?"[54]

Pennington formally entered the race two weeks later in front of supporters at the Fairmont Hotel and those in attendance listened closely as he vowed not to be a one-issue candidate. But he began his announcement by talking about crime and how he would "cut the murder rate in half . . . again," if he was elected mayor. He then took aim at the city's legacy of political corruption. "When you are serious about weeding out corruption, you don't drown it with rhetoric. You rip it out from its roots." He went on to mention that he would make economic development a priority by conducting a national search for a director; require all city employees to sign an ethics code; and introduce a CITYSTAT program, modeled after the NOPD's COMSTAT system, which would track complaints, evaluate the city's response, and hold city departments accountable. He closed out the event by announcing that he would take an unpaid leave from the NOPD to enter the race under the advisement of Mayor Marc Morial. His decision to go on leave made some citizens uncomfortable since the Sugar Bowl, the Super Bowl, and Mardi Gras were approaching in the post 9/11 climate. Nonetheless, Pennington decided to step down.[55]

Although Pennington had won national awards and received high praise from all segments of New Orleans, he was not necessarily well liked by the rank-and-file of the NOPD. During his tenure Pennington either arrested, fired, or replaced 350 members, which was roughly 20 percent of the 1,750-member force, and he had also made history by asking the FBI to scrutinize his own department. Consequently, Pennington did not receive an endorsement from either of the city's three major police organizations. Ironically, the Black Organization of Police (BOP) did not endorse him. When questioned about the lack of an endorsement from the BOP, a Pennington spokesperson stated that Sergeant Ira Thomas, BOP president, held a personal grudge against Pennington because the chief suspended him after violating the NOPD's private detail policy. Thomas, however, denied the allegations and argued that Pennington failed to meet with the BOP and that black officers received harsher discipline than white officers.[56]

Pennington finished second in the primary easily and he was now in a runoff with Ray Nagin, a fellow African American and CEO of Cox Communications of New Orleans. Nagin was a relatively unknown figure, and he did not have any prior political experience. The thinking in black political circles was that the white corporate community enticed Nagin to run since the previous mayor, Marc Morial, had effectively limited their involvement in city affairs. Pennington fired the first salvo of the campaign by labeling Nagin a closet Republican and referring to him as "Ray Reagan." Although Nagin was offended by the remark, it was clear that Nagin was not running the traditional campaign of a black mayoral candidate. He avoided black churches during the campaign, surrounded himself with black moderates and members of the white business elite, and pledged his support to the controversial Bureau of Governmental Research proposal that would create a special citizens committee to evaluate bids for city contracts. This proposal was seen in the black community as a way to limit black access to lucrative city contracts, something that virtually every African American mayor throughout America utilized to help black-owned businesses. In many respects the Nagin strategy was a virtual carbon copy of the deracialized Barthelemy effort of 1985.[57]

While the majority of New Orleanians appreciated the work he had done as the city's top cop, Pennington was not able to convince voters that he had the skills to develop the city economically and voters were also looking for a fresh face to run the city. He lost a in a tight race to Nagin and then he took the helm of the Atlanta Police Department. Prior to departing for Atlanta, Pennington told a local reporter that he did not want "a lot of pomp and circumstance" as a farewell. "Every day on the street, everywhere I go, people walk up to me and say they appreciate what I've done for the city. That's more than enough for me."[58]

A STREET COP BECOMES CHIEF

Although Mayor-Elect Nagin formed the Police Chief Search Committee in an effort to find a suitable replacement for Pennington, it was clear to many insiders that Nagin would select his next chief from the existing ranks of the NOPD. The committee received a total of forty-two resumes, but the list of finalists consisted of all NOPD veterans. Patrick Evans, Nagin's director of transition communications, stated that Nagin, however, did not want to exclude any potential applicants from the pool. "He's always said that he believed there would be strong candidates within New Orleans, but he owed it to the residents of the city of New Orleans to overturn every rock and look into every nook and cranny." After the interview process, Nagin appointed forty-two-year-old Eddie Compass, an African American, to the top job of the NOPD.[59]

At a news conference to announce his appointment as chief of the NOPD, Compass made it clear that as a native son he would not forget his roots. "Even though the mayor has blessed me with this position and made me chief of police, which I'm honored and humbled by, I'm still a policeman. And I will never forget that I was a policeman. I will always be a policeman because I feel the pain of the men and women in the street. I think that's been the secret to my success." He also stressed that although he admired his former boss, Pennington, they were two different people. "Chief Pennington did an outstanding job as chief of this department. Chief Pennington had his style, I have my style. And I'm going to define the department my way. I'm a community-oriented person. I'm a street cop. I embrace the community. And I plan on being just as successful as Chief Pennington was, if not more." As a lifelong member of the NOPD, Compass had the support of the rank-and-file largely because he had come up through the ranks as a patrolman, then as director of the COPS, and finally as captain of the First District. Under Compass's leadership, the COPS unit was extremely successful. Crime in the three housing projects it patrolled dropped and murders decreased by 73 percent. His agenda as chief was straightforward: "Basically, you're on the front lines. You meet with the community . . . It's very, very-manpower intensive. You have to go and actually go door to door talking to people. You have to get involved in the community. You have to make the people in the community feel as though you're a part of the community. And then they will give you information about drug activity that's going on in their area."[60]

The Compass agenda had six main components: (1) enlist ministers and religious leaders to help establish a witness support program; (2) start Boy Scout troops in the city's housing projects; (3) aggressively enforce a citywide curfew for youngsters; (4) raise NOPD salaries; (5) expand the city job program into the housing projects; and (6) work with the Housing Authority of New Orleans to increase the police presence. In late August, the Compass Agenda was sidetracked when nine people were murdered in the span of one week. Compass blamed the murders on turf wars, the heroin trade, and domestic disputes. But he was at a loss as to what to do to stop the killing. "We have to learn to get involved in the community," he said.[61]

At the end of his first year in office, Compass was faced with an escalating murder rate. By April 2003, the city had witnessed eighty-seven murders, a 47 percent increase ahead of 2002. Although he accepted respon-sibility, he wanted citizens to know that the city's murder rate did not necessarily reflect the quality of its policing. "When the murder rate is low, the chief of police gets too much credit. And when it's high, he should take the blame, because that goes with the territory." Despite the murder rate in-crease, crime was down by an unprecedented 21 percent and Compass could be optimistic that things would go better during his second year as chief.[62]

In an effort to cut the city's crime rate, Compass doubled street patrols in the city's high-crime areas and partnered with the housing authority to develop an autonomous eighty-cop squad to exclusively patrol the proj-ects. For Compass the goal was to get weapons off the street by conduct-ing "stop and frisk" checks. "We're going to treat law-abiding citizens with respect, but we're going to handle the criminals that are responsible for all this violence like the thugs that they are." These special patrols weren't the only initiatives Compass launched. He also expanded outreach programs through the COPS for Kids Program, and he wanted to develop late-night basketball.[63]

The initiatives were effective. By late September 2003, murders in the high-crime areas were down 43 percent, 150 guns had been seized, 155 sus-pects had been arrested in connection with confiscated guns, and 1,751 peo-ple had been arrested for a variety of drug charges. At a hastily called news conference, Compass stood behind a table full of confiscated guns, includ-ing semiautomatic rifles. "One of the reasons this press conference is being called is so we can show the community something is being done. We're do-ing everything we can."[64]

While Compass was busy fighting, the rise in crime his department was spiraling out of control with officer misconduct. In July 2003, Officer Ab-reace Daniel, a fifteen-year veteran, was accused of raping a Florida tourist; three months later, Officer Alvin Poole, Jr., was booked with malfeasance in office for trying to extort sex from a woman in exchange for a promise to delete her criminal record from a master database; and later that month, five officers were dismissed from the NOPD in a statistics-cooking scandal in which hundreds of violent crimes were downgraded to "miscellaneous incidents" and never investigated. Although the crime was inexcusable, the motivation to downgrade the incidents was to help their respective districts win the NOPD's quarterly crime-reduction awards. In January 2004, two Eighth District officers were arrested on charges that they threatened to arrest people who would not withdraw money from a French Quarter ATM.

Two high-ranking officers were suspended later that month when it was revealed that they inadvertently destroyed evidence from 1999–2002 that included narcotics, rape kits, DNA evidence, and weapons submitted by investigators as evidence. The overzealous housecleaning included evidence in more than 2,500 rape cases. In April, Officer Tawanda McAfee was booked with shoplifting after being caught on videotape at a drugstore for stealing a tube of chap stick. During the investigation of McAfee, local media reporters discovered that she had just been reinstated to the force after her common-law husband, Lawrence Brown, was booked with possession and intent to distribute crack.[65]

The misconduct continued in 2004 and 2005. Officer James Adams was arrested in April 2004 and indicted on charges of aggravated kidnapping, extortion, and malfeasance, while Officer Gregory Augustine, Jr., was arrested after conspiring to rob a bank. In June 2004, the corruption continued as Officer Tiji Sherman was arrested for soliciting prostitution, and in April 2005 Officer Corey Johnson was booked and charged with rape after he busted into a residence and forced a woman to give him oral sex. By the summer of 2005, Compass and the NOPD were in trouble: morale was low, officers were leaving the force, public confidence was near rock-bottom, salaries were not competitive, and crime was raging out of control. Coupled with the lack of financing, coordination, and interest, it was clear that the NOPD was in trouble. But Compass's biggest battle wouldn't be against criminals or rogue-cops. It came in the form of a natural and man-made disaster named Katrina.[66]

EPILOGUE

POLICING KATRINA

As the dire predictions about Hurricane Katrina controlled public discussion in New Orleans and the Gulf Coast throughout the month of August, the New Orleans Police Department (NOPD) did not make any definite emergency plans until thirty-six hours before landfall. At a meeting on Saturday, August 27, the NOPD command staff was instructed to tell officers that first and foremost they were to ensure the safety of their families. Second, the command staff was told to prepare for storm duty at police headquarters by 4:00 p.m. on Sunday afternoon. Although meteorologists and hurricane experts predicted that New Orleans would get hit hard, NOPD brass felt that police headquarters was safe.[1]

On Sunday, Mayor Ray Nagin issued a mandatory evacuation for the entire city. Although he had been warned weeks before that Katrina would be vicious, Nagin waited until just hours before anticipated landfall to evacuate a city in which between 80,000 and 100,000 people, mostly African American, did not own vehicles. After the evacuation order, officers went throughout the city telling citizens to leave. They stayed out in the streets until the winds reached fifty to fifty-five miles per hour. In giving the order, Nagin gave all police personnel the authority "necessary to cope with the local disaster emergency."[2]

Once the storm hit New Orleans at approximately 2:00 a.m. Monday morning, lawlessness and disorder settled into the city. First, the electricity went out throughout the city; second, flood waters swamped police headquarters; and third, the department's radio system stopped working after a piece of glass punctured the radiator atop the Entergy Tower. Thus, just one hour into the storm, the NOPD had no reliable way to communicate with its personnel. When the floodwaters breached the levees later that day, the NOPD received more than six hundred 911 calls within twenty-three minutes. But they were "helpless to assist." As the levees continued to breach throughout the city, the NOPD began to resemble a rag-tag group of independent police officers who were without effective radio communication, vehicles, boats, ambulances, ammunition, and weapons. With more than 20 percent of the city in water, the NOPD was sinking into chaos as evacuees filled the Louisiana Superdome. Once the Seventeenth Street levee failed Tuesday morning, more than 80 percent of the city was covered in water and the NOPD had no effective way to respond.

As New Orleanians found themselves stranded in attics, on rooftops, on porches, at the Superdome, and at the supply-less Convention Center, the NOPD was structurally not equipped to handle a catastrophe of this magnitude without the help of other law enforcement agencies. Officers soon found themselves trying to keep order in a city without order. They battled looters, carjackers, shooters, thieves, and armed gangs, without the possibility of backup and with limited weaponry and ammunition. Nonetheless, they rescued people from water-logged homes, recovered dead and bloated bodies, fought against looters, and continued to conduct dangerous patrols in a city without water, electricity, or telephones. Further, they set up makeshift living quarters, "supply depots, infirmaries in hotels, schools and nursing homes. They siphoned scarce gas from inoperable pumps using little more than hoses and a generator. They rigged car batteries for electricity, hot wired golf carts, and improvised boat repairs." The most remarkable feat of the NOPD, however, was keeping peace at the Ernest Morial Convention Center, where approximately 20,000 people had gathered without food or water. Despite the tales of murder, rapes, and just general mayhem, only six people died at the Convention Center, and none of the deaths were related to violence.[3]

Paul Toye, a fifty-three-year-old narcotics officer, had an experience typical of NOPD personnel. After securing his family's safety, Toye and his son began rescuing people on their boat. "I'll keep driving my boat until there's nobody left. I'll keep working as long as we're needed." Many officers such as Toye had begun working around the clock and many did not have a change of clothes, a place to sleep, or a place to relieve themselves. Officer John Pfeiffer told one reporter, "I borrowed my jeans from a friend and my own house is under water." Pfeiffer wasn't alone in losing his house. More than 80 percent of all NOPD officers lost their homes in the storm.[4]

Shortly after flooding began that Tuesday, the NOPD shifted from traditional police work to search and rescue. "Our priority was to save as many lives as possible," Riley said. "This was the ultimate enemy. What do you do when the enemy has cut off your supply routes, your food, your water, and puts you in a situation where your rescuers had to be rescued. Nothing prepares you for this," he exclaimed. The first people rescued by the NOPD were fellow officers. Close to three hundred officers were stranded by flood water and more than eighty off-duty officers were stranded on rooftops and attics. As they began rescuing fellow officers and then civilians, they often came under heavy fire. When Officer Tim Bruneau responded to a looting call at a pharmacy, his flashlight and siren were greeted with gunfire. On the Danzinger Bridge in New Orleans East, officers exchanged gunfire with an alleged sniper, killing two civilians instantly. But the NOPD did suffer one fatality. During the first day of the storm, one unnamed officer was murdered. Chief Compass was proud of the way his officers performed, considering the circumstances. "The bulk of this police department stood intact, we fought the most unbelievable war imaginable' and we survived. Some officers lost their houses and they're still out there. Some officers lost their family members and they're still out there."[5]

Despite the heroism of the majority of officers, a small portion of the NOPD used Katrina to continue the NOPD's tradition of law-breaking. Mayor Nagin's proclamation giving the NOPD "the authority necessary to cope with the local disaster emergency" led to looting by officers. The first sign of trouble appeared when officers were seen driving brand-new Cadillac Escalades and other cars from Sewell Cadillac Chevrolet in Metarie, a New Orleans suburb, and as far away as Texas. Dan Stead, president of the dealership, told reporters that he was on his way to Lafayette, Louisiana, when an employee notified him about seeing their vehicles being driven by some members of the NOPD. In all, the dealership lost two hundred cars during the storm and approximately forty officers were involved. Although the NOPD had the authority to use the cars for emergency use, they improperly failed to lock and secure the dealership. The second major case of NOPD lawlessness occurred at a local Wal-Mart, not far from downtown, where officers were seen looting non-essential merchandise such as DVDs, flat-screen televisions, and jewelry. One witness told a local reporter that one officer broke the DVD case so that people would not injure themselves in getting the merchandise. Other incidents of police misconduct involved police officers looting homes, officers turning a hotel into a private club and chilling beer with a generator stolen from Tulane Hospital, and officers taking refuge in a suburban Holiday Inn and threatening local cops when questioned. Former Chief Richard Pennington was not surprised at this behavior. "When some officers don't see their commanders, they become renegades. Troops will wait for instruction and guidance. I had no policy of allowing officers to commandeer things. It would have gotten out of control."[6]

While some officers served heroically and others became lawbreakers, 289 NOPD officers either failed to report, abandoned their post, or defied orders. Many officers, however, left to take care of their families. Officer Danna Aubert, twenty-five, spent the first two days after Katrina attending to patients at Memorial Hospital in New Orleans East. After being rescued by boat and taken to safety, she was distraught over the whereabouts of her five-year-old daughter and sixty-eight-year-old mother. After searching frantically for two weeks, she found them in a motel in Tunica, Mississippi. She was suspended and subsequently fired for failing to report. Similarly, Officer Nekeisha Barnes worked the first few days after the storm helping a group of hotel guests get to Baton Rouge; upon arriving in the state capital, she located her daughter in Opelousas, Louisiana, and took her to Atlanta. At a disciplinary hearing Barnes took offense to being called a coward and a deserter. "I'm a good police officer. I'm a tough police officer. It wasn't about me being a coward. It wasn't about me being scared. My only objective was to take care of my family." Officer Eric Doucette took his family to Tylertown, Mississippi, and then stayed there for the next three weeks removing fallen trees and cleaning streets. "I'm a man and I don't have anything to prove to anybody. They talk about desertion, but I took an oath to my family before I took an oath to the city." Assistant Chief Martin Defillo did not accept these excuses. "Dealing with personal issues is not a defense," he said. "Prior to the storm, police officers were given instructions to secure their families and get them out of harm's way. A lot of officers procrastinated." Officer Alan Bartholomew quit in the middle of a search and rescue operation. He later told a reporter, "Look, man, I stayed that whole week. No electricity, no radio communications. I hadn't heard from my wife and kids. I decided that my family was more important."[7]

Assistant Chief Warren Riley stated that those who left the force "couldn't handle the pressure," and that the NOPD did not need them any longer. Lieutenant David Banelli, president of the Patrolmen's Association of New Orleans (PANO), felt that the true deserters should be fired. "For those who left because of cowardice, they don't need to be here. If you're a deserter and you deserted your post for no other reason than you were scared, then you left the department and I don't see a need for you to come back."[8]

In the days and weeks after Katrina, the NOPD came under nationwide criticism. Stories about police lawlessness, police not stopping looters, and officers deserting the force led to the perception that somehow the NOPD was to blame for the storm, the levee breaches, and the resultant human devastation. Chief Eddie Compass stated eloquently to one reporter that "we [NOPD] faced the greatest challenge that any city has faced in the history of mankind." Despite his efforts to praise the heroics of his officers, he resigned weeks later as Mayor Ray Nagin looked for a scapegoat to cover up his own failures before and during the storm. At a press conference in which he took no questions, Compass did not offer a reason for his resignation. "I have taken this department through some of its toughest time in its history. But every man in a leadership position must know when it's time to hand over the reins to someone else."[9]

Nagin forced Compass out for several reasons: first, because of the widespread perception that the department was out of control; second, because it was rumored that Compass had left the city after the levee breech and did not return until three days later; and third, because of his unsubstantiated comments about babies being gang-raped and armed thugs terrorizing evacuees at the Convention Center. These comments were perhaps Compass's greatest mistake since it created a climate of fear that caused Federal Emergency Management Agency (FEMA) to both pull its medical personnel from the Superdome and temporarily suspend search and rescue efforts. However, Nagin was just bowing to public pressure in asking Compass to resign, feeling that the city's police department needed new leadership during the recovery period.[10]

The dismissal of Compass ushered in a new era for the NOPD. Nagin then appointed twenty-three-year veteran Deputy Chief Warren Riley as the city's top cop. At the press conference announcing his appointment, Riley sounded optimistic. "Hurricane Katrina washed away so much, but she also gave us a fresh start. We will rebuild this city better, stronger, and most importantly safer." At a U.S. Senate Hearing on Hurricane Katrina and law enforcement, Riley concluded his remarks by reminding the Homeland Security and Governmental Affairs Committee that despite the bad press the NOPD received during Katrina, "91% of the members of the NOPD, protected, sacrificed, served, prayed, and stayed all the way through Katrina and its seemingly endless devastation." One can only hope that this will

represent a new start for the New Orleans Police Department and its relationship with the African American community.[11]

CONCLUSION

For African Americans in New Orleans the issue of police brutality was by
far the most important civil rights issue in the postwar period and they
made a connection between fair police protection and democracy. Because
every African American could be an unfortunate victim of police brutality,
the issue of police violence cut across class lines and other artificial barriers to racial unity in New Orleans. In a community that was divided along
socioeconomic lines, skin color distinctions, and cultural norms, police brutality served as the catalyst for periods of unprecedented racial unity. Consequently, the fight for fair police protection galvanized black protest and it
also triggered the creation of countless organizations that pledged to make
the NOPD more responsive to the needs of the African American community. Although historians have not given the issue of black activism against
police violence the attention it deserves, the case of New Orleans illustrates
that the fight for equitable law enforcement has been a consistent struggle since the 1940s and throughout the remainder of the century. In the
1940s, African Americans made concerted demands for black police officers
by suggesting that an integrated NOPD could reduce the high rate of crime
in the black community. After integrating the NOPD, black officers were often forced to patrol without uniforms, could not arrest whites, and were
often harassed by African American civilians who questioned their authority. During the period of the civil rights movement, the NOPD intensified
its brutality through violent attacks upon civil rights demonstrators. Years
later, the NOPD and the Black Panther Party engaged in a number of highly
publicized confrontations as tensions between the police and the African
American community reached an all-time high in the sprawling Desire Projects. The Mark Essex killings in 1973 touched off a wave of pro-police legislation that was designed to empower local police against black radicalism.
As the number of African American officers on the force increased in the
aftermath of court-ordered mandates, labor strikes, and an increase in the
overall black population, the Black Organization of Police (BOP) attempted
to demand wholesale changes in police behavior and policy. These efforts
were enhanced when Ernest Morial was elected mayor in 1977, making him
the city's first black mayor.

With Morial's election the city's black residents were eager to see him use his office to dramatically reform the NOPD. However, Morial was overly cautious in his approach to transform the troubled department and it resulted in the highly controversial police killings of four African American civilians in the community of Algiers in the fall of 1980. After a series of protests, which included a takeover of city hall, a boycott of Canal Street, and marches throughout the city, black residents were successful in getting the police chief fired, a guilty conviction against the offending officers, and the creation of a civilian review board, the office of municipal investigation (OMI). While the OMI was established to monitor and prosecute police misconduct, its success was short-lived as the city fell into the abyss of white-flight, economic distress, and a high murder rate fueled by crack cocaine. Because of its low pay, the NOPD quickly became a haven for rogue cops, many of whom were African American, who engaged in a wide range of illegal activity such as drug smuggling, sexual assault against women, and outright murder of civilians.

Mayor Marc Morial and Police Chief Richard Pennington embarked on an ambitious plan to reform the NOPD upon taking office in 1993. Over the next eight years, Pennington reorganized and reformed the department, and in the process he cut crime and restored public confidence in the NOPD. However, after a failed bid for city hall by Pennington, he departed New Orleans for Atlanta and upon his departure there was a return to the NOPD's decades-old tradition of lawlessness. This unfortunate reality continues to haunt African American residents of New Orleans and other cities across the country.

NOTES

INTRODUCTION

1. Gail O'Brien, *The Color of the Law: Race, Violence, and Justice in the Post–World War II South* (Chapel Hill: University of North Carolina Press, 1999), p. 143; Mary Dudziak, *Cold War Civil Rights: Race and the Making of American Democracy* (Princeton: Princeton University Press, 2002); Frank Donner, *Protectors of Privilege: Red Squads and Police Repression in Urban America* (Berkeley: University of California Press, 1992); Kenneth Kusmer, "African-Americans in the City Since World War II: From the Industrial Era to the Post-Industrial Era," *Journal of Urban History* vol. 21, no. 4 (May 1995): 458–504; Raymond Mohl, "The Transformation of Urban America Since the Second World War," in *Essays on Sunbelt Cities and Recent Urban America,* ed. Raymond Mohl, Robert Fairbanks, and Kathleen Underwood (College Station: Texas A&M Press, 1990). Since African Americans knew that filing a formal complaint against white officers would prove fruitless, they instead went to local civil rights offices for help. After receiving a complaint, the local organization would then contact the local black press and the story would often be in the next issue of the paper. For good studies that look at the nascent conservative ideology among whites during the postwar period, see Kevin Kruse, *White Flight: Atlanta and the Making of Southern Conservatism* (Princeton: Princeton University Press, 2005), and Matthew Lassiter, *The Silent Majority: Suburban Politics in the Sunbelt South* (Princeton: Princeton University Press, 2005).

2. O'Brien, *The Color of the Law,* p. 251.

3. The following community studies mention the fractured relationship between the police and African Americans and for the most part they note that the race riots of the 1960s were triggered by police brutality: Thurgood Marshall, "The Gestapo in Detroit," *Crisis* 50 (August 1943): 232–247; Karl Johnson, "Police-Black Community Relations in Post-War Philadelphia: Race and Criminalization in Urban Social Space, 1945–1960," *Journal of African-American History* 89, no. 2 (March 2005): 118–135; Matthew Countryman, *Up South: Civil Rights and Black Power in Philadelphia* (Philadelphia: University of Pennsylvania Press, 2005); Heather Thompson, "Rethinking the Collapse of Postwar Liberalism: The Rise of Mayor Coleman Young and the Politics of Race in Detroit," in *African-American Mayors: Race, Politics, and the American City,* ed. David Colburn and Jeffrey Adler (Urbana: University of Illinois Press, 2001), pp. 227, 230–231; Heather Thompson, *Whose Detroit? Politics, Labor, and Race in a Modern American City*

(Ithaca: Cornell University Press, 2004); Ronald H. Bayor, *Race and the Shaping of Twentieth Century Atlanta* (Chapel Hill: University of North Carolina Press, 1996), pp. 177–184; Leonard Moore, *Carl B. Stokes and the Rise of Black Political Power* (Urbana: University of Illinois Press, 2002); Robert O. Self, *American Babylon: Race and The Struggle for Postwar Oakland* (Princeton: Princeton University Press, 2005); Chris Romberg, *No There There: Race, Class, and Political Community in Oakland* (Berkeley: University of California Press, 2004); James B. Lane, "Black Power and its Limits: Gary Mayor Richard B. Hatcher's Administration, 1968–1989," in *African-American Mayors: Race, Politics and the American City*, ed. David Colburn and Jeffrey Adler (Urbana: University of Illinois Press, 2001), p. 73; Gerald Horne, *The Fire This Time: The Watts Uprising and the 1960s* (Charlottesville, University of Virginia Press, 1995); Raphael Sonenshein, *Politics in Black and White: Race and Power in Los Angeles* (Princeton: Princeton University Press, 1993); Kamozi Woodard, *A Nation Within a Nation: Amiri Baraka and Black Power Politics* (Chapel Hill: University of North Carolina Press, 1999), pp. 78, 258. For a discussion on the relationship between local police and the Mexican American community, see Edward Escobar, *Race, Police, and the Making of a Political Identity: Mexican Americans and the LAPD, 1900–1945* (Berkeley: University of California Press, 1999).

4. For a good discussion of these relationships between city hall and black political organizations, see Arnold Hirsch, "Simply a Matter of Black and White: The Transformation of Race and Politics in Twentieth Century New Orleans," in *Creole New Orleans: Race and Americanization*, ed. Arnold Hirsch and Joseph Logsdon (Baton Rouge: Louisiana State University Press, 1992), pp. 262–319.

5. For a good discussion on this brand of leadership, see Charles Payne, *I've Got the Light of Freedom: The Organizing Tradition and the Black Freedom Struggle* (Berkeley: University of California Press, 1995).

6. U.S. Department of Justice–Civil Rights Division, *Study on Police Department Complaints 1984–1990* (Washington, D.C.: U.S. Government Printing Office, 1992); "Cops or Criminals," *A&E Investigative Reports*, 1993; "NOPD Blues," *Sixty Minutes Television Program*, 1994; Human Rights Watch, *Shielded From Justice: Police Brutality and Accountability in the United States* (New York: Human Rights Watch, 1998); *Times-Picayune*, April 9, 2006.

7. August Meier and Elliott Rudwick. *CORE: A Study in the Civil Rights Movement* (Urbana: University of Illinois Press, 1975), p. 367; Kruse, *White Flight;* Robert O. Self, "The Black Panther Party and the Long Civil Rights Era," in *In Search of the Black Panther Party*, ed. Jama Lazerow and Yohuru Williams (Durham: Duke University Press, 2006), pp. 28–29; Dwight Watson, *Race and the Houston Police Department, 1930–1990* (College Station: Texas A&M Press, 2005); W. Marvin Dulaney, *Black Police in America* (Bloomington: Indiana University Press, 1996); Marilynn Johnson, *Street Justice: A History of Police Violence in New York City* (New York: Beacon Press, 2003); Dennis Rousey, *Policing the Southern City: New Orleans 1805–1889* (Baton Rouge: Louisiana State University Press, 1996); Dennis Rousey, "Black Police Officers in New Orleans During Reconstruction," *The Historian* (February 1987): 223–243; William Ivy Hair, *Carnival of Fury: Robert Charles and the New Orleans Race Riot of 1900* (Baton Rouge: Louisiana State University Press, 1986); Christina Metcalf, "Race Relations and the New Orleans Police Department, 1900–1972" (senior honors thesis, Tulane University, 1985); Louis Marchiafava, "The New Orleans Police," unpublished paper. Some of the more notable works that address police brutality and police oppression in the African American community are Paul Chevigny, *Police Power* (New York: Oak Tree Publications, 1969); Ellis Cashmore and Eugene McLaughlin *Out of Order: Policing Black People* (New York: Routledge, 1991); Robert Wintersmith, *Police and the Black Community* (New York: Lexington Books, 1974); Charshee McIntyre,

Criminalizing a Race (Kayode Publications, 1993); John L. Burris, *Blue versus Black: Let's End the Conflict between Cops and Minorities* (New York: St. Martin's Press, 1999); Jill Nelson, *Police Brutality* (New York: Norton, 2000); Andrea McArdle and Tanya Erzen, eds., *Zero Tolerance: Quality of Life and the New Police Brutality in New York City* (New York: New York University Press, 2001); James Skolnick, *Police and the Excessive Use of Force* (New York: Free Press, 1994); Homer Hawkins and Richard Thomas, "White Policing of Black Populations: A History of Race and Social Control in America," in *Out of Order: Policing Black People*, ed. Ellis Cashmore and Eugene McLaughlin (London: Routledge, 1991), pp. 65–86; David H. Bailey and Harold Mendelsohn, *Minorities and the Police: Confrontation in America* (New York: Free Press, 1969); *National Advisory Commission on Civil Disorders* (New York: Bantam Books, 1968).

8. Human Rights Watch, *Shielded from Justice*, pp. 47, 258–259.

9. For a good study on the culture of big-city police departments, see Rodney Stark, *Police Riots* (Belmont, CA: Focus Books, 1972); Wintersmith, *Police and the Black Community*; Burris, *Blue versus Black*; Kenneth Bolton, Jr., and Joe R. Feagin, *Black in Blue: African American Police Officers and Racism* (New York: Routledge, 2002).

10. See Wintersmith, *Police and the Black Community*.

11. See Bolton and Feagin, *Black in Blue*.

12. See Marilyn Johnson's work *Street Violence*, for an excellent discussion on how the targets of police repression changed over time.

13. For more on the New Orleans NAACP and Tureaud, see Adam Fairclough, *Race and Democracy: The Civil Rights Movement in Louisiana, 1915–1972* (Athens: University of Georgia Press, 1997); Sharlene Sinegal, "The Making of a Civil Rights Leader: Alexander Pierre Tureaud, 1927–1952" (M.A. thesis, Louisiana State University, 2001); and Hirsch, "Simply a Matter of Black and White."

CHAPTER 1

1. Bayor, *Race and the Shaping of Twentieth Century Atlanta*, p. 175; Laurie Green, *Battling the Plantation Mentality: Memphis and the Black Freedom Struggle* (Chapel Hill: University of North Carolina Press, 2007), pp. 81–83.

2. *Louisiana Weekly*, March 3, 1945. Similar protests occurred throughout the urban South and especially in Atlanta. For more in the Atlanta protest, see Bayor, *Race and the Shaping of Twentieth Century Atlana*; Ronald Bayor, "Race and City Services: The Shaping of Atlanta's Police and Fire Departments," *Atlanta History* 36 (Fall 1992): 19–35.

3. Edward F. Haas, *DeLesseps S. Morrisan and the Image of Reform* (Baton Rouge: Louisiana State University Press, 1974), pp. 13, 18, 24–25.

4. *Smith v. Allright*, 321 U.S. 649 (1944); Darlene Clark Hine, *Black Victory: The Rise and Fall of the White Primary in Texas* (New York: Millwood Press, 1979).

5. *Louisiana Weekly*, May 12, 1945.

6. *Louisiana Weekly*, May 12, 1945; "Petition, Requesting the Appointment of Negro Police Officers," Alexander Pierre Tureaud Papers, Amistad Research Center, Tulane University. Hereafter referred to as Tureaud Papers.

7. *Louisiana Weekly*, July 27, 1946.

8. *Louisiana Weekly*, August 31, 1946.

9. Haas, *DeLesseps S. Morrison*, pp. 32–33.

10. Haas, *DeLesseps S. Morrison*, p. 101.

11. *Louisiana Weekly*, June 29, 1946; July 13, 1946; Haas, *DeLesseps S. Morrison*, pp. 100–101.

12. *Louisiana Weekly*, November 2, 1946; January 25, 1947; February 1, 1947; "Medical Report of Earnest Raphael," January 1, 1947, Tureaud Papers; Affidavit of Milton Bienamee, Otis Fisher, Ernest Raphael, James Russell, June 1947, Tureaud Papers.

13. *Louisiana Weekly*, October 26, 1946.

14. *Louisiana Weekly*, December 21, 1946; February 1, 1947.

15. *Louisiana Weekly*, November 16, 1946; December 14, 1946.

16. *Louisiana Weekly*, May 3, 1947.

17. *Louisiana Weekly*, January 17, 31, 1948; M. Prevost et al. to New Orleans NAACP, January 9, 1948, Folder 53, State of Louisiana NAACP Records, Earl K. Long Library, University of New Orleans. Hereafter referred to as LA-NAACP Papers.

18. *Louisiana Weekly*, January 31, 1948.

19. *Louisiana Weekly*, March 13, 1948.

20. *Louisiana Weekly*, June 19, 1948; "Police Patrolman Registers," October 25, 1949, Tureaud Papers; African Americans throughout the South argued that black officers would help reduce crime in the black community. See "Negro Police are Urged as a Means of Preventing Racial Fiction," in *Negro Year Book, 1931–1932*, ed. Monroe Work (Tuskegee: Tuskegee Institute, 1931); "Negro Policeman and Crime Prevention," in *Negro Year Book, 1941–1946*, ed. Jesse Parkhurst Guzman (Tuskegee: Tuskegee Institute, 1952), pp. 275, 320.

21. *Louisiana Weekly*, August 28, 1948.

22. *Louisiana Weekly*, August 28, 1948.

23. *Louisiana Weekly*, October 23, 1948; "Biography of Carlton Pecot," Tureaud Papers.

24. Leroy Williams to Louisiana NAACP, January 1949, Container 58, LA-NAACP Papers; *Louisiana Weekly*, January 15, 29, 1949; February 5, 12, 1949; Frank Charles, Jr., to Tureaud, January 29, 1949, Folder 58, LA-NAACP Papers; Haas, *DeLesseps S. Morrison*, pp. 114–115.

25. *Louisiana Weekly*, February 5, 19, 26, 1949.

26. *Louisiana Weekly*, March 19, 1949.

27. *Louisiana Weekly*, March 26, 1949.

28. *Louisiana Weekly*, May 7, 1949.

29. *Louisiana Weekly*, June 4, 1949; Hass, *DeLesseps S. Morrison*, p. 77; "Civil Service Test Score of Carlton Pecot," Tureaud Papers; "State of Louisiana, EX REL Carlton Pecot v. Honorable Delesseps S. Morrison and Joseph Scheuring," June 1, 1949, Tureaud Papers; A. P. Tureaud to Milton Bienamee, June 15, 1949, Tureaud Papers; Alfred Hobart to Tureaud, May 11, 1950, Tureaud Papers; Tureaud to Hobart, May 12, 1950, Tureaud Papers.

30. Hass, *DeLesseps S. Morrison*, p. 77; "City of New Orleans—Civil Service Law," October 1944, Tureaud Papers.

31. Hass, *DeLesseps S. Morrison*, p. 67.

32. *Louisiana Weekly*, June 18, 1949.

33. *Louisiana Weekly*, June 8, 1950; May 27, 1950; "Minutes of a Meeting for the Organization of a Citizens Committee for Negro Police," May 10, 1950, Tureaud Papers; *Times-Picayune*, May 11, 1950.

34. *Louisiana Weekly*, June 24, 1950; January 12, 19, 1952; Hass, *DeLesseps S. Morrison*, p. 78; New Orleans Urban League to A. P. Tureaud," May 18, 1950, Tureaud Papers; For more on the first wave of black police officers in the twentieth century, see Elliott Rudwick, *The Unequal Badge: Negro Policeman in the South* (Atlanta: Southern Regional Council, 1962); Louis Marchiafava, "The Houston Police, 1878–1948," *Rice University Studies* 63 (Spring 1977): 11–13; Harold C. Fleming, "How Negro Police Worked Out in One Southern City," *New South* (October 1947); Elliott Rudwick, "The Southern Negro Policeman and the White Offender," *Journal of*

Education 30 (Fall 1961): 3–5, 7; Elliott Rudwick, "Police Work and the Negro," *Journal of Criminal Law, Criminology, and Police Science* 50 (July–August 1960): 596–599.

35. *Louisiana Weekly*, April 12, 1952.

36. *Louisiana Weekly*, October 4, 1952.

37. *Louisiana Weekly*, October 25, 1952; November 22, 29, 1952; George Dalmas to Delesseps S. Morrison, September 20, 1955, Box S56, Folder 29, Delesseps S. Morrison Papers, New Orleans Public Library. Hereafter referred to as Morrison Papers.

38. *Louisiana Weekly*, January 10, 1953; March 14, 1953; Elliott Rudwick, "The Negro Policeman in the South," *Journal of Criminal Law, Criminology and Police Science* 61 (July–August 1960), pp. 273–276. For an overall picture of black police officers in the South during the era of integration, see Elliott Rudwick, "Negro Police Employment in the Urban South," *Journal of Negro Education* 30 (Spring 1961): 102–108.

39. *Louisiana Weekly*, June 6, 20, 1953; June 19, 1954; October 2, 1954.

40. *Louisiana Weekly*, February 5, 1955; May 21, 1955; July 23, 1955; Provosty Dayries, Superintendent of Police to Carlton Pecot, July 13, 1955, Box SPR 60, Folder 7, Morrison Papers; George Dalmas to Delessepps S. Morrison, September 20, 1956, Box S56, Folder 29, Morrison Papers.

41. Dalmas to Morrison, September 20, 1956, Box S56, Folder 29, Morrison Papers.

42. *Louisiana Weekly*, September 17, 1955.

43. *Louisiana Weekly*, September 17, 24, 1955.

44. *Louisiana Weekly*, June 26, 1954. For more on the central role of these organizations, see Peter Feuille, *Police Unionism: Power and Impact in Public Sector Bargaining* (Lexington, MA: Lexington Books, 1973), and Tim Bornstein, "Police Unions: Dispelling the Ghost of 1919," *Police Magazine* 1, no. 4 (September 1978): 25–29.

45. *Louisiana Weekly*, November 5, 12, 1955; December 10, 1955. For more on the early history of African American female officers, see Janis Appier, *Policing Women: The Sexual Politics of Law Enforcement and the LAPD* (Philadelphia: Temple University Press, 1998), and Lois Higgins, "Historical Background of Policewomen's Service," *Journal of Criminal Law, Criminology and Police Science* (1951).

46. Haas, *DeLesseps S. Morrison*, pp. 205, 211; *Report of the Special Citizens Investigating Committee of the Commission Council of New Orleans—the New Orleans Police Department*, vols. I–VI, April, 1954, New Orleans Public Library. Also see *Organized Crime in Interstate Commerce: Hearings before the Special Committee to Investigate Organized Crime in Interstate Commerce, Eighty-Second Congress, First Session, Part 8: Louisiana, January 25, 26, February 7, 1951*. This report was a catalyst for the SCIC probe.

47. See Kruse, *White Flight*.

48. *Louisiana Weekly*, March 19, 1955.

49. *Louisiana Weekly*, March 19, 1955.

50. *Louisiana Weekly*, March 26, 1955.

51. *Louisiana Weekly*, January 14, 1956; For more on the resistance of ordinary African Americans on Jim Crow buses, see Robin Kelley, "'We are Not What We Seem,': Rethinking Black Working-Class Opposition in the Jim Crow South," *Journal of American History* (June 1993): 75–112, and Stewart Burns, ed., *Daybreak of Freedom: The Montgomery Bus Boycott* (Chapel Hill: University of North Carolina Press, 1997).

52. *Louisiana Weekly*, March 28, 1959.

53. *Louisiana Weekly*, December 5, 1959.

54. *Louisiana Weekly*, December 5, 1959.

55. *Louisiana Weekly*, December 12, 1959.

56. *Louisiana Weekly*, December 26, 1959; January 9, 1960.

57. *Louisiana Weekly*, March 26, 1960.

58. *Louisiana Weekly*, May 11, 1960.

59. *Louisiana Weekly*, July 16, 1960.

60. Prophet A. M. Calhoun to Delesseps Morrison, June 15, 1960, Box SPRO-60, Folder 7, Morrison Papers.

61. Hirsch, "Simply Matter of Black and White," p. 276; Haas, *DeLesseps S. Morrison*, pp. 68–75.

CHAPTER 2

1. Major Dominic Palmisano, Intelligence Division, NOPD, to Joseph Giarrusso regarding "Progress Report relative to Racial Activities during the month of September 1960," October 10, 1960, Box SPR-60, Folder 6, Morrison Papers; Oretha Castle Haley Interview, Amistad Research Center; Haley Interview, Xavier University Archives. For a fuller history of the civil rights movement in New Orleans, see Kim Lacy Rogers, *Righteous Lives: Narratives of the Civil Rights Movement* (New York: New York University Press, 1993); Ruby Bridges, *Through My Eyes* (New York: Scholastic Press, 1999); Barbara Worthy, *Blacks in New Orleans from the Great Depression to the Civil Rights Movement, 1930–1960* (New Orleans: SUNO-CASS, 1994).

2. *Louisiana Weekly*, September 17, 1960; Press Release by Mayor Morrison, September 12, 1960, Box SPR-60, Folder 7, Morrison Papers; Haas, *DeLesseps S. Morrison*, p. 217. The black community was optimistic about Giarrusso's ability since he had the reputation of being somewhat liberal.

3. Press Release announcing Joseph Giarrusso's appointment as chief, August 12, 1960, Box SPR60-7, Morrison Papers; Speech by Joseph Giarrusso to Police Officers, August 20, 1960, Box S60-3, Victor Schiro Papers, New Orleans Public Library. Hereafter referred to as Schiro Papers.

4. *New Orleans States-Item*, November 14, 1960; *Times-Picayune*, November 15, 1960; Fairclough, *Race and Democracy*, pp. 244, 250–251; Rudy Lombard Interview. For a more detailed look at the school crisis, see Lisa Baker, *The Second Battle of New Orleans: The One-Hundred Year Struggle to Integrate the Schools* (New York: HarperCollins, 1996); Morton Inger, *Politics and Reality in an American City: The New Orleans School Crisis* (New York: Center for Urban Education, 1969); U.S. Commission on Civil Rights, *The New Orleans School Crisis* (Washington, D.C., 1961).

5. *New Orleans States-Item*, November 15, 1960; Betty Wisdom Interview.

6. *New Orleans States-Item*, November 16, 1960; W. McFerrin Stone, "Willie Rainach and the Defense of Southern Segregation in Louisiana: 1954–1959" (Ph.D. dissertation, Texas Christian University, 1997). For a general history of the white citizens council, see Neil McMillan, *The Citizen's Council: Organized Resistance to the Second Reconstruction, 1954–1964* (Urbana: University of Illinois Press, 1994), and Ross Barnett, *Strength Through Unity* (Greenwood, MS: Greenwood Citizen's Council, 1960).

7. *New Orleans State-Item*, November 16, 1960; *Times-Picayune*, November 17, 1960; *Louisiana Weekly*, November 26, 1960; Joseph Giarrusso Interview, Xavier University Archives; Jonathan Sokol, *There Goes My Everything: White Southerners in the Age of Civil Rights, 1945–1975* (New York: Random House, 2007), p. 129.

8. *New Orleans States-Item*, November 16, 1960.

9. *New Orleans States-Item,* November 29, 30, 1960; December 1, 2, 5, 9, 1960; Fairclough, *Race and Democracy,* pp. 248–249; Haas, *DeLesseps S. Morrison,* p. 271; Giarrusso Interview; Iris Kelso Interview, Xavier University Archives.

10. *Louisiana Weekly,* January 21, 1961; Arthur Chapital to District Attorney Richard Dowling, June 4, 1961, Container 54, New Orleans NAACP Papers, Amistad Research Center, Tulane University. Hereafter referred to as NO-NAACP Papers.

11. *Louisiana Weekly,* February 25, 1961.

12. *Louisiana Weekly,* June 3, 1961; Arthur Chapital to District Attorney Richard Dowling, June 4, 1961, Container 54, NO-NAACP Papers; Interview with Alice Hite, wife of Thomas Foster, May 31, 1961, Container 54, NO-NAACP Papers; "Parents Authorization to Investigate Shooting of Allen Foster," May 31, 1961, Container 54, NO-NAACP Papers.

13. Statement of Helen Holloway, June 13, 1961, Container 54, NO-NAACP Papers.

14. Arthur Chapital to *Times-Picayune,* June 18, 1961.

15. *Louisiana Weekly,* July 1, 8, 1961; "Mass Meeting Resolution Passed at St. Mark's to Dowling," June 4, 1961, Container 54, NO-NAACP Papers; Burke Marshall to Arthur Chapital, June 4, 1961, Container 54, NO-NAACP Papers.

16. *Louisiana Weekly,* September 2, 1961.

17. *Louisiana Weekly,* September 2, 1961.

18. *Louisiana Weekly,* December 23, 1961.

19. *Louisiana Weekly,* December 23, 1961.

20. Edward Haas, "The Expedient of Race: Victor Schiro, Scott Wilson, and the New Orleans Mayoralty Campaign of 1962," *Louisiana History* 42 (Winter 2001): 17–18, 22.

21. Fairclough, *Race and Democracy,* pp. 335–336.

22. *Louisiana Weekly,* April 22, 1964; Alexander was involved in a similar affair months later when he attempted to integrate the Tango Restaurant and Bar. See "Statement of Rev. Avery C. Alexander," July 21, 1964, Box 28-54, NO-NAACP Papers; Alexander Interview; Revius Ortique Interview, Xavier University Archives.

23. For more on the Birmingham Police Department, see Glenn Eskew, *But For Birmingham: The Local and National Movements in the Civil Rights Struggle* (Chapel Hill: University of North Carolina Press, 1997), especially chapter 3.

24. *Louisiana Weekly,* March 16, 1963; "Alleged Police Brutality in New Orleans," New Orleans CORE, March 14, 1963, Box S63-19, Schiro Papers.

25. Oretha Castle, New Orleans CORE to Joseph Giarrusso, March 14, 1963, Box S63-19, Schiro Papers; *Louisiana Weekly,* March 23, 1963. Also see February 8, 1964; May 16, 1964; September 4, 1965; September 2, 1961.

26. *Louisiana Weekly,* January 11, 1976.

27. *Louisiana Weekly,* February 26, 1966. For more on civilian review boards and black demands for them, see American Civil Liberties Union, *Police Power and Citizen's Rights: The Case For an Independent Police Review Board* (New York: ACLU, 1966), and J. Hudson, "Police Review Boards and Police Accountability," *Law and Contemporary Problems* 36 (Fall 1971): 515–538. The New York City Police Department established a civilian review board in 1966. See Dulaney, *Black Police in America,* p. 73.

28. Horne, *The Fire This Time.*

29. *Louisiana Weekly,* April 16, 1966; Don Hubbard Interview, Xavier University Archives.

30. *Louisiana Weekly,* July 2, 1966.

31. Don Hubbard, CCPM to Joseph Giarrusso, April 25, 1967, Box S67-18, Schiro Papers; See the affidavits of Nancy Hollins and Alexcear Hollins for a typical statement taken by the

CCPM, April 24, 1967, Box S67-18, Schiro Papers; "Complaints of Police Brutality, January 1964–June 1966, October 12, 1966," Box S66-21, Schiro Papers.

32. *Louisiana Weekly*, February 25, 1967; "Citizens Inquiry Card," Box S67-17, Schiro Papers; Aaron Kohn, Metropolitan Crime Commission to Arthur Chapital, February 15, 1967, Box 28-220, NO-NAACP Papers.

33. *Louisiana Weekly*, February 25, 1967; Arthur J. Chapital to New Orleans City Council, February 14, 1967, Box 28-220, NO-NAACP Papers; "Press Release on Stop and Frisk Law and Citizen Inquiry Cards," February 17, 1967, Box 28-221 NO-NAACP Papers.

34. *Louisiana Weekly*, March 25, 1967; "Stop and Frisk Ordinance," City of New Orleans, January 12, 1967, Box 28-220 NO-NAACP Papers; "Repeal the Stop and Frisk Law," New York Civil Liberties Union, undated, Box 28-220, NO-NAACP Papers; "Stop and Think Instead of Stop and Frisk," undated, Box 28-203, NO-NAACP Papers.

35. *Louisiana Weekly*, April 1, 1967; Joseph Giarusso to Mayor Schiro, Box S67-18, July 3, 1967, Morrison Papers; New Orleans City Council Meeting Minutes, March 23, 1967, Box 77, City Council Papers, New Orleans Public Library. Hereafter referred to as City Council Papers; Milton Upton, Interdenominational Ministerial Alliance to the New Orleans City Council, February 19, 1967, Box 28-220, NO-NAACP Papers; Chapital to New Orleans City Council, March 6, 1967, Box 28-220, NO-NAACP Papers.

36. Joseph Giarrusso to Victor Schiro, July 3, 1967, "Stop and Frisk Law Statistics," Box S67-18, Schiro Papers.

37. Horace Bynum to Joseph Giarrusso, October 3, 1966, Box S67-17, Schiro Papers; Joseph Giarrusso to Mayor Victor Schiro, "Proposed Summer Program . . .," April 13, 1967, Box S67-17, Schiro Papers; "Summer Program Outline," April 13, 1967, Schiro Papers; Michael Banton, *The Policeman in the Community* (New York: Basic Books, 1964). The President's Commission on Law Enforcement and Justice suggested that police departments should establish better relationships with minority groups.

38. "Activities of the CRD," undated, Box S67-18, Schiro Papers; For a more complete description of the division's activities, see *New-Orleans States-Item*, March 16, 1970.

39. *Louisiana Weekly*, July 1, 1967; "Statement of Marietta Camp," June 1967, Box 28-53, NO-NAACP Papers.

40. *Louisiana Weekly*, April 6, 1968; June 22, 1968. Despite the outrage, New Orleans never experienced a major race riot in the 1960s, while virtually every other major city in American had some sort of racial disturbance. Although the NOPD ruled with an iron fist, black residents were rather restrained. In other cities police brutality was the catalyst for major race riots. See Robert Fogelson, "From Resentment to Confrontation: The Police and the Outbreak of the Nineteen-Sixties Riots," *Political Science Quarterly* 83 (June 1968): 217–247; Paul Jacobs, "The Los Angeles Police: A Critique," *Atlantic Monthly* (December 1966): 95–101; John Hersey, *The Algiers Motel Incident* (New York: Bantam Books, 1968); Moore, *Carl B. Stokes*, especially chapter 2.

41. *NOLA Express*, no. 3, 1968; Kent Germany, *New Orleans After the Promises* (Athens: University of Georgia Press, 2007), p. 129.

42. *Louisiana Weekly*, July 26, 1969; Ad Hoc Police Committee of Community Relations Council to Community Relations Council Roundtable on Police Matters, June 1970, Box 1, Folder 12, Community Relations Council Papers, Amistad Research Center, Tulane University. Hereafter referred to as CRC Papers; "Major Recommendations of the Human Relations Round Table's study of The New Orleans Police Department of October 1969," Box 3, Folder 12, CRC Papers; "Report of the New Orleans Police Department Budgeting and Finance," October 13, 1969, Box 3, Folder 12, CRC Papers.

43. *Louisiana Weekly,* January 18, 1969; Statement by Black Police for Positive Action, undated, Box 1, Folder 12, CRC Papers; Human Relations Committee of New Orleans, Monthly Report, April 1969, Box 47, Folder 10, LA-NAACP Papers. For more on the development of black police organizations, see Dulaney, *Black Police in America,* pp. 65–80.

44. "Report for the Police Committee of CRC Roundtable Assembly," May 28, 1969, Box 28-195, NO-NAACP Papers. The issue of black officers in urban police forces captured the attention of the mainstream press several years later. See "The Lonely Struggle of the Black Cop," *Readers Digest,* March 1971, pp. 123–127, and "The Black Cop," *Newsweek,* August 16, 1971, pp. 19–20.

45. *Louisiana Weekly,* April 7, 1969; *NOLA Express,* April 11, 1969; May 9, 1969; Kalamu ya Salaam Interview, Amistad Research Center. For a more complete discussion of the black power movement on college campuses, see William Van Deburg, *New Day in Babylon* (Chicago: University of Chicago Press, 1992), pp. 64–82; Vincent Harding, "Black Students and the Impossible Revolution," *Journal of Black Studies* 1 (September 1970): 75–100; Max Stanford, "Black Nationalism and the Afro-American Student," *Black Scholar* 2 (June 1971): 27–31.

46. *Louisiana Weekly,* April 10, 1969; Kalamu ya Salaam Interview.

47. Kalamu ya Salaam Interview.

48. NAACP-Urban League Joint Statement, April 9, 1969, Box 37, Folder 6, LA-NAACP Papers; Kalamu ya Salaam Interview.

49. *Louisiana Weekly,* May 3, 1969; Hirsch, "Simply a Matter of Black and White," p. 293; Moon Landrieu Interview, Amistad Research Center.

50. Hirsch, "Harold and Dutch Revisited: A Comparative Look at the First Black Mayors of Chicago and New Orleans," in *African-American Mayors: Race, Politics, and the American City,* ed. David Colburn and Jeffrey Adler (Urbana: University of Illinois Press, 2001), pp. 109–110.

51. Hirsch, "Simply a Case of Black and White," pp. 289–290.

52. Human Relations Committee Round Table to Moon Landrieu, July 17, 1970, Box 1, Folder 2, CRC Papers.

53. Human Relations Committee Round Table to Moon Landrieu, July 17, 1970, Box 1, Folder 2, CRC Papers.

54. Human Relations Committee Monthly Report, July 1969, Box 47, Folder 11, LA-NAACP Papers; Arthur Chapital, Sr., to Joseph Giarrusso, June 19, 1969, Box 2, Human Relations Committee Papers, New Orleans Public Library, hereafter referred to as HRC Papers; NAACP Press Release, July 7, 1969, HRC Papers, Box 2; Joseph Giarrusso to Arthur Chapital, Sr., December 17, 1969, Box 3, Folder 12, CRC Papers

55. Paul Sazenbach to William E. Hagerty, December 22, 1969, Box 1, Folder 1, CRC Papers; Revius Ortique to Joseph Giarrusso, September 30, 1969, Box 1, Folder 11, CRC Papers; W. Findley Raymond to Louis Sirgo, August 31, 1970, Box 1, Folder 12, CRC Papers; *The Police and the Rest of Us.* Human Relations Committee of New Orleans, 1969, Box 3, Folder 12, CRC Papers.

CHAPTER 3

1. *NOLA Express,* October 2, 1970.

2. *Louisiana Weekly,* September 17, 1970; National Committee to Combat Fascism to Businessmen of the Greater New Orleans Area, re: Free Breakfast Program," undated, HRC Papers; Hirsch, "Simply a Matter of Black and White," p. 298; Orissa Arend, *Showdown in Desire: People, Panthers, Piety and Police: The Story of the Black Panther Party in New Orleans, 1970* (New Orleans: Arend, 2003). For a fuller discussion of the Black Panther Party and local police departments, see Huey P. Newton, "War Against the Panthers: A Study of Repression in

America" (Ph.D. dissertation, 1980, University of California–Santa Cruz); for general studies of the Panthers, see Charles Jones, ed., *The Black Panther Party Reconsidered* (Baltimore: Black Classic Press, 1998); Kathleen Cleaver, ed., *Liberation, Imagination, and the Black Panther Party* (New York: Routledge, 2001); Philip Foner, ed., *The Black Panthers Speak* (New York: Lippincott, 1970).

3. Robert Tucker's description of the social ills in the Desire Projects was echoed by WWL-TV. See WWL-TV Editorial on the Desire Crisis, September 16, 1970, Reel 59, Landrieu Papers. For an earlier view of public housing in New Orleans, see Housing Authority of New Orleans, "Public Housing in New Orleans," 1947, and Marnie Mahoney, "The Changing Nature of Public Housing in New Orleans, 1930–1974," (M.A. thesis, Tulane University, 1985). Desire was the largest housing project in the South and it was an example of everything that was wrong with public housing. For a broader look at the intersection of race and public housing consult, see Arnold Hirsch, *Making the Second Ghetto: Race and Housing in Chicago, 1940–1960* (Chicago: University of Chicago Press, 1992), and John F. Bauman, Roger Biles, and Kristen M. Szylvian, eds., *From Tenements to Taylor Homes: In Search of an Urban Housing Policy in 20th Century America* (University: Pennsylvania State University Press, 2000).

4. Self, "The Black Panther Party," pp. 45–47; Worth K. Hayes, "No Service Too Small: The Political Significance of the Survival Programs of the New Orleans Black Panther Party," pp. 4–5, www.xula.edu/xulanexus/issue3/BBP.html; for richer discussion on the importance of the survival programs of the Black Panther Party, see JoNina Abron, "Serving the People: the Survival Programs of the Black Panther Party," in *The Black Panther Party Reconsidered*, ed. Charles Jones (Baltimore: Black Classic Press, 2000), pp. 177–192.

5. *Louisiana Weekly*, September 17, 1970.

6. *Times-Picayune*, September 19, 1970.

7. *Times-Picayune*, September 19, 1970.

8. *New Orleans States-Item*, September 15, 1970.

9. *Times-Picayune*, September 15, 17, 19, 1970.

10. *Times-Picayune*, September 16, 1970.

11. *Times-Picayune*, September 16, 1970. There were similar Panther-Cop confrontations throughout urban America. The most infamous of course were in Oakland, New York City, and New Haven, Connecticut. See Paul Chevigny, *A Study of Provocation* (New York: Pantheon, 1972), and Donald Freed, *Agony in New Haven: The Trial of Bobby Seale, Ericka Huggins, and the Black Panther Party* (New York: Simon and Schuster, 1973).

12. *Times-Picayune*, September 16, 1970; *States-Item*, September 15, 1970.

13. *Times-Picayune*, September 16, 1970; "Exposure of Raymond Reed, Bootlicker, Puppet, and Nigger-Pig," in Box 4, HRC Papers; *New York Times*, September 19, 1960.

14. *Times-Picayune*, September 16, 1970; Statement by Joseph Giarrusso to Press, September 15, 1970, Moon Landrieu Papers, Reel 59, New Orleans Public Library. Hereafter referred to as Landrieu Papers.

15. *Times-Picayune*, September 16, 1970.

16. *Times Picayune*, September 16, 1970; Statement by NOPD regarding the disturbance in Desire, September 15, 1970, Box 4, HRC Papers.

17. *Times-Picayune*, September 17, 1970.

18. *Times-Picayune*, September 17, 1970.; "Transcript of Mayor's News Conference," September 16, 1970, Box 4, HRC Papers, New Orleans Public Library; Statement by Moon Landrieu, September 16, 1970, Reel 59, Landrieu Papers.

19. *Times-Picayune*, September 18, 1970.

20. *Times-Picayune*, September 26, 1970; Statement by anonymous concerned citizens to Landrieu, undated, Reel 59, Landrieu Papers. The NAACP echoed many of these same sentiments. Harvey Britton to Moon Landrieu, September 22, 1970, Reel 59, Landrieu Papers.

21. *Times-Picayune*, September 17, 1970.

22. *Times-Picayune*, September 17, 1970.

23. *Louisiana Weekly*, September 26, 1970.

24. *Louisiana Weekly*, October 3, 10, 17, 31, 1970.

25. *Louisiana Weekly*, November 7, 1970.

26. *Times-Picayune*, November 21, 1970.

27. *Times-Picayune*, November 20, 1970; Robert Tucker to Sidney Cates, "Follow-Up Action in Desire Area," September 22, 1970, Reel 59, Landrieu Papers.

28. *Times-Picayune*, November 20, 1970.

29. *Times-Picayune*, November 20, 1970.

30. *Times-Picayune*, November 20, 1970.

31. *Times-Picayune*, November 20, 21, 24, 25, 1970.

32. *Times-Picayune*, November 25, 1970.

33. *Times-Picayune*, November 25, 1970.

34. *Times-Picayune*, November 27, 1970; "Resolution by Concerned Clergy and Citizens of New Orleans Protesting Impersonation of Clergyman by Police," December 4, 1970, Box 4, HRC Papers; "Statement of Panthers on Raid," by the NCCF, Box 4, HRC Papers,

35. *Times-Picayune*, November 27, 1970.

36. *Louisiana Weekly*, December 3, 1970.

37. *Louisiana Weekly*, November 28, 1970.

38. *Louisiana Weekly*, December 12, 1970; Injunction against NCCF, Civil District Court, December 7, 1970, Box 4, HRC Papers.

39. *Louisiana Weekly*, January 2, 1971.

40. *Louisiana Weekly*, January 16, 1971; Statement by Joseph Giarrusso, January 11, 1971, Reel 59, Landrieu Papers; "Police Department Report on Desire Area Fire," January 11, 1971, Reel 59, Landrieu Papers.

41. *Times-Picayune*, March 24, 1972.

42. *Times-Picayune*, April 8, 1972; September 2, 1972. The creation of the felony action squad was part of the NOPD's "law and order" plan. The term *law and order* became a codeword for "take back the streets from thugs, criminals, and black folks," after President Richard M. Nixon taped a commercial alluding to the breakdown of law and order in America. Throughout the period there was a major concern over crime and Nixon popularized the term in an effort to attract white southern support. See Dan T. Carter, *The Politics of Rage: George Wallace, The Origins of the New Conservatism, and the Transformation of American Politics* (Baton Rouge: Louisiana State University Press, 1995), pp. 348–349.

43. *Times-Picayune*, September 14, 1972.

44. *Times-Picayune*, September 19, 1972.

45. *Louisiana Weekly*, September 23, 1972; *Times-Picayune*, September 19, 1972.

46. *Louisiana Weekly*, September 30, 1972; *Times-Picayune*, September 23, 1972.

47. *Louisiana Weekly*, September 30, 1972; *Times-Picayune*, September 25, 1972.

48. *Louisiana Weekly*, October 7, 1972.

49. *Times-Picayune*, October 26, 1972; New Orleans City Council Meeting Minutes, October 5, 1972, Box 94, City Council Papers, New Orleans Public Library. Hereafter referred to as City Council Papers.

50. *Times-Picayune*, October 26, 1972; Louis Charbonnet to Clerk of City Council, August 27, 1972, City Council Papers; Black Legislative Caucus Statement, undated, City Council Papers; New Orleans City Council Meeting Minutes, October 5, 1972, City Council Papers.

51. *Times-Picayune*, October 26, 1972; *Louisiana Weekly*, October 14, 1972.

52. *Times-Picayune*, October 11, 1972; New Orleans City Council Resolution on the Felony Action Squad, October 12, 1972, Box 94, City Council Papers.

53. *Times-Picayune*, October 12, 13, 1972; New Orleans City Council Meeting Minutes, October 19, 1972, Box 94, City Council Papers.

54. *Louisiana Weekly*, October 21, 1972; New Orleans City Council Meeting Minutes, October 19, 1972, Box 94, City Council Papers.

55. *Louisiana Weekly*, October 14, 1972; *Times-Picayune*, October 18, 1972.

CHAPTER 4

1. Peter Hernon, *A Terrible Thunder: The Story of the New Orleans Sniper* (New York: Doubleday, 1978), p. 51; New Orleans Police Department, "Official Report on the Mark Essex Shootings," p. 215, New Orleans Public Library. Hereafter referred to as Essex Report.

2. *Times-Picayune*, January 10, 1973; *New York Times*, January 11, 1973.

3. Hernon, *A Terrible Thunder*, p. 53; Essex Report, p. 215.

4. *Times-Picayune*, January 10, 1973.

5. Essex Report, p. 215; *Times-Picayune*, January 10, 1973; *New York Times*, January 11, 1973; Hernon, *A Terrible Thunder*, pp. 52–53.

6. Hernon, *A Terrible Thunder*, p. 23; Essex Report, p. 215.

7. Essex Report, p. 216; Hernon, *A Terrible Thunder*, pp. 24–25; *Baton Rouge Advocate*, January 11, 1973.

8. Hernon, *A Terrible Thunder*, pp. 35, 38; Essex Report, p. 216.

9. Essex Report, p. 216; Hernon, *A Terrible Thunder*, p. 19.

10. Hernon, *A Terrible Thunder*, pp. 25–27, 36–37.

11. Hernon., *A Terrible Thunder*, pp. 39–40.

12. Hernon, *A Terrible Thunder*, pp. 52–53, 63–64, 66; Essex Report, p. 216; *Baton Rouge Advocate*, January 11, 1973.

13. Hernon, *A Terrible Thunder*, pp. 71, 74, 80–82; Essex Report, pp. 216, 219; The New York branch of the Black Panther Party received considerable publicity in the early 1970s, when twenty-one members of that chapter were arrested but later acquitted of conspiring to bomb parts of New York City. The "Panther 21," as they are often referred to, have been the subject of several studies. See Peter Zimroth, *Perversions of Justice: The Prosecution and Acquittal of the Panther 21* (New York: Viking Press, 1974); Kuwasi Balagoo, *Look For Me in the Whirlwind: The Collective Autobiography of the New York 21* (New York: Random House, 1971); Murray Kempton, *The Briar Patch: The Trial of the Panther 21* (New York: De Capo Press, 1973).

14. Hernon, *A Terrible Thunder*, p. 88; Essex Report, pp. 217, 219–220.

15. Hernon, *A Terrible Thunder*, pp. 99–102; *Times-Picayune*, January 30, 1973; Marcus Cox, "From Patriotism to Rebellion: African-American Attitudes Toward Military Service and Training, 1941–1973" (Ph.D. dissertation, Northwestern University, 2001), includes a detailed discussion of the Southern University shootings.

16. Essex Report, pp. 43, 46; Hernon, *A Terrible Thunder* p. 20.

17. Essex Report, pp. 50–55; Hernon, *A Terrible Thunder*, pp. 43, 49; *Times-Picayune*, January 2, 1973.

18. *Times-Picayune*, January 2, 3, 6, 1973.

19. Hernon, *A Terrible Thunder,* pp. 95–96; Mark Essex to Pastor of First New St. Mark Baptist Church, in Essex Report, p. 290; Essex Report, pp. 56–57.

20. Essex Report, pp. 59–61; Hernon, *A Terrible Thunder,* pp. 103–105.

21. Essex Report, p. 71; Hernon, *A Terrible Thunder,* p. 114; *Times-Picayune,* January 18, 1973.

22. Essex Report, pp. 77–79; Hernon, *A Terrible Thunder,* p. 115; *Baton Rouge Advocate,* January 9, 1973.

23. Essex Report, pp. 32, 156–159; Hernon, *A Terrible Thunder,* pp. 116–118.

24. Essex Report, p. 32; Hernon, *A Terrible Thunder,* p. 120.

25. Hernon, *A Terrible Thunder,* p. 162; Essex Report, pp. 34, 139–140.

26. Hernon, *A Terrible Thunder,* p. 163; Essex Report, p. 35.

27. Hernon, *A Terrible Thunder,* p. 212; Essex Report, pp. 164–169; The killing of Sirgo would be a major setback for police-community relations since he was next in line to become chief. Sirgo had a reputation for being an enlightened administrator and he represented the progressive-thinking wing of the NOPD.

28. Essex Report, pp. 41–42; Hernon, *A Terrible Thunder,* pp. 250–251; "Howard Johnson Hotel Guest List," Reel 19, Landrieu Papers; List of Fatalities During Essex Shootings, Reel 19, Landrieu Papers.

29. *Times-Picayune,* January 9, 10, 1973; *Louisiana Weekly,* June 16, 1973; Press Conference, January 8, 1973, Reel 19, Landrieu Papers. The Essex incident was the second such incident in the twentieth century for New Orleans. In 1900, Robert Charles launched an all-out attack on the NOPD in a rather similar fashion. See Hair, *Carnival of Fury.*

30. Hernon, *A Terrible Thunder,* pp. 260–261; *States-Item,* January 10, 12, 1973; Anonymous letter to Moon Landrieu and Joseph Giarrusso, Reel 19, Landrieu Papers; "Free The Land," Republic of New Afrika Newsletter, undated; "The New Afrikan Journal," undated.

31. Hernon, *A Terrible Thunder,* pp. 255–256; Essex Report, pp. 236–238; *Times-Picayune,* January 13, 1973; *States-Item,* January 13, 1973.

32. *New York Times,* January 12, 1973; *Times-Picayune,* January 12, 1973; Hernon, *A Terrible Thunder,* pp. 266–268.

33. *New York Times,* January 14, 1973.

34. *Times-Picayune,* June 9, 1973.

35. *Times-Picayune,* June 13, 1973.

36. For more on black vigilante organizations and their broader meaning, see Larry Moss, *Black Political Ascendancy: Urban Centers and Black Control of the Local Police Function* (San Francisco: R & E Research Associates, 1977).

CHAPTER 5

1. Manning Marable, *Race, Reform, and Rebellion: The Second Reconstruction in Black America, 1945–1990* (Jackson: University of Mississippi Press), p. 126.

2. *Louisiana Weekly,* October 13, 1973; the Black Organization of Police immediately became a member of the National Black Police Association, see NBPA Memo, Box 54, Folder 18, LANAACP Papers; *NOPD Annual Report, 1973.* The formation of the BOP was part of a larger pattern of black officers becoming increasingly more aggressive in their quest for equality on the force. For more on these developments among black officers, see Dulaney, *Black Police in America,* pp. 71–80.

3. *Times-Picayune,* October 27, 1973; November 9, 1973.

4. *NOPD Annual Report, 1973; Times-Picayune,* March 10, 1973; *Louisiana Weekly,* March 17, 1973. Other black police organizations filed lawsuits as well; see Dulaney, *Black Police in*

America, p. 78. For a broader discussion on the issues facing black officers, see Ina Friedman, *Black Cop* (Philadelphia: Westminster Press, 1974); Valencia Campbell, "Double Marginality of Black Policemen," *Criminology* 17 (February 1980): 477–484; James Bannon and G. Marie Wilt, "Black Policemen: A Study of Self-Images," *Journal of Police Science and Administration* 1 (March 1973): 21–29; Elliott D. Lee, "Blacks in Blue," *Black Enterprise*, February 1982, pp. 87–90; Donald B. Walker, "Black Police Values and the Black Community," *Police Studies* 5 (1983): 20–28.

5. *Times-Picayune*, April 27, 1973.

6. *Times-Picayune*, June 29, 1973.

7. *Times-Picayune*, September 14, 1973.

8. *Louisiana Weekly*, February 9, 1974; *Times-Picayune*, February 5, 1974; Clarence Giarrusso to Gustave Thomas, April 28, 1975, Box 2, HRC Papers.

9. *Louisiana Weekly*, May 25, 1974.

10. *Louisiana Weekly*, March 29, 1975.

11. *Louisiana Weekly*, September 20, 1975.

12. *Louisiana Weekly*, June 5, 1976; *Times-Picayune*, May 28, 1976; Gustave Thomas to Clarence Giarrusso, April 17, 1975, Box 2, HRC Papers; New Orleans City Council Meeting Minutes, May 27, 1976, City Council Papers; *NOPD Annual Report, 1976*.

13. *Louisiana Weekly*, February 19, 1977.

14. *Louisiana Weekly*, December 21, 1974.

15. *Louisiana Weekly*, April 19, 1975.

16. *Louisiana Weekly*, April 26, 1975; May 24, 1975.

17. *Louisiana Weekly*, April 26, 1975; October 18, 1975.

18. *Louisiana Weekly*, June 14, 1975; July 5, 1975; August 9, 1975.

19. *Louisiana Weekly*, June 26, 1976.

20. *Louisiana Weekly*, October 23, 1976; City Council of New Orleans Meeting Minutes, October 14, 1976, City Council Papers; *Times-Picayune*, October 15, 1976.

21. *Louisiana Weekly*, December 25, 1976; January 8, 1977.

22. *Times-Picayune*, December 5, 1976.

23. *Times-Picayune*, December 18, 197; January 2, 6, 13, 1977. For one response to Giarrusso's plea, see the letter to the editor from officers of the American Law Enforcement Association, *Times-Picayune*, January 2, 1977.

24. "Public Hearing of the New Orleans City Council on Police Brutality and Civilian Review Board, January 7, 1977," City Council Papers; New Orleans City Council Resolution, January 6, 1977, Box 6, A. L. Davis Papers, New Orleans Public Library. Hereafter referred to as Davis Papers. American Law Enforcement Association Remarks before the New Orleans City Council, January 7, 1977, Box 6, Davis Papers; *Louisiana Weekly*, January 15, 1977; *Times-Picayune*, January 8, 1977.

25. "Public Hearing of the New Orleans City Council on Police Brutality and Civilian Review Board, January 7, 1977," City Council Papers.

26. City Council of New Orleans Meeting Minutes, January 13, 1977; *Louisiana Weekly*, January 29, 1977.

27. Resolution by Councilman A. L. Davis, Box 6, Davis Papers; City Council of New Orleans Meeting Minutes, January 13, 1977, City Council Papers.

28. Resolution by Councilman A. L. Davis, Box 6, Davis Papers; City Council of New Orleans Meeting Minutes, January 13, 1977, City Council Papers.

29. City Council of New Orleans Meeting Minutes, January 20, 1977, City Council Papers; *Times-Picayune*, January 14, 23, 1977.

30. City Council of New Orleans Meeting Minutes, January 20, 1977; Press Release by Citizen's Observers Committee, Box 6, Davis Papers; *Times-Picayune*, January 20, 1977.

31. City Council of New Orleans Meeting Minutes, January 20, 1977, City Council Papers; *Times-Picayune*, January 21, 23, 27, 28, 1977.

32. *Louisiana Weekly*, March 5, 12, 19, 1977; *Times-Picayune*, March 3, 1977.

33. *Louisiana Weekly*, March 12, 1977; Press Release by Ad Hoc Committee on the Wayne Smith Murder, Box 6, Davis Papers.

34. *Louisiana Weekly*, March 19, 1977.

35. *Louisiana Weekly*, March 19, 1977.

36. *Louisiana Weekly*, March 19, 1977; *Times-Picayune*, March 11, 1977.

37. *Louisiana Weekly*, March 26, 1977; Statement by the Ad Hoc Committee March for Wayne Smith, Box 6, Davis Papers.

38. *Louisiana Weekly*, April 2, 1977; *Times-Picayune*, March 25, 1977.

39. *Times-Picayune*, March 25, 27, 1977.

40. *Times-Picayune*, April 27, 1977; May 5, 1977.

41. *Times-Picayune*, April 29, 1977.

42. *Times-Picayune*, May 30, 1977; June 1, 6, 1977.

43. *Times-Picayune*, December 13, 1977.

44. *Times-Picayune*, January 4, 1978.

45. *Times-Picayune*, January 6, 28, 1978.

46. *Times-Picayune*, January 15, 26, 1978.

47. *Times-Picayune*, January 20, 1978; March 14, 30, 31, 1978; April 5, 1978.

CHAPTER 6

1. For a good overview of the dilemmas faced by African American mayors, see David R. Colburn and Jeffrey S. Adler, eds., *African American Mayors: Race, Politics, and the American City* (Urbana: University of Illinois Press, 2001).

2. Marc Morial, "Development of Black Politics in New Orleans," pp. 22–23, 26, unpublished paper in possession of the author; Hirsch, "Simply a Matter of Black and White," pp. 305–310.

3. *Times-Picayune*, date unknown, January 12, 1978; Information regarding Police Superintendent Search, Office of Mayoral Transition, Box B12, Dutch Morial Papers, New Orleans Public Library. Hereafter referred to as Morial Papers I; Dutch Morial Interview, Amistad Research Center; Morial Interview, Xavier University Archives. For a closer look at Morial's early political career, see Arnold Hirsch, "Race and Politics in Modern New Orleans: The Mayoralty of Dutch Morial," *American Studies* 35 no. 4 (April 1990): 461–484; Hirsch, "Simply a Matter of Black and White," pp. 262–319; Huey L. Perry and Alfred Stokes, "Politics and Power in the Sunbelt: Mayor Morial of New Orleans," in *The New Black Politics: The Search for Political Power*, ed. Michael Preston (New York: Longman, 1987).

4. *Times-Picayune*, February 25, 1978; March 15, 18, 19, 1978; Committee for Accountable Police Position Paper, February 1978, Box B5, Morial Papers I. Whenever a city elected an African American to city hall for the first time, expectations were high for police reform and one of the main concerns was adding more blacks to the force. See Peter Eisinger, "Black Employment in Municipal Jobs: The Impact of Black Political Power," *American Political Science Review* 76 (June 1982): 380–392; Roger Biles, "Black Mayors: A Historical Assessment," *Journal of Negro History* 77 (Summer 1992): 109–125.

5. Background information on Police Chief Candidates, Box B12, Morial Papers I; Resume

of Joseph Rouzan, Box B12, Morial Papers I; *Times-Picayune,* April 25, 27, 28, 29, 1978; May 11, 16, 1978.

6. Hirsch, "Race and Politics," p. 471.

7. *Times-Picayune,* May 17, 1978; *Louisiana Weekly,* May 27, 1978; Ratings of Candidates, Box B12, Morial Papers I; Task Force to Recommend a Superintendent of Police, April 13, 1978, Box B12, Morial Papers I.

8. Statement by Carl Galmon of the New Orleans Citizens for Action League, October 2, 1980, Box B5, Morial Papers I.

9. *Times-Picayune,* May 17, 1978; *Louisiana Weekly,* May 27, 1978.

10. *Times-Picayune,* May 18, 1978.

11. Amos Townsend to Mayor Earnest Morial, May 9, 1978, Box B12 Morial Papers I; *Times-Picayune,* May 20, 1978; Statement by Carl Gowman, October 2, 1980, Box B5, Morial Papers I.

12. *Times-Picayune,* May 23, 24, 25, 26, 28, 1978; June 1, 2, 13, 1978.

13. "Re-organization plan of Chief James Parsons," Box 71, Folder 12, Dutch Morial Papers, Amistad Research Center. Hereafter referred to as Morial Papers II; *Times-Picayune,* July 7, 8, 15, 1978; *Louisiana Weekly,* July 15, 1978.

14. *Times-Picayune,* August 4, 1978; *Louisiana Weekly,* August 12, 1978.

15. *Times-Picayune,* August 4, 5, 1978; *Louisiana Weekly,* August 12, 1978.

16. *Times-Picayune,* September 1, 1978; *Louisiana Weekly,* September 9, 1978.

17. *Louisiana Weekly,* September 2, 1978.

18. *Louisiana Weekly,* October 7, 1978.

19. *Louisiana Weekly,* October 21, 1978; November 18, 1978.

20. *Louisiana Weekly,* December 2, 1978.

21. *Times-Picayune,* January 4, 5, 6, 1979; *Louisiana Weekly,* January 13, 1979; Hirsch, "Race and Politics." For more on police unionism and strikes, see Harvey Juris and Peter Feuille, *Police Unionism: Power and Impact in Public Sector Bargaining* (Lexington, MA: Lexington Books, 1973).

22. *Times-Picayune,* January 18, 25, 1979.

23. *Times-Picayune,* February 7, 8, 1979; Mayor's Press Conference, February 6, 1979, Tape 10, Side 2, Morial Papers I.

24. *Times-Picayune,* February 9, 10, 11, 12, 13, 14, 17, 1979; Mayor's Press Conference, February 9, 1979, Tape 11, Side 1, Morial Papers I.

25. *Times-Picayune,* February 16–23, 1979; *Louisiana Weekly,* February 24, 1979; Mayor's Press Conference, February 15, 1979, Tape 11, Side 2, Morial Papers I; Mayor's Press Conference, February 23, 1979, Tape 13, Sides 1–2, Morial Papers I.

26. *Louisiana Weekly,* February 24, 1979.

27. *Louisiana Weekly,* March 3, 1979.

28. *Times-Picayune,* March 5, 1979; Mayor's Press Conference, March 4, 1979, Tape 14, Side 1, Morial Papers I.

29. *Louisiana Weekly,* May 12, 1979; June 16, 1979.

30. *Louisiana Weekly,* June 30, 1979; July 7, 21, 1979; September 8, 1979.

31. *Times-Picayune,* October 4, 1979.

32. *Times-Picayune,* October 4, 1979; *Louisiana Weekly,* October 13, 1979.

33. *Times-Picayune,* January 26, 1980; *Louisiana Weekly,* February 16, 1980.

34. *Louisiana Weekly,* September 6, 1980.

35. *Times-Picayune,* September 3, 4, 1980; *Louisiana Weekly,* September 6, 1980.

36. *Times-Picayune,* September 26, 27, 1980; *Louisiana Weekly,* November 8, 1980; City Council of New Orleans Meeting Minutes, September 25, 1980, City Council Papers.

37. *Times-Picayune,* September 28, 1980.

38. Notes from the City Council Meeting, October 2, 1980, Box B5, Morial Papers I; City Council of New Orleans Meeting Minutes, October 2, 1980, City Council Papers; *Times-Picayune,* October 3, 1980; *Louisiana Weekly,* October 11, 1980; November 8, 1980.

39. *Louisiana Weekly,* November 15, 1980.

40. *Times-Picayune,* January 10, 1980.

41. *Times-Picayune,* January 10, 1980.

42. *Times-Picayune,* January 10, 1980.

CHAPTER 7

1. Marable, *Race, Reform, and Rebellion,* pp. 155, 175.

2. *Times-Picayune,* November 9, 1980; The People for Justice to Arnold Broussard and Cherly Craver, Box B5, Morial Papers I.

3. *Times-Picayune,* November 9, 1980; City Hall Press Release on the death of Gregory Neupert, undated, Box B6, Morial Papers I.

4. *Times-Picayune,* November 11, 13, 1980.

5. *Times-Picayune,* November 13, 1980.

6. Statement of Johnnie Brownlee, undated, Box B5, Morial Papers I; Statement by the Liberation League, Box B5, Morial Papers I; *Louisiana Weekly,* December 13, 1980; *Times-Picayune,* November 21, 1980; The People for Justice to Arnold Broussard and Cheryl Craner, undated, Box B5, Morial Papers I.

7. *Times-Picayune,* November 14, 1980, February 6, 1981; *Louisiana Weekly,* November 22, 1980; Arrest Warrant for Reginald Miles, Box B5, Morial Papers I; "The Shooters in the Algiers Execution," Box B5, Morial Papers I.

8. *Times-Picayune,* November 14, 1980.

9. *Times-Picayune,* November 14, 1980.

10. "Justice for the Algiers Victims," Statement by the Liberation League, misc. unsorted materials, CRC Papers; *Times-Picayune,* November 15, 1980; *Louisiana Weekly,* November 22, 1980.

11. *Times-Picayune,* November 16, 1980.

12. *Times-Picayune,* November 18, 1980; *Louisiana Weekly,* November 22, 1980; "Your Present D. A.'s office in action," Liberation League, misc. unsorted materials, CRC Papers.

13. Statement by Mayor Dutch Morial, November 17, 1980, Box B5, Morial Papers I; *Times-Picayune,* November 18, 1980.

14. *Times-Picayune,* November 20, 1980.

15. *Times-Picayune,* November 21, 1980.

16. *Times-Picayune,* November 23, 24, 1980;

17. Coalition of Community Organizations to Mayor Dutch Morial, misc. unsorted materials, CRC Papers. For more on the issue of "use of force," see James J. Fyfe, *Above The Law: Police and the Excessive Use of Force* (New York: Free Press, 1994) and two other works also by Fyfe, "Who Shoots? A Look at Officer Race and Police Shootings," *Journal of Police Science and Administration,* 9 (1981), pp. 367–382, and "Race and Extreme Police-Citizen Violence," in *Race, Crime, and Criminal Justice,* ed. R. L. McNeely and Carl Pope (Sage: Beverly Hills, 1981).

18. *Times-Picayune,* November 25, 29, 1980; *Louisiana Weekly,* November 29, 1980; Mayor's Press Conference on Parson's Resignation, November 24, 1980, Tape 35, Side 1, Morial Papers I; "Police Brutality Committee," Brotherhood of Taxi Drivers Bulletin, August 1981, misc. unsorted materials, CRC Papers.

19. Mayor's Press Conference, April 16, 1981, Tape 38, Side 1, Morial Papers I; *Times-Picayune*, November 30, 1980; April 17, 1981; *Louisiana Weekly*, November 29, 1980; April 25, 1981.

20. Statement by Mayor Dutch Morial, December 11, 1980, Box B5, Morial Papers I.

21. City Council Meeting, December 11, 1980, Tape 83, Sides 1–2, Morial Papers I; Statement by Police Brutality Committee, misc. unsorted materials, CRC Papers; *Times-Picayune*, December 12, 1980; *Louisiana Weekly*, December 20, 1980; City Council Meeting Minutes, December 11, 1980, Box B5, Morial Papers I. For more on civilian review boards, see the following books by Samuel Walker: *Police Accountability: The Role of Citizen Oversight* (New York: Wadsworth, 2000) and *The New World of Police Accountability* (New York: Sage, 2005).

22. Peoples Conference on Police Brutality—Schedule of Events, Box B5, Morial Papers I; *Times-Picayune*, December 16, 19, 1980; *Louisiana Weekly*, December 27, 1980; "Don't Shop on Canal Street—Questions and Answers About the Selective Buying Campaign," misc. unsorted materials, CRC Papers.

23. *Times-Picayune*, December 21, 28, 1980; January 4, 1981; Internal memo on Kalamu Ya Salaam to James J. Coleman, Box B5, Morial Papers I.

24. *Louisiana Weekly*, January 17, 1981.

25. Liberation League Statement, February 21, 1981, Box B5, Morial Papers I.

26. Police Brutality Committee—Statement and Petition, undated, Box B5, Morial Papers I.; The People for Justice to Arnold Broussard and Cheryl Craner, undated in Box B5, Morial Papers I.

27. *Louisiana Weekly*, May 9, 1981; Kalamu ya Salaam to Morial, undated, Box 71, Folder 5, Morial Papers II; "Take it to the Next Phase—A Rally To Seek Solutions Featuring Ben Chavis," February 3, 1981, misc. unsorted materials, CRC Papers; "End Police Terror," flyer issued by the Liberation League announcing a rally, Box B5, Morial Papers I.

28. *Times-Picayune*, May 12, 1981; *Louisiana Weekly*, May 16, 1981; "The Right of Self-Defense," undated, Box B5, Morial Papers I; Mayor's Press Conference on the Orleans Parish Grand Jury Report, May 11, 1981, Tape 39, Folder 1, Morial Papers I; Statement by Mayor Dutch Morial, May 11, 1981, Box B5, Morial Papers I.

29. Concerned Citizens of Algiers to Morial, Connick, and Volz, undated, Box 71/Folder 5, Morial Papers II; Liberation League Press Release, February 21, 1981, Box B5, Morial Papers I.

30. *Times-Picayune*, May 13, 1981; *Louisiana Weekly*, May 16, 1981.

31. *Times-Picayune*, May 18, 1981; "The Community Strikes Back," Police Brutality Committee Press Release by Kalamu ya Salaam, undated, CRC Papers; Police Brutality Committee Appeal for Unity Letter, May 28, 1981, CRC Papers; Press Release by Coalition of Community Organizations, May 13, 1981, Box B5, Morial Papers I.

32. "Police Brutality Committee—Unity Banquet," May 18, 1981, Program, Box 71, Folder 10, Morial Papers II; *Times-Picayune*, May 19, June 13, 1981; Kalamu ya Salaam and Bill Rouselle to Friends, May 28, 1981, misc. unsorted materials, CRC Papers.

33. *Louisiana Weekly*, June 27, 1981; *Times-Picayune*, June 19, 1981; "Blow the Whistle on Dutch," Community Action Now and Police Brutality Committee flyer, Box 71, Folder 10, Morial Papers II; "Unity in the Black Community—List of Demands," undated, CRC Papers.

34. *Louisiana Weekly*, June 27, 1981; *Times-Picayune*, June 19, 1981.

35. *Times-Picayune*, June 20, 1981; *Louisiana Weekly*, June 27, 1981.

36. *Times-Picayune*, June 20, 1981; *Louisiana Weekly*, June 27, 1981; Community Action Now and Police Brutality Committee Rally Flyer, Box 71, Folder 10, Morial Papers II.

37. "Dutch Fun Affair," flyer, Box 71, Folder 10, Morial Papers II; United Front for Justice Letter to Friends," June 19, 1981, Box 71, Folder 10, Morial Papers II.

38. U. S. District Court, "An Indictment for Conspiracy to Violate and Violation of Civil Rights versus John McKenzie, Dale Bonura, Stephen Farrar, Stephen Reboul, Ronald Brink, Thomas Woodall, and Richard Leblanc," Box 71, Folder 14, Morial Papers II; *Times-Picayune*, July 10, 11, 16, 1981; *Louisiana Weekly*, July 18, 25, 1981; Morial to Morris, re: Stephen Reboul, May 18, 1981, Box 71, Folder 6, Morial Papers II. As this letter illustrates, Reboul had a long history of misconduct. In fact, the city of New Orleans had paid out more than $800,000 in damages to civilians as a result of lawsuits filed against him.

39. U.S. Attorney, Eastern District of New Orleans, "Press Release," July 9, 1981, Box 71, Folder 14, Morial Papers II; *Times-Picayune*, September 11, 12, 13, 17, 1981; *Louisiana Weekly*, September 26, 1981.

40. *Times-Picayune*, March 29, 1983; April 2, 3, 7, 1986; New Orleans Mayor's Office Independent Investigation Report on Algiers Killings, Box B5, Morial Papers I.

41. *Louisiana Weekly*, March 27, 1982. Although the city put the agreement of the decree in effect in 1982 it was not official until 1987. See *Times-Picayune*, May 28, 1987; Leroy Aucoin, Assistant Chief Administrative Officer to Henry Morris, May 27, 1981, Box 71, Folder 6, Morial Papers II.

42. *Times-Picayune*, October 6, 8, 13, 1981; NAACP Legal Defense Fund to Ralph Dwyer, re: NOPD Personnel Statistics, December 3, 1980, Box 71, Folder 6, Morial Papers II; *NOPD Annual Report*, 1980, NOPL.

43. *Times-Picayune*, October 14, 17, 1981; *Louisiana Weekly*, October 17, 1981. For more on affirmative action and police departments, see Samuel Walker and Tara Shelley, "Affirmative Action, Diversity, and Law Enforcement," in *Police and Policing: Contemporary Issues*, ed. Dennis Kenney and Robert McNamara (New York: Praeger, 1999), pp. 187–199.

44. *Times-Picayune*, October 14, 15, 1981; *Louisiana Weekly*, October 17, 31, 1981; November 30, 1981; Morial to Rochon, April 1, 1981, Box 71, Folder 8, Morial Papers II; "Discussion topics for the Mayor concerning black police candidates and tests," Box 71, Folder 7, Morial Papers II.

45. *Louisiana Weekly*, October 24, 27, 1981; *Times-Picayune*, October 15, 16, 1981.

46. *Louisiana Weekly*, December 18, 25, 1982; *Times-Picayune*, December 17, 24, 1982.

47. *Louisiana Weekly*, January 24, 1981; February 7, 1981; *Times-Picayune*, January 29, 30, 1981; Police Brutality Committee Agenda For Meeting with White Business Leadership, misc. unsorted materials, CRC Papers; Joseph Giarrusso to Mayor Dutch Morial, January 16, 1981, Box B5, Morial Papers I.

48. *Times-Picayune*, March 13, 1981; *Louisiana Weekly*, March 21, 1981; "Fact Sheet on the Proposed Office of Municipal Investigation," Helen Matlick to Morial, November 21, 1980, misc. unsorted materials, CRC Papers; "Draft of Job Requirements for Director of Office of Municipal Investigation," misc. unsorted materials, CRC Papers.

49. Morial to Henry Morris, re: Stephen Reboul, May 18, 1951, Box 71, Folder 6, Morial Papers II.

50. *Times-Picayune*, November 26, 1981.

51. *Times-Picayune*, May 18, 1982.

52. *Times-Picayune*, September 29, 1982.

53. *Times-Picayune*, September 24, 1982; "Why the OMI?" misc. unsorted materials, CRC Papers.

54. *Times-Picayune*, November 11, 1982.

55. *Times-Picayune*, June 22, 1983.

56. *Times-Picayune*, November 1, 1982; May 26, 1983.

57. *Times-Picayune*, September 24, 1982.

58. "Ordinance-City of New Orleans," regarding OMI, June 19, 1980, misc. unsorted materials, CRC Papers; *Louisiana Weekly*, November 17, 1982; March 5, 1983. The city of Chicago had a similar agency, the Office of Professional Standards. See S. Letman, "Chicago's Answer to Police Brutality: The Office of Professional Standards," *Police Chief*, 1980, pp. 16–17, and "The Office of Professional Standards: Six Years Later," *Police Chief*, 1981, pp. 44–46. For a comparative look at what other cities did in regards to police oversight, see Samuel Walker and B. Wright, *Civilian Review of the Police: A National Survey of the 50 Largest Cities* (Omaha: University of Nebraska-Omaha, 1985).

59. *Louisiana Weekly*, November 17, 1982.

60. "Why the OMI?" CRC Papers; *Times-Picayune*, February 23, 1983; March 16, 1983. The city of Detroit had a municipal agency similar to the OMI. See E. Littlejohn, "The Civilian Police Commission: A Deterrent to Police Misconduct," *University of Detroit Journal of Urban Law* 59 (1981): 5–62.

61. "Off the Top of My Head," Mtumishi St. Julian, misc. unsorted materials, CRC Papers; *Times-Picayune*, April 21, 1983; *Louisiana Weekly*, April 16, 1983; City Council of New Orleans Meeting Minutes, April 21, 1983, City Council Papers.

62. *Times-Picayune*, June 7, 1983.

63. *Times-Picayune*, August 9, 1983; October 7, 1983.

64. *Times-Picayune*, September 2, 3, 11, 1983; *Louisiana Weekly*, September 17, 1983.

65. *Times-Picayune*, September 11, 1983.

66. *Times-Picayune*, September 14, 23, 24, 27, 1983; *Louisiana Weekly*, September 17, 1983.

67. *Louisiana Weekly*, October 1, 1983; *Times-Picayune*, October 20, 1983.

68. *Times-Picayune*, October 20, 27, 1983; February 9, 10, 1984; August 24, 1985; May 22, 1986; November 16, 17, 18, 19, 20, 21, 22, 1986; *Louisiana Weekly*, February 11, 1984; December 28, 1985.

69. *Times-Picayune*, May 17, 1984; June 12, 1985; July 4, 1985.

70. Human Rights Watch, *Shielded from Justice*, pp. 57–58.

71. Human Rights Watch, *Shielded from Justice*, pp. 57–58.

72. *Times-Picayune*, December 27, 29, 1984; January 20, 1985; *Louisiana Weekly*, January 5, 1985. For more on the experience of the first wave of black police chiefs, see Dulaney, *Black Police in America*, pp. 81–103.

73. *Times-Picayune*, December 29, 1984; *Louisiana Weekly*, January 5, 1985.

74. *Times-Picayune*, December 29, 1984; *Louisiana Weekly*, January 5, 1985.

75. *Times-Picayune*, January 30, 1985; February 1, 1985; April 28, 1985; *Louisiana Weekly*, February 9, 1985.

76. The experiences of policewomen have always been challenging. For a more detailed discussion on the issues facing policewomen, see Joseph Balkin, "Why Policemen Don't Like Policewomen," *Journal of Police Science and Administration* 16 (March 1988): 29–38, and Daniel Bell, "Policewomen: Myths and Reality," *Journal of Police Science and Administration*, 10 (1982): 112–120.

77. *Times-Picayune*, January 30, 1985; *NOPD Annual Report, 1984*.

78. *Louisiana Weekly*, January 5, 1985; *NOPD Annual Report, 1985*.

79. *Times-Picayune*, July 28, 1985; *NOPD Annual Report, 1985*. For more on the neighborhood policing movement, see Lee Brown, "Neighborhood-Oriented Policing," *American Journal of Police* 9 (1990): 197–207.

80. *Times-Picayune*, July 28, 1985.

81. Hirsch, "Simply a Matter of Black and White," pp. 313–315; Lyle Perkins, "Failing the

Race: An Historical Assessment of New Orleans Mayor Sidney Barthelemy, 1986–1994" (master's thesis, Louisiana State University, 2005), pp. 9–10.

82. Perkins, "Failing the Race," pp. 8–9, 15–16; Hirsch, "Harold and Dutch Revisited," p. 125; Hirsch," Simply a Matter of Black and White," pp. 317–318; Sidney J. Barthelemy Interview, Xavier University Archives.

CHAPTER 8

1. *Times-Picayune,* July 11, 1986; October 4, 10, 23, 1986.

2. *Times-Picayune,* December 21, 1986.

3. *Times-Picayune,* January 14, 16, 1987.

4. *Times-Picayune,* January 18, 19, 1987.

5. Minutes of Police Meeting, June 21, 1988, Box 94, Folder 1, in Sydney J. Barthelemy Papers, New Orleans Public Library. Hereafter referred to as SJB Papers; Ronald J. Cannatella to Congressman Richard Baker, June 30, 1988, Box 90, Folder 4, SJB Papers; *Times-Picayune,* July 17, 1987.

6. *Times-Picayune,* March 8, 1987.

7. *Times-Picayune,* March 8, 1987.

8. *Times-Picayune,* March 8, 1987.

9. *Times-Picayune,* March 8, 1987.

10. *Times-Picayune,* July 19, 1988; *NOPD Annual Report, 1987.*

11. *Times-Picayune,* July 19, 1988; *Louisiana Weekly,* April 16, 1988.

12. *Times-Picayune,* November 13, 15, 24, 1988.

13. *Times-Picayune,* May 19, 1989.

14. *Times-Picayune,* July 3, 1989.

15. *Times-Picayune,* August 16, 1990.

16. *Times-Picayune,* October 6, 1990.

17. *Times-Picayune,* January 8, 1988; March 18, 29, 30, 1988; April 23, 1988; June 17, 1988; October 27, 1988; November 7, 1989; November 3, 6, 10, 1990; Allen Johnson, "How Good Are the Police," *New Orleans Magazine,* June 1990, pp. 32–28.

18. *Times-Picayune,* March 23, 1990.

19. *Times-Picayune,* November 19, 20, 1990; March 21, 1991.

20. *Times-Picayune,* December 2, 12, 14, 23, 1990; February 16, 1991; March 29, 1991; *NOPD Annual Report, 1990.*

21. *Times-Picayune,* April 2, 1991; *NOPD Annual Report, 1991;* Biography of Arnesta Taylor, Box B5, Morial Papers II.

22. *Times-Picayune,* April 2, 1991; "Highlights of NOPD Reorganization," Box B9, Folder 11, SJB Papers.

23. *Times-Picayune,* April 11, 17, 1991; February 11, 1992. For good books on the Rodney King affair, see Lou Cannon, *Official Negligence: How Rodney King and the Riots Changed Los Angeles and the LAPD* (New York: Westview Press, 1999), and Horne, *The Fire This Time.*

24. *Times-Picayune,* August 29, 30, 1991; September 1, 2, 1991.

25. *Times-Picayune,* September 5, 6, 1991.

26. *Times-Picayune,* September 8, 1991.

27. *Times-Picayune,* May 15, 1992; June 19, 1992; July 9, 1992.

28. *Times-Picayune,* November 20, 1991, March 12, 13, 1993; April 28, 30, 1993.

29. *Times-Picayune,* April 30, 1993; March 19, 1993.

30. *Times-Picayune*, May 7, 18, 1993.

31. *Times-Picayune*, July 24, 1993.

32. *Times-Picayune*, August 25, 30, 1993.

33. Hirsch, "Harold and Dutch Revisited," p. 126.

CHAPTER 9

1. Morial Campaign Plan, "A Blueprint for Change," Box 71, Folder 2, Marc H. Morial Papers, New Orleans Public Library. Hereafter referred to as MHM Papers; *The NOPD Revisited*, International Association of Chiefs of Police, 1994, Box 33, Folders 1–3, MHM Papers.

2. Morial Statement on Federal Funding for NOPD, May 12, 1994, Box 57, Folder 1, MHM Papers; Morial Administration Crime Initiative, May 16, 1994, Box 57, Folder 1, MHM Papers.

3. Morial Statement on Police Chief Search Committee, March 29, 1994, Box 57, Folder 1, MHM Papers; Morial Press Release on List of Finalists for Superintendent, June 5, 1994, Box 57, Folder 1, MHM Papers; *Times-Picayune*, October 14, 1994; April 9, 22, 1994; Morial Statement on Richard Pennington, October 13, 1994, Box 57, Folder 3, MHM Papers; Morial Statement on Joseph Giarrusso, May 20, 1994, Box 57, Folder 1, MHM Papers. Giarrusso would be the administrations liaison to the district attorney's office and other state and federal agencies.

4. *Times-Picayune*, October 14, 1994.

5. Morial Statement on *60 Minutes* Segment, October 31, 1994, Box 57, Folder 3, MHM Papers; *Times-Picayune*, November 10, 1994; *NOPD Annual Report, 1994*.

6. *Times-Picayune*, December 6, 1994.

7. *Times-Picayune*, December 6, 1994.

8. *Times-Picayune*, November 7, 1994.

9. *Times-Picayune*, January 24, 1995.

10. *Times-Picayune*, December 9, 1994; January 15, 1995; *NOPD Annual Report, 1994*.

11. *Times-Picayune*, December 9, 1994; *NOPD Annual Report, 1994*.

12. *Times-Picayune*, December 14, 1994.

13. *Times-Picayune*, December 21, 1994; April 16–27, 1996; December 19, 1996. For a similar ring inside the LAPD, see Juan Juarez, *Brotherhood of Corruption: A Cop Breaks the Silence on Police Abuse, Brutality, and Racial Profiling* (Chicago: Review Press, 2004).

14. *Times-Picayune*, December 18, 1994; *New Orleans Police Department 1996 Action Plan*, New Orleans Public Library.

15. *Times-Picayune*, February 5, 1995; July 18, 20, 1995; Chuck Hustmyre, *Killer With a Badge* (Berkley: Berkley Press, 2004).

16. *Times-Picayune*, March 5, 6, 1995.

17. *Times-Picayune*, March 5, 1995.

18. *Times-Picayune*, March 6, 1995.

19. *Times-Picayune*, March 7, 8, 9, 1995.

20. *Times-Picayune*, March 10, 1995; Paul Keegan, "The Thinnest Blue Line," *New York Times Magazine*, March 31, 1996.

21. *NOPD Annual Report, 1994*.

22. *Times-Picayune*, December 20, 1994; *NOPD Annual Report, 1994*; *NOPD Transition Report, 2002*, MHM Papers.

23. The literature on community policing is voluminous. For a good overview of community policing, see Robert Trojanowicz and Bonnie Bocquerox, *Community Policing: A Contemporary Perspective* (Cincinnati: Anderson Press, 1990); J. R. Greene and S. D. Mastrofski, eds.,

Community Policing: Rhetoric or Reality? (New York: Praeger, 1998); D. P. Rosenbaum, ed., *The Challenge of Community Policing: Testing the Promise* (Thousand Oaks, CA: Sage, 1994); Robert Friedmann, *Community Policing: Promises and Challenges* (New York: St. Martin's Press, 1992).

24. *Times Picayune*, January 11, 1995; *NOPD Annual Report, 1995.*

25. *Times-Picayune*, February 6, 1995; *NOPD Annual Report, 1994.*

26. *Times-Picayune*, January 11, 1995; February 1, 1995; *New Orleans Police Department Annual Report 1996; NOPD Transition Report, 2002.* The NOPD's community policing efforts paid off in a major reduction in crime. See Provanda Kennedy, "The Impact of Community Policing on Crime in New Orleans Public Housing Developments" (master's thesis, University of New Orleans, 2000). The NOPD foot-patrol program was modeled after a pilot program in Flint, Michigan. See Robert Trojanowicz, *Neighborhood Foot Patrol Program in Flint Michigan* (East Lansing: National Neighborhood Foot Patrol Center, undated).

27. *Times-Picayune*, January 12, 1995; *NOPD Transition Report.*

28. *NOPD Annual Report, 1994.*

29. "The Pennington Plan," January 19, 1995, Box 57, Folder 4, MHM Papers; "Police Early Warning System Guidelines," Box 56, Folder 1, MHM Papers; "Personal Performance Enhancement Program," Box 56, Folder 1, MHM Papers; *Times-Picayune*, January 13, 1995; *NOPD Annual Report, 1995.*

30. *Times-Picayune*, January 17, 19, 1995.

31. *Times-Picayune*, January 3, 6, 28, 1995; February 17, 1995.

32. *Times-Picayune*, February 17, 1995; March 13, 1995; April 6, 9, 1995; June 2, 6, 8, 14, 15, 21, 1995; *NOPD Annual Report, 1995.*

33. *Times-Picayune*, June 30, 1995; *NOPD Annual Report, 1995; NOPD Annual Report, 1996; NOPD 1996 Action Plan.*

34. Morial Statement on Federal Grant to Supplement Community Policing Program, July 27, 1995, Box 56, Folder 2, MHM Papers; *Times-Picayune*, August 12, 19, 1995; March 21, 1996.

35. *Times-Picayune*, September 20, 1995; *NOPD Report, 1995.*

36. *Times-Picayune*, October 9, 1995.

37. *Times-Picayune*, October 9, 1995.

38. Morial and Pennington Statement on NOPD Crime Lab, October 6, 1995, Box 56, Folder 1, MHM Papers; Pennington Progress Report on NOPD Corruption and Murders, October 10, 1995, Box 56, Folder 1, MHM Papers; *Times-Picayune*, October 11, 1995; *NOPD Annual Report, 1995.*

39. *Times-Picayune*, November 9, 1995.

40. NOPD Reform Timetable, Box 57, Folder 4, MHM Papers; *Times-Picayune*, March 13, 1996; *NOPD Annual Report, 1996.*

41. *Times-Picayune*, May 28, 1996; *NOPD Annual Report, 1996.*

42. Morial and Pennington statement on Second Phase of Police Reform, March 25, 1996, Box 56, Folder 6, MHM Papers; *Times-Picayune*, August 9, 10, 11, 12, 17, 27, 1996; *NOPD Annual Report, 1996.*

43. *Times Picayune*, December 19, 31, 1996; February 21, 1997; *NOPD Annual Report, 1997.*

44. *Times-Picayune*, February 21, 1997.

45. *Times-Picayune*, February 21, 1997; March 4, 23, 1997; April 22, 1997; Morial and Pennington Statement on Police Recruitment Campaign, April 25, 1997, Box 58, Folder 1, MHM Papers.

46. *Times-Picayune*, April 13, 1997; *NOPD Annual Report, 1996; NOPD Annual Report, 1997.*

47. *Times-Picayune*, April 20, 1997; May 6, 1998; "History of COMSTAT," in *NOPD Annual Report, 2001;* Jack Maple, *Putting The Bad Guys Out of Business* (New York: Broadway Press,

2000); William Bratton and Vincent Henry, *The Compstat Paradigm: Management Accountability in Policing, Business, and the Public Sector* (New York: Looseleaf Law, 2002); Phyllis McDonald, *Managing Police Operations: Implementing the NYPD Control Model Using COMPSTAT* (New York: Wadsworth Press, 2001).

48. *Times Picayune*, April 20, 1997; *NOPD Annual Report, 1997*.

49. *Times-Picayune*, April 22, 1997.

50. *Times-Picayune*, April 22, 1997; October 12, 1997; May 9, 1998; December 25, 1998.

51. Morial Statement on Washington's Police Chief Search, March 19, 1998, Box 58, Folder 7, MHM Papers; *Times-Picayune*, March 20, 24, 25, 1998.

52. *Times-Picayune*, April 1, 1998; August 28, 1998; September 15, 25, 1998; October 2, 16, 1998.

53. *NOPD Transition Report; NOPD Annual Report, 1999; NOPD Annual Report, 2000*. For examples of other police reform success stories, see William Bratton, with Peter Knoeller, *The Turnaround: How America's Top Cop Reversed the Crime Epidemic* (New York: Random House, 1998); George Kelley, *Fixing Broken Windows: Restoring Order and Reducing Crime in Our Communities* (New York: Free Press, 1998).

54. *Times-Picayune*, November 8, 2001.

55. *Times-Picayune*, November 21, 2001.

56. *Times-Picayune*, January 31, 2002.

57. *Times-Picayune* February 12–14, 2002.

58. *Times-Picayune*, May 24, 2002.

59. *Times-Picayune*, April 23, 30, 2002.

60. *Times-Picayune*, May 22, 25, 2002.

61. *Times-Picayune*, August 30, 2002.

62. *Times-Picayune*, April 27, 2003.

63. *Times-Picayune*, May 1, 2003; June 26, 2003.

64. *Times-Picayune*, September 25, 2003.

65. *Times-Picayune*, July 24, 2003; October 22, 24, 26, 27, 28, 2003; January 9–11, 2004; April 2, 2004.

66. *Times-Picayune*, April 16, 2004; August 9, 16, 27, 2004; April 16, 2005.

EPILOGUE

1. Testimony of Warren Riley before the Senate Homeland Security and Governmental Affairs Committee, "Hurricane Katrina: Managing Law Enforcement and Communications in a Catastrophe," February 6, 2006. Hereafter referred to as Riley Report.

2. Warren Riley Testimony; Dan Baum, "Deluged: When Katrina hit, where were the police?" *The New Yorker*, January 9, 2006, p. 54.

3. *Times-Picayune*, December 18, 2005; *Spiegel Magazine*, September 7, 2005.

4. *Spiegel Magazine*, September 7, 2005; Riley Report.

5. Riley Report; *Times-Picayune*, September 4, 2005; December 18, 2005.

6. *Times-Picayune*, August 30, 2005; September 2, 2005; Baum, "Deluged," pp. 56–57.

7. *Times-Picayune*, April 9, 2006; Baum, "Deluged," p. 63.

8. *Times-Picayune*, September 27, 2005.

9. *Times-Picayune*, September 28, 29, 30, 2005; *New York Times*, September 28, 2005.

10. *Times-Picayune*, September 28, 2005.

11. Riley Report.

BIBLIOGRAPHY

MANUSCRIPT COLLECTIONS

Collections at the Amistad Research Center, Tulane University
Hazel Augustine Papers
Daniel Byrd Papers
Community Relations Council of Greater New Orleans Papers
Congress of Racial Equality Papers
Adam Fairclough Papers
Free Southern Theater Papers
William Jefferson Papers
Ernest Morial Papers
Marc Morial Papers
NAACP Papers, Field Office of Louisiana
Revius Ortique Papers
Morris Reynaud Papers
Jim Singleton Papers
Alexander Pierre Tureaud Papers
Urban League of New Orleans Papers

Collections at City Archives, New Orleans Public Library
Sidney Barthelemy Papers
Troy Carter Papers
Abraham Lincoln Davis Papers
Joseph DiRosa Papers
Joseph Giarrusso Papers
Human Relations Committee Papers
Moon Landrieu Papers

Robert Maestri Papers
Ernest Morial Papers
Marc Morial Papers
Henry Morris Papers
Delesseps S. Morrison Papers
New Orleans City Council Papers
New Orleans Police Department Records
Victor Schiro Papers
Dorothy Taylor Papers
Oliver Thomas Papers

Collections at Earl K. Long Library, Special Collections, University of New Orleans
New Orleans NAACP Papers
A. P. Tureaud Papers

Oral Histories
Amistad Research Center
Oretha Castle Haley
Moon Landrieu

Kim Lacy Rogers-Glenda Stevens Collection, Xavier University Archives
Avery Alexander
Sidney Barthelemy
Daniel Byrd
Raphael Cassimere
Thomas Dent
Lolis Elie
Joseph Giarrusso
Oretha Castle Haley
Don Hubbard
Moon Landrieu
Rudy Lombard
Helen Mervis
Ernest Morial
John P. Nelson
Revius Ortique
Jim Singleton
Jerome Smith
Llewellyn Soniet
Alice Thompson

Betty Wisdom
Skelly Wright
Kalamu Ya Salaam
Andrew Young

NEWSPAPERS AND PERIODICALS

Baton Rouge Advocate
Black Enterprise
Figaro
Gambit Weekly
Louisiana Weekly
NOLA Express
New Orleans Magazine
New Orleans States-Item
New Orleans Times-Picayune
Newsweek
New York Times
New York Times Magazine
The New Yorker

GOVERNMENT DOCUMENTS

Organized Crime in Interstate Commerce: hearings before the Special Committee to Investigate Organized Crime in Interstate Commerce, Eighty-Second Congress, First Session. On file at the New Orleans Public Library.
Report of the Special Citizens Investigating Committee of the Commission Council of New Orleans—the New Orleans Police Department. On file at New Orleans Public Library
U.S. Department of Justice-Civil Rights Division. *Study on Police Department Complaints, 1984–1990.* Washington, DC, 1992.

TELEVISION PROGRAMS

A&E Investigative Reports. "Cops or Criminals." 1993
60 Minutes. "NOPD Blues." 1994.

SECONDARY SOURCES

Abbott, Carl. *The New Urban America: Growth and Politics in Sunbelt Cities.* Chapel Hill: University of North Carolina Press, 1987.

Abron, JoAnn. "Serving the People: The Survival Programs of the Black Panther Party." In *The Black Panther Party Reconsidered,* edited by Charles Jones, pp. 177–192. Baltimore: Black Classic Press, 2000.

American Civil Liberties Union. *Police Power and Citizen's Rights: The Case for an Independent Police Review Board.* New York: American Civil Liberties Union, 1966.

Appier, Janis. *Policing Women: The Sexual Politics of Law Enforcement and the LAPD.* Philadelphia: Temple University Press, 1998.

Arend, Orissa. *Showdown in Desire: People, Panthers, Piety and Police: The Story of the Black Panther Party in New Orleans, 1970.* New Orleans: Arend, 2003.

Bailey, David H., and Harold Mendelsohn. *Minorities and the Police: Confrontation in America.* New York: Free Press, 1969.

Baker, Lisa. *The Second Battle of New Orleans: The One-Hundred Year Struggle to Integrate the Schools.* New York: HarperCollins, 1996.

Balagoo, Kuwasi. *Look for Me in the Whirlwind: The Collective Autobiography of the New York 21.* New York: Random House, 1971.

Balkin, Joseph. "Why Policemen Don't Like Policewomen." *Journal of Police Science and Administration* 16 (March 1988): 29–38.

Bannon, James, and G. Marie Wilt. "Black Policemen: A Study of Self-images." *Journal of Police Science and Administration* 1 (March 1973): 21–29.

Banton, Michael. *The Policeman in the Community.* New York: Basic Books, 1964.

Barnett, Ross Robert. *Strength Through Unity.* Greenwood, MS: Greenwood Citizen's Council, 1960.

Baum, Dan. "Deluged: When Katrina Hit, Where Were the Police?" *The New Yorker,* January 9, 2006, p. 54.

Bauman, John F., Roger Biles, and Kristen M. Szylvian, eds. *From Tenements to Taylor Homes: In Search of an Urban Housing Policy in 20th Century America.* University: Pennsylvania State University Press, 2000.

Bayor, Ronald H. "Race and City Services: The Shaping of Atlanta's Police and Fire Departments." *Atlanta History* 36 (Fall 1992): 19–35.

———. *Race and the Shaping of Twentieth Century Atlanta.* Chapel Hill: University of North Carolina Press, 1996.

Bell, Daniel. "Policewomen: Myths and Reality." *Journal of Police Science and Administration* 10 (1982): 112–120.

Bernard, Richard M., and Bradley R. Rice, eds. *Sunbelt Cities: Politics and Growth Since World War II.* Austin: University of Texas Press, 1984.

Biles, Roger. "Black Mayors: A Historical Assessment." *Journal of Negro History* 77 (Summer 1992): 109–125.

Bolton, Kenneth, Jr., and Joe R. Feagin. *Black in Blue: African American Police Officers and Racism.* New York: Routledge, 2002.

Bornstein, Tim. "Police Unions Dispelling the Ghost of 1919." *Police Magazine* 1, no. 4 (September 1978): 25–29.

Bratton, William, with Peter Knoeller. *The Turnaround: How America's Top Cop Reversed the Crime Epidemic*. New York: Random House, 1998.

Bratton, William, and Vincent Henry. *The Compstat Paradigm: Management Accountability in Policing, Business, and the Public Sector*. New York: Looseleaf Law, 2002.

Bridges, Ruby. *Through My Eyes*. New York: Scholastic Press, 1999.

Brinkley, Douglas. *The Great Deluge: Hurricane Katrina, New Orleans, and the Mississippi Gulf Coast*. New York: HarperPerennial, 2007.

Brown, Lee. "Neighborhood-Oriented Policing." *American Journal of Police* 9 (1990): 197–207.

Burns, Stewart, ed. *Daybreak of Freedom: The Montgomery Bus Boycott*. Chapel Hill: University of North Carolina Press, 1997.

Burris, John. L., with Catherine Whitney. *Blue versus Black: Let's End the Conflict between Cops and Minorities*. New York: St. Martin's Press, 1999.

Campbell, Valencia. "Double Marginality of Black Policemen." *Criminology* 17 (February 1980): 477–484.

Cannon, Lou. *Official Negligence: How Rodney King and the Riots Changed Los Angeles and the LAPD*. New York: Westview Press, 1999.

Carter, Dan T. *The Politics of Rage: George Wallace, the Origins of the New Conservatism, and the Transformation of American Politics*. Baton Rouge: Louisiana State University Press, 1995.

Cashmore, Ellis, and Eugene McLaughlin. *Out of Order: Policing Black People*. New York: Routledge, 1991.

Chai, Charles. "Who Rules New Orleans: A Study of Community Power Structure." *Louisiana Business Survey* 16, no. 5 (1972): 2–11.

Chevigny, Paul. *Police Power*. New York: Oak Tree Publications, 1969.

———. *A Study of Provocation*. New York: Pantheon, 1972.

Cleaver, Kathleen, ed. *Liberation, Imagination, and the Black Panther Party*. New York: Routledge, 2001.

Colburn, David R., and Jeffrey S. Adler, eds. *African-American Mayors: Race, Politics, and the American City*. Urbana: University of Illinois Press, 2001.

Countryman, Matthew. *Up South: Civil Rights and Black Power in Philadelphia*. Philadelphia: University of Pennsylvania Press, 2005.

Cox, Marcus. "From Patriotism to Rebellion: African-American Attitudes Toward Military Service and Training, 1941–1973." Ph.D. dissertation, Northwestern University, 2001.

Dent, Tom. "New Orleans Versus Atlanta." *Southern Exposure* 7 (Spring 1979): 66–68.

Donner, Frank. *Protectors of Privilege: Red Squads and Police Repression in Urban America*. Berkeley: University of California Press, 1992.

Dudziak, Mary. *Cold War Civil Rights: Race and the Making of American Democracy*. Princeton: Princeton University Press, 2002.

Dulaney, W. Marvin. *Black Police in America*. Bloomington: Indiana University Press, 1996.

Dyson, Michael Eric. *Come Hell or High Water: Hurricane Katrina and the Color of Disaster*. New York: Basic Civitas Books, 2007.

Eisinger, Peter. "Black Employment in Municipal Jobs: The Impact of Black Political Power." *American Political Science Review* 76 (June 1982): 380–392.

Escobar, Edward. *Race, Police, and the Making of a Political Identity: Mexican Americans and the LAPD, 1900–1945*. Berkeley: University of California Press, 1999.

Eskew, Glenn. *But For Birmingham: The Local and National Movements in the Civil Rights Struggle*. Chapel Hill: University of North Carolina Press, 1997.

Fairclough, Adam. *Race and Democracy: The Civil Rights Struggle in Louisiana, 1915–1972*. Athens: University of Georgia Press, 1995.

Feuille, Peter. *Police Unionism: Power and Impact in Public Sector Bargaining*. Lexington, MA: Lexington Books, 1973.

Fleming, Harold C. "How Negro Police Worked Out in One Southern City." *New South* (October 1947).

Fogelson, Robert. "From Resentment to Confrontation: The Police and the Outbreak of the Nineteen-Sixties Riots." *Political Science Quarterly* 83 (June 1968): 217–247.

Foner, Philip, ed. *The Black Panthers Speak*. New York: Lippincott, 1970.

Freed, Donald. *Agony in New Haven: The Trial of Bobby Seale, Ericka Huggins, and the Black Panther Party*. New York: Simon and Schuster, 1973.

Friedman, Ina. *Black Cop*. Philadelphia: Westminster Press, 1974.

Friedmann, Robert. *Community Policing: Promises and Challenges*. New York: St. Martin's Press, 1992.

Friedrichs, David. "The Role of the Negro Minister in Politics in New Orleans." Ph.D. dissertation, Tulane University, 1967.

Fyfe, James. *Above the Law: Police and Excessive Use of Force*. New York: Free Press, 1994.

Germany, Kent. *New Orleans After the Promises*. Athens: University of Georgia Press, 2007.

Goldfield, David. *Black, White, and Southern: Race Relations and Southern Culture, the 1940s to the Present*. Baton Rouge: Louisiana State University Press, 1990.

———. *Cotton Fields and Skyscrapers: Southern City and Region, 1607–1980*. Baton Rouge: Louisiana State University Press, 1982.

Green, J. D., and S. D. Mastrofski, eds. *Community Policing: Rhetoric or Reality?* New York: Praeger, 1998.

Green, Laurie. *Battling the Plantation Mentality: Memphis and the Black Freedom Struggle*. Chapel Hill: University of North Carolina Press, 2007.

Gregory, James. *The Southern Diaspora: How the Great Migrations of Black and White Southerners Transformed America*. Chapel Hill: University of North Carolina Press, 2006.

Guzman, Jesse Parkhurst, ed. *Negro Year Book, 1941–1946*. Tuskegee: Tuskegee Institute, 1952.

Haas, Edward F. *DeLesseps S. Morrison and the Image of Reform*. Baton Rouge: Louisiana State University Press, 1974.

———. "The Expedient of Race: Victor Schiro, Scott Wilson, and the New Orleans Mayoralty Campaign of 1962." *Louisiana History* 42 (Winter 2001): 5–29.

Hair, William Ivy. *Carnival of Fury: Robert Charles and the New Orleans Race Riot of 1900*. Baton Rouge: Louisiana State University Press, 1986.

Harding, Vincent. "Black Students and the Impossible Revolution." *Journal of Black Studies* 1 (September 1970): 75–100.

Hawkins, Homer, and Richard Thomas. "White Policing of Black Populations: A History of Race and Social Control in America." In *Out of Order: Policing Black People*, edited by Ellis Cashmore and Eugene McLaughlin, pp. 66–86. London: Routledge, 1991.

Hayes, Worth K. "No Service Too Small: The Political Significance of the Survival Programs of the New Orleans Black Panther Party," pp. 4–5, www.xula.edu/xulanexus/issue3/BBP.html.

Hernon, Peter. *A Terrible Thunder: The Story of the New Orleans Sniper*. New York: Doubleday, 1978.

Hersey, John. *The Algiers Motel Incident*. New York: Bantam Books, 1968.

Higgins, Lois. "Historical Background of Policewomen's Service." *Journal of Criminal Law, Criminology and Police Science* (1951).

Hine, Darlene Clark. *Black Victory: The Rise and Fall of the White Primary in Texas*. New York: Millwood Press, 1979.

Hirsch, Arnold. "Harold and Dutch Revisited: A Comparative Look at the First Black Mayors of Chicago and New Orleans." In *African-American Mayors: Race, Politics, and the American City*, edited by David Colburn and Jeffrey Adler, pp. 109–110. Urbana: University of Illinois Press, 2001.

———. *Making the Second Ghetto: Race and Housing in Chicago, 1940–1960*. Chicago: University of Chicago Press, 1992.

———. "New Orleans: Sunbelt in the Swamp." In *Sunbelt Cities: Politics and Growth since World War II*, edited by Richard M. Bernard and Bradley R. Rice, pp. 100–137. Austin: University of Texas Press, 1983.

———. "Race and Politics in Modern New Orleans: The Mayoralty of Dutch Morial." *American Studies* 35, no. 4 (April 1990): 461–484.

———. "Simply a Matter of Black and White: The Transformation of Race and Politics in Twentieth Century New Orleans." In *Creole New Orleans: Race and Americanization*, edited by Arnold Hirsch and Joseph Logsdon, pp. 262–319. Baton Rouge: Louisiana State University Press, 1992.

Hirsch, Arnold, and Joseph Logsdon, eds. *Creole New Orleans: Race and Americanization*. Baton Rouge: Louisiana State University Press, 1992.

Honey, Michael. *Going Down Jericho Road: The Memphis Strike, Martin Luther King Jr.'s Last Campaign.* New York: Norton, 2007.

Horne, Gerald. *The Fire This Time: The Watts Uprising and the 1960s.* Charlottesville: University of Virginia Press, 1995.

Hudson, J. "Police Review Boards and Accountability." *Law and Contemporary Problems* 36 (Fall 1971): 515–538.

Human Rights Watch. *Shielded from Justice: Police Brutality and Accountability in the United States.* New York: Human Rights Watch, 1998.

Hustmyre, Chuck. *Killer With a Badge.* Berkeley: Berkeley Press, 2004.

Inger, Morton. *Politics and Reality in an American City: The New Orleans School Crisis.* New York: Center for Urban Education, 1969.

Jacobs, Paul. "The Los Angeles Police: A Critique." *Atlantic Monthly* (December 1966): 95–101.

Johnson, Karl. "Police-Black Community Relations in Post-War Philadelphia: Race and Criminalization in Urban Social Space, 1945–1960." *Journal of African-American History,* 89, no. 4 (March 2005): 118–135.

Johnson, Marilynn. *Street Justice: A History of Police Violence in New York City.* New York: Beacon Press, 1993.

Jones, Charles, ed. *The Black Panther Party Reconsidered.* Baltimore: Black Classic Press, 1998.

Juarez, Juan. *Brotherhood of Corruption: A Cop Breaks the Silence on Police Abuse, Brutality, and Racial Profiling.* Chicago: Review Press, 2004.

Juris, Harvey, and Peter Feuille. *Police Unionism: Power and Impact in Public Sector Bargaining.* Lexington, MA: Lexington Books, 1973.

Keegan, Paul. "The Thinnest Blue Line." *New York Times Magazine,* March 31, 1996.

Kelley, George. *Fixing Broken Windows: Restoring Order and Reducing Crime in Our Communities.* New York: Free Press, 1998.

Kelley, Robin. "'We are Not What We Seem': Rethinking Black Working-Class Opposition in the Jim Crow South." *Journal of American History* (June 1993): 75–112.

Kempton, Murray. *The Briar Patch: The Trial of the Panther 21.* New York: De Capo Press, 1973.

Kennedy, Provanda. "The Impact of Community Policing on Crime in New Orleans Housing Developments." Master's thesis, University of New Orleans, 2000.

Kruse, Kevin. *White Flight: Atlanta and the Making of Southern Conservatism.* Princeton: Princeton University Press, 2005.

Kusmer, Kenneth. "African-Americans in the City Since World War II: From the Industrial Era to the Post Industrial Era." *Journal of Urban History* 21 (May 1995): 458–504.

Lane, James B. "Black Power and its Limits: Gary Mayor Richard B. Hatcher's Administration." In *African-American Mayors: Race, Politics, and the American City,* edited by David Colburn and Jeffrey Adler, pp. 262–319. Urbana: University of Illinois Press, 2001.

Lassiter, Matthew. *The Silent Majority: Suburban Politics in the Sunbelt South.* Princeton: Princeton University Press, 2005.

Lazerow, Jama, and Yohuru Williams, eds. *In Search of the Black Panther Party.* Durham: Duke University Press, 2006.

Lee, Elliott D. "Blacks in Blue." *Black Enterprise,* February 1982, pp. 87–90.

Lemann, Nicholas. *The Promised Land: The Great Black Migration and How it Changed America.* New York: Vintage Books, 1992.

Letman, S. "Chicago's Answer to Police Brutality: The Office of Professional Standards." *Police Chief* (1980): 16–17.

———. "The Office of Professional Standards: Six Years Later." *Police Chief* (1981): 44–46.

Littlejohn, E. "The Civilian Police Commission: A Deterrent to Police Misconduct." *University of Detroit Journal of Urban Law* 59 (1981): 5–62.

Mahoney, Marnie. "The Changing Nature of Public Housing in New Orleans, 1930–1974." M.A. thesis, Tulane University, 1985.

Maple, Jack. *Putting the Bad Guys Out of Business.* New York: Broadway Press.

Marable, Manning. *Race, Reform, and Rebellion: The Second Reconstruction in Black America, 1945–1990.* Jackson: University of Mississippi Press, 1991.

Marchiafava, Louis. "The Houston Police, 1878–1948." *Rice University Studies* 63 (Spring 1977).

———. "The New Orleans Police." Unpublished paper.

Marshall, Thurgood. "The Gestapo in Detroit." *Crisis* 50 (August 1943): 232–247.

McArdle, Andrea, and Tanya Erzen, eds. *Zero Tolerance: Quality of Life and the New Police Brutality in New York City.* New York: New York University Press, 2001.

McDonald, Phyllis. *Managing Police Operations: Implementing the NYPD Control Model Using COMPSTAT.* New York: Wadsworth Press, 2001.

McGirr, Lisa. *Suburban Warriors: The Origins of the New American Right.* Princeton: Princeton University Press, 2005.

McIntyre, Charshee. *Criminalizing a Race.* Kayode Publications, 1993.

McMillan, Neil. *The Citizen's Council: Organized Resistance to the Second Reconstruction, 1954–1964.* Urbana: University of Illinois Press, 1994.

Meier, August, and Elliott Rudwick. *CORE: A Study in the Civil Rights Movement.* Urbana: University of Illinois Press, 1975.

Metcalf, Christina. "Race Relations and the New Orleans Police Department, 1900–1972." Senior honors thesis, Tulane University, 1985.

Mohl, Raymond. "The Transformation of Urban America Since the Second World War." In *Essays on Sunbelt Cities and Recent Urban America,* edited by Raymond Mohl, Robert Fairbanks, and Kathleen Underwood, pp. 8–32. College Station: Texas A&M Press, 1990.

Moore, Leonard. *Carl B. Stokes and the Rise of Black Political Power.* Urbana: University of Illinois Press, 2002.

Morial, Marc. "Development of Black Politics in New Orleans." Unpublished paper.

Moss, Larry. *Black Political Ascendancy: Urban Centers and Black Control of the Local Police Function.* San Francisco: R&E Research Associates, 1977.

National Advisory Commission on Civil Disorders. New York: Bantam Books, 1968.

Nelson, Jill. *Police Brutality.* New York: Norton, 2000.

Newton, Huey P. "War Against the Panthers: A Study of Repression in America." Ph.D. dissertation, University of California–Santa Cruz, 1980.

O'Brien, Gail. *The Color of the Law: Race, Violence, and Justice in the Post–World War II South.* Chapel Hill: University of North Carolina Press, 1999.

Payne, Charles. *I've Got the Light of Freedom: The Organizing Tradition and the Black Freedom Struggle.* Berkeley: University of California Press, 1995.

Peralta, David. "Organized Labor in the Criminal Justice System: Mardi Gras and the New Orleans Police Department." M.A. thesis, University of New Orleans, 1994.

Perkins, Lyle. "Failing the Race: An Historical Assessment of New Orleans Mayor Sydney Barthelemy, 1986–1994." Master's thesis, Louisiana State University, 2005.

Perry, David, and Alfred Watkins, eds. *The Rise of Sunbelt Cities.* Beverly Hills: Sage, 1978.

Perry, Huey. "Black Politics and Mayoral Leadership in Birmingham and New Orleans." *National Political Science Review* 2 (1990): 154–160.

Perry, Huey, and Alfred Stokes. "Politics and Power in the Sunbelt: Mayor Morial of New Orleans." In *The New Black Politics: The Search for Political Power,* edited by Michael Preston, Lenneal Henderson, and Paul Puryear, pp. 228–236. New York: Longman, 1987.

Quinn, Michael. *Walking with the Devil: The Police Code of Silence.* Quinn and Associates, 2004.

Rogers, Kim Lacy. *Righteous Lives: Narratives of the Civil Rights Movement.* New York: New York University Press, 1993.

Romberg, Chris. *No There There: Race, Class, and Political Community in Oakland.* Berkeley: University of California Press, 2004.

Rosenbaum, D. P., ed. *The Challenge of Community Policing: Testing the Promise.* Thousand Oaks, CA: Sage, 1994.

Rousey, Dennis. "Black Police Officers in New Orleans During Reconstruction." *The Historian* (February 1987): 223–243.

———. *Policing the Southern City: New Orleans 1805–1889.* Baton Rouge: Louisiana State University Press, 1996.

Rudwick, Elliott. "Negro Police Employment in the Urban South." *Journal of Negro Education* 30 (Spring 1961): 102–108.

———. "The Negro Policeman in the South." *Journal of Criminal Law, Criminology and Police Science* 61 (July–August 1960): 273–276.

———. "Police Work and the Negro." *Journal of Criminal Law, Criminology, and Police Science* 50 (July–August 1960): 596–599.

———. "The Southern Negro Policeman and the White Offender." *Journal of Education* 30 (Fall 1961).

———. *The Unequal Badge: Negro Policeman in the South.* Atlanta: Southern Regional Council, 1962.

Self, Robert O. *American Babylon: Race and the Struggle for Postwar Oakland.* Princeton: Princeton University Press, 2005.

———. "The Black Panther Party and the Long Civil Rights Era." In *In Search of the Black Panther Party,* edited by Jama Lazerow and Yohuru Williams, pp. 15–58. Durham: Duke University Press, 2006.

Sinegal, Sharlene. "The Making of a Civil Rights Leader: Alexander Pierre Tureaud, 1927–1952." M.A. thesis, Louisiana State University, 2001

Skolnick, James. *Police and the Excessive Use of Force.* New York: Free Press, 1994.

Sokol, Jonathan. *There Goes My Everything: White Southerners in the Age of Civil Rights, 1945–1975.* New York: Random House, 2007.

Sonenshein, Raphael. *Politics in Black and White: Race and Power in Los Angeles.* Princeton: Princeton University Press, 1993.

Souther, J. Mark. *New Orleans on Parade: Tourism and the Transformation of the Crescent City.* Baton Rouge: Louisiana State University Press, 2006.

Stanford, Max. "Black Nationalism and the Afro-American Student." *Black Scholar* 2 (June 1971): 27–31.

Stark, Rodney. *Police Riots.* Belmont, CA: Focus Books, 1972.

Stone, W. McFerrin. "Willie Rainach and the Defense of Southern Segregation in Louisiana: 1954–1959." Ph.D. dissertation, Texas Christian University, 1997.

Sugrue, Thomas. *Origins of the Urban Crisis: Race and Inequality in Post-War Detroit.* Princeton: Princeton University Press, 1996.

Thompson, Heather. "Rethinking the Collapse of Postwar Liberalism: The Rise of Mayor Coleman Young and the Politics of Race in Detroit." In *African-American Mayors: Race, Politics, and the American City,* edited by David Colburn and Jeffrey Adler, pp. 57–79. Urbana: University of Illinois Press, 2001.

———. *Whose Detroit? Politics, Labor, and Race in a Modern American City.* Ithaca: Cornell University Press, 2004.

Trojanowicz, Robert. *Neighborhood Foot Patrol Program in Flint, Michigan.* East Lansing: National Neighborhood Foot Patrol Center, undated.

Trojanowicz, Robert, and Bonnie Bocquerox. *Community Policing: A Contemporary Perspective.* Cincinnati: Anderson Press, 1990.

Van Deburg, William. *New Day in Babylon.* Chicago: University of Chicago Press, 1992.

Walker, Donald B. "Black Police Values and the Black Community." *Police Studies* 5 (1983): 20–28.

Walker, Samuel. "Citizen Complaints and the Community. In *Police and Policing: Contemporary Issues,* edited by Dennis Kenney and Robert McNamara, pp. 200–215. New York: Praeger, 1999.

———. *The New World of Police Accountability.* New York: Sage, 2000.

———. *Police Accountability: The Role of Citizen Oversight.* New York: Wadsworth, 2000.

Walker, Samuel, and Tara Shelley. "Affirmative Action, Diversity, and Law Enforcement." In *Police and Policing: Contemporary Issues,* edited by Dennis Kenney and Robert McNamara, pp. 187–189. New York: Praeger, 1999.

Walker, Samuel, and B. Wright. *Civilian Review of the Police: A National Survey of the 50 Largest Cities.* Omaha: University of Nebraska–Omaha, 1985.

Watson, Dwight. *Race and the Houston Police Department, 1930–1990.* College Station: Texas A&M Press, 2005.

Winston, George, III. "To Protect and Serve? Police Brutality and Attempted Reform in New Orleans During the first Morial Administration." M.A. thesis, University of New Orleans, 2004.

Wintersmith, Robert. *Police and the Black Community.* New York: Lexington Books, 1974.

Woodard, Komozi. *A Nation Within a Nation: Amiri Baraka and Black Power Politics.* Chapel Hill: University of North Carolina Press, 1999.

Work, Monroe, ed. *Negro Year Book, 1931–1932.* Tuskegee: Tuskegee Institute, 1931.

Worthy, Barbara. *Blacks in New Orleans from the Great Depression to the Civil Rights Movement, 1930–1960.* New Orleans: SUNO-CAAS, 1994.

Zimroth, Peter. *Perversions of Justice: The Prosecution and Acquittal of the Panther 21.* New York: Viking Press, 1974.

INDEX

9 780807 177372